Plains Woman

Plains Woman

THE DIARY OF MARTHA FARNSWORTH 1882–1922

EDITED BY

Marlene Springer and Haskell Springer

INDIANA UNIVERSITY PRESS
BLOOMINGTON AND INDIANAPOLIS

First Midland Book Edition, 1988

Manufactured in the United States of America

Library of Congress Cataloging in Publication Data

Farnsworth, Martha, 1867–1924.
  Plains woman.

  Bibliography: p.
  1. Farnsworth, Martha, 1867–1924. 2. Pioneers—
Kansas—Biography. 3. Women pioneers—Kansas—
Biography. 4. Kansas—Biography. 5. Kansas—Social
life and customs. I. Springer, Marlene.
II. Springer, Haskell S. III. Title.
F686.F37A37   1985   978.1′031′0924 [B]   84-43169
ISBN 0-253-34510-3 (cl.)
ISBN 0-253-20480-1 (pbk.)

    3   4   5   6   92   91   90   89   88

Contents

Illustrations

Introduction

The first words of Martha VanOrsdol Farnsworth's diary, begun in 1882, are "At home." She then recorded the day's visitors and the direction of the wind. All three topics might be considered metaphors for the writer's life, for she was "at home" in Kansas most of the time; she received thousands of visitors; and the direction of the wind, both physical and political, remained one of her prime concerns until her death in 1924. This woman, who was born in Iowa in 1867, moved to Kansas at age five to stay the rest of her fifty-seven years, keeping a daily record of her life from the age of fourteen. She grew up in frontier Kansas to become a housewife, a bereaved mother, a young widow, and a wife again. An avid reader, a teacher, waitress, theater-goer, church member, suffragist, social worker, and political cartoonist, she skated and swam into middle age, would walk alone virtually anywhere, and always found her life worth living. Martha Farnsworth was not a celebrity; but the story revealed in her diary is compelling for what it tells about one woman, and for what it illustrates about the lives of countless people who experienced both the frontier and rapid social change, and who managed to adapt with dignity, strength, and humor.

The diary is a long one (about four thousand pages), making it unusual for private writings, most of which tend to be kept only in times of crisis or passage—and the volumes themselves, sixteen in all, are revealing. The majority are legal-size ledger books, from which the frugal Martha sometimes took left-over pages for scrap paper. In especially difficult times when money or privacy was at a premium, she used much smaller stationery pads. The handwriting is large, easy to read; the grammar and spelling are good for someone of her time and education. The pages are usually neat, the confident hand supplemented occasionally by red borders of hearts for marriages and engagements, wide black borders for deaths and funerals. The early years contain much of the red and the black. Sometimes there are doodles, small sketches to mark a special day, and a few afterthoughts are recorded—another visitor she forgot to mention, an adjective (precise but never profane) to describe a politician she knew.

Many attitudes and influences—social, personal, even literary—combine to determine the format, content, and style of a diary. Martha's record is intriguing not only because of the events it describes, but also for what it reveals about her own attitude toward her diary, and the influence of this attitude on the way she wrote. By her own account, she let no one read this record; indeed, her first husband never knew she was keeping one. Yet what she included and what she omitted suggest that she did consider the possibility that her diary would be read, and that she was therefore dutifully conscious of her style. For example, she read parts of it aloud to a group of her Sunday-school students, and she subsequently used it as an historical record to settle arguments among them. And as if she were considering the possibility of an uninitiated reader in the distant future, she identified by kinship, occupation, or relationship many of the people she mentioned, continuing to do so when they reappeared. She often saved newspaper clippings to embellish her accounts of both public and personal events. And she protected, with unfortunate foresight, her sexual life from whoever might read her diary. (On one occasion, when single, she stayed overnight in a hotel with three friends, two men and one woman, but the diary tells of it with convincing innocence. The morning after her wedding was recorded without reference to change. That she had sexual relations with her husband at all is evidenced only by her miscarriages.) Her friendships, jealousies, hurts are described, but those aspects of her life that might embarrass her about herself, then or now, she preferred not to examine—leaving them for future readers who could (can?) draw their own conclusions from the factual clues she leaves. As with so many Victorian women, her adventuresome spirit could not overcome her prudishness.[1]

In addition to these clues in her tone which indicate an imagined audience, evidence suggests she was concerned about her style. At those times when she wanted to move from the immediate to the internal or the universal, she was acutely aware of herself as a writer; and as author she drew from the sentimental style of the novels she read so often in her youth. The full extent of her reading is lost to us, for she did not record every book in the early years of the diary (in contrast to her later habit of commenting on all the movies she saw). But intermittent references and a list of "names and authors of the various books I've read" jotted on the back of her father's business card ("Jas. O. VanOrsdol/Dealer in Patent Tree Protectors") give us some insight into her taste and the sources of her prose.

By the time she was sixteen, Martha was attending, with her father and sisters, "Literary," a type of educational group activity that often took place at the local schoolhouse. Her reading as a result was catholic, sometimes trivial, and often dictated by availability. Colonel Charles Greene's "thrilling stories of heroic adventures" are prominent on her list, but so are *Robinson Crusoe* and *Ivanhoe*. Most revealing, however, is her reading of the sentimental best-sellers: Augusta Evans' *Inez, A Tale of the Alamo* which she read around 1884; Evans' *St. Elmo*; Marion Harland's *At Last* (also ca. 1884); Mary J. Holmes' *Lena Rivers*; and of course *Uncle Tom's Cabin*. That Martha read these books is not surprising: the popularity of Harriet Beecher Stowe's novel is legendary, and *St. Elmo* won an audience that places it "securely among the ten most popular novels ever published in the United States," according to Helen Papashvily.[2]

The recurrent pattern of these novels is obvious to anyone who has read even several, and the style is insidiously contagious. The melodrama surrounding each crisis; the pious moral sentiment infusing each action; the lesson that true happiness comes from suffering, submission and repression; the domestic turmoil that always has a clear villain and heroine; and most important, the elevated language that makes it all sound so noble—all were standard for the domestic novels of the period. The formula, in turn, was reflected in Martha's life, including the ways she perceived and wrote of herself, especially during her courting days and her wretched years with her first husband. This is not to say that Martha consciously turned her life into art. But the stylistic formality and thematic piety of what she was reading did seep into her story. When the plot was thick, for example, she waxed extravagant:

> . . . . *tonight I am so wretched*, that I *feel dazed* and *as if I must awake from some terrible night-mare. Four years ago a Bride, hoping to be happy. Tonight a widow in abject misery.* I *know* my *heart aches* as *much over his* death, as if *I had loved* him, *for it is terrible* to *have one die, not a christian*, and *especially one, who was much to us at some time in our life.*

And her style shows the novels' biblical cadences and allusions, as well as their judicious use of flashback.

If Martha's writing recalls the sentimental novels of her time, so can much of her early life be compared to the stock heroine's existence. In fact, the standard heroine of Augusta Evans's fiction fits Martha's adolescence to a startling degree. The Evans heroine usually is an orphan or has a wicked stepparent. Because of her situation she usually enters the house of a benefactor, and is well cared for. But dependence strikes hard at the pride of the heroine, and she is determined to better herself—wasting no tears on her plight. She faces everything with Christian forbearance, and relies heavily on the Bible and theology for support. She acquires whatever education she can, and studies independently for one of the careers open to women—teaching, singing, writing, even painting. Ultimately she and her kind marry. In the domestic novel as a genre it is often a "loveless marriage"; that is, the man loves passionately, threateningly, but the woman marries to save her family, her honor, her mother's secret, *ad infinitum*. Or conversely, when the woman falls in love and displays it, she pays a bitter price for the weakness: abandonment, disinheritance, death often result.[3] There are endless variations in this formula, in Evans's novels in particular and in the genre as a whole, but the formula holds. Martha herself did not face the marriage forced upon a drugged bride, the occasional poisons, miscellaneous disinheritances, innumerable deaths by consumption that were standard fictional fare, but she did come dangerously close. Another editor might easily cast her early life as a *Tempest and Sunshine* or *Folly as It Flies*: She lost her mother at age three, fought with a rigid and unsympathetic stepmother, lost a sister at nineteen, accepted and rejected several proposals of marriage, guiltily lamented the attempted suicide of a rejected suitor, married a con- sumptive, alcoholic brute, suffered through a miserable pregnancy, lost the child, and was a widow—all before she was twenty-six!

Martha's father, James VanOrsdol, came from a large family, and these relatives are constantly mentioned in the diary. During the Civil War, he fought for the Union (Company K, 4th Iowa Cavalry) and afterward returned to Mount Pleasant, Iowa, where Martha, his first child, was born April 26, 1867. When she was five, the family moved to Kansas, to a village near Winfield founded only two years before, where the buffalo and Indians still roamed nearby. Less is known about her mother, who came from a family of Southern slaveholders. She died when Martha was three years old, during the birth of Belle, Martha's youngest sister. The death might have been precipitated by her closely spaced pregnancies, for five months after giving birth to Martha she was pregnant with May (born October 9, 1868) and then seven months after May's birth with Belle, born January 20, 1870. Two years after her death, James remarried, but Martha's relationship with her stepmother, as she records it in her diary, was not a happy one. By 1883, when she was sixteen, her problems at home intensified and she went to live with a neighboring family, essentially to make her own way. She never returned permanently to her own family; and in September of 1887 she left Winfield, where she had lived for fifteen years, and moved to Topeka, which became her permanent home.

In those early years Martha was quite independent, frequently going to dances, staying out with her friends until 4 A.M., and, in spite of her already tight financial situation, giving little indication that she would later become an impressively industrious person. Her education dur- ing these years was erratic, although she attended school whenever one was available, and in June 1883, for example, mused "I wish I could always go to school." In 1886, however, she implied that her stepmother had made her give up school, and she directed her energies toward courtship and her livelihood rather than education.

Martha's attitudes toward courtship, and toward men in general, are an interesting psychological study, for while she is bluntly objective about both her conquests and her losses, she nonetheless often reveals more than she knows. In her young womanhood she toyed with men—used them brutally at times—and then she paid, and paid, and paid. Her first proposal came at age sixteen, but she chose to stay in school. By the time she was eighteen, having carefully collected admirers, she had had three proposals and two engagements. The complexity of her nature is graphically illustrated when at one point she determined to conquer a man who had angered her by his casual flirtations with her and others, won his love in the time she allowed herself, rejected him, and was then haunted by him and his unhappy existence for the rest of her life.

Martha's sister May married in 1885 at age seventeen, Belle died of typhoid in 1886, and Martha, now virtually on her own, inexorably drifted toward marriage, in spite of repeated qualms. Even as she set her wedding date she feared she would be unhappy. She married Johnny Shaw, eight years her senior, on September 4, 1889, after a year's courtship. The problems began three days later with their first quarrel. Their first serious fight came within two weeks, and by April of 1892 things had deteriorated to the point where he threatened to shoot her. Their four-year life together was a true melodrama without a brighter tomorrow. The domestic tragedies were broken only by the boredom she frequently complained of in the early months of marriage. (Nothing so well illustrates the dullness of the former frontier after the buffalo and Indians had gone than the fact that she went to the Wizard Oil Medicine Troupe show thirteen times during its two-month stay in town). Johnny's insane jealousy and volatile temper, his drinking, which shocked and dismayed Martha; her several miscarriages; his consumption, which she claimed gave his body an odor of death that made him repulsive to share a bed with, her forced trip by wagon to Colorado while pregnant—all were borne before he, to her guilty relief, died. With a masochistic devotion to duty Martha stayed with him through it all, even though he offered her her freedom, for she did not believe in divorce for herself—although she never condemned it for others.

Her attitude toward marriage was reinforced by her first experience with it. She was very much in favor of the institution—for other people. Yet, with inexplicable contradiction, she married a second time, only seven months after Johnny's death. Her second husband, Fred Farnsworth, had been a friend of Johnny's and a pallbearer at his funeral, as

well as at their daughter's. Martha went, inwardly kicking and screaming, to the altar and almost fainted during the ceremony, but fortunately her fears this time were unfounded. The marriage of twenty-
nine years was, to all appearances, highly successful.

Fred Farnsworth, a postman, and a year older than Martha, was
from one of Topeka's pioneering families. His father had been an
Indian agent in the frontier town of Council Grove, Kansas, but later
had moved to Topeka, about fifty miles to the northeast, and had been
elected to the first Kansas State Senate. Fred's brothers, John, Will, and
Coit, seem to have gone on to financially successful careers, but Fred
spent his life in forced frugality, content with equanimity rather than
fortune. He appears to have been slow-moving, even lethargic—especially in contrast to Martha's constant activity—but he enjoyed his life,
and deeply loved his wife. He treated her with what she deemed
infinite kindness: Martha wrote, "he has no faults." In 1906 when he
went to visit relatives, Martha recorded that it was her first night alone
since their marriage twelve years before. On her one extended trip
alone, to Philadelphia in 1908, she wrote to him every day. Their only
recorded marital problem was childlessness, a continual cause of pain
for Martha.

In 1908 Martha sent a friend a congratulatory wedding card on
which she had pasted the pictures of twelve children and added a
caption: "May *these* be *all* your troubles." The card tells much about her
attitude toward children. While married to Johnny she miscarried
three times before her daughter was born, and the successful pregnancy was a saga of sickness, suppressed whenever possible so that her
extremely unsympathetic husband would not know. Johnny was antag-
onistic to the pregnancy, even suggested an abortion, but then posses-
sively reversed himself after the birth, insisting that he alone name the
baby. Martha truly delighted in this child, obviously and consciously
transferring her thwarted affection from husband to daughter. When
the baby became ill while they were living in Colorado, she took her
only meaningful action in defiance of her husband and returned to
Topeka for medical help without asking or waiting for Johnny's consent. When the child died at the age of six months, Martha was more
deeply hurt than she knew how to say. She commemorated the birth
and death of baby Inez in her diary for most of the rest of her life, and
her words on the twenty-first anniversary of the child's death are as
poignant as those on the fifth.

There followed a long series of surrogate children: Besides a foster
child, Roy Penwell, and a niece, Freda Gilbert (born on the same June
day on which Martha's baby had died three years earlier), whom she
reared for almost ten of the child's first thirteen years and supported

for many years thereafter, she also occasionally took in wards of the juvenile court; and ultimately her Sunday-school class of boys became a consuming interest for more than a decade.

With the exception of this class, these attempts at mothering were not entirely successful: Roy was suddenly returned to his relatives because Martha found him uncontrollable. Her quick change of attitude toward the boy she called "our son" is another fascinating element in the diary, for Martha makes no attempt to justify her seemingly contradictory behavior. Freda also became a constant source of pain. Fred and Martha fed and clothed her, encouraged her in music and art, and nursed her at the hospital and at home when she was severely ill; yet Freda's mother, May, abruptly moved Freda and her other children back to Colorado, out of Martha's reach. Again, she chooses to ignore the implications of her sister's departure (which may have been a defensive move on May's part, since Martha had begun to talk of them as "our children"). Although Freda occasionally returned to Topeka, she never brought consolation, only consternation. Ultimately, after two marriages and—to Martha—shocking behavior, Freda's only contacts with them were requests for money, to which Martha and Fred responded with generosity and sacrifice.

Martha began teaching her Sunday-school class of ten-year olds, later to be called the "Play Square Gang," in 1908. According to tradition, the boys would have graduated to other teachers as they got older, but the group refused and, by threatening a boycott, forced Martha's promotion. The group varied in size and loyalty, but newspaper notices of her success credit her with reaching more than two hundred boys. A nucleus of about thirty adopted her as their "auntie," and for nearly a decade many of them spent Sundays, holidays, and much of their vacations with her. She fed and entertained them constantly; she became intimately involved with their emotional lives, and later with their courtships. She attended their ball games, withholding all Christian charity from their opponents and the umpires; she anguished over them when they were at war; every summer she and Fred took a group of the boys, and later their girlfriends, camping. By 1916 the boys had supplanted her relatives as her prime concern, and in 1924 they made the arrangements for her funeral. Martha often noted that these boys made life worthwhile for her and Fred, and one is constantly struck by the "top gallant delight" she had in them. But she was not allowed to forget that they were not hers. Their parents were often jealous of her closeness to them and reminded her of her position. And when the boys came home from the war in 1919, only wives and parents were allowed at the station; Martha and others had to wait at the Statehouse. Martha must have been painfully aware of her own childlessness at times like these, and despite her strong faith this personal injustice sometimes rankled; she did not resist a few moralistic judgments on some parents she knew.

Martha was also taken advantage of in other ways—not only by her family but also by some of her boys, who were always willing to eat her food, seemingly without awareness of what it cost. Martha felt herself amply repaid, and was never indignant—but she and Fred were also always short of money, and Martha worked as hard as she could to stay out of debt.

Early in her life, and then especially during her days with Johnny Shaw, Martha took jobs out of economic necessity, but she also saw this work as a blessing, in the latter case as an escape from Johnny and his contagious consumption. During this period she was employed as a reluctant waitress, refusing to get a better job because it would prevent her from nursing her husband. Her daily schedule became: 6 A.M.— walk seventeen blocks to work; 2 P.M.—walk home to fix Johnny's lunch (although he was not at all incapacitated); 4–7 P.M.—back at work; and 7 o'clock—home to fix supper (having walked a total of five miles). She gave all her earnings to her husband, apparently happily, though legally she had little choice. Later she worked as a live-in nurse; in addition, before her first marriage, she had done a brief stint as a teacher, and in 1886 traveled alone to the frontier town of Medicine Lodge, Kansas, to work in a hotel, where she was happy and popular.

When she married Fred, Martha gave up all salaried employment, but she never gave up work. Her production and hours are astonishing: She cleaned, canned, gardened, and cooked interminably. To overcome the "high cost of living" which was her nemesis, she sold eggs and milk, raised her own vegetables and fruits, and supplemented the family income by designing tombstones for the local monument company.

In spite of her energy and Fred's steady job, their financial position was always precarious. After twenty years with the Post Office, Fred made $116 a month. When first married, Fred protectively kept his debts from her; she soon realized the situation and took their finances in hand, managing some of Fred's absent brothers' business affairs as well. Martha knew how to manage money, and she made Fred's meager salary go a long way; but it was her own generosity that often kept them in financial straits. She fed "her boys" regularly, tithed to the church, and gave generously to charities: In 1919 she listed a January contribution of $5.00 to the Jewish Armenian Relief fund, $5.00 to missions in February, $3.75 to the "colored church" and $3.00 to "help give a girl a home" in April, $5.00 to the Salvation Army in August— and these months are by no means exceptions. That same year, when post-war prices were terribly high, she and Fred rarely ate meat, and turkey on Thanksgiving was a sacrifice; yet she gave several welcome-home parties for the boys, and fed the crowd huge meals. In 1921 she guiltily paid $10.50 for her first new hat in many years, though she freely spent $8.50 for a wedding gift for one of her boys. Getting the hat was unusual for her; the wedding present was not. She often sent money to family members in Colorado, and regularly gave away food she had canned and baked. To survive with such generous habits and such a limited income, she kept a very close budget, even itemizing "small sack of table salt, $.09." But even with Martha's careful planning, money remained a problem. In 1903 she was suspended from the Grand Army of the Republic for nonpayment of dues; when Fred was sick in 1915 they were, at one point, down to about $50, had a three-month grocery bill outstanding, and held little health insurance. They never had any substantial savings, and they never, with the exception of two trips to Colorado and one to Oklahoma to see relatives, went on pleasure trips during Fred's vacations. Martha was able, in later years, to blame their situation on war profiteering—but that Fred had to work so hard for so little she could only blame on the Government in general and the Democrats in particular.

Martha, like many Kansans, took her politics seriously, and public events get a degree of attention unusual in women's private writings.[4] In 1884 she recorded matter-of-factly that a man was shot down on the streets of Winfield for speaking out, in this case, in favor of a Republican. Her political persuasions were influenced by her family and friends, but they also had an immediate practical basis: neither Johnny's nor Fred's postal job was protected by Civil Service. In February 1897, thanks to the spoils system, Fred's salary was reduced by $200 a year and he was put on a long foot route because his horse route was given to a "low down Democrat." Martha's political activities, however, went far beyond her loyalties to her heritage, her party, or Fred's federal job. They were certainly not auxiliary to her husbands' involvements, for neither Johnny nor Fred was allowed to do political work. Martha was clearly an intelligent woman limited by education, family connections, and her own expectations. Had she gone to college, had she gotten support from her family and friends, had she been born fifty years later, she could have been a candidate. As things were, she remained a resolute, and successful, campaigner for others.

She was a member of the Women's Republican Club and rode in parades under its banner. In 1905 she and the governor's wife were voted into the prestigious, somewhat eclectic Good Government Club, a local women's organization devoted largely to social reform but occasionally partisan in the support of candidates. The Club was pro-segregation ("separate-but-equal"), quite intolerant of "socialists" and "reds"; and its stance on temperance in Carry Nation's home state was usually predictable. But it was militantly pro-woman suffrage, and newspaper reports indicate it took up other causes as well: judicial reform, non-discriminatory voter registration (the Club led the successful fight against having to reveal one's exact age at registration), white slavery (particularly aimed at saving the young girls used by Fort Campbell), non-sexist laws for determining the age of majority (some legislators wanted majority to depend on marital status, giving a husband control of his young wife's money), and clean-up campaigns aimed at city government and drinking "joints." Also defended with vigor was the Club's determination to lend its support to the WCTU's anti-cigarette bill; its endorsement of the Ministerial Union's Sunday-closing bill, calling for the prohibition of Sunday theater, baseball games, and the like; its opposition to all fraternities and sororities in high schools; and its protests against payment into the city treasury of fines from "disreputable houses."

Martha's own position on many of these topics placed her squarely in the majority and helped her get elected first treasurer and then president. On the question of temperance, however, she was undoubtedly more conservative than many of her fellow Club members. In 1880 Kansas had become the first state in the Union to have constitutional Prohibition, but the laws were difficult to enforce. Moreover, spirits could legally be sold in drugstores for "medical, scientific, and mechanical" purposes. Drugstore "joints" suddenly appeared everywhere. Non-Kansans were amazed at the number of ailments (cholera, cancer, indigestion) liquor was said to cure—and at the number of sickly Kansans. But even though Prohibition was generally unpopular, all efforts at repeal (supported by Democrats, opposed by Republicans) failed, thanks in part to Carry Nation's crusade in 1900, when she led an army of followers through Topeka smashing saloons. Martha noted on a clipping enclosed in the diary that she had visited Carry Nation in jail, had brought food to her, and had been part of her "army." (Unfortunately the volumes for the years when she knew Nation have disappeared.) Throughout her life she was a "dry"—and her experiences with Johnny Shaw confirmed for her the rightness of her position. (Many women, in fact, supported Prohibition primarily because they were bound to alcoholic husbands.) Martha found Fred drinking only once, before their marriage. She made him take the pledge, saying she would leave him if he ever drank again. He believed her, and apparently never did. In 1909 the sale of whiskey for medical purposes was outlawed, surely to Martha's satisfaction. Though national Prohibition was repealed in 1933, in 1985 the Kansas constitution still forbids the "open saloon."

Although Martha was more rigid than many other Club members on the alcohol question, on racial issues she seems to have been more liberal than most. She did occasionally use the word "nigger," and while the term was less pejorative at that time than it is now, it does indicate a streak of bigotry. But this was an infrequent lapse. When she wrote "Negro," she capitalized it, something it took Southern newspapers until recent times to accomplish. True to her era, she noted "colored" after every name in her diary to which the designation applied. But she also was on very easy terms with her black neighbors, she admonished her ward to be respectful to blacks, and she went to a black church for services and once for Thanksgiving dinner. There is little question that by more recent standards Martha's racial attitudes were patronizing, that she was always aware of color. But unlike so many of her contemporaries, Martha's compassion, friendship, and charity were color blind. And she did not wish to be "separate," especially from "Mrs. Brown (colored)," a helpful neighbor.

Socialists, however, did not receive such benevolent consideration, and "red" was a color safely abhorred by all good Kansans. In 1914 the Good Government Club had at least one internal battle in which an apparently leftist group tried to stage a coup, but Martha's side won, and the members all returned to mutually agreeable topics such as suffrage.

The battle for woman suffrage was one of the hardest-fought campaigns in Kansas history. From the beginning of statehood in 1861, women could vote in district school elections, making Kansas the first state to grant this right. (Kentucky had a school suffrage law earlier, in 1838, but it was limited to widows with school-age children.) In 1875, in *Minor* v. *Hapersett*, the U.S. Supreme Court had ruled that it was up to individual states to decide which of their citizens could vote, and to establish voting regulations. Kansas's Governor St. John, in 1882, announced his third-term candidacy and ran on a pro-Prohibition and woman-suffrage ticket. His attempt to break the two-term tradition and his support of the suffrage bill are credited with his defeat. But agitation for full state suffrage was building. Some of the pressure was relieved in 1887 when Kansas became the first state to give women suffrage in municipal elections. The state suffrage amendment went to the legislature in 1894 and was defeated, as it had been in 1867 when, for the first time in the nation's history, the question of woman suffrage had been submitted to a popular vote. This second defeat slowed the movement for a time, but various organizations continued to work for the cause. In 1907 the Good Government Club went on record in support of Governor Hoch's unsuccessful recommendation that the invidious distinction between male and female be struck from the state's constitution, and by 1910 the state suffrage organization had decided that the time was right to make another appeal to the voters.

Martha and her fellow club members became active in the amendment campaign. Martha herself had long urged women to vote in local elections for women candidates and, conversely, had refused male politicians who sought her help, saying that until she was good enough to vote for them, she was not good enough to work for them. Once this campaign began, she marched, distributed literature, and stood at the polls on voting days. She lobbied, cajoled, drew political cartoons for a special suffrage issue of the Topeka *Sunday Capital*, and, of course, prayed. Fortunately she did not have to divide her loyalties, for Kansas Republicans stood staunchly for suffrage as well as for Prohibition; the Democrats were again openly opposed, as were the Populists. Martha was an impatient, partisan observer in the legislative gallery as the bill was debated. On February 9, 1911, the governor signed the suffrage resolution passed by both houses, and the issue went to the people in the general election of 1912. The campaign at this point gained national recognition, bringing money and suffragists to Kansas from all over the country. Martha recorded her euphoria when the bill was finally passed, and she somehow managed to keep a copy of her first ballot, which she inserted in the diary; appropriately, it was for the Republican primary.

The Kansas bill of 1912, however, did nothing to ease Martha's frustration with the national political situation—especially when she saw the United States being drawn into war, first with Mexico and then with Germany. Her attitude toward World War I was painfully ambiguous. She felt that Wilson's temerity had led the country into war; a Republican, she believed, could have kept it out. But she felt that once involved, America was duty-bound to fight. Martha was intensely patriotic—she flew the flag at every holiday and encouraged her Sunday-school boys to enlist. She was harsh toward those she deemed "slackers," listing them often in her diary, pressuring them to enlist, and supporting the local girls who refused to date them. But she also anguished over her "boys" in service, and became a local celebrity for her faithful correspondence with the troops and for her other war work. Her hatred for "Kaiser Bill" and the Germans was appropriately feverish, and she later opposed home rule for the Irish, partially because they had supported the Germans during the war. To her joy, all her "boys" returned alive—but they were not unscathed; several were deeply depressed by their experiences, especially those who had been in France. One suffered from "nerves" for years afterward. Martha saw the return of all these young men as divinely ordained, and even skeptics might admit that it was unusual that not one of the fifty or more whom she watched over was killed or seriously wounded. Martha would humorously contend that God protects Kansans.

Such Kansas chauvinism is a strong theme in the diary. All of Martha's worries about political inequity and about the high cost of living could not dampen her joy in living in what she considered the best state in the Union. She reveled in the change of season, the rich soil, the bright blue sky. Not the 100°-plus heat, the below-zero cold, nor the tornadoes were held against Kansas by her, and she delighted in the fierce lightning storms. To enjoy a snowstorm as one walked through it to milk the cow, knowing that every flake that fell near the house would have to be shoveled, takes a deep-seated loyalty to "place." Martha had it.

Her sense of place, then, was central to her personality—and in her case, provincialism did not necessarily lead to boredom. Nor, in Martha's life, did it mean resistance to change. With a Victorian faith in progress, Martha was able to assimilate with some ease, occasionally even to embrace with enthusiasm, most of the social changes that profoundly altered her life. The coming of the railroad to southern Kansas was the earliest important innovation. As early as 1870 Kansas was spanned by an east-west line, but not until the 1880s did construction really boom. In 1880 Kansas had 3,100 miles of track; in 1890, nearly 8,800 miles.[5] This efficient network shrank long distances, and travel and social contacts grew proportionately. Later on, these same railroads, on which Topeka was a major junction, became the source of much of Martha's socializing. Friends or kin, extremely important to her, were always arriving from somewhere, and Martha was always meeting them at the station, mostly to her delight.

Second only to the railroad as a catalyst for social change was the telephone system, an advance that Martha viewed with some skepticism. Her ambivalence about the invention is explicit: On November 1, 1908, she ordered one for her house, but on November 13 she wrote that she did not really want one; on November 14 her phone was installed, and on November 15 and 16 she talked on the phone almost all day. The convenience of the system was obvious to her, but so was the physical loneliness that resulted from its use. The neighborly "porch call" was soon supplanted by the telephone call, and Martha missed the face-to-face contact. As people cut down their visiting, they gradually drifted into the psychic isolation that has continued to intensify with more modern technologies.

Martha met other elements of modernization with more enthusiasm.

In 1903 the Farnsworths installed indoor plumbing. In 1907 she took her first ride in an automobile, and she liked cars, although she was later to fear for life and hat as she careened across rural Colorado at fifty miles an hour. In 1911 electric lights were installed in her home, and they were followed some years later by an electric iron and an electric vacuum cleaner. On September 23, 1913, she watched her first talking movie, and soon the easy availability of such entertainment seemed to leave little time or inclination for social tours of the insane asylum—where she had commonly taken visitors at the turn of the century.

Martha's loyalties to Kansas, electricity, and the Atchison, Topeka, and Santa Fe line help to explain her. Three aspects of her personality are striking: her independence, her continued energetic joy in living, and her deep religious faith. Yet none of these aspects is without its own complexity, its own ambiguity, for the public persona Martha so carefully constructs is sometimes at odds with the self-portrait inadvertently revealed. That she acted independently is clear from the earliest entries recording her riding across the countryside at will and seeming to move from one situation to another with ease. Later she commented that two relatives did not like her because she had "too much dirty, nasty independence." Paradoxically, however, she did not relish confrontation, and apparently never really argued with her second husband, or even his family. But in subtle ways she exerted her power; it was Martha who negotiated for a piece of property while Fred stayed home with her sister's children. Nor was she afraid to try something new. (Fred was less inclined to take risks.) At age thirty-eight, she took up roller skating, promptly breaking her arm (and then nearly dying from an overdose of chloroform when the doctor set it). At age forty-two she was the first woman in Topeka to swim across a local lake—initially with water wings, then without. And she walked anywhere alone at any time, as long as she had her huge hatpins with her. We are convinced she would have used them.

Along with the independence went fierce energy, and relish of the everyday. She usually arose at 5:30 A.M., even when she had had company late the night before, and still had immense stamina. She did the housework, including all the gardening and canning, in the morning, leaving her afternoons and evenings free for club and lodge meetings, visits, lectures, concerts, movies, plays, ballgames, and other events. In 1899 she took up painting, and later began painting lessons at Mr. Beardsley's studio. For years she went to the studio almost every afternoon when it was open, for social as well as for artistic reasons. In 1905, after Beardsley had to close his studio, Martha was at loose ends for a time, but she then took up photography with equal energy, learning to develop and print her own pictures so as to save money. On some afternoons she developed as many as 150 photographs.

The rest of her "free" time seems to have been equally full. She was very active, for example, in her lodge, the Knights and Ladies of Security, and in 1897 was elected to its second highest office. This lodge gave her the opportunity to travel to Philadelphia to participate with its drill team in a national competition. Her energetic sight-seeing in Philadelphia exhausted all her companions. In later years she gave most of her energy to the Good Government Club, but she was also variously a member of the Coterie Club, Ladies of the Grand Army of the Republic, Golden Rule Club, Go-As-You-Please Club, Eastern Star, Woman's Kansas Day Club, Ladies' Aid Society, and other groups. Nor did she slight the local entertainment; she and Fred sometimes seem to have attended everything in town. In 1921 alone, they saw twenty-four movies, in addition to a large number of high school and church concerts and graduation ceremonies. The sheer volume of her activities is impressive, all of them engaged in with enthusiasm. She even liked her climb up into the state Capitol dome in 102° heat.

Martha never lost this *joie de vivre*, and she frequently thanked God for giving her the health and energy to do all she did, repaying the debt with a lifetime of religious loyalty. From the time of her very first entries, Martha was an inveterate churchgoer. She noted that she was a descendant of John Rogers, who was burned at the stake for his religion in Smithfield, England, in 1554. With the blood of such a martyr in her veins, she was true to her heritage throughout her life. In her courting days some of the attraction of church was clearly social. When she married Fred she settled her loyalties on the First Christian Church of Topeka, and she remained active there for the rest of her life. Martha's diary shows her to have been a sincerely devout woman who thoroughly enjoyed religion. Sometimes she went to church twice on Sunday, and occasionally she heard three different sabbath sermons. She was relatively tolerant, toward everyone except Mormons. (She recorded her surprise at seeing her first "real live Mormon," and never lost her conviction that they were adulterers, even though Fred's brother, John, was a devout member of the Church of Jesus Christ of Latter Day Saints. She consistently tried to convert any Mormon missionary who unsuspectingly came to her door.)

Although unquestioning faith sustained her, Martha enumerated enough of her woes to make her contrasting assertions of happiness believable. She suffered, for example, through some major illnesses and dangers, and her responses to these times of helplessness and fear were all recorded. Perhaps the worst period came when she was married to Johnny Shaw, and often feared that their marital proximity would give her his consumption. She had the usual childhood ailments: measles, chicken pox—serious enough in her time—and then malaria and typhoid, the disease that had killed her sister the same year. After she broke her arm, in her thirties, the bones slipped, requiring resetting; and at age forty-eight she permanently lost the sight of one eye.

Even during these periods of anguish, Martha considered herself blessed, and her response to both illness and worry was confident. She was intelligently cautious about disease: Johnny vaccinated her against smallpox, and she was careful not to enter houses of friends who had contagious ailments. Neither did she panic when a flu epidemic struck Topeka. When she broke her arm, she withheld the information from Fred for fear of worrying him. Later, facing an eye operation and fearing another overdose of chloroform, she secretly prepared for her death by setting her affairs in order to spare her husband as much worry as possible. She was neither maudlin nor melodramatic about it.

It is Martha's response to death that as much as anything reveals her religious confidence. The death of her sister at age sixteen was her first searing confrontation, made even harsher by the family's failure to call her to the deathbed in time for farewells. Martha reacted to the tragedy with despair and disbelief, and with a desire to die herself, confident that she would then be reunited with her sister. Her response to her own child's death was the same: a willingness to return the child to God because of its suffering, but a poignant plea for her own death. In later years, when several of her Sunday-school boys died, she did not go so far as to wish for death, but she expressed full confidence that they were safe in heaven and waiting for her. Only rarely, as when typhoid killed her sister May's young husband, leaving her a twenty-seven-year-old widow with three young children, do we see Martha question the divine will.

Martha's personality, then, was essentially provincial, adaptive, independent, sympathetic, buoyant, and so deeply religious that she could counter death with hope. Admittedly, there were disturbing elements too. A streak of self-righteousness, an intolerance born of unshakable moral conviction, occasionally surfaces. So too do we see a willingness to ignore some of her own faults: the impatience the naturally healthy have with the sick; the refusal to allow fatigue that the energetic often inflict on the phlegmatic; her inexplicable unwillingness to follow through on child-rearing. Martha's personality was not a simple one. Nonetheless, she is admirable for her confidence, her strength, and for her sustained ability to marvel, to maintain her curiosity and a sense of wonder about her existence—but she was probably difficult to live with.

Philip Greven, in *The Protestant Temperament*, remarks that moderate Protestants in Puritan times were self-approving people with little self-doubt; therefore their diaries record what they did, rather than what they thought.[6] Martha Farnsworth is in this tradition, though much of what she thought can be inferred from how she did what she did. The enthusiasm, the climate of an era, even the repression that Martha brings to her diary are intriguing. Her easy visiting among her neighbors, her devotion to kin, her frequent outings to public events, her enthusiasm for the mundane, her devoutness, her constant willingness to greet the present and the unseen with a cheer—all are nostalgic reminders of a world seldom seen in the literature of today. But lest we forget, the diary also reminds us of other aspects of this recent past: long hours of housework in prostrating heat; disenfranchisement; the haphazard nature of medical care, and death from typhoid, tuberculosis, smallpox; public lynchings; and national Prohibition. Perhaps this backward glance at the daily accountings of a Kansas woman who wanted to write a book but did not have the time will not make readers yearn for simpler days and simplistic pleasures. But it may make them marvel, as we did, over one woman's energy and enterprise, and lead them into more profound speculation about the psychological make-up of a woman who lived precariously in the lower middle class of second generation pioneers. Most certainly it will give an intriguing look at how it feels to be a woman in a legally defined man's world; at the changes wrought by the conversion of prairie to small town; of what it felt like to meet a woman who had not seen another woman for six months; of life with hated alcohol; of the frustrations of being a suffragist and a patriot; of loving the enigma of the land even while welcoming the railroad. The list goes on through a lifetime. Perhaps, finally, it will move them to find time to keep diaries themselves—thereby coming to realize that art does indeed shape the truth of life.

Notes

1. For a fine interpretation of how to read women's private writings in a social context, see Elizabeth Hampsten's *Read This Only to Yourself: The Private Writings of Midwestern Women, 1880-1910* (Bloomington: Indiana University Press, 1982). Hampsten's work indicates that Martha's reticence here is somewhat unusual. However, Martha's careful recording of her miscarriages and her open references to her husband's insistence that she have an abortion are in keeping with the kind of detail recorded by women of the period.

2. Helen White Papashvily, *All the Happy Endings* (New York: Harper and Brothers Publishers, 1956), p. 152.

3. Ibid., pp. 153-67

4. See Hampsten, p. 25.

5. William F. Zornow, *Kansas: A History of the Jayhawk State* (Norman: University of Oklahoma Press, 1957), p. 137.

6. Philip Greven, *The Protestant Temperament* (New York: Alfred A. Knopf, 1977), p. 299.

Acknowledgments

We thank the following for their willing and helpful aid in this project: the staff of the Kansas State Historical Society—especially Pat Michaelis, who helped us discover Martha Farnsworth; George Griffin and the staff of the Kansas Collection at the Spencer Research Library, The University of Kansas; Ralph Kingman and family; Thomas Averill; Patricia Deery; Edith Springer; the University of Kansas General Research Fund; the Research Council of the University of Missouri-Kansas City; and David Katzman, for his reading of the Introduction.

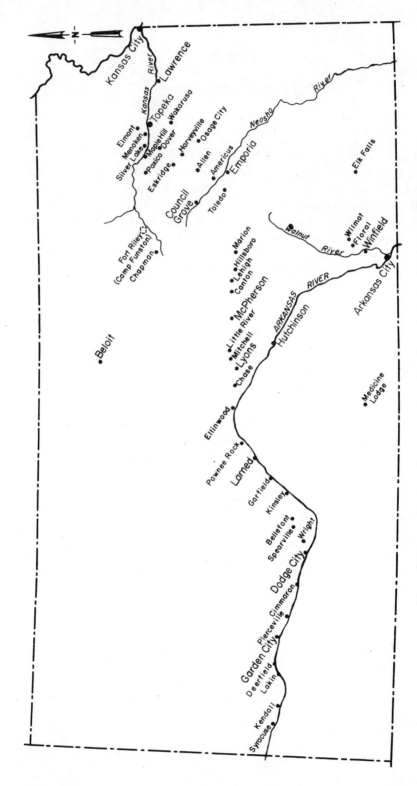

Map of Kansas showing places mentioned in diary (*map drawn by John Hollingsworth*).

THE DIARY OF
MARTHA FARNSWORTH,
1882–1922

Editorial Note

Martha Farnsworth's diary, located in the Manuscript Department of the Kansas State Historical Society, covers the years 1882–1922, but the books for 1900–1902 and 1923 are missing. These volumes are probably lost, rather than unwritten, for Martha was obviously a compulsive recorder. She filled every day of the extant diaries, even when she was so sick with malaria that she could only note, "At home all day and night sick. Wind blew from the south." The early entries are short; as her life became more complex and her insights more mature, the entries develop accordingly, and the diary becomes increasingly exciting. The text is spelled as Martha spelled it, with errors and inconsistencies intact, except that where her mistakes or oversights might create reading difficulties we have made silent corrections. We also have removed many of her excessive and distracting commas and have supplied missing punctuation where necessary for comprehension. Italicized editorial notes are included to clarify, or to summarize a relevant section that had to be omitted because of length. In order to pare thousands of manuscript pages to hundreds, six relatively uneventful years, 1897–99, 1904, 1907, and 1917, have been left out, as were months and days from other years because they reveal nothing new about her activities or her personality. The condensed diary, then, accurately displays the variety of the diarist's life—a rich mixture of the common and the dramatic.

[1882]

Martha began her diary in 1882 at age fourteen with no indication of her plans for it, nor any sign that she hoped to continue it for the rest of her life. The fact that she lived on the plains is immediately suggested by her continual references to the wind, a concern she maintained throughout the early years of the diary. The first year of her diary is not notable either for its content or its style. The entries are brief, reflecting both her youth and the recurring similarity of her days. Striking to the modern reader is the continuous stream of visits—primarily to and from relatives, but also from friends. Also evident from the earliest entries are her fine penmanship and fairly good grammar, reflecting at least some degree of education even in this remote, sparsely populated area of Kansas.

January

Sunday 1   At home. Anna & Alex Boomershine came over. In the evening I and Mrs. Keidney went to call on Mrs. Pontious. South wind.

Tues. 24   A cold day, wind blew from South. At school all day. At home all night. . . . George Rogers run a Wolf by the School-house, on his pony, "Pet," but did not catch it.

Thurs. 26   . . . . A grand wolf hunt took, was to take place. About 100 out; no wolves caught. Plenty of other game. Wind blew from North-west. Mrs Rhinehart and Annie Irwin at school.

February

Mon. 6   At home all day: sick and did not go to school: Strong south wind. At home all night. Fanny Pontious here in the evening.

Feb. 8–28 carry the refrain "At home all day and night sick," the only variation being in wind direction. She does not return to school until March 29—a 53-day fight with malaria.

March

Fri. 31   At school all day. The last day of Fanny Pontious' school, at Prairie Grove.[1] Had a nice dinner and a "spelling-school" at night. Wind blew from south.

April

Wed. 26   At home all day planting corn: at home all night. Wind blew from the north. Geo. Rogers was here. My birthday. Aged 15.

May

Fri. 12   At home all day and night. Got the chicken-pox.[2] Wind blew from the north. Geo. Stalter, Ella Weber and Hettie and Mary Plunkett were here.

November

Fri. 17   Anna Boomershine and Elfy White stayed all night here. At home all day, there being no school. Wind blew from the north, Dottie Pontious and Bert Plunkett were here. Went to "Literary" at night.[3]

December

Thurs. 28   At home all day: Fannie Pontious here all day: south wind. Went to "Singing-school" at night.[4] Frank Schock wanted to come home with me, but I had to give the poor fellow the "mitten."[5]

Fri. 29   Went to Mrs. Limerick's, to practice "pieces" for the Concert. At home all day. . . . South-east wind. Went to the schoolhouse at night and went from there to Mrs. Limerick's with Frank Schock. Bert Plunket brought me home.

[1883]

During this year Martha's interest in boys increased, and she devoted much energy to typical adolescent affairs of the heart. Again, there is little detail. It is interesting to note her late hours on some of these occasions, an indication of a decidedly un-Victorian freedom she was to enjoy throughout her dating years.

January

Tues. 2
At school all day: sisters May and Belle & I went to Singing-school in the evening at the schoolhouse. Mr. Hittle teaches. Bert Plunket walked home with me. Here are our descriptions. I am fifteen years old, black hair, & big, black eyes. My hair curls. Bert is 15, just my height, has blue eyes and light hair. We are both *heavy* for our ages, and everyone says, we are *"an awful cute little couple."* Bert is 6 months the oldest.

Fri. 5
At school. Went to Literary in the evening with Pa, & sisters. Bert Plunket walked home with me. We have just the jolliest, best, times at Literary.

Sun. 7
At home. We live on our farm, 12 miles north of Winfield, our nearest Railroad point. We call our farm "Sunny Slope" for our house is built on the south Slope of a hill and is so sunny in winter.

Mon. 8
At school. We all have such good times at school.

Tues. 9
At school. Went to "Singing" in the eve. Bert walked home with me. Irve Schofield and Emery Savage want to go with me and some others too, but I'll stick to Bert, I think.

Sat. 20
At home. This is sister Belle's birthday: she is a sweet, pretty, little, black-eyed sister and I love her, very much.

Tues. 23
At school. Went to "Singing" in the evening with Pa, May & Belle, and Bert Plunket walked home with me. My step-mother says, if I don't quit letting the boys walk home with me, she will put us all to bed, for we are only children: *she can't put me to bed, anyhow.*[1]

Thurs. 25
At school. We play Base-ball at school, at noon, every day and have such good times: the Boys have their "9,"

and we girls our "9" and when we play against the Boys we beat them every time: We all play together a good deal.

Fri. 26   At school. In the evening, the school gave a *"Neck-tie Festival"*[2] at the school-house and *cleared $38.22*: I went with my sisters, but Bert came home with me. I ate supper with Luman Phelps. Sister May was voted a "cake," for being the *"handsomest"* girl present.

Sat. 27   At home. I made some new *"mashes"* last night: wonder if my step-mother would put me to bed if she knew it.

March

Wed. 14   Went to school in the morning and came home at the forenoon "recess," sick with the "measles". Hated, Oh! so much to have to leave school.

Thurs. 15   At home with the *measles.* The hateful things won't *break out* and they are soaking me full of tea.

Fri. 16   At home.

She remains ill with measles for approximately two weeks. The entries during this period are primarily "At home" so she must have been quite ill. Her only lament is that school has closed by the time she has fully recuperated (March 27).

April

Sun. 1   Went to Mr. Wm. Plunket's in the morning and staid until after dinner, when Kirk Thompson came there, for me to go to their house and stay this summer and I went home with him.[3]

Mon. 2   At Mr. John R. Thompson's, one of our neighbors, about 4 or 5 miles from home. . . .

June

Mon. 4   At Mr. Thompson's; they want to *adopt* me; "the very idea;" I would not be anyone's girl but Pa's and I wish my stepmother was good to me, so I could stay home more.

James Ogden VanOrsdol,
Martha's father, in his Civil
War uniform. Courtesy
Ralph A. Kingman, Topeka.

Sat. 30   At Mr. T. Went home this evening to stay all night. Rode
home on horse-back; rode Kirk's 3 year old, colt,
"Queen," wild as a *deer* and never had the saddle on her
before. Pa said I *should* not come home again, until I
could have a more gentle horse to ride. But I *Dearly love
daring*, am a good rider, for I've rode all my life, and
inherit some of my good horsemanship from my father,
and have rode nearly every kind of animal, from a
Jack-(Jass-ack), Burro, Cows, Hogs, Young Steers, Stal-
lions and all, but for *solid fun* give me a colt to *break*.

August

Sun. 26   At Mr. Thompson's. Went to S. S. [Sunday School] in
the morning with the family and in the afternoon Lennie & his mother brought me over home to stay, as my
"step-mother" is sick and needs me: hope I'll be a little
better treated, now I'm needed. Lennie took me to see
Anna Boomershine awhile in the afternoon. I hated—
just a little—to come home, for I was having such a good
time and my stepmother is none to kind to me.

September

Wed. 12   At home. In the evening I went to a Party at Mr. Baker's, with Sam Dent. We went on horse-back, had a *jolly good* time and got home at 3:30 A.M. Sam is a good boy, but I'm *not stuck.*

November

Mon. 1   At school. School commenced this morning with John Clemence Bradshaw as teacher; he is tall, with blue eyes, very light complection, and not over 20 years old, and seemingly very bashful. Oh! what a time we girls will have, if he is: we will make life miserable for him.

Thurs. 4   At school. Teacher blushes everytime I look at him and so do I. I wish he wouldn't look at me; the girls say he is *"stuck"* on my big, black, eyes: he needn't be. I never *fall in love* with my teachers.

December

Fri. 7   At school. Went to Literary in the evening with Pa and sisters. Jozie Calvin walked home with me after Literary: Bert is *"not in it"* so much this winter, he is a jolly, handsome, little fellow tho, but I've "got my eye" on a "new fellow" who came into the country, this Fall: he is a *giant*. Jozie is short, with black eyes and the prettiest black mustache. I'm the envy of all the girls, but they can have Jozie, for I'm going to catch this "new fellow," before the winter is over. I'm acquainted with him now, but only a little.

Wed. 12   At school. Went to a "Party" in the evening, at uncle Zeke Roger's, with Jozie Calvin and just had the best time. The "new fellow," *Mr. Carman* was there, and we had lots of games together. . . .

Mon. 31   At school. We just have the, *"maddest, merriest"* times, at school. This is the last day of the "Old Year." I wonder what the "New Year" will bring me. It is going to bring me a new "beau" if I *am* a little girl and my step-mother says I'm too young to go with the Boys. I'm 16 and not very small, either, 'cause I'm *awful fat.* my legs, measure 14 inches around the "calf" and I'm big all over. *I'm* big enough to go, whether *I'm* old enough or not. I weigh 129. My hair is just as curly and one girl told me the other day, that if I was only *white* I'd be the "prettiest girl in the country." She is a blond is why she said it. I'm Brunette.

[1884]

January

Tues. 1

At school: a very cold day. The coldest "New Year" I've ever seen in Kansas, and I came to Kansas Dec. 10, 1872 from Mt. Pleasant Iowa.

Thurs. 3

At school. Went to Uncle Zeke Rogers' after school in eve, and after supper went with them and cousin Will Sapp, to a "dance" at Mrs. Boomershine's. I danced everything that was danced during the whole evening except two "Quadrilles" and everyone said I danced so nicely, tho' I was never on the floor, but once before, in my life: and this is the first dance I ever went to. But it was "*born in me*" to dance, for my parents before me were good dancers. "*Mr. Carman*" was my "Partner" more than any one else, during the eve, and Uncle Neal Anderson who brought his sister Carrie, and my sisters brought us all home at 1:30 A.M. after a most happy evening.

Tues. 29

At school. Carrie Anderson, Will & John Johnson and Jack Schrubshell were at school today. Jack was trying to make a "mash" on me, but I'm not so easy mashed; he is as ugly as a "*mud fence staken rided with bull-frogs*" and I can "mash" on *prettier faces* if I like.

Thurs. 31

At school. In the evening, I went to a "Dance" at Mrs. Boomershine's, with Jamie Carman. We just had the *jolliest best* time. I danced the Quadrilles, Waltzs, Schottisches & Polkas and hardly left the floor from time I got there until we left for home at 4 o'clock in the morning. Everyone says I'm such a pretty dancer. I dearly love to dance, and I get all I want of it too, for every young man wants me to dance with him.

March

Sat. 1

At school. The "*Last Day*" and we are all, *awfully* sorry, for it has been a most *jolly, happy* school term. Clem Bradshaw is such a good teacher. We had a "big dinner" and Oh! *such a jolly time* . . . . After supper, Minnie, sisters and I went to "spelling school" at school house, after which our "*best Boys*" walked home with us again.

Sun. 2   In the morning sister Belle & I hitched up old "Barney & Prince" to the wagon and hauled two Barrels of water, about 1/2 mile from a nice Spring. We have to be Pa's "boys" for we have no brothers and our wells are getting low so have to haul water, sometimes. After dinner cousin Minnie Weber came and we got on the two horses "bare-back" and rode to Mr. Cunningham's, Nelse Sapp's and Mrs. Boomershine's. We had a lovely ride of about 10 miles and all just for the "sport" there was in it, for we two "tom-boys."

Tues. 4   Am going to Winfield next week to go to school.[1] I dearly love to go to school, but I hate awfully to leave my friends here at Prairie Grove.

Fri. 7   At home. Went to Literary in the evening with Pa & sister May & Belle. We had just the jolliest time at Literary and I hate to think that I'm going way and can't come any more. Jamie Carman walked home with me after Literary and when we got right on top of the hill, near the house, he looked down at me (for I only come to his shoulders) and says "*Mattie I want to make a bargain with you.*" I had noticed that he was rather quieter than usual, but I little dreamed, of what was coming, and replied, "*alright*," when he says, rather abruptly, "*Will you marry me*"? Well, it was so sudden and unexpected that I answered, simply, "*Yes*" without hardly knowing what I was saying. I wonder if that is the way everyone "*gets engaged.*" I always thought people "made love" first, and he has never made love to me; I have never went with him very much, tho', and he hasn't had a chance and he wanted to ask me, before I went away to school and will "*make love*" afterwards. He says we will get married when ever I get ready to quit school. This is my first "*proposal*": just think! I'm the first one, of all this crowd of school-girls and boys to be engaged, and I'm *young, too young*: just "*sweet 16*" and Jamie is 20. Morris is his name, but Clem Bradshaw "nicnamed" him "Jamie" at a dance one night. I wonder what Pa will say, but he won't know it, for we won't marry for *ever-so-long*, tho' Jamie says he is ready to marry any time: this Spring, in the Fall, or when ever I'm ready, but I must go to school a long time first. I'll have to give up my other "sweet hearts" when we get married, so I'm going to wait a long time: Jamie asked me to "kiss" him goodnight and I had to do it: but I don't think he is near so nice for doing it. I never kissed him before. I don't like to *kiss boys*.

Sat. 8   Went down to Grandpa Anderson's in the morning to borrow a spool of thread. Roy Cass, Mr. Darling and Belle Anderson were here. I feel just like I always do, if I am "engaged": how funny it sounds.

Mon. 10   Pa & Ma took me to Winfield, very early in the morning to Mr. Devore Parmer's where I am to Board and then to Mrs. Limerick's, where Minnie Weber came and Pa & Mrs. Limerick went with us to the Central school building, where Minnie & I entered school under Miss Lois Williams, in Grammar Department. Minnie in "B Grade" & I in the "A," where in two months if I pass good examinations I will be promoted to High School. I went up town in the evening to buy some school-books.

Tues. 11   At school. Called at Mrs. Limerick's few minutes in the morning, before school. Mrs. L. is an old teacher of mine and I love her very much. Mr. Parmer's seem to be very nice people: She is going to let me help her with her work, to pay for my Board, because my stepmother didn't want me to come and this will settle the "expense" question.

Wed. 19   At school. Was at Mr. A. J. Thompson's few minutes in eve to get some milk. I'm getting awfully "home sick" to see all the young folks at Prairie Grove. I'm going out there Friday night to Literary if I have to walk the whole 12 miles. I would like to see Jamie but no more than the rest of the folks.

Sun. 23   . . . Mr. Mount treated me to "Beer" the first I ever tasted and I think it *awfully, nasty, bitter* stuff. He had better leave it alone, for he has drank up his home and everything he ever had.

Tues. 25   At school. Went over to Mr. Thompson's in the evening to get some milk and was introduced to Gene McInturff & Will Finch while there. Will is tall with blue-eyes and light mustache, and seems so quiet. Gene is short, with blue-eyes, smooth face and quite talkative. I think I will like him the best of the two, tho' I'm not making "*mashes*".

Fri. 28   At school. I saw a Chinaman today; the first in my life. . . .

April

Sun. 6	At Mr. Parmer's all day: Rained most all afternoon. Mrs. Thompson & children spent the evening with us. I believe I'm beginning to think Mr. McInturff and especially Mr. Finch, are quite nice boys: tho' Gene seems to be the jolliest.
Mon. 7	At school. Went up town from school, in the eve. I like school here very much and am making many new friends.
Sun. 13	Went over to Mrs. Thompson's after dinner and went with Anna Hook to Sunday-school at the Methodist church, after which I went back to Mrs. T's with her and in eve went to church with her at the Methodist. Gene McInturff and Will Finch both wanted to go to church with me and neither wanted to go with Anna, and as they could not agree between themselves, who should go with me, they both "*slyly*" excused themselves to me and stayed at home and let us go alone.
Mon. 14	At school. Spent the evening at Mrs. Thompson's very happily, and Gene McInturff walked over home with me. I see I've made two "conquests" in Gene Mc & Will Finch: wonder who will come out "best." Gene is ahead now. Poor Jamie Carman is being forgotten I'm afraid. Well I *don't love* him anyway and never did, and people ought to *love* when they marry. I like Jamie only as a friend. Link Frederick, an old *admirer* of mine at Prairie Grove, is 21 years old today: he has blue eyes. All my "*sweet hearts*" have. Bert, Jamie, & now Gene & Will.
Mon. 21	At school. Mrs. Thompson & Mrs. Parmer have been trying to get Will Finch & I to going together, but Gene & I seem to "Match" better. I'm 16, and Gene is 18: Will is 21 and seems much older to me: but both are nice boys.
Sat. 26	Went up town in the afternoon. This my 17th birthday and I've had to keep out of sight of Gene & Will all day, for they were determined to give me a whipping. Anna Boomershine sent me a pretty glass cup, Mr. Parmer gave me some candy, Mrs. Parmer, a gold "Breast-pin" & Eliza Johnson a pretty collar and all for my Birthday presents.
Sun. 27	Went to Mrs. Thompson's for milk as usual this morning and Will Finch caught me, turned me across his

knee and whipped me awfully hard with the Clothes-brush, he said to make me remember my 17 birthday and I always will. Minnie Weber took me out to her home in the morning and we went to S.S. at Walnut Valley church in the morning and after dinner we went to Mr. Corbon's and played "Authors" awhile, then drove back to town and got Eliza Johnson and all three went to see Anna Hook at Mrs. Thompson's and Will Finch went to Baptist church with we four girls, in eve but we made Will walk with Anna. After church Will & I took Anna home, then took a short walk around two or three blocks and then home. Will scolded because I would not walk to church with he and Anna, instead of making him walk alone with Anna: He said I knew that I was the only one of the "bunch" that he wanted to go with. Of course I knew it, but I wanted to *tease* him.[2]

Wed. 30   At school. Went to Mr. Mount's in the evening after school, to Mary's "wedding." Mary Mount and Fred Gross were married at 8 o'clock P.M. by Judge Garrs: had a real nice time: Mary was so happy & proud of Fred. I don't feel a bit like I would be happy if I married Jamie, I guess I'm beginning to like some one else better—*Will, for instance.* I hope Mary & Fred will always be happy. Mary is the first girl I became acquainted with when I came to Kansas. . . . I was only 5 years old then and Mary & I have always been friends. Ed Mount walked home with me after the wedding.

May

Sat. 3   Went up town in the afternoon and called at Mrs. Limerick's. I know Pa won't like it very well, because I had my ears *pierced* last night: he says that is the way Indians do.

Sun. 4   Minnie Weber and Eliza Johnson came in the afternoon for me to go *walking* with them. We went to the West R.R. Bridge, over the Walnut River, where a year or so ago, Charlie Cobb—a 19 year old Boy—was hung by a Mob for killing Sheriff Shenneman, while trying to arrest him.[3] We went to Bliss Mill too: had a long walk, then I came home and Will Finch came and took me to meeting. I had a jolly time today.

Sat. 10   Cora Finch came and went to the school house, where we scholars all went to get our "Promotion" Cards. Cora & I were both *promoted* to High School.

Wed. 14   . . . Mrs. Parmer said she would give me $2.00 a week to stay with her this summer. *Pa* would rather I was at home. *I* would rather be here, where I can see Will.

Sun. 18   Minnie Weber & Eliza Johnson came in afternoon and we went to the Park where we met Nellie Gretsinger then we all went . . . to the Baptist church to meeting, taking Hallie Hunt & Maggie Early with us. After meeting, all but Eliza walked home with me. This morning I wrote a letter to Jamie Carman, "breaking our engagement." I like Will Finch better and there is no need of Jamie's thinking I'll marry him when I won't. Jamie is a good friend but I *can't* love him so why be engaged to him.

June

Tues. 3   At Mr. Parmer's. I went up town in the afternoon with Anna Hook. In the evening Will Finch & Anna Hook came over. Anna went upstairs and talked with Mrs. Parmer and left Will & I to ourselves and we sat on the Porch and talked all evening: this little love affair is mutual, and in dead earnest; not like it was with Jamie: With Will & I it was "love at first sight" tho' both of us were engaged to someone else; but I've broken mine and it waits to be seen whether Will can his or not. I hope he can.

Fri. 6   At Mr. Thompson's for breakfast and there until noon when the folks came home. Cora Finch came to see me awhile . . . and after supper she & Will came for me and we all went to the Ice-cream Parlor, then to Rose Hixon's where we spent a jolly hour or two . . . and then Will & I came home and sat on the Veranda and talked until 11 o'clock. These talks with Will are getting very serious and mean very much to both of us.

Mon. 9   Cora Finch came in P.M. & she and I went to the Brettun Hotel to see Emma Weber and also to Mr. Mount's. In eve I went to Opera House with Anna Hook to hear "Helen Gougar" lecture on *Womans Rights*.[4]

Fri. 20   At. P's. Mrs. Parmer & children, & I spent the evening at

Mrs. Thompson's. No wonder Will & I are "falling so much in love," we see each other, day and night and all the time.

Sun. 22 Went to Sunday-school in the morning, to the United Brethren church. In afternoon Will & I went down to his father's and got Cora & Rose Hixon and went to the Park for the afternoon. We all went to Rose's from the Park and at church time to Catholic church, but it was so crowded we went back to Rose's awhile then home.

Mon. 30 Mrs. Thompson & children & Anna Hook, spent the evening with Mrs. P. & I. Mrs. T. & Mrs. P. are trying to interfere with Will & I. Want Will to go with Anna and me get a new fellow; *not much.*

July

Fri. 4 Up bright & early and packed my Lunch basket . . . then up town to see the Parade and to the Fair Grounds to the Fourth of July Celebration. Will ate dinner with us and spent all the time he could with me. I went home for supper and after supper Will and Gene McInturff— who has been out of city for some time—came for me to go down town with them to see the Fireworks, which were just grand; after they were over, Will came home with me and we talked till mid-night. This has been such a *very, very* happy day to me. I know I'm so happy because Will loves me so much. I saw poor Jamie today, but dared not speak to him, lest I should encourage his love, that I do not want: he looked *wretched* and I'm sorry for him, but most too happy in my new love, to feel very sorry. Jamie is too be pitied if he cares for me as I do for Will, and I have every reason to think he does. It would break my heart to lose Will, tho' we are not engaged. Cora Finch introduced me to Charlie Jenkins, today; he is an old beau of hers or wants to be one, and appears very nice.

Tues. 15 Rained hard most all day: Will Finch got word today from Elk Falls, Kans. to come on, at once and accept a position in a Mill over there so about 4 o'clock P.M. he came over and bid me good-bye and took the 5 o'clock train for Elk Falls: it just broke my heart: I've been so "blue" all evening, I couldn't eat any supper and I've nearly cried my eyes out. I didn't know I did care so much for him, until now he is gone: how can I ever stand it.

Wed. 16   Went over to Mr. T's in eve awhile to see Emma Weber who is "sewing" there, but it is so lonesome there, without my Will, I could not stay. . . . I've cried all day today when ever I was alone. I'm so lonesome.

Wed. 23   Clem Bradshaw came up in the evening to see me and we went for a walk and after our return he stayed and talked until 11 o'clock. He said I was the one, among all the girls at Prairie Grove, that he wanted to go with and I would never give him a chance to go with me, always kept "shy" of him—well, I never fall in love with my teachers. He *proposed* to me and I told him I would not marry until I was an "old maid" and that would be 13 years from now: he said he would wait 13 years, if he could have me in the end. I told him *"alright"*: he would think his chances *"slim"* if he knew how much I cared for Will.

Thurs. 24   At Mr. Thompson's awhile in the morning and got an introduction to Harvey McClellan while there. Oh! how I do want to see Will and every one is trying to get me to take Jamie back again, because he is so broken-hearted and tried to "commit suicide" by taking Strychnine but his mother caught him, just in time. I'm sorry for poor Jamie, but I can't love him. Will has me heart and soul, tho' we are not engaged yet, but he *loves* me I know.

Sun. 27   At Pa's until after dinner when Cousin Will Sapp and Jamie Carman came and took Cora, sister May & I back to Winfield, Cora & I rode in the seat with Will: they all had a good time but me and I wanted Will. Jamie was glad to be near me, even if I wouldn't ride with him. I didn't want him along: it made me feel *"cheap"* after [the] way I've treated him.

Thurs. 31   . . . . Clem Bradshaw came in the evening and we went down town for ice cream and he staid until almost mid-night after we came home. He is wasting his time, for I will *never* love any one but Will, I know.

August

Sun. 10   Went to the Depot this morning to meet my Will and he came at 10 o'clock. I had to tell a *"fib"* to the folks for everyone is now opposing my going with him and I told them I was going to S.S. I went with Will to his father's and staid all day: after dinner he & I took a short walk, to the Santa Fe R. R. Bridge. He had to return on the 5 P.M. train and Cora, Gene McInturff & I went to Depot with him, where he kissed me good-bye and nearly broke my heart, going away again. Cora then walked home with me and in about 1/2 hour, Gene Mc & George McClellan came and took us out driving. We drove about 7 miles out in the country, and it was a lovely drive, but I wanted Will all the time, tho' it was a very jolly evening, as it was.

Mon. 11   At Thompson's awhile in the morning: the folks know that I saw Will yesterday and are *mad* about it, but I am *very* happy, tho' it makes me more lonesome.

Sun. 17   Minnie Weber came for me, bright and early and we drove out to Prairie Grove, to Pa's and stayed until 1:30 P.M. when cousin Will Sapp came and he, Minnie & I all drove up to Green Valley, to Mr. Carman's. I didn't want to go, but they all insisted: they are trying to get me to "go back" to Jamie again and I can't love him. We did not get out of the Buggy, but talked about an hour to Jamie and then drove back to Winfield, cousin Will riding at least 6 or 7 miles with us and then walked back.

Sat. 23   In the afternoon, without any "warning" who should come, but Jamie Carman: how I hated to see him, but in *spite* of my *heart's protest*, "we talked over," the *past* and now are *"engaged"* again. I could not "hold out" against his *"pleadings"* when I saw the tears streaming down his cheeks and saw his whole body trembling, for *very love* of me. Poor boy, I wish I could love him, but I know I'll *never* love anyone but Will, but I *must bury my own heart* now, and try to *like* Jamie all I can. After we "made up" we went down town together and Jamie seemed *so* happy. Oh! how *can I ever marry him.*

Sun. 24   At Parmer's. Oh! so lonely for I'm used, at least on Sunday, to being with a *dear one* and now to know I never will be again: *how can I tell Will* what I've done, for he will be so disappointed, tho' he wasn't out of his other engagement. I *don't love* Jamie and *never can.*

Tues. 26   At Thompson's awhile in the morning. I wish Will had stayed here, then Jamie could not have had a chance to "coax" me back. Oh! Well I may get over it; a girl of 17 is not expected to know *what* or *who* she wants and is excusable for most anything she does. I'll try to be good to Jamie.

Fri. 29   At Parmer's all day; so *much more lonely*, now there is *no hope*.

Sat. 30   Went down town in afternoon and got a letter from Will. At Thompson's in eve: they & Parmer's are glad, Jamie "came on the scene"; they think that ends all between Will & I. Harvey McClellan asked me to drive with him tomorrow and I said I would: Jamie sent me word he was coming down but maybe I can run away, for I'd rather drive with Harvey.

Sun. 31   Minnie Weber came early in afternoon, also Jamie Carman also Harvey McClellan, for the promised drive, and Jamie looked so *pitiful*, I had to *fib* to Harvey and stay at home with Jamie. I think I have a *few* "too many strings to my bow." I will just have to *drop* Jamie.

September

Mon. 1   Thompson's & Parmer's think I treated Harvey Mc badly, yesterday, but I didn't "go to." I wish so many didn't "fall in love with me," or what-ever it is. . . .

Tues. 2   Minnie Weber, came on "horseback" in afternoon and I got on behind her, and we rode out in the country to her father's and stayed until after dark: and I enjoyed myself very much, if *I am* "engaged" to *one*, in love with *another*, and *several more* strings to my bow, I might spare.

Tues. 9   At Parmer's. Got a letter from Will today: he feels *very badly* to think I've gone back to Jamie but says Jamie has first right to me; poor Will is so unselfish, I know his heart is breaking so is mine and I never will marry Jamie.

Sun. 14   Jamie Carman came to see me, just a little past noon and later he & I called at Dr. Bull's for Idola Moore & Jess Kuhn and went to Riverside Park for the afternoon. We stopped at Rose Hixon's on our way home. I knew Jamie wanted to have me all to himself, but I can't bear to be alone with him, for he "loves me to death" and can do nothing but tell me about it over and over, and I can't *bear* to hear it; it is hateful to me, for I can't love him the least bit in return and he overwhelms me with love I do not want. I *pity* the poor Boy, but that is all. He stayed with me until "plum" midnight. I'm glad he only comes down every two weeks.

Tues. 23 Aunt Emma Van Orsdol died today noon, leaving a pretty little, 5 year old daughter, Vella, that she gave us. Uncle Will & Neal Anderson came in for me in the eve and I went out home to Pa's.

Thurs. 25 Came back to town this morning with cousin Nelson Sapp. My Will is over from Elk Falls. I went to the *Fair* in the afternoon with Minnie Weber and met Will there and was so glad to see him, I cried. Jamie Carman is down too, but I wouldn't let him come out to see me. Minnie ate supper with me and then we went down town where we met Will & a fellow for Minnie and we all went to the Theatre, and took the longest way home afterwards. I've been so happy with Will today. Minnie always helps us to get together: she is just the dearest, best girl and does everything for me.

October

Thurs. 2 At school. Wrote a letter to poor Jamie telling him to release me from my engagement with him. I can't love him, so why go on this way.

Fri. 3 At school. Pa and Ma were down today to have "adoption papers" made out for cousin Vella Van. I don't think they ought to adopt her at all: it is enough to keep her and alright, but I don't want her adopted.

November

Sat. 1 My Dear old Will came over from Elk Falls today and sent me a note, so I met him down town in eve at Court House and went to the Theatre with him. I have to meet him in secret always now.

Sun. 2 At Parmer's. . . . Minnie came in afternoon. Jim Finch came in afternoon with a note from Cora wanting me to come down but the folks mistrusted Will was home and I dared not go, but I wasn't to be beaten and in eve Minnie Weber pretended to go home, I went to my room, and the folks went to bed, and soon there was a low call of "Mattie" at my window from Minnie; I pulled off my shoes, stole lightly down the stairs and out the door and was soon with Will, hid behind the hedge at the gate. Wasn't I happy tho'. He staid some time, then took my dear Minnie home.

Mon. 3   At school until noon. I went down after dinner and met Will at P.O. where soon Minnie Weber & Frank Spring met us with a "double rig" and we all drove 12 miles out to Akron to cousin Lulu Roger's, where she had a *party* in honor of her 18th birthday. Rained on us hard most of the way, but we had a splendid *rig* and kept dry: it was 12:30 A.M. when we got home and how I did enjoy myself with Will. The folks don't know he is over from the "Falls," I told them I was going to the *Party* after school with another fellow, but *"All is fair, in love and war,"* if it was a *fib*.

Tues. 4   At school. Very little studying tho', as it is Election Day, and teachers & pupils alike—being almost every one, Republicans—are very much interested and Politics, more than lessons, were discussed. Prof. Gridley went down town real often for us, to get the latest *returns*. God grant the Republicans may gain a grand victory and elect Blaine & Logan, President and Vice-Pres. of the United States, over Cleveland & Hancock Democrats.

Fri. 7   At school. In eve after school, drove up to Green Valley, 16 miles North of here, with Dell Stalter, her mother & two little brothers, to a dance at her sister's Lou Snyder: Got there in good time and commenced dancing at 8 o'clock and such a jolly time as we had. Jamie Carman was there, and *I had to dance with him*, but not one word, was said, about our recently broken engagement, tho' I knew how much he felt, by the way his hands trembled, as he took mine in dancing. Poor Jamie, I'm sorry for him. Dell & I staid all night. Dance broke up at 3 A.M.

Sat. 8   About 10 A.M. Dell and I walked to her mother's from Snyders and at 4 P.M. All left for Winfield again and when about halfway, met Pa, who had been at W—and I went home with him to Floral, where my folks have moved, about 4 miles from Prairie Grove. Went to meeting at Baptist church in eve with sisters May & Belle & little Vella. Charlie Fletcher a young colored man— Republican—was shot & killed in Winfield this eve, for *"hurrahing"* for Blaine and Logan, by Mr. Burghe, who is a Democrat and was drunk. Fletcher shot Burghe badly before dying.

Thurs. 13   At school. At Thompson's in eve. Packed my trunk when I went up to bed, for I'm going to "run away" from Parmer's and find a new boarding place. They are *fighting* Will all the time and I have to meet him *clandestinely* when ever he comes over to see me, and I'm going to leave. Wonder what Pa will say. Will is better than the "P's & T's".

Sat. 15 At Mr. Finch's all day except few minutes in A.M. Jimmie Finch took Cora & I to Mr. Clark's and Mrs. C. not being very strong, with two Babies thought I could help her a good deal in the care of them and go to school, so now "I've run away," that is [the] way I'm to pay my board and still go to school. Went to town with Cora in eve and then to Clark's to stay all night and make my home awhile. Little Hugh Parmer is 5 years old today. Mr. Clark's seem very nice. Have two little girls Ada & Ora.

December

Tues. 16 At school until noon. My dear Will came over today and gave me a *most happy* suprise. I played "*hookey*" and spent the whole afternoon with him at his father's and went to the Theatre in eve with him, and he didn't hurry home after, we came home from the Theatre to Mr. Clark's: I've been so happy all P.M.

Wed. 17 Didn't go to school today for Will was here to see me. I went to a "Ball" with him in eve and had such a good time with him as I always do.

Thurs. 18 Didn't go to school today, for Will was here. In eve went to a Dance at Mr. Hodges, on east 9th Ave. While waltzing, another couple jostled against me and pushed my elbow right thro' a nice glass door, and of course Will paid for it. Oh! we did have such a jolly good time and it was after 1 o'clock when we got home. Will was so happy, and so was I, but had to bid him good-bye as he goes home in A.M.

Fri. 19 Stayed at home to rest, after my three nights "*disapating*."
Went to school in afternoon tho'.

[1885]

Notable in this year is Martha's constant round of parties, visiting, and other entertainment; she often wrote that she was enjoying her life. Church continued to be a major factor in local life, but for the young people its function was social more than religious, and they were eclectic in their attendance. Martha joined the Christian Church on June 7th and was to remain a member throughout her life, but she also variously attended the Baptist, the Holiness and the United Brethren Churches. Nearly every entry mentions some aspect of her love life. She had already had two engagements and three proposals, though not yet nineteen years old. Along with dancing, church, and courting, she also found time to help her father who had taken in ten boarders, and to attend a "Normal School" for four weeks, hoping to improve her teaching skills.

January

Thurs. 1   At home all day: Began the "New Year" good by going to Prayer-meeting in eve, at Baptist church, with Rose Hooker, May & Belle & little Vella, and Susie Ferguson. Cousin Will Sapp came in eve to get me to go to a dance at his brother Nelson's, but I wouldn't go because my Will F. couldn't be here to go with me and I know Jamie Carman would be sure to be there and I must keep away from him.

Mon. 12   At school till noon when I went to P.O. with Cora F. and meeting Will there, they both insisted on my going home with them for dinner, which I did. At 4 P.M. Cora had to go up town, and so it left Will & I alone, just the chance he wanted, and after Cora left, he told me, he had broken his engagement, with the other girl, because he loved me more, and then asked me to marry him. I was so happy, I cried. I don't think there is two happier people any where, than Will & I are. After the "*Proposal*" he walked part way home with me, then went up town and came back by Clark's to bid me good-bye, as he had to take the 5:25 P.M. train to Elk Falls again. I hated to have him go, but have something to look forward to now; a time when I'll be with him always. I believe I'm the happiest girl on earth. I've never been so happy in all my life before and Will seemed brimming over with joy and happiness.

Tues. 13   At school until after my Grammar class in the P.M. when I got "excused" and came home and at 6 P.M. went to the Opera House to Rehearse in the Play, "*The Tennessee Scout*" to be given by the G.A.R.[1] by "home talent," under management of L. D. Dobbs, who is also the Author of the Play, and travels with Mr. Devendorff, Mr. Cooper and Mr. Johnston, taking "home talent" for rest of Play. *Jessie Stretch*, as "Miss Alice Coleman," a Nurse, Hattie Andrews, as "Bessie Fox" a housemaid, Cora Finch, as "Aunt Jemima" and I as Maria Carey were the only girls in the play, except the 9 Tableaux girls. I was highly complimented on my acting by all. After "Rehearsal" Cora F. came home with me and staid all night.

Thurs. 15   At Mr. Clark's. Went to the Opera house in the eve to Play in the Tennessee Scout, this being first night. I was most highly complimented by the Manager, L. D. Dobbs, the Soldiers and *loudly cheered* by the Audience. All did just splendidly, but I had the funny part, and had to *rush into my lover's arms* and *kiss him on his "return from the war."* Everyone said I was so "original"; may be they think I have not had a *little practice* before I went into this play, ha! ha! Frank Waverling was my lover, in the play, and all the Soliders told me, they envied him. I had compliments enough tonight, to turn many a head. Mr. Clark took me to the Opera House and Mr. Trump brought me home after the Play.

Fri. 16   At Mr. Clark's. Mr. Trump took me to the Opera House in the eve, to take part again in the Play. I was "*applauded to the skies* and *back*" and the G.A.R. Post, all made a great deal over me. We girls all wore "Soldier Caps" during most of the Play and were prettily dressed. I wore my *Cap* thro' all the Play, at the request of the Soldiers who said it "become" me *very* much. The Play is said to be the best that has ever come to Winfield: everyone speaks highly of it. Mr. Clark brought me home after the play.

Sat. 17   At Mr. Clark's. Went to Mr. Trump's in the eve and went with them to the Opera, to Play again in the Tennessee Scout, this being the last night. Compliments came to me from every side and introductions were sought by more than one. I was told the Soldiers were all in love with me. I didn't try to attract anyone. I only tried to do my part as best I could and so succeeded in making many friends. I think it was the part I played that was so popular, instead of me. After the Play was over, the Soldiers all came and shook hands and bid the "Soldier Girl"—as they called me—goodbye. Mr. Dobbs the manager bid me good-bye telling me I had done my part *well*, had pleased the audience and pleased him, then shook me by the hand saying, "*God bless you, my girl, I hope we may meet again, good-bye*" and then we parted, all speaking a kind word, and "shaking hands" with me as I left the Stage. I have been very happy thro' all this, but one dear name has ever been in my heart, had my constant thought: thro' it all there was a constant Wish for Will. I came home from the Play with Mr. Trump's and then ran across the street home.

Sun. 25   Went for a short walk in afternoon with Lettie Davis & Jennie Wells. Mr. Welch, who took part in the Play—Tennessee Scout—last week was accidently shot and killed this morning by his room mate.

Mon. 26   At school. Had examination in Grammar today and my "standing" was 91%. Pretty good I think, considering how little I study. I have Will "on the brain" too much for study.

February

Mon. 23   At Mr. C's. Went to the "Central Hotel" in eve and staid all night. Am going to help Mr. Axtel, until he gets another girl. I must get work of some kind to do, for Will & I are to be married this Fall and I will have to get my clothes, for it will be against my folks' wishes I know.

Fri. 27   At the Central till noon, when Pa came for me to go out home. I hated so much to leave Winfield and my many friends, but had to, as Pa says they need me at home, so bid folks good-bye, went to Mrs. Clark's and Mrs. Trump's and Mr. Finch's and bid them good-bye, then to school-house and got my Books and came home to Floral with Pa. Got a letter from Will, today noon.

March

Tues. 3   At home. In eve went to Library meeting, at the school-house, with sisters, May & Belle, & Anna Graves and Lura Hart. Oh! dear how lonesome it is out here.

Sun. 8   Cora Finch & I went to S.S. at U.B. [United Brethren] church in the morning after which to the Baptist church to Mrs. Houck's funeral and then called at Mr. Mater's, finding Mrs. Mater just barely alive. After Dinner, Lettie Davis & Fred Dunham came and Lettie & Frank, Fred & I all went to the Park to go Boat-riding, but boatman being gone, could get no boats, so took a ramble thro' the woods, and came out, by West road bridge, where we saw an Indian Camp; coming back thro' the woods or Park went to A.T. & S.F. R.R. bridge where we saw another Indian camp and Indians preparing their dinner. After stopping at the Mill-dam awhile, came thro' town, to Cora's, again and in eve, Cora, Frank & I went again to Lettie's and got her, and started for the Colored church, but didn't know where it was, so went to Mr. Clark's awhile, got Richard Clark and all took Lettie home, then Richard & Cora, Frank & I went back to Mr. Finch's where I staid all night.

April

Mon. 6   Commenced teaching a short term of school this morning; so rainy looking, only 13 scholars present. I don't know whether I can change myself from a "romping tom-boy" to a sober little school ma'am, or not, but I can try.

Wed. 8   Teaching school. Went to a "Party" at Mr. Seigler's, in the eve, with Bert Freeland: had a jolly time at the Party, but quarreled with Bert coming home and wont go with him again. I never did like him any too well.

Thurs. 9   Teaching school. Went to prayer-meeting in eve, with May & Belle and Mr. Ferguson, Sue & Anna, stopping for Minnie Freemole, after which Lyman Gilbert walked home with May, & Bert Freeland thought to spite me by walking home with sister Belle, I walked behind and all alone. Bert will find me *independent* enough and soon see how little I care about him.

Fri. 10   Teaching school and like it real well: find some of my pupils quite mischevious. Staid all night with Minnie Freemole. After supper she & I went to P.O. and Bert F. walked with us, or rather Minnie for I never spoke one word to him: he puts himself in my way all he can. *Never spoke one word* to Bert. Went to meeting at Christian church, in eve, with sisters.

Mon. 20   Didn't teach today as the "water" is so high, few could get to school: have had heavy rains. I went on horseback, to uncle Zeke Rogers, for dinner, then to Cousin Nelson Sapp's, Grandpa Anderson's, uncle Joe Anderson's and Mrs. White's, then home: found the Creeks very high, but dared to "*plunge in*" and cross.

Mon. 27   At home making preparations for my Birthday Party tonight. I had sent over 100 invitations but it rained awfully hard and Creeks so high, only 34 got here, but we had just the *jolliest, best* time. Every one said they had a most splendid time. I was dressed in White and received compliments from every side. Also many handsome presents.

May

Sat. 2   Teaching school to make up for Monday. Just as I reached home, after school, who should ride up, on horse-back, but that dear boy, Will, in company with Jamie Carman, who came to show him the nearest way. Jamie is a noble boy, for not many would take their *rival* to see one they loved as dearly, as Jamie does me. Jamie went home. Will & I took a short walk and later went to Mr. Edward's and for a walk, to the Creek, from there. His father is worse and he had to come home so rode out 12 miles to see me and made me very happy by doing so: had to go home tho' at 7:30 P.M. and I went to a Party, at Mr. Freemole's, then, up at Lone Tree, 8 miles north of here, with Sue & Charlie Ferguson, Minnie Freemole and Lafe Maxwell. Came home at 1:35 A.M. had a jolly time. . . .

Wed. 13   At home. Had to give up school on account of so much rain and high water: pupils couldn't get to school.

June

Fri. 12   At home all day. Staid all night at Mr. Edwards. Belle went away this morning saying she was going to see

Ida Hedric. I believe she has "run off," for she has threatened to do so several times. Our Stepmother is so cross we can hardly live together and dear Belle is too independent to take much from her.

Sat. 13   Came home from E's, early this A.M. only to find my suspicions of last night true. My darling sister, Belle has "run off". I got on a horse early as could and started out to find her. Went to Mr. Hedric's, Uncle Joe Anderson's and Mr. White's. Elfy White rode back to Floral with me, where we called at Mr. Stone's and to Edward's where we staid until the Mail came in and then went to P.O. from there with sister May, Sue & Anna F. and Minnie Freemole. Then went home, without any traces of Belle. I never undressed all night but lay [down]. after midnight, tho' I could not sleep. No one knows how unkind our stepmother is to us. God watch and guard thee, with tender mercy darling sister and bring you safe home again.

Sun. 14   May, Vella & I went to Mr. Edwards in A.M. and he took me to Winfield to hunt up my dear Belle. I took dinner with Lettie Davis after which I went to Mr. Freeland's at Commercial Hotel where I found my darling sister and Mr. Edwards took us back to Floral, where we arrived in time for church and Belle & I went together to the Baptist church. Belle didn't want to come home at all, but I coaxed so hard she had too. I wish our Stepmother was kinder to us; poor Belle and [the] rest too have to take some pretty hard talk.

Sun. 21   In A.M. went to S.S. at Christian church with May & Belle and after a good sermon by Rev. Frazee, the whole Congregation and some others, went to the old Baptismal place on Timber Creek, near John Bush's, where I was Baptized into the Christian church by Rev. J. H. Irwin. It was about 1 o'clock and a most beautiful day: the bank of creek was a solid mass of people to see me Baptized and everyone said, I looked so "sweet and pretty," and "took it" so calmly & quietly, and [they] never saw anyone Baptized so nicely. I rode to the Creek with Bert Plunket & his folks and after changing my clothes at Mr. Bush's, Pa brought me home, with Vella, Belle & Minnie Freemole who took dinner with us. . . . in eve went to meeting again where Rev. Frazee preached again and Belle & I came home together.

There was an awful large crowd at church this evening also this A.M.

July

Thurs. 30   At Normal [School]. Called and went to P.M. session with Alma K. In eve . . . went to the normal social at McDougal Hall. Jim Mc & Cora B. took me to get ice cream, and then walked home with me. I surely enjoy life.

August

Mon. 10   Sue & Anna Ferguson took dinner with me, . . . after supper Charlie F. and Lafe Maxwell walked up after Sue F. and all went to McGlynn's camp to another dance.[2] They have a "platform" for dancing, in a little Walnut Grove, and it is just lovely dancing in the open air in the moonlight. After the dance my "*little, irish dude*" walked home with me (Pat McGlynn), also Anna F. who staid all night with me. I expect we girls' parents will "*give it*" to us, when they find we are going to these dances. It's all done on the *sly*, but the folks are all so nice and it is delightful dancing these beautiful summer nights and we can't resist the temptation.

Sat. 29   At E[dward]'s. Bennie McGlynn came down this morning and bid Belle & I good-bye and at 10 o'clock A.M. all camps left for Belle Plaine. I hated to see them go, for have made many pleasant acquaintances among the young folks. . . . Sent Will a letter today that I'm sure will "*break us up.*"[3]

September

Sat. 5   At Edward's. Quite nervous all day expecting a letter from Will & got it, asking me to release him from his engagement with me. I'd rather have died, than live to see this day. Will, that woman does not and never will live, who will love you as I do, and you *will* live to regret this day, most bitterly; when you let your temper, get the best of your better nature. *I* suffer now, *you* will suffer later.

Mon. 7	At E's. Rained all day. Wrote a letter to Will today releasing him from our engagement.
Tues. 8	At E's. Am heart-broken, over my trouble with Will.

Will is not mentioned again until October 17. The intervening days are busy ones, replete with visiting and miscellaneous parties.

October

Sat. 17	At E's. Got a letter from Elfy White, Dick Clark and my dear Will, but Oh! his letters are so cold, they almost break my heart, for I love him as dearly as ever.
Tues. 27	At school. In eve I went with Charlie Roby in a buggy with Carrie Plunket & Will Files, up to Wilmot (or as we Floralites call it, *Needmore*) to a neck-tie social and such a time we had, getting there. The night was "dark as pitch," "wind blowing a gale" and "cold as Greenland," a wild team that was on a dead run, part of time: in crossing R.R. track missed crossing and were nearly up set, ran into a wire fence, where a road had been changed and finally got lost on the Prairie, but found a road and got there at last. Twas light coming home and had no trouble.

November

Sun. 1	At E's. In P.M. J. W. Cottingham, one of the Deacons of the church, called and talked about two hours to me, trying to get me to quit dancing, but I would not promise, for I do not think it wrong: he was after a number of others too. . . .
Tues. 3	At E's. No school as 'tis "Election Day" Mr. E's are moving to my father's today: are going to board at Pa's so I'm home again. Pa now lives right in town, in a house of Mr. Stone's. After supper Belle & I went to hear the Blind man Lecture on "Love Courtship & Marriage." Twas just splendid.
Wed. 4	At school. Went with Charlie Roby to Mr. Sidle's in eve where there was to be a dance, but so stormy no musicians came and hardly anyone else. I think so much of *Will* and yet am having such a good time, guess my heart won't break.
Sat. 7	At home. For once there is nowhere to go tonight.

December

Fri. 11   At school until 3 o'clock P.M. when the teachers and all
the school went to the Baptist church to the funeral of
little Minnie Seigler. Happy you are now, darling Minnie, resting in the arms of Jesus. Oh! little school-mate,
how we will all miss you. No more will the sweet, childish
face, run to meet me as I go into the school yard; no
more, will the bright, smiling face, prattle by my side,
the dear, little hands clasp mine on our way home from
school. We all loved little Minnie—9 yrs old—very
much. I staid all night with Mrs. John Pollock.

Sat. 19   At 7:30 A.M. Pa took Lizzie Roby & I to Winfield we took
dinner with Mrs. Clark. Will Finch is in town and I was
to have a talk with him is why I came down, but I could
hardly find courage to go to their house, but Lizzie & I
went at 2:30 P.M. and at 6 o'clock Will came home and
greeted me in his old, friendly way. How glad I was to
see him and yet my heart was breaking to know that
trouble had come between us. We sat up alone, talking,
until 1:30 A.M. I cried the whole time, for we could come
to no understanding and I was willing to concede everything.

Sun. 20   At Mrs. Finch's all day and night. Will & I had the day to
ourselves except at dinner as his mother is in Junction
City and all rest went out, to give us the day, as they are
anxious to see us married. I cried my heart out today
and I'll never be the same again. Will has promised to
come to me in one year.

Mon. 21   At 8 o'clock A.M. Lizzie Roby & I went to Frisco Depot
and took train for home. Will & Cora going to Depot
with us, where I bid my dear Will good-bye for one year,
then he is coming to see me and it means *to get married* "if
all is well," tho' 'twas not said in so many words, but I feel
better any way. Arrived home at 9:30 in a rain and went
from Depot to school, there rest of day. Not well; cried
myself sick.

Thurs. 24   At home in bed most of the day.

Fri. 25   A most beautiful Christmas Day. At 1:30 P.M. took a
short ride, in a big lumber wagon, drawn by a span of
big mules, with sister Belle, Bob Pollock, Brilla Read,
Anna Graves and Joe Moore, after which I went for a
long drive with Charlie Roby driving until Sun-down
when came home, dressed, and at 7:30 went to the

Christmas Ball in the Bahutge Building with Joe Moore. Had the jolliest time and at 11:30 stopped just long enough for supper after which danced till 3:40. I danced everything, danced all the eve, only [missed] what was danced while I was at supper and came home feeling better than when I went to the Ball.

Thurs. 31   At 1 P.M. Uncle Zeke, Aunt Mary & Gerty took me to Pa's where at 4 P.M. sister May was married to Lyman Gilbert by Rev. Childs. Carrie & Al Anderson, Will & Ella Mundy, Sam Gilbert & wife, Mr. & Mrs. Edwards Uncle Zekes folks and our own family were all that was at the wedding. Sister was an awful sweet little Bride, but so young: only 17 in Oct. She has got an excellent husband tho. Sister Belle is sick in bed, and they were married in her room. After the "Wedding supper" at 4:30 The whole crowd walked up to the Depot and I took the 5:30 train for Winfield as Will wrote for me to be sure and come. Mr. Williams also went down on same train and walked out to Mrs. Finch's with me. I was terribly disappointed not to find Will at home, but he had received a "dispatch" to go at once to Chapman, Ks. where he was offered a good position in a Mill and left at once on this P.M. train leaving "*regrets*" for me. . . . So ends the most eventful year of my life. Christmas-day was to have been Will's & my wedding day, but next Christmas may be the "Day."

[1886]

January

Sun. 3

Cora Beach & Alder Rogers called in late P.M. and I went to meeting at Bapt. church, with them in evening. Charlie Roby wanted to walk home with me, but I gave him "*G. B.*" and let Al Korns walk home with me. Charlie is trying to *play sweet* on me and another girl, at same time, and that won't go with me. He can go with me when *I'm* doing that, if he wishes, but I won't go with him when *he* is doing it. *Independence.*

Wed. 27

We have such jolly times at home, but our step-mother makes it hard for us, threatening to "mash our mouths" or do something dreadful for the least little thing. She doesn't want Belle and I at home at all, and says if we don't leave she will. Pa doesn't know 100th part of how she treats us and some times seems to take her part.

February

Sun. 21

Went to Christian church in A.M. to S.S. & meeting after which, with Charlie & Virrilla Roby, went to Cemetery to Burial of Mr. Geo. Anderson, after which went to Pa's with May & Lyman Gilbert. At 3 P.M. went to Temperance-meeting with Dick Johnson, after which, to Pa's again, with Charlie Roby. At 4:30 started to Depot with May & L. and was joined by Al Korns who walked with me. Charlie Hollister, came in on the train and walked back to Pa's with me and in eve Charlie Roby took me to meeting, then home to Yarbaugh's. Think I've had *fellows* enough for one day. They all know, "*they are not in it*" but are satisfied, if I'll even talk with them.

April

Fri. 16

Lizzie, Virrilla, & Mattie Roby, Retta Freeman & I, all went up town, then to Jim Roby's where all staid for supper except Retta. My folks so strongly oppose Charlie that he had me go to Jim's for supper, so he could

WINFIELD DAILY COURIER

Artist's conception of
Winfield, Kansas, 1878.
(Martha lived here as a
young girl.)

meet me there, and take me to "Singing-school." All of
us had our wraps on, ready to go and I was talking to
Charlie, when Jamie Carman drove up and called for
me. I went out, and he asked me to drive 8 miles, with
him to a dance at Mr. Stalter. I went in, put on my hat
and without one word—not even good-night—to Charlie, walked out, got in the Buggy with Jamie, went home
and changed my dress, and went to the dance. Danced
from 9 P.M. to 4:45 A.M. and had Oh! such a jolly time,
but Jamie begged me, all the way home, to marry him:
he loves me so passionately and won't give up. Poor
Charlie loves me just as much as Jamie and see how I
have treated him tonight, but he knows I don't love him,
and a little more such treatment will convince him I
guess. I think everything of Charlie as a friend, but can
never marry him.

Sat. 17 . . . . Met Charlie there [at Depot] and really, after way I
treated him last night, I felt ashamed to look at him, and
he walked home with me. Poor Boy, I never saw anyone
so heart-broken. I ought not to have treated him so,
even if I don't love him; he gives me all the love of his
heart, a pure, honest love, that I ought to respect, even
if I cannot return it, tho' I have no heart to give him. He

never *scolded* me one bit, but talked so good and kind, that a less heartless girl than I, would surely, have asked forgiveness and promised at once to marry him. I only laughed at him. He took me for a lovely drive in eve. There was a *"full moon"* and it was a grand night. My heart was joy, Charlie's breaking.

Mon. 26 — Went early to uncle Will Weber's and Willie & Myrtle Weber took me to Frisco Depot for my trunk, then to Judge Torrance's [in Winfield] where I am to stay awhile. How I hated to leave and Charlie felt awfully bad but my step-mother don't want me home, and better I don't see so much of Charlie as I'm not going to marry him. Am 19 today.

Tues. 27 — At my new home at Judge Torrance's. I wish my step-mother was willing for me to stay home, I can't bear to be away from dear sister Belle.

May

Wed. 5 — Charlie Roby was down from Floral today, to see me. Poor boy, he can't give me up and I can't marry him so what's to be done; I like Charlie, but can't love him.

Sun. 9 — . . . at 6 P.M. Lettie, Lula, Cora, Lizzie & I went to "Frisco Depot," to meet sister Belle and my old beau, Charlie Roby; the girls, with sister all came home with me and then we called at Rev. J. H. Irwin's and then all went to Cora's where Charlie Roby & Will Files came. Jim Finch with Lettie Davis, Will Files with Cora and Charlie with me all walked out to Mr. Thompson's with Lizzie and sister Belle, then Charlie brought me home and staid until 11 o'clock; the last time I'll ever go with him, for at 4 A.M. he goes to Topeka to be married to Mila Bair, tho' he *begged* me to change my mind, and marry him: He says he will *never* love Mila, *never* be happy with her because he wanted me and said he *never* tried so hard in his life, to win a "girl's love" as he had mine and *vows* he will always love me and said if I would only say the *word*, he would marry me now and never go to Topeka. I cried for an hour after Charlie left. I felt so sorry for him and hate to see him marry this way: he was always so good to me, but I don't want to marry him.

Mon. 10 — Charlie left at 3 A.M. today and will be married this eve to Mila Bair in Topeka. How I pity him but hope he will forget the love he has for me and learn to love her dearly and fondly and be very happy with her.

Thurs. 20 Spent the eve at uncle Bill Weber's. . . . My aunt said she "never seen me look *so sweet* as I did tonight." "*Auntie mine don't flatter*." What good is "*Beauty*": it *doesn't* make my step-mother kind, so I can stay at home: one gets tired of so much *praise* away from home, and constant "*ding donging*" at home.[1]

Sun. 23 Home, My dear Belle & Bob Pollock, Minnie Weber & Joe Moore were in to see me in eve and poor Belle cried so hard: she is not very strong and our step-mother doesn't want she & I at home, and she is such a "Papa girl" and loves me so dearly, it nearly *breaks her heart* to be separated from me. Poor dear, I wish we could be together all the time.

Fri. 28 In eve, drove out to Floral, with Bob Pollock, to an ice-cream supper at Baptist church. . . . Charlie Roby & his new wife were there and I avoided Charlie all eve, till nearly time to go home, he came to me in spite of everything and talked so long, I had to leave him lest people should remark, the attention he was paying me, to the neglect of his Bride. We all drove to Mr. Roby's at 12 o'clock and as it looked so very rainy, went in the house awhile; later in going out to our Buggies, Charlie left his wife to walk with Will & Lizzie, while he walked alone with me—Bob having gone ahead—his arm about me all the time and kissed me "over and over," so passionately. He told me this eve, he loved me *best* and would always be sorry he married who he did, and night he was married, he tried to think he was marrying me; said he never would get over it: he seemed *heart-broken*, poor boy: *it is too bad* but I have the consolation of knowing, *I never for a moment encouraged him.*

June

Wed. 2 . . . went to Theatre with Link Frederick. The Play was the *Wild West* and tho' everything all thro' was good, this country is *too new* for that sort of thing, and didn't enjoy it at all. Have seen too much of such things off the stage.

Tues. 29 Lee Johnson called in eve, to engage my company for a dance tomorrow eve, but I told him "*nixy*". He is too badly "*stuck on me.*" Why can't a girl go with a fellow a *few times* any way, without his getting so stuck on her, that she must either marry him, or quit going with him. *Foolish boys.*

July

Sat. 3   Celebration of the "Fourth" today and I took morning train to Floral, to help celebrate; found the whole community drawn up in *Procession* at Depot, ready to go to the Park. A wagon drawn by 6 horses—Will Gross driver—finely decorated, in red, white & blue was filled with girls, dressed in white, carrying small banners, and each representing a state. I joined them representing *Virginia.* A Procession a mile long, with Pa as *Marshall* and Edwards, Purcell, and Snodgrass his staff. Had a splendid good time, with hosts of friends and old *admirers*, until 12:30 when with Rose Hooker and a lot of others took the train for Winfield to finish the day. Went . . . to the Fair Grounds, where I spent a very jolly afternoon. At 5 P.M. Mr. Pollock brought me home. After supper Ruby Whipple & I went up town awhile and later Mr. Pollock called, with *finest team* in town, and took me for a drive, then to see Fireworks—which were grand—and finished the day by attending the Ball at the Skating Rink; came home at Mid-night. I've had the *grandest, merriest* time today; the *happiest "Fourth"* of my life. If Will could have seen how happy I was, he would have seen how little he was necessary to my happiness. He has *acted* heartless to me because he *felt sure* of me: *today he could not have added to my happiness.* The only thing to *mar my perfect happiness,* was that my little dog, *Trip* got killed at noon today, out home. My sisters were both there and looked very sweet and my darling Belle, couldn't kiss me enough. After all kissed me, as I got ready to take train back to Winfield, she kissed me again, saying "I must have the last kiss." Dear little sister she is so sweet I can hardly bear to be away from her, but have to. *Oh! this has been such a happy Fourth.*

Sat. 10   Called at Emma Adams, in early eve. About mid-night, a "Burglar" got into the room where Ella Utterback and I were sleeping. Ella *scared* him out, by *screaming*, while I could only stand and laugh, to see him *git* thro' the window he'd come in at.

Sun. 18 John Hubbell, an old friend from Medicine Lodge called to see me this eve and wants me to go home with him.[2]

Tues. 20 Bid my friends good-bye and with John Hubbell, took the 10:20 A.M. train for Medicine Lodge. John lives at the Grand Central Hotel, where we arrived at 4 P.M. very tired. Passed thro' some lovely country today: saw one Prairie-dog town, and a *few* sod-houses.

Wed. 21 At the Grand Central, "happy as a *lark*" to meet my old friends again, Mr. Strong, Prop. of the Hotel says he will pay me well, if I'll help them at whatever they may want done, odd jobs etc, and I guess I will for my step mother gets angry everytime Pa spends a "penny" on we girls. None of my folks know I came here and Pa will be awfully angry if I stay here to work, but I can't see any harm in it.

Thurs. 22 At the "Grand," my home, for the present. Have fell quite in love with the little Village on the Plains, tho' it seems funny to see Stage-coaches etc.

Mattie Farnsworth, date un-
known. Courtesy Ralph A.
Kingman, Topeka.

August

Sun. 1	Home. Making lots of new friends here.
Mon. 2	Home. I'd like the town better, if there were no "Saloons" here. *"Prohibition doesn't Prohibit here."*
Sun. 15	I'm deeply distressed because I can't hear from dear, sister Belle. I wrote her nearly a month ago.
Tues. 17	Home. I wish *I was home* with Papa & sisters.
Fri. 20	Home. Got a letter from Cousin Minnie Weber, of Winfield, this eve, saying my dear sister Belle is very sick, but I can't believe it, for my folks would surely send me word.
Sat. 21	Home. Just worried to death, about dear Belle. I'm afraid she *is* sick, or she would have written, and yet I can't believe it, for the folks would surely send me word.
Mon. 23	I pray God every day, if my dear Belle is sick, to spare the precious life to me, who loves it more than my own life.
Tues. 24	Was awakened at 5 A.M. by a *terrible* dream, of a storm, in which I saw my darling sister *die*. And at 9 A.M. received a *Telegram*, telling me my *poor darling sister* was dead. Oh! how *cruel* the folks have been, not to send me word, so I could have gone home, in time. God *have mercy. How can I ever bear it.* I *loved* and *worshipped* my darling sister, above *everything* else in the whole world. She died at 5:30 this morning. I took the 11 o'clock A.M. train for home. At Winfield Minnie Weber & Rev. J. H. Irwin got on the train and we arrived at New Salem at 5:30 P.M. Rev. Irwin hired a "rig" and drove we three home to Floral, where, he preached a *short*, but *most beautiful* sermon then, my darling, was taken to the Cemetery, followed by *Oh! such a long procession* of loving friends, and just after Sunset, my *dear, precious* sister was laid in her last resting place. Oh! God *pity* and *comfort* my broken heart; it is *so hard* to give her up. What will my life be without her, my hearts *dearest treasure*. But dear Lord, *Thy* will, *not* mine, be done. Rest in peace dear Belle. You have gone home to a dear, Angel mother where some day I hope to meet you both. Minnie & I staid all night at Pa's.
Wed. 25	. . . *Oh! I am so* lost without dear Belle. They tell me she was sick 3 weeks, with Typhoid fever and tho' suffering *very* much was very patient throughout her sickness. She talked of me *constantly* and asked so often, for them to

write, for me to come home, but they kept "putting her off" until it was *too late.* How could they be so cruel, when they knew how much we were to one-another. Darling Belle, they have wronged you & I *so much.* They dared not allow my name mentioned before her. She was conscious when death came and willing to die, calling each one—by name—to her and kissing them goodbye. She looked *so sweet* in her coffin. Six young men, who use to go with her—one being her teacher, the others school-mates—were her Pall-bearers. She was 16 years, 7 months and 4 days old, and so *sweet* and *pretty* and *good.* I gave my darling, the *very last kiss* of all, for she always wanted my last kiss, when going anywhere and *so my lips must be the last to touch hers,* and were.

Inserted at this leaf are pressed flowers with the following note on a scrap of paper:
Some of the flowers of the wreath of sister Belle's coffin.
Died Tuesday 5:30 A.M. Aug 24, 1886.

Mon. 30   At Pa's, but am going back to Medicine Lodge where my friends think the world of me. I must go away until I get a little over dear Belle's death. I feel the folks have wronged us both, and so must go away awhile until I can reconcile myself a little.

Tues. 31   At Pa's. All the world is so *dreary* with out my dear Belle. Yet I cannot wish you back, my *precious one*; instead, I wish I were with you, for *I know* you are so much better off. Oh! it draws my heart nearer heaven to know a dear mother, a precious sister are waiting for me there.

September

Tues. 7   Bid uncle's folks good-bye and with Minnie Weber & Katie Reigle went to S.K.R.R. Depot, but train again so much late, we went to Riverside Park until noon, then came back to Depot, where met Joe Moore & Bob Pollock, and they, with Minnie W. took train with me at 1 o'clock P.M. to go as far as Wellington with me, on reaching there they persuaded me to get off and visit the "Wellington Fair," which I did. We had a pleasant afternoon at the "Fair" and staid all night at "Phillips Hotel."

Wed. 8   At "Phillips Hotel" in Wellington, until 10:30 A.M. when Minnie, Joe & Bob, took me to S.K. Depot, where I took 11:30 P.M. train for Medicine Lodge, arriving there at 4 P.M. receiving a most *hearty welcome* from my friends at "Grand Central." Mac Reed met me in the Hall and almost "smothered" me with kisses, before I knew what he was about. He has been very much in love with me for some time, but might have asked for the kisses.

Fri. 10   Home. *I'm so lost* since dear Belle's death.

Thurs. 30   Home. Sometimes, I tell my friends—just to hear what they will say—that I'm going back to Floral, and how they will talk to me and coax me not to go: they say, "what will Medicine Lodge be, without you, Mattie; you are *the life* of us all." I get so many compliments from my friends.

October

Wed. 6   Home. I ought to be happy here, with so many good friends who are *continually* paying me some *pretty* compliment. A girl friend told me today that everyone were saying they, "never knew a *jollier* girl than Mattie Van." How little they know, how my heart is *bleeding* for dear Belle. "Many a *broken-heart*, is covered by a smiling face."

Sun. 17   Home; Mr. Jake Knier said to me today, "I've never met, so *jolly* and *lively* a young lady as you"—little German—and said he wanted to *build a little home for two*, but I, "turned the subject" and wouldn't take the hint: He is nice, but I don't want to marry and don't think I've seen the *man*, yet, that I'll marry.

Wed. 20   Home; feeling quite sick.

Thurs. 21   Home; Feeling no better and called Dr. Lackwood, who says he is afraid I'm going to have a hard spell of fever.

Sun. 24   Home. Afraid I'll have to go home to Pa and don't want to, for know my step-mother doesn't want me.

Thurs. 28   Feeling so badly, had to bid my friends good-bye and take 2 P.M. train for Winfield. I hated *so much* to leave and none of my friends wanted me to go. I arrived in Winfield, just after dark and went to uncle Will Weber's and staid all night.

Fri. 29   Cousin Willie Weber took me to "Frisco Depot" in A.M. and I took 9:30 A.M. train out to Floral. My step-mother treated me very cool, and I feel an unwelcome guest.

Sat. 30	At Pa's, feeling so sick: Have "Typhoid-fever." Dr. Stine, who boards with Pa's is doctoring me.

November

Wed. 3	At Pa's. Wish I was back in Medicine Lodge, for my step-mother is so cross to me.
Thurs. 4	Home. very sick.
Mon. 8	At Pa's, sick: wish I might never get well, it is so lonely with out dear Belle.
Tues. 9	At Pa's sick with typhoid fever, which my sister died with.

November 10–December 5 have no entries other than ditto marks.

December

Mon. 6	At Pa's sick. Pa's moved today, into their own home, about 1/4 mile from here and as I cannot even "stand" yet and can't stand *"jaring"* Pa, Lyman Gilbert, Mr. Edwards and Dick Johnson carried me to the new home, on a "stretcher": the shaking from moving hurt me quite a little, tho' a short distance.
Mon. 13	Sick and weak but improving: typhoid fever.
Sat. 25	Christmas-day: One year ago today was to have been my *wedding day with Will F.*
Tues. 28	Today, Pa helped me out to dinner: first time I've been out of my room since I took sick and was *so weak* I could hardly move, *hand or foot.*
Wed. 29	My old sweet-heart, Will Finch, gave me a great surprise this morning, by coming to spend the day with me. I didn't know he was within 200 miles of me, until he opened the door and walked in, about 10 o'clock A.M. I was real glad to see him and enjoyed his visit, but he wanted me to promise to marry him, as soon as I was strong enough, which I could not do. The old love is gone: *killed* by his own *heartlessness.* He knew I loved him and felt *so sure* of me, that he thought to let me suffer on, to his own good time. I was not in the wrong and my heart has felt his unjustness and resented it, so far as to lose its love for him. He took the 5:30 P.M. train back to Winfield.

Thurs. 30   Am still improving. I think I treated Will most *too cool* yesterday, for he is *so good*: but my heart would not respond to his "overtures of love"; instead it resented, and felt repulsive to every loving word and look: he let my heart suffer and *break* unjustly, and lost the *purest, best* love a woman ever gave to man, by doing so.

Fri. 31   Improving Oh! so slowly and wish my life might go out, with the old year. Life is so dreary. Dear Belle is dead, my step-mother *so cross* and *unkind* and my heart has lost its dearest love: has been disapponted in one it thought *noble* and *good*.

[*1887*]

January through April entries of this year are very brief. Much of March is spent going places alone, which is unusual for her. After her move to Topeka in September, she spends several months reacquainting herself with her relatives, and these entries, especially those on the first days in Topeka, are terse.

January

Sun. 2   Seem to be gaining strength rapidly and can get out doors with help.

Tues. 11   At Pa's: back in bed again. Relapse of Typhoid-fever.

Thurs. 27   At Pa's. Am getting *well* at last, I guess.

February

Tues. 1   Dick Johnson took me to "Singing" in eve at Baptist church: my "first night out" since I took sick in Oct.

Wed. 2   At Pa's: my stepmother says I "*have to go*" as soon as I am strong enough tho', and I want to stay home *so much.* "*Groundhog*" saw his *shadow* today for 'twas a pretty day.

Mon. 14   At 1 o'clock P.M. went to make my home at Mr. Edwards for a while.[1] Am not *strong yet,* but my step mother doesn't want me at home. God *pity* a girl, that can call *no place home.* In eve Len Honnold & I went to a Concert, given by 3 blind people, at the old stone school-house. It was just splendid: grand.

March

Fri. 4   At E's. Pa came early this morning to bid me good-bye, as he starts with Ramie's folks for Colorado, to build up another Home, in the *far West.* I love *Frontier life* and wanted to go too, but he wouldn't let me, for I'm not strong enough yet.

Mon. 16   "Singing" met here this eve, but rained and not many came. We have a new "Telegraph Operator" here, and

Dr. Stine says to me today "Sis there is another chance for you." Thank you, I *don't want it.*

Sun. 22 Went to S.S. in A.M. and in P.M. to Singing at Hotel, with Mr. & Mrs. Edwards and Tom Dickens. Seen our New Telegraph Operator, at Singing this P.M. and tho' not introduced, learned his name, which is "Mr. Kettlewell," and he is about as long as name. He is the most *everlastingly,* longest man I ever saw.

Mon. 23 Singing met here this eve and we had such a jolly time. The new Operator was here, but I didn't get an introduction, tho' think I'll "mash" him, to see what he's made of.

June

Sun. 12 Went to S.S. in A.M. and Mr. Maurice Butts & I went home with Will Gross and Sue Ferguson to dinner. We four came back to *meeting* at 4 P.M. and at 5:30 we four went to Hotel to Singing: And Oh, what a nice *flirtation* Mr. Kettlewell & I carried on. I believe he is an awful *Flirt,* Mr. Butts brought me home and spent evening with me.

Fri. 15 Went to Winfield on 5:25 P.M. train, going to Cora Finch's. After supper, Cora & I went up town and to Cora Dawson's then Cora F., Fairy Dawson and Jim Finch went to Depot with me where I took 9 P.M. train home to Floral, and O.K. walked over home with me. Oren Kettlewell, talks so *awful much* love to me, and I *don't* like it: it sounds *too soft,* so this evening I remonstrated, as I've done before and told him I'd rather he didn't come any more, for if he was in earnest, he'd best quit, as I didn't want to marry: he replied, that he was only *flirting,* that he could not marry me if he wanted too, as he was engaged to a girl some where else: he said when he came to this little Village, he thought it such a little *country* place, he'd have a great time *mashing* all the girls and I pleased him most and he wanted to go with me. How like a *flash* the thought, came to me what to do. I told *him* he could come if he *wasn't* "*on the marry.*" And to *myself* I made this *vow.* I don't love Oren K. and know he is an *awful* Flirt, but will *show* him, that *Flirting* is a game *two can play,* and *I vow, I will make him love me and he will ask me to be his wife before three months from now; now see if I don't. See if I don't prove to be the best flirt of the two. I feel sorry for the other girl, but I shall leave nothing undone, to win him; even tho' I should learn to love him* in winning him and die of a broken heart. *I'll do it.*

She begins to see O. Kettlewell regularly now. Throughout the months of June and July he visits her often and stays late.

Mon. 18   Home: didn't see O.K. *all day for a wonder.*

August

Fri. 5   . . . Went for a drive with Oren in eve. Am doing nicely in my *flirting.* I *exert every effort* to be fascinating and am succeeding beyond expectation.

Mon. 8   Oren couldn't come this eve as a young man from Atlanta was down to see him. I *study* Oren and do everything in my power to please him as a means of *wining* him. I'm sure to prove to be the best *Flirt* and how I'll *glory* in it, tho' I don't approve of it and *never deliberately flirted* with any one, before.

Wed. 10   . . . . Oren went to church with me in eve. He is my *shadow* now and *talks marry* a *big lot* but 'twill be *no go.*

Tues. 16   . . . . Last night of meeting, and the *very* Rev. being a Widower, with any amount of children, some older than I, was *very much smitten* with me, but didn't give him a chance to *propose.* Had my pictures taken today.

Wed. 17   Oren took me to prayer-meeting in eve: he is getting *awfully awful* sweet on me, but I'm going to Topeka next month and he will have a chance to *transfer* his *sweetness* to some other girl.

Sun. 21   Oren went to S.S. with me in A.M. and spent evening with me. He is getting very much in earnest, as I can see by the earnest glance of his blue eyes, and the tender tone of his voice: his *flirting* is *fast* changing to *seriousness.*

September

Sat. 3   Went to Depot with *O. K.* in eve to meet sister May, who came up on the *early train* and staid all night with me. Had "Singing" here this eve and of course O.K. was here and staid *long* after the singers left. People are beginning to notice his *marked attention* and some say he is *completely infatuated.*

Mon. 5   Sister May & Little Zaidee spent most of the day with me.[2] Oren came in afternoon, again in eve, but was late as he walked home with another girl first. We quarreled about it too, for he won't let me do that way. I dare not look, talk or write, to any of the *male sex.* I quarrel every chance I get, to hurt him: he picked on the wrong one to *flirt* with, or ought not to have told me so, for *I'll break his heart* if *I break my own doing so.*

Sun. 18   Went S.S. in A.M. with Oren. "*God be with you till we meet again,*" was sung as a farewell to me as I leave tomorrow for Topeka: Oren came right after dinner and we went to the *Park* till 3:30 P.M. when we went to Temperance-meeting at Bapt. church, and sang in a *Duet* together, with Mr. & Mrs. Edwards, or rather a Quartette. After we sang, I left him and went alone to the Cemetery, to bid good-bye to the grave of my darling sister Belle, then went home, and Oren came at 5 P.M. and I went to train with him and staid for *No 2* when he came home with me and staid all night. He wouldn't leave me, but sat talking the whole night thro' imploring me to stay and marry him, not to go to Topeka: He *cried* almost the whole night, but I would not give up, and now *I have him at my feet,* where I *vowed three months ago I would have him,* and I think it shows me to be the best *Flirt.* I think a great deal of him, but not enough to stay here and marry him. He left me about 5 o'clock A.M. to go to Depot and seemed almost broken-hearted.

Mon. 19   Mr. & Mrs. Edwards & Oren went to Depot with me at 5:40 A.M. where at 6 o'clock, with Mila and Charlie Roby I took train for Winfield and there with Mila, took 7:10 A.M. train for Topeka, where we arrived at 3:45 P.M. and was met by Harry Bair and went home with him; Mollie Mitchell also came on a later train, from Winfield.[3] I wanted to come here to visit, but hated to leave Floral, where I've lived most of my life, for some way I have a *presentiment* that it will never again be my home, and I have grown up there, from a little girl, and the place is very dear to me: none of my friends wanted me to leave but I felt that I must do it, or I would yet give in to Oren's *pleadings* and marry him against my better judgment, and he is not one I care to marry.

Thurs. 22   At Harry & Lizzie's. Went to Santa Fe Depot, with Mila Roby in P.M. I got *Poisoned* on *Ivy* in the woods yesterday.

Sat. 24   Went to town in A.M. with Mollie Mitchell, to see a doctor, as I am badly poisoned and feel real sick. My face is badly swollen, one eye being entirely closed, the other almost. Got a letter from Oren, saying I *just must* promise to return and marry him, so I'll just tell him *"alright, it is a go."* It will be easy enough to get out of it again; I'll *never* marry him, but sat down and answered at once, saying I would.

Fri. 30   Seems like a *month* since I had left Floral. Harry & Lizzie Bair, Mollie Mitchell & I spent a very jolly evening at Mr. J. M. Bair's. On our way, we stopped at Mr. Cook's "accomadation" P.O. and got our mail. I got an awful *sweet letter* from Oren and a pretty gold Pin, he sent me: he seems happier since we are *"engaged"*.

October

Mon. 17   . . . Mila & I called on Mrs. J. C. Douglas in afternoon, and she wanted me to come and stay with her, so I promised her I would, so that will keep me in Topeka awhile. I had promised to return to Floral in Nov. but if I do, I'd be persuaded into marrying, so I'll stay here till that *"falls thro'."* I'm to be one of the family at Mrs. Douglas as long as I'll stay.

November

Wed. 16   Home. Trouble is coming between O.K. and I.[4]

December

Sun. 11   Went to meeting at Christian Church in A.M. In P.M. went to "Vespers" at Catholic, with Maggie & Hallie Powell and Sadie McArdle. In eve to Methodist with Sadie Mc, Aggie Bokay & Millie Kersten.

Thurs. 15   Went to Prayer meeting at Christian church in eve and D. L. Carson, walked home with me. Our little Mail carrier has been talking *sweet* for some time: *he is cute but not in it.*

[*1888*]

April 26th of this year marked Martha's twenty-first birthday. She was quite independent by this time, obviously a young adult concerned with her financial future, but also determined not to sell herself precipitously on the marriage market.

January

Sun. 1   "*New Years Day*," and wonder "what of *Joy*, what of *sorrow*," will "1888" bring to me: the past one has been quite a happy year, the loss of dear sister being the only dark spot. Went to meeting, at Christian Church, in evening.

Mon. 2   Home. No letter lately from O.K. We have quarreled so much, we are about to "*quit*".

Wed. 11   Home: my heart has troubled me very much all day. Our little Mail carrier, *No 11* seems bound to make a *mash* on me.

Sat. 14   Home. Got letter from O.K. How little *No 11* does *tease* me about my letters. I get real cross, sometimes.

Sat. 28   Down town in P.M. Just awfully muddy: got to walk part of way with my little Mail-Carrier—he is just a little dandy. Pretty brown eyes, and awfully cute. Don't know his name, but he is *No 11*; he tries hard to make a mash on me, guess I'll *flirt* with him, to make O.K. jealous. He told Sadie today, in my presence, that I was "*sweet enough to be kissed*." I don't like such remarks at all.

Mon. 30   Home. If O.K. doesn't "lookout" he is going to get left. Postman No 11 is awfully cute and I may succomb to his smiles.

Tues. 31   Home. No letter today from O.K. tho' I use to get them every day. We have quarreled so much I guess he is ready to *quit*, and I know, I am. I don't want to marry such a man. When some good, honest man comes along and wants a wife, I've got a *whole heart* to give him.

February

Mon. 6   Home. O.K. and I keep quarreling, yet he won't release me from "our engagement" and *insists* that we will marry. As we can't *settle* affairs by "letter writing," think I'll run down to Floral, and settle matters by *talking*.

Wed. 22   When starting to "Dressmakers" this morning met little Carrier *No 11*: told him was going away: he says "write to me", I replied, "I don't know you," he says, "don't you know me? I'm John W. Shaw." So now I know his name but was disappointed to find such a *cute* little fellow, with such a *homely* name. At 1:40 P.M. took Santa Fe for Winfield; after changing cars, at Florence, Collector L. P. Slavens started up a conversation with me, and I had a very pleasant trip rest of way, where arrived at "*Wn*" at 9:30 P.M. and Mr. Slavens—who stops in Winfield—walked out to my Auntie Weber's with me, where I took them all by surprise. Mr. S. did not stay, but cousin Myrtle & Minnie having beaus we all staid up talking, till 5 o'clock A.M.

Fri. 24   Spent the whole day in Floral, but things seem changed. After Breakfast at Mr. Snodgrass, Oren came for me, to go to the Depot with him, like I used to do. Well I went, and took dinner with him at noon, at Mr. Al Manker's and spent whole P.M. with him at Depot. At 4 P.M. I called at Mr. Stone's and Mr. Snodgrass' with him, where bidding them good-bye went to Depot and took 4:45 P.M. train for Winfield where staid all night with my *Chum* Cora Finch and so am in a "*Peck of trouble*". Oren would not hear to our engagement being broken, and Will Finch my old lover, is at home. I told him a good while ago, if I ever came to Winfield, while he was here I would marry him, but under the circumstances I can't, so what am I to do. A girl likes to keep on the *good side* of all these nice Boys. God bless them, what would we do without them. The *very thought of marrying now*, is *so distasteful* to me, that I can't do it. Will asked me at "Bed-time," to stay up later to talk to him, which I did. What a pleasure it would have been at one time, but now I care *absolutely nothing* for him and would not let him speak of the *past* to me: his tears did not soften me. I would not kiss him, when he *begged so hard for one last kiss*: begged and pleaded, Oh! so hard, as tho' pleading for his life. I could see those tears fall, without a tremor. But I thought of a time, when my own had fallen and thought retribution was coming to him. He had my love once and could have kept it *forever*, now I do not even feel a *friendship* for him: he said, "he wished he was lying at my feet dead; that I might look in his coffin at his dead face, then my *hard heart* might soften." But it wouldn't, for I don't love him: the very thought of loving or marrying him, was *repulsive* to me, so I went to bed and left him: Poor boy it is too bad, but I had not *one* thought of pity for him and it will disappoint his whole family, for they were anxious for the *"Match."*

Sat. 25   . . . I took 7:10 A.M. train for Topeka where I arrived at 4 P.M. Twas very cold. Saw my little Postman, most as soon as I got home. Have hardly slept any since I have been gone, so was too tired to go to "Choir-practice" and went to bed at 8 o'clock P.M. Would have staid in Winfield, had it not been for "Kettlewell & Finch" who are both determined to marry me, so it is better to stay, where I won't see them and be bothered. The "Finches" were rather cool to me, because they know I've not taken Will "back" and he would not look at me, this A.M. tho' gave his hand without turning his head, to say good-bye to me.

Sun. 26   . . . . Had a nice time down home, but couldn't accomplish what I went for. Well Oren will get tired after awhile.

Wed. 29   Home. Our little Mail-carrier, Mr. Shaw is most awfully cute; such a jolly little fellow.

March

Sun. 4   Went to S. S. Concert at Christian church in eve. I sing in the Choir, and in looking over the congregation, just as we commenced to sing who should I "spy" near the front, but our little, Postman, *No 11*. I felt like I'd go thro' the floor, for some way I felt he was there for my sake: he gave me a pretty smile of recognition, and after the Concert walked home with me. He is very pleasant. *Throughout the month of March she makes sporadic references to seeing "No. 11," Mr. John Shaw.*

Tues. 27   Home. Got a letter from O.K. today and wrote in reply

	that he *was free*: that *I wouldn't* marry him if he was the last man on earth. *I don't want* him.
Thurs. 29	Went to Harry Bair's at 3 P.M. and got there for a "*Picnic*." Mila & Charlie Roby live with them and a 9 pound girl—a little beauty—was born to them just as I stepped in the house. Mila had a hard time. Got a Telegram from O.K. this eve: he won't give me up. Went to Prayer-meeting in eve alone.
Sat. 31	Home. Got *two* letters from Oren Kettlewell today, saying, *he does not want his freedom*: he wants to marry me: they were awfully sweet. I like Oren so much and have shed *bitter tears* over this affair—he is such good company, but I feel in my heart, that I *must not* marry him: that I *would not* be happy with him.

April

Mon. 2	Town in P.M. In eve went to the "Monday Easter Ball," at Metropolitan Hall, with Mame, Sadie and Cris. Devlin. Came home at 2:20 A.M. *Never was so angry* in my life before. I thought there was too many rough people present and wanted to come home; the rest wouldn't do it, and I couldn't come alone. I *never* will go anywhere again, with those girls, *never*.
Thurs. 26	Church in eve. I am 21 years old today.

May

Wed. 23	Went to the Jones Building on West 6th St. in eve to the opening of a "Short-hand School." Which I am going to attend. Mrs. Mary West of Kansas City, is teacher. Got home at 9 o'clock.
Fri. 25	To School in eve. Wrote letter to O.K. today, "breaking off" our engagement *for sure* and *for good*. I'm not going to fool about it any longer.
Sat. 26	Went with Mr. J. W. Shaw, in eve, to a Euchre Party at Mr. Gists on Prospect street. Had a nice time and got home at 1 A.M. and he staid till 5 A.M. quarreling hard as we could all the time. I *despise* him and told him *never* to come again.
Sun. 27	Just as I was ready to go to church this eve Mr. Shaw came: I am so angry at him that I wouldn't go to church with him, and if went alone, he would follow, so I staid

home and *he staid* with me, tho' I tried to make him go home, and talked so *hateful* to him, that he shed tears. He wants to be a friend at least.

Mon. 28   To School in eve and Mr. Shaw came, and walked home with me, in spite of my protests. I wouldn't let him "take my arm," and told him to "go about his business," but it done no good. *Oh! it makes me so mad.*

Tues. 29   To School in eve and Mr. Shaw home with me. I guess I never will get *rid of him.*

June

Fri. 1   School in eve. Mr. Shaw walked home with me. *I never hated anyone so bitterly in my life as I do him.* He comes and I can't help myself, and seems to think a great deal of me. Like Stenography very much: It is *very facinating* to me. *Cross's* system is one taught.

Sun. 3   Took Jennie Douglass to church with me in eve to prevent Mr. Shaw's having a chance to come home with me, if he should be there. He was there and came in and sat down behind me. After meeting, asked to walk home with me: told him, *very emphatically no*: but done no good. He walked out of church behind me and walked beside me, all the way home, tho' I wouldn't let him "take my arm." *What am I to do.*

Sun. 10   . . . . In eve J. W. Shaw came and I went to church with him. I don't like to miss church and he *will* come, so I just as well treat him good, as bad.

Tues. 12   School in eve. Shaw home with me.
Wed. 13   School in eve. Shaw home with me.
Sun. 17   Went to church in eve, with Mr. Shaw.
Tues. 19   School in eve. Mr. J. W. Shaw walked home with me.
Thurs. 21   School in eve. Shaw home with me.
Sat. 23   Mr. J. W. Shaw—*No 11*—spent evening with me.
Sun. 24   Spent P.M. at J. M. Bair's. Virrilla Roby came home with me and went to church with Mr. Shaw & I; her brother took her home.
Mon. 25   School eve. Shaw home with me.
Tues. 26   School eve. Shaw home with me.
Wed. 27   School eve. Home alone.
Thurs. 28   School eve. Shaw home with me.
Fri. 29   School eve. Home alone: Shaw came too late.

July

Wed. 4   A hot "Fourth of July." P.M. went to Fair Ground with Mr. Shaw to the races: he got very much out of patience, going, because had to wait so long for street-car. Home for early supper, then at 8 P.M. we went to Garfield Park to see "Pinafore", it being played on Soldier Creek. *Such an immense crowd* prevented our seeing much, and like to have *never* gotten home. Everything "sold out" on the Grounds. Paid 10 cts per glass, for Creek water, put in a barrel with ice. *A hot day and evening: An awful crowd. Beautiful* Fireworks, everywhere: And quite a pleasant day for me.

Thurs. 5   School in eve: Mr. Shaw home with me.

Wed. 11   Called at J. N. Stauffer's in A.M. and in eve went there to stay. Mrs. Stauffer has just been confined; has a sweet Baby girl, and I am to take care of the two: it is 1260 Topeka Ave and Mr. Shaw does not carry mail down there so I shall be quite lonely, as I begin to like the Boy, he is so good to me.

Sun. 15   Attended meeting at 1st Congregational church in eve with Mr. Shaw.

Fri. 20   School in eve. Last night of school—*so sorry.*

Sun. 22   Mr. Shaw, took me to meeting, at Presbyterian church in eve, after which he staid with me to watch the Moon go into "*Total Eclipse*" at mid-night. Twas such a beautiful night, perfectly, cloudless so had a good view of the Eclipse, watching it *on* and *off* and the Moon, being Full, 'twas a *grand* sight. *Beautifully, wonderfully,* grand.

Mon. 23   Home. So few attended school, didn't pay, so closed. Mr. Eberts a nice young man. Cousin to notorious Younger Brothers.[1] He said I must *never* give up "Short Hand" as I'd make an *Expert* and was equally good on Typewriter.

Wed. 25   Home. Mr. Shaw delivers mail in two blocks of me so, I get to *flirt* with him from the door every day.

August

Wed. 1   Home. Mr. Shaw seems very devoted and some say he would *love* me if I'd let him; some say he is *very much in love* with me and *all* say it is *shameful* way I treat him and I'll be sorry. Everyone likes him so much.

Fri. 10	A letter today from Oren Kettlewell says he wants to marry me. "*Not much* old, boy," there are people I like better, in this world.
Tues. 14	Home. Begin to like Mr. Shaw much better.
Tues. 21	Uncle Frank and cousin Will Van Orsdol came about 1 P.M. and I went to Santa Fe Depot with them to see my father who is on his way from Springfield, Colo. to Mt. Pleasant, Iowa to a Reunion of his old Company, the 4th Iowa Cavalry Boys. Train stopped over 1/2 hour, so I had a nice little visit. Haven't seen him for 1 1/2 years. Was so glad to see him. Mr. Shaw spent the evening with me.

September

Wed. 19	Went alone to the State Fair in P.M. at Fair Grounds and some kind of a *creature* in "the shape of a man" tried to "make a mash" on me, but didn't find me *soft enough*. How I *utterly detest* such men. Mr. Shaw spent eve with me.
Thurs. 27	Downtown in P.M. with Mrs. Stauffer. To Prayer meeting in eve and Mr. Shaw came to take me home; tho' I *hated, despised,* him once, I like him very much now: he is so good and kind to me, and is a good Boy.

October

Fri. 5	With Mr. Stauffer's, attended Reunion in P.M. A *Sham Battle* by U. S. Troops, was grand.[2] Speeches made at Hall were excellent. Judge Usher—only living member of Lincoln's Cabinet—Sen. Plum and Commander-in-Chief of G. A. R., Warner, were prominent speakers.[3]
Sat. 6	Poor Mr. Shaw is sick and couldn't come up this eve.
Mon. 8	Home. Wish I could see Mr. Shaw to know how he is.
Tues. 9	Home. Really feel *Blue* because haven't seen Mr. Shaw, for several days: guess I like him better than I thought. He is so good and kind.
Wed. 10	Got a letter from Mr. Shaw this A.M. and in afternoon, on *persuasion* of others went down to see him: found him able to be up and so glad to see me.
Sat. 27	Home. Mr. Shaw spent eve with me: he is winning me over, thro' his goodness and kindness. I've always had a *presentiment* that I would marry that man and I don't

want to, at all, yet I seem to be drawn on and on, towards him, against my own will.

Wed. 31   Home. Got a short, cranky note from O.K. today: he first *coaxes*, then *pleads* and then gets *cranky*.

November

Tues. 6   Home. "Election Day" Latest returns at Bedtime, announced election of "Cleveland and Thurman" ("Democrats") but I sincerely hope not.

Wed. 7   Home. Harrison & Morton (Republicans) were *elected* by a *fine* majority, and now old Grover C. can go *fishing* every day, if he wants to. *Kansas went Republican 82000 majority.*

Fri. 9   Home. Snowed hard all day, till 8 P.M. Snow two feet on level. Democrats got great snowing under: hope they will never get out again.

Wed. 14   . . . . There being a *Rally* to *Ratify* the *Election* of "*Harrison & Morton*" as *President & Vice* of *U. S.* I went out on the street, after supper with Lucy Blood, Kissie Boyd & Lucian Stauffer and meeting Col. Boyd, he took us all up to his Room in the Windsor Hotel, where we could see and be out of the Crowd, which I believe was biggest I was ever in: the streets were a solid mass of people; Flambeau Clubs,[4] Bands, people blowing every manner and kind of horns and whistles, ringing bells, beating pans and doing every thing to make a loud noise, till it was almost impossible, to be heard in conversation: but it was *grand* and I enjoyed it, until Mr. Shaw came up, and would not come near me and when I went to speak to him, he was so *angry* he would not look at me and it was some time before I could find out the cause, to be *jealousy* of an old man, old enough to be my Grandfather. *How ridiculous: yet I was very much hurt*, to see him act so, without any cause what ever. I begged Mr. Shaw so hard to take me home, but he wouldn't do it, so I went back with Mr. Stauffer when they got ready to go home at midnight, I was so heart-broken, to have Mr. Shaw treat me so *unjustly*, for *God knows I was innocent* of any wrong doing and my heart *rebelled* at his unjustness and soon as I got home, I sat down and wrote him a long letter, expressing myself very plainly. Wonder how he will take it.

Thurs. 15   Got a letter from Mr. Shaw this A.M. saying he was very sorry for way he acted last night: he will get mine at noon. Went to Prayer meeting in eve and Mr. Shaw was there and walked home with me. He was cross about the letter I wrote, but I talked him out of it, and he went home in a good humor, and I'm happy again.

Wed. 21   Mrs. Stauffer & I went down town in P.M. I bought a new *"Corset and Bustle"* and coming home, met Mr. J. W. Shaw, Mr. Geo. Yount, Mr. Sad Hodgins and Mr. Wes Brown—Carriers—it *"plagued* me half to death" for was afraid they could tell what I had, but of course "Boys" don't know that "girls" wear such things.

December

Sat. 22   Mr. Shaw spent the eve with me. He is 29 years old today.

Tues. 25   "Christmas Day." A sleety, drizzly one, but I was happy enough. The Cases and Boyds were here for dinner. Mr. Shaw sent me a nice Book—Nature's Serial Story, by E. P. Roe—as a present, and tho' very stormy he came up and spent the evening with me: it has been a very happy "Christmas" to me.[5]

Mon. 31   Down town in P.M. got new pair of shoes to wear to the Ball tomorrow night. So closes the year 1888. I wonder what '89 will bring me. I hope, more happiness than 1888, tho' 1888 has been very happy since I got O. Kettlewell off my Hands. I liked Oren very much, but do not want to marry him: he is splendid company, but I feel, deep down in my heart, that he won't do to marry. He is going with another girl down home and deceiving her: she thinks he means to marry her, and all the time he is begging me to marry him and writes me awful letters about her. Says she threw herself in his way and he has no use for her, but would like to *"swing her about 6 months and throw her over."* Now that is no way for an honorable young man to do, and I can't bring myself to marry such a man. *No I'll never* marry Oren, *never.*

[1889]

January

Thurs. 10   At noon an old, "Gypsy-woman" came and insisted on telling my fortune, which I unwillingly let her do: 'twas great fun and cost me a dollar. She told me all my *past* life, as well as I know it myself and here is some things she told of the *future*: she says Oren Kettlewell will be here to see me before the month is out, and insist on my marrying him, but I must not do it: says Will Finch wants me too, but not to marry him: says Mr. Shaw loves me too, but I must not marry him, nor any one I know at present. Says I'll be in a crowd at a Party the middle of February and be introduced to a man whose name commences with "*D*" that I've never seen, nor even heard his name, he is married, has children and must have nothing to do with him: says in March I'll have a little sick spell; severe but short: says I must not become *engaged* to any one till after first of May. Says I'm to take a trip in June and will then meet the man I must marry: he is tall, light and has blue eyes. I will return again and Topeka will always be my home and I'll be very happy, and married and in my own home before next winter and Oh! so much I can't remember half. Now we will see how much comes true. At 2 P.M. took Lucian Stauffer and called at Col. Douglass', then went to a Dog & Pony Matinee at "Crawfords'": didn't like it; come home before it was out. Went to Prayer-meeting in eve and Mr. Shaw walked home with me.

Thurs. 24   Mr. Shaw called in afternoon to see me and again in eve and took me to Prayer meeting. He goes to Kansas City tomorrow on his Vacation and talked very much of *Matrimony* tonight: says for me to study about the matter till he comes home.

Sat. 26   Home and what an eventful day it has been to me. At 8:20 A.M. received Telegram that O. Kettlewell would be here during the day—no good news to me for I don't want to see him—At 8:30 the Postman brought me a letter from Mr. Shaw and how glad I was. God bless, dear Winnie boy. And at 9 o'clock A.M. O. Kettlewell came—so this much of my Gypsy fortune has come true—staid till 11 o'clock then went downtown and back again at 3 P.M. staying till 4 o'clock A.M. and all the time begging and pleading with me to marry him: says he would marry me tomorrow if I would only say the word: Oh! how hard he cried and walked the floor, half the time. I pitied him and was half afraid of him he was so desperate yet I could not think of marrying him for I do not love him and I do love Winnie. Oren says he will have me yet, but he never shall: he seemed completely *broken-hearted* when he bid me good-bye at 4 A.M.

February

Sat. 2

In afternoon Mr. Shaw & I went for a ride on "Eastside-circle" out to Cottage Grove. We spent the eve at Mr. Geo. Weymouths on Lincoln St, playing cards and when we got home near midnight, came something that makes me very happy: the happiest girl that lives. My, dear "Winnie Boy," *asked me to be his wife*, and I am Oh! so happy; he is so good and honest I know he will always be true and good to me, yet I don't think I ever shed so many tears, for some way, I don't feel just satisfied; I feel half afraid and yet I love him so much, yet there is an uneasiness I cannot explain; but I am happy.

Thurs. 28

Mr. Shaw spent eve with me: he says I must call him by his right name, "Johnny" but I'll never get used to it I know.

March

Sat. 2

Downtown in afternoon. Went with Johnny Shaw to State House in eve, it being the last night of the Legislature. Met several of my old friends from Winfield—my old home in southern Kansas—and had a splendid time but Johnny got quite *spunky* at me for not introducing him to a friend, when I had hardly more than a chance to speak to them: it is these little *fits* of *temper* that I'm afraid of: makes me feel that trouble may come of it, in the future, after marriage.

May

Sat. 11   Down town in afternoon, and Met Johnny who walked most of way home with me. He came in eve and took me to get ice-cream: after we got home, he *vaccinated* me on my left arm, as there is considerable Smallpox scare here.

June

Tues. 4   Great excitement in City today over the shooting of A. J. Rogers & wife at 4 o'clock A.M. by a Burglar. The burglar—Nat Oliphant—was caught about 9 A.M. Mr. Rogers died at 10 o'clock A.M. 9 P.M. mob commenced to break into jail and at 11 P.M. prisoner was hung at or near 6 & Quincy St: estimated near 15,000 people saw the hanging.[1] Mr. & Mrs. Stauffer went and I kept their children. Mr. Shaw staid with me till 10:30 when he went down in time to see the hanging. I could hear the pounding and hear the shouts of the mob, which was

Picture taken June 5, 1889, the day after Nat Oliphant was lynched on this spot.

enough for me. Mr. Rogers was very prominent here: his wife is in a critical condition but may recover.

Wed. 5   Went in P.M. with Hannah Peterson to Stoker's Under-taker's office to see Nat. E. Oliphant, Burglar & murderer, who was hanged last night by the mob. It was a dreadful sight: thousands of people in line, passing thro', to get a look at him and not one with a thought of pity: all seeming to think he got what he deserved. Poor man tho' he did a dreadful thing, *he had a soul* to save and seems like he ought to have been spared and given a chance to become a better man. There are other punish-ments. Johnny spent eve with me.

Mon. 10   In eve Johnny & I went out to Lowman Hill and called on . . . to bid them good-bye, as I leave for Winfield, Wednesday, to spend the summer and get ready to marry this Fall.

July

Thurs. 4   "*Fourth of July.*" Went down town in A.M. to see the Parade with the family and with them in eve to see the "Fire-works." But all rest of day, home alone. I was too lonesome to enjoy the *Fourth* without Johnny, so staid home.

Fri. 12   Cousin Emma Adams came in afternoon and went downtown with me to buy my "*wedding dress.*" I think I had splendid luck, and got a pretty dress of white satin, and Valiencennes lace, and tulle veil. I hope it will please my Boy. I never got such a thing for any other man and never will again: it is my *first* and *last wedding dress.* I never was so lonesome as I am away from Johnny. After the *wonderful dress* was bought we went to an ice cream Parlor and I *treated* to ice-cream.

Mon. 22   After delays and a long, hot, tiresome trip, reached Topeka at Daylight and Johnny took me to Mrs. Kes-sler's near 7th & Tyler where I'm to board awhile and he called in eve few minutes. I was awfully tired.

August

Thurs. 1   Still at Mrs. Kessler's. Johnny called in eve and he & I carried over to his house a lot of my dishes I have bought to go to housekeeping with. We will be married September 4th and while I think I'm very happy, there is a constant kind of dread or presentiment, that, "all will not be well" and I shall be unhappy; but I drive such fears away, for my boy is *very good* and *kind*.

September

Mon. 2   Called at Uncle Marian's few min. this morning then to Uncle George's, who with aunt Samanthe & cousin Fred drove few min. to uncle Charlie's with me, then brought me to Mrs. Shaw's in Topeka. Johnny was home when we got in. Rained on us, coming to town. Quite a gloomy day, which seemed to me a dark omen to my approaching wedding day. How lovely the "Buckwheat" smelled this morning as we passed the farms, coming in. Johnny took me out to Mr. Weymouth's awhile in eve. Staid all night at Shaws.

Tues. 3   . . . . My last day, of "*Single Blesedness*," so must make the most of it: it all seems so strange, yet I'm happy as can be. All night at Mrs. Shaw's.

Wed. 4   *My Wedding Day*, and I pray God to bless it. The morning dawned, bright and clear, grand and beautiful. Went with Johnny early in A.M. to 1st Christian Church and from there with Mrs. Weymouth to get some flowers to Decorate with. Very busy all day, going to and from the church, getting things ready and the Minister was there too, to *drill* us: commenced raining about 11 o'clock A.M. and rained hard rest of day, until little after 6 P.M. I have felt *so sad* all day and it has been hard to keep back the tears: my eyes have been full, most all day but not one dropped. I'm determined not to cry on my wedding day. I love Johnny and I know he does me, yet it seems as tho' he has thought more of how things shall look, at the wedding, than of me; he has hurried me all day and not given me one little pleasant word concerning what is to be. My heart feels hungry and not satisfied. I suppose more because it has been so gloomy, than anything else. At 7 o'clock P.M. I commenced dressing; my dress is white Satin and Valiencennes lace, long veil, of Tulle; long train low, square neck, no sleeves, long gloves. At 8:20 P.M., with a bright moon peeping from a few clouds Johnny and I drove to the church where we were married by Rev. B. L. Smith. Miss Lila Goodhue playing "Clayton's Grand March" on Piano as we went up centre isle and "Mendolson's Wedding March" as we came out. A large crowd was at the church to see us married and the Mail carriers with some of their wives and friends and Johnny's folks, came to our house after the wedding, where had light lunch and Johnny "set up" the Beer. We got some handsome presents; especially the set of silver from Mail-carriers. We went straight from church to Johnny's home at 411 West 9th st. where we will live.

Thurs. 5   This has been such a beautiful day; I feel very happy to find myself, Mrs. J. W. Shaw instead of Mattie Van Orsdol. It seems funny to commence housekeeping for one's self: it is more like keeping "Play house." Geo. Weymouth called in morning. Johnny not working today but had to go down town and "set up" the Cigars.

Sat. 7   Home. Frank & Rosie Shaw and Mrs. Weymouth called in eve and went with us to a "Beer Party" at Mr. C. Kerle's, and Johnny & I had our *first misunderstanding* in married life. I don't approve of Liquor of any kind and he does very emphatically: so he felt little out of patience with me, that was all.

Sun. 8   Home and a *very dear home, to me*, too. Sad Hodgins came home with Johnny from P.O. at 4 P.M. and took dinner with us: the first of the P.O. Boys we've entertained: it seems like play.

Tues. 10   Home. It seems so funny to be married, I feel like I wasn't in the right place, but am very happy.

Wed. 11   Home. Ironed today. Am getting down to business.

Thurs. 19   Went to the State Fair, at "Fair Grounds" in P.M. with Johnny and he got so *awfully* angry at me he tried to run off from me, just because I wanted him to take me into Exposition Hall as he promised to do, of his own free will, then didn't want to—tho' had plenty of time— fearing he would miss some Racing and wouldn't tell me; Oh! he acted so *shamefully* and would not speak to me. I was so unhappy I nearly cried my heart out. And when we got home I had to coax for an hour or more to get him to eat supper: then he wanted to leave me to go down town, but I finally got him in a better humor so he let me go to P.O. with him. This is the *stubborn temper*, I felt afraid of before marrying him. *Oh! I've been so unhappy today.*

October

Fri. 4	Mrs. Mila Roby & Mrs. Lizzie Bair called in P.M. In eve Johnny & I went down town. It is so nice to be married.
Sat. 5	Cousin Will Van Orsdol ate dinner with us today. In eve Johnny & I went to a Beer Party at Frank Shaw's. I *hate* these Parties, but must go to please Johnny, or he will think me "*cranky.*"
Sat. 12	The "Beer Party" met at our house in evening. Large crowd, mostly Mail Carriers, present and Johnny introduced me to Fred Farnsworth a nice, quiet boy, a good friend of Johnny's, whom I've seen so much of, and been in same crowd with so much yet never have been introduced to. I had to finish out a table of four, to play cards and my partner was Mr. Geo. Yount of whom Johnny became almost *insanely* jealous: he was so nice and kind to me, till the crowd left then he began cursing and abusing me most dreadfully and he had no cause, as Mr. Y. paid more attention to others than me. I think it must have been the Beer he drank that caused it.
Sun. 13	A rainy, bad day. Johnny still very angry at me and I'm so unhappy. I will never submit to another Beer Party coming to our house, if it is to cause me such trouble.
Mon. 14	Home and Oh! so unhappy. I try so hard to please Johnny and nothing pleases him. He won't hardly notice me.
Wed. 16	Home: how I wish Johnny wasn't so stubborn, he hardly treats me respectful, and I feel so badly.
Thurs. 17	Home. Johnny is awfully mad at me again: it is dreadful to have him get so angry, and without the slightest cause: he is so awfully high tempered and abuses me terrible.
Fri. 18	Spent the P.M. with Mrs. Geo. Weymouth. In eve Johnny and I went to hear the *great* Evangelist—D. L. Moody—Preach. Liked him very much: a pleasant, earnest speaker. He is short of stature and heavy, with gray hair and beard.[2]
Sat. 19	Went alone at 4 P.M. to M. E. church to hear Rev. D. L.

Moody: in eve went to P.O. with Johnny to work up his Mail: have him in a good humor again.

Sun. 20   Johnny so angry with me, I'm heart-sick, but he took me to hear Evangelist Moody's *farewell* sermon at M.E. church, which was just splendid.

Mon. 21   Home. I can't feel contented and happy for the constant dread, that in some way, I may displease Johnny, for what pleases him one time will displease the next: *he has an awful temper.*

Thurs. 24   Home. How nice is it, when Johnny is in good humor. I would be so, Oh! so happy if he would never get cross at me.

Thurs. 31   Home and not feeling at all well. Johnny I know loves me dearly, but every little thing offends him and it seems like I so often offend, tho' always without knowing it. I've already shed many bitter tears.

November

Fri. 1   Home. In bed most of day. Mis-carriage: missed just one month: feel awful bad.

Sat. 2   Home, a most unhappy girl, for Johnny is so angry at me again and *I don't know* why. I am not a bit well and can't bear to have him get so cross at me: it is enough, to *tear the heart right out* of a person, for I love him and it is dreadful to be treated so by one, who should treat you the best.

Thurs. 7   Home. A cold rainy day. In eve had a good hot supper waiting for my Boy, with his slippers and dry clothing near a good, warm fire; coal, and kindling, in: everything cozy and snug so Johnny would have nothing to do on his return from work and I was happy in the thought, that I had our little home so cheerful and waited patiently for his coming, but one, two hours passed—and I began to cry with uneasiness as the presentiment came to my heart that all was not right—and the hours dragged by, 'till he was more than four hours late, when at last I heard his welcome step, but when the door opened and I went to give my welcoming kiss he *staggered into the room drunk.* Oh! God have mercy on my *wretched, miserable* life. Oh! the disgrace and shame of having my dear, dear Boy come home in such a condition. Only a Bride yet and this so soon. Oh! what is my life to be. How could my Boy do so. Oh! dear God, take me from this world before I ever see my Boy drunk again. Oh! what a time I had with him.

Fri. 8 Johnny hardly over his *spree* this morning, but managed to work. I'm so unhappy, I don't want to live. Oh! if God would only let me die: it is a terrible blow to a trusting, loving young wife: the shame and disgrace is *terrible, terrible*. Johnny could eat nothing all day and I could not for my heart is broken. I've cried so bitterly all day.

Sat. 9 Johnny is getting over his "drunken spree" enough to be cross and has abused me shamefully all day, when home; my tears will fall tho' I try to hide them and I'm so heart broken it makes him cross and he *cursed me so hard* this evening. Oh! God, have mercy on me and let me die. I don't want to live. My Boy does not love me, or he would not *curse* me: no man would *curse* a woman he loved. I can't bear this, and live. God look down in pity and take me home to Thee.

Sun. 10 Johnny sober today and took me to church in evening, but I *never will* be happy again for my confidence is gone. I trusted him once completely: I had implicit faith in him but he has broken it, and I *cannot* trust again.

Mon. 11 Home.

Tues. 12 Home. So miserably unhappy. Ah! a girl should listen to her heart and when it feels afraid stand back. While Johnny was always so good and kind to me, yet I caught glimpses of Temper, that made me feel all would not be well with one who would marry him. But too late, now; it is done, and for life.

Sat. 16 Johnny & I went to a Beer Party at Mr. Weymouths in eve. Oh! how I despise these Parties and yet I must go for the sake of peace. But *Peace* or *no Peace* I will never go to another one.

Fri. 22 Home. Johnny is so good & kind when he is in a good humor, and makes me very happy.

Sat. 23 My dear Boy, came home sick at noon and I watched anxiously by his bedside until an hour or more after mid-night, when his fever abating, I lay down for a little rest.

Wed. 27 Went to the Doctor's in the evening for Medicine and when I returned, found Mr. Fred Farnsworth, with Johnny, having brought us a fine Turkey, Oysters and

Celery, as a present, from himself and the other Carriers for our "Thanksgiving" dinner tomorrow. The
P.O. Boys are all so kind and good.

Thurs. 28   *Very, very, very* cold. Mrs. Shaw rooms with us and leaving her to look after Johnny, I went to the Doctor's
about 9 A.M. I [am] awfully worried about Johnny, as he
is so *low* and gets no better.

Fri. 29   I went for a new Doctor this A.M. and got Dr. Roby. He
says Johnny has Pneumonia.

Sat. 30   Doctor Roby called this A.M. Says Johnny is little bit
better, but I don't exactly like him: he seems to know all
about him, without asking anything about his previous
condition.

December

Sun. 1   Dr. Menninger—Dr. Roby's partner—called this A.M.
and gave Johnny a thorough examination. And we are
very much pleased with him.[3]
Dr. Menninger calls at the home daily for the next 6 days.

Sun. 8   A very beautiful day and my Boy sat up quite awhile;
most too long I thought for the first time, but I can do
nothing with him. He got so very angry at me this eve
and cursed me so hard, and was so mad he wouldn't take
his medicine, because he thought I took more time than
I needed, to eat a lunch. I've done everything I know
how for him and am worn out with care and worry over
his sickness, yet he curses me so, when I hardly take time
to eat.

Mon. 9   Down town in A.M. to get some things for Johnny. He
hardly lets me take time to breathe. He *curses* me if I'm
gone longer than he thinks I ought to be, or if I take a
few minutes to gulp down a few bites to eat: Oh! he is so
unreasonable: is all my life to be so *unhappy?* Doctor
called this A.M. Says he is much improved.

Sun. 15   Home and happy to see Johnny getting well.

Fri. 20   Johnny & I went down town in afternoon. The Store
windows are trimmed very prettily for the Holidays.
How good it is to have my Boy out again, tho' he is very
weak yet.

Wed. 25   A grand, old Christmas-Day, just like summer. Mother
Shaw and I went to hear Christmas services at Catholic
church at 4 o'clock A.M. Church beautifully decorated

and fine music. Johnny & I attended mail-carriers Fourth Annual Ball in eve, at Metropolitan Hall which was grand success in every particular. Hecks Orchestra: Hall full, to overflowing. Grand March, led by Postmaster J. L. King and wife. Johnny not strong enough to dance, but I danced. Home at 2 o'clock A.M.

Mon. 30   Johnny & I spent day and night at uncle Frank Van's and Johnny went hunting with the Boys.

Tues. 31   A pretty day and still at Uncle Frank's, where they are busy preparing to give a big "*New Year's* Dinner" tomorrow. We are having a splendid visit and Johnny is looking ever so much better.

And so ends the year 1889, the most eventful one of my life; it is with such conflicting emotions of *Joy* and *Sorrow* that I look back over the past Year. Joy, that every young girl feels, when she becomes the Bride of one, in whom she has the most *implicit faith*. Sorrow that *crushes* the heart, when that faith is broken, by the abuse from one it has most loved.

Oh! God give us many blessings in the New Year.

[1890]

January

Wed. 1   Johnny (my husband) and I, spent the day at uncle Frank Van Orsdol's, at Silver Lake. They gave a *big* "*New Year*'s dinner," to a *big* crowd of people. We younger people spent the forenoon "running races", *jumping* and with rifle, shooting at "*marks*", and danced all afternoon. I danced with uncle Frank and every young man present. We had such a happy day and I hope it is a foreruner of a *happy year*, but I have *forebodings*.

Mon. 6   Johnny went to work this morning, but will work in the Stamp Department until stronger.

Fri. 10   I don't find much to do in our little home so fret the hours away, because of my poor husband's ill health.

Tues. 14   We have a Mr. & Mrs. Page (they call themselves Mr. & Mrs. George Brown) rooming with us. He is *Foreman* of the Stonecutters, who are building the North and South wings and Dome of the State House. They are very pleasant.[1]

Tues. 21   I had *thought, to be so happy*, but *don't believe* I am.

Thurs. 23   Some days, Johnny has to "lay off," not being well enough to work and it makes him so angry, because he is so ambitious to work and get a home.

Tues. 28   Johnny breaks my heart, when he gets so cross and ill-tempered.

Wed. 29   Mr. Brown *drinks* and I don't believe *she* is extra happy either, like me.

Fri. 31   How I pray, Johnny may get well. My poor husband, I would give him my own good health, if I could.

February

Thurs. 6   My *Honeymoon*, should not be over, yet, and what a world of trouble has already come.

Tues. 11   Johnny and I are studying his case and trying to learn what would be best to restore his health.

Wed. 12   Doctors here (especially D. H. W. Roby) want to operate on Johnny for a Fistula but I don't want them to; I am afraid it is Tuburculis. I don't believe he will get well.

Mon. 17   We have decided Johnny must go to Chicago to be doctored and I cry and cry.

Tues. 18   Mother and Rosa Shaw here. Johnny left for Chicago at 3 o'clock P.M. over Santa Fe and I went to depot with him.

Wed. 19   I went to Frank Shaw's and spent the afternoon. I was dreadfully hurt because Johnny would not let me go to Chicago with him; and he needs me so much. I stay alone tho', the Browns have rooms with us.

Tues. 25   Another night of tears and I suppose I will keep it up, as long as Johnny is away. I am so lonely, I can hardly live.

Wed. 26   Johnny writes he had to have an operation and came very near dying. Now I *knew* I ought to have been with him.

March

Tues. 4   I am a *miserable* girl, if there *ever* was one. I don't *cook, eat* or *work*, since Johnny left. Mother Shaw stays with me much of time.

Mon. 10   Life is all tears and heart-ache. Why *must* I suffer so. I get so lonely to see Johnny. Mrs. Brown has gone to Ohio to visit her people and I nearly die. He sleeps in his rooms at night, but I don't know when he is home.

Tues. 11   I have made up my mind, I am going to Chicago and see my husband.

Thurs. 13   I just packed my *grip*, borrowed some money from our roomer, Mr. Geo. Brown and left for Chicago at 3 o'clock this afternoon over the Rock Island. I bought a second-class ticket, for $6.50. Was raining a little, when I left Topeka and tonight it is just *pouring*. We are flying thro' Missouri and Iowa and I cannot sleep becase I am going to Johnny. Some old *masher* sat in front of me, and tried to flirt with me and I was so glad of the company of a dear old lady, as far as Fairfield Iowa. She said I was too *young* and *pretty* to be *traveling alone*, but I'll bet I can take care of myself against any old fool of a *masher* that shows up. I refused all overtures to talk and would not even look at him. I told him I had a husband and he would not believe it.

Fri. 14   Crossed the Mississippi River this morning at Davenport Iowa, just at dawn, but was so foggy, could not see much. Saw some pretty places, passing thro' Illinois. I arrived in Chicago about 11 o'clock A.M. and took a Hack and drove straight to the *Emergency Hospital,* on Wells St., and La Salle Ave, where my husband is. He was surprised beyond words, but we were *so glad* to see one another. I went to a little Hotel on Clark St. and got my dinner, then spent a very happy afternoon, in the Ward with Johnny. Mrs. Metz, the Matron, says I may board at the Hospital, if I will occupy a room with some convalescence, and I am so glad, because I will be near Johnny all the time.

Sat. 15   My! what a big noisy place, Chicago is. From Hospital windows I can see nothing but *City* in any direction I may look. How happy I am to be here with Johnny.

Mon. 17   I walked down town alone, crossed the Chicago river and went to the South-side. I was never in a real City before and was gone so long, the Hospital folks thought I must be lost, but I was only going thro' some big Stores. I had never been out of the State of Kansas, since going to it when a little girl, five years old, and so I find much to see in a big City, like this noisy, smoky, dirty old place. I am glad I do not live here.

Tues. 18   Went down town again today, during the hours I could not be with Johnny: they allow me to go in the Ward to see him, a few minutes at 9 o'clock, and for one hour at 11 o'clock, then all the afternoon and a few minutes in the evening. I caught a terrible cold on the train.

Wed. 19   This is a German Hospital and I am the only English person "on my feet," tho' many of them can speak *English.* I have a room with Jennie Paulson, Emma Munz and Letta Uldsholdt, who are here awaiting treatment or operations.

Thurs. 20   I am so happy because Johnny is growing better, but he is in bed all the time. My throat is very sore and Doctor Isham says I have "Quinzy."[2]

Fri. 21   I have suffered greatly today with my throat and was only allowed the tiniest glimpse of my husband. "Quinzy" is terrible. The Doctors and Nurses would not allow me out of Hospital.

Sat. 22   I feel some better today, tho' I nearly choked to death, last night and could not take any food or my medicine. But Dr. Hill has had me gargle, every half hour all day, with clear *hot water; very hot water*, and it is getting the best of my Quinzy. I was in quite serious condition.

Sun. 23   I slipped away from the Nurses this morning and went to Church, with Emma Munz at D. L. Moody's Church on La Salle St. and after service, we walked down to the shore of Lake Michigan and got my first look at a large body of water. A lovely day with just wind enough, to make pretty waves. Except I've taken a big risk today.

Mon. 24   Did not leave the Hospital today, but don't believe I am the worse, for going yesterday.

Tues. 25   A rainy bad day and I did not leave the Hospital. I am "picking up" many German words and getting so I understand lots of it; don't believe it would be hard to learn.

Thurs. 27   Didn't leave Hospital today. They have almost every *Nationality* here, and *surely* every kind of disease and Surgical case, ever heard of. A Hospital is most interesting.

Fri. 28   They tell me I can take Johnny home now whenever I learn to *dress* the wound, made by operating, so I went into the Operating room with the Doctor and Nurse this morning but it looked so badly, I could not bear to touch him. Went down town and to the Auditorium with Lettie Uldsholdt. And went to a Saloon, and bought some table-Beer Johnny wanted and doctors said he could have, or rather, *want* him to have. I wish no such stuff was made. I hate it.

April

Thurs. 3   Johnny and I told our Hospital friends good-bye soon after dinner, Shopped a little and took 6 o'clock P.M. train, for "*Home sweet Home*." It rained, thundered and lightened awfully as our train pulled out of Depot.

Fri. 4   Arrived home at noon and tho' Johnny stood the trip well, he is very tired and weak. He bought a number of things for himself in Chicago, just before he left, and not a *single* thing for me. I could not help feeling a little hurt, especially as he was not in need of fancy Ties, Stick-pins, collars and cuffs by wholesale. But I never let him know I felt this selfish neglect.

Thurs. 17   Johnny improves in health and is cross as a Bear.

Sat. 26   *I am 23 years old today* and have had a *world of care*: I feel

like there was little in the World worth living for and life
has only begun too. Johnny and I went down town this
evening, just for a walk.

Wed. 30   Are having such *lovely* days. *Wish I could be as happy* as the
Spring is beautiful, but *I have found one can't be happy* with a
cross husband, even if his *crossness does indicate* returning
health. It is a *pretty good thing too*, that he *doesn't read* my
Diary. I *don't* think he knows I keep one.

May

Sun. 4   I *climbed* to the *State House Dome* this morning on *ladders*
and *trestle work* on a *wager* with Foreman, George Page-
Brown who *did not believe I could do it*: it *was very dangerous*, but *I felt no fear*. He went up, but his wife and
Johnny *could not*. Johnny and I went to church this eve.

Mon. 5   Washed this morning. *My! what a climb* I had yesterday
and my muscles *are sore* today. The Dome is *not finished*
and are *no* floors: one just looks *down, down, down* into
black space. Some of the workmen are made dizzy and
several have been killed but I was *not the least dizzy* and
absolutely without fear. Some of the ladders were *roped
together* to make them longer and it made *very long climbs*,
from one trestle to *another* before one could rest, *but I
just went up like a Squirrel.*

Fri. 23   The Browns and us went to a Re-Submission-meeting,
at the State House, this evening; it was "n.g." *O I hate the
thought of Re-submission* and *liquor*, but for the *sake of
peace*, I must go to such meetings, with my husband, who
is *fond of his Beer*.[3]

June

Mon. 2   My *busy* day. I sometimes think I had better have married, Will or Charlie or Oren and I might have been
happy. I don't *like* to think these things but they *will come
up*, when Johnny gets an ugly spell.

Wed. 4   Married nine months, today and don't know what to
think of the life: sometimes I am happy and *sometimes*,
utterly miserable; and I *know marriage* has brought *more
tears*, than *smiles*: and *drink* and *temper*, cause of it.

Thurs. 5   Busy, "playing" keep-house.

Thurs. 26   I don't find enough to do, to keep busy in this "play-house" *existence.*

July, August, and September continue the lament about Johnny's volatile temperament. The entries are very short and give no indication of the sources of their marital difficulty. The only interesting event during these months is the arrival of the "Wizard Oil Medicine Troupe," which Martha sees 13 times!

September

Thurs. 4   Our *first Wedding Anniversary,* and the year has been *so full* of tears. I pray God, the coming year may be more happy. I *cannot* admit, even to myself, that I am un-happy, and yet I *know* I am *not* happy. Johnny has an ungovernable temper, and I never know when he is angry at *me* or some one else, but whomever it may be, he takes his *spite* out on me. I *know* he loves me, is *proud* of me but he lets his temper rule him and make him unkind.

October

Thurs. 2   We, and the Browns, went to the Wizard Concert this evening, *just splendid.* I am not at all well.

Fri. 3   In bed all day with high fever. It means I might have been a mother, but will not this time. *I'm sorry.*

Sat. 4   In bed all day again and my *fever very high* Johnny went to Forepaugh's *Circus,* tonight with the Browns and left me *all alone* in the house. I felt hurt, that he would go and leave me at such a time, with only his own *pleasure* in mind, while *I* am sick at home because of him. But I let him go with a kiss and a smile and he *never dreamed* how my heart *ached.* I find him a very selfish man. I wanted him home tonight so much.

Sun. 5   Sat up a little today, but 'twas a big risk to do so; but Johnny doesn't like to have me in bed.

Wed. 8   I walked out around the State House today tho' I suppose I should not, but I feel strong.

Fri. 10   Went up town this morning to see a Parade of School Children, Old Soldiers and our *President Benjamin Harrison;* was a perfect mass of people on the street. Our President is a fine looking man. This afternoon,

Johnny, mother, Mrs. Brown and I, went to the Reunion at the Fair Grounds, which was simply *grand*. We
listened to an address by President Harrison, and wit-
nessed a *splendid* "Sham Battle" tho' it seemed very
dangerous.

Sat. 11   We went to Wizard Oil Concert tonight. The Company
is going to leave the City soon.

Tues. 14   Just resting today. Thro' the Summer, Johnny seemed
to have regained his health, but now that Fall has come
he is not real well and I feel he *never will* be well—O its
dreadful.

Wed. 15   The Browns are preparing to move away from the City,
and we shall miss them greatly.

Thurs. 16   I just sit at home and wonder what the future has for me
and I *dread* it, because of the *forebodings* that come to me.
O, if Johnny could only be strong.

Fri. 17   I went with Mr. & Mrs. Brown, thro' the State Insane
Assylum and the City and County Jails, this afternoon.
Both are *terrible* places, but I would rather lose my mind,
than be a Criminal.

Tues. 21   Went Shopping this afternoon, but my Shopping *always*
means buying the *bare necessities*.

Wed. 22   Mrs. Brown asked me to go *shopping* with her this afternoon and this evening, Johnny and I were the guests of
the Browns for Supper, at the largest Restaurant in
town. They left on the 11 o'clock P.M. train, for a new
home in Denver.

Mon. 27   Johnny *coughs* so much, I am dreadfully worried.

Fri. 31   Mother and I, went to the Grand Opera House this
afternoon to hear *Ex-Governor Robinson*, talk on "Re-
submission" of Prohibition law.⁴ I only *cared to see the
man*, as *Kansas' first Governor*, for I'm *decidedly against
Resubmission*.

November

Wed. 5   I so love to be at home, tho' it is none too happy because
Johnny is so cross most of the time and his cough worries me nearly sick. I believe he is *going into Consumption*
and will *never* get well, and it *nearly kills me. He* believes
he will get strong, and *never suspects anything serious*, and
I *must be brave* and never let him know the terrible
forebodings and *premonition*, that comes to me; but I feel

sure *he will never* be a *well man again and it's hard to be cheerful.*

Thurs. 6 *Never a day passes,* that Johnny *doesn't take his drink,* and I am so *radically against such things,* so of course *am most unhappy over it* but never oppose his wishes and allow him to keep liquor in the house all the time, which *he would do anyway, for he knows how bitterly I hate the stuff* and know it's harmful to him.

Mon. 24 I went to town this afternoon. Johnny *grows no better* and we have *made up our minds* to *visit* my people in *Colorado, hoping* the *change of climate* will *help* him *grow strong.* We *can't afford* the trip, but have *got to take* it, for he *wont get well here.*

Thurs. 27 *"Thanksgiving Day,"* and Mother and Brother Jim's family came for dinner and *we were quite happy together,* tho' *worried* and *anxious* as Johnny is *having Hemorages.*

December

Tues. 2 Sold some of our things and *"storing"* the rest. *Breaking up housekeeping* and *we had only just begun.* Our *last day in this little home,* and while I *have been more unhappy,* than *happy, in it,* I *hate* to leave it, for *here* we *began our married life* and had *hoped* to *be so happy.* I *feel all the time* a *presentiment* of *trouble ahead.* We came to brother Jim Shaw's to stay all night.

Wed. 3 We went out to Geo. Weymouth's and to Frank Shaw's to tell them *good-bye* and took the *1:15 P.M. Santa Fe train,* for a visit to my father and sister, at Springfield Colo. *Johnny thinks we are going for only two weeks* but *I know we will have to stay all Winter.*

Thurs. 4 Arrived in Lamar Colo. at *5 o'clock A.M.* and was *met* at train by *my brother-in-law, Lyman Gilbert who immediately started with us,* for his home, a *50 miles drive, due South;* we stopped for Breakfast just as passed the Sand Hills. Had *Antelope* for *Breakfast, and was mighty good.* Arrived at Lyman's 7:30 this evening *very tired* tho the day was *fine* but *cool* to us.

Fri. 5 Awakened, after a good night's rest, to find a *very foggy* morning. How strange this new country seems. *Fifty miles from a Railroad* and in a *sparsely settled, Ranch country,* with nearly *all* the Settlers in *"Dugouts"* and *Sod Houses:*[5] Lyman, sister May and children drove with us, this morning, three miles to my father's. We gave Pa a *big surprise*, as we had not let him know we were coming. *Haven't seen him, nor any of the folks since I was married.* My little niece, Zaidee, *could not talk*, when *I last saw her* and she has grown so: and sister has *such a sweet baby boy*, little James, four months old. Zaidee is a *nice little* girl, inclined to be a little *timid* and is a *little droll*, or *old fashioned*. We staid all night with Pa who lives in a Dug-out. A fine big one. Lyman's is rather small.

Wed. 10   At sister's: O I do enjoy her babies. This is a lovely country and the air fine, but its so new there must be deprivations and hardships.

Sat. 13   At Sister's. A beautiful day and *this morning* I *saw* the *most wonderful* and *beautiful Mirage*; a *new* and *most interesting sight to me; one just gazes in wonderment.*

Thurs. 25   *"Christmas Day" in the far West.* May and Lyman and Children, spent the day at Pa's and it was a lovely day: *no snow* and *warm.* We *were out most of the afternoon, hunting "specimens"*—pretty stones—and found many, among them, large quantites of Moss Agates. This evening, May & Lyman, Johnny & I, walked over to Springfield, to a *"Masked Ball." We "masked"* in *our Wedding clothes*— my dress of white satin and lace; I took off the train. We had a *very jolly time* and *found* a *number of good dancers there.*

Sat. 27   We are at Pa's: we like the novelty of being in a new country, but would not want to *live* away from all civilization, although there is something facinating about Pioneer life.

Wed. 31   At Pa's. *"Blew-up"* very cold today, giving us a taste of a Colorado Winter. Johnny is much better than when we came. We brought ten dollars worth of medicine with us and I don't believe he will need any more. I hope my heart-ache and worries are all over, with the ending of the *Old Year.*

[1891]

January

Thurs. 1

"*New Years Day*" and *so bitter cold*, we staid the entire day in the house; no one "*coming* and *no one going*." Johnny's cough is *so much better* and I pray God, for his complete recovery in this new year.

February

Mon. 9

Still at my sister's. There is a *very pitiful side* to the question of "*Rangers*" or Range Cattle. These cattle *must rustle their living* on the *prairies*, and the *cold* and *snow*, drive them *here*, by *hundreds*, from the *North*: to *protect* their own Stock who *need* this pasture, the *Settlers*, *drive them back again* and *many perish from hunger. I think there should be a law*, to *not allow these big Ranchmen* to *keep more cattle* than *they can properly feed* and *take care of*; its *cruel*.

March

"Deer Hunt"

Wed. 4

This morning with my father and husband, I *started* on a *Deer Hunt* to the "*Cedars*," 30 miles away. We arrived *just* at *Dusk* and *set up our Tent* and *set a large Cedar-tree afire* and *got our Supper.* Oh! *it is so grand.* A *great Forest* of *mammoth Pine* and *Cedar*; *great* Canons and Mesas, and *entirely away* from all habitation; just the *sublimity* of *wild nature*, that *inspires one with awe, in contemplating* the *greatness* of God, who *created all this granduer.* In many places, the Cedars look as if set by human hands in some great Park.

Some wood haulers came up with us for wood.

Thurs. 5

We *moved Camp*, today, *at noon*, just a short way, *around the Hills*, to near the Stone Ranch, which is *only a ruins*. It was a *home*, or a *Fort* in a *very early day*, built near a *small pond* of water, *fed by a Spring.* Whoever occupied the place--and we are told it was Soldiers—were *attacked* by the Indians and the *place destroyed*; it all happened so long ago, that it has all been *forgotten*, or there is *no one left to tell the story*, but there are *six graves*, about the ruins, that remain, as *mute witnesses* of the *Tragedy*.

Wed. 11
Started for home today and *camped tonight* near *Interstate*. I *was very loth to leave the "Paradise of the Cedars,"* but it *will ever be a beautiful "memory-picture" to look back upon* and I have *enjoyed every moment spent out here, in wild nature.*

Fri. 20
At sister's and not at all well. I was two months, or more, in Maternity and had so much hoped, and was *so happy in the hope* of being a mother, only to meet with most bitter disappointment this morning, so have been in bed all day. O it is dreadful.[1]

Sun. 22
Sisters folks all down to Pa's today, where I try to keep quiet, but must stay up, for I cannot tell them of my *disappointment*, since I had not let them know of my expected joy, wishing to keep it for a sweet surprise. How full of disappointment is this old world, *especially for me.*

Fri. 27
Pa started with us for the Railroad at Lamar, this morning, going by my Sister's, to bid them good-bye. Oh! I so hated to leave them all and especially, little Zaidee and James. Bright and warm, but snow very deep and had to shovel thro' the snowbanks several places and could only reach Butte Creek, in time to go into Camp for the night.

Sun. 29
Arrived in Topeka at 4:30 P.M. and went to brother Frank Shaw's to stay all night. Clear and windy here; no snow.

Mon. 30
We went to P.O. this morning to see the Boys—Letter Carriers—Hunting a house, to move into. Took supper with Mr. & Mrs. Geo. Yount, newly married. Met Dr. Menninger on street this morning and he says, Johnny *is not yet strong* enough, to live here and must go back at once and stay at least three years.

April

Wed. 1
Rained all day, today, but we *moved* anyway and have a good house, with two bed-rooms and a very large store room, up-stairs and Parlor, dining-room and kitchen down-stairs and a cellar, and barn at 1211 Lincoln St., all for *five dollars per month.*

Mon. 27   Mr. P. L. Doane, one of the Letter Carriers, died today and sometimes I am so unhappy I wish I could die, and be free from it all.

May

Fri. 1   I am so happy to be in my own home, but Johnny is so cross, he causes me to shed many tears. However, he has "*cursed*" me so many times for the tears that come unbidden at a cross word, that I have gotten so I can control them better and keep them back, until alone and only let him see my smiles.

Mon. 25   Raining. The *peculiarity* of *Johnny's sickness* and *my unusual good health* causes me to *wonder*, if there is not a reason for it, especially his morning sickness.[2]

June

Fri. 5   Have begun to feel badly myself, of mornings, and I think I know why it is.

Sun. 7   I get so deathly sick of mornings, and I am very sure it means "maternity." I have been sick this way, on other occasions when in such a condition and I know its symptoms.

Sat. 13   Busy with my little bit of Saturday work. I get up so sick of mornings, but get better during day.

Sun. 14   Just lazy at home. Johnny wont go to Church with me.

Mon. 15   I don't believe Johnny was ever in better health in his life, except for this *morning sickness* and yet he is cross as a bear.

Thurs. 18   I went to town this afternoon and bought me a new dress of French mull—Lavender. I always have to ask Johnny's consent before I buy anything for myself and take him along or show him a sample.

Sun. 21   Wonder what it would seem like, to have a husband who was kind and good, or how it would feel, to be happy.

Mon. 22   Went to town with Allie W. this morning.

Wed. 24   *I have to make a fight*, to *be allowed* to *become a mother*, for Johnny says, *if it is a fact*, that I am pregnant, as everything indicates, I *must* do *something* to prevent it; that *he is not ready to commence* to raise a family and that *I shall not bear the child.*

Thurs. 25	I wish I did not have to be so sick, mornings.
Fri. 26	Every day, I coax and coax Johnny, to "lets raise a family;" let me bear this child, and tell him, *how nice "our Baby"* would be, and he gets so angry, he curses me, until my heart *can bear no more* and I go away by myself and *cry* and *cry.* I want the little one, Oh! so much and he *will not* listen to it. He says "*sometime* we will have a family, *but not now."* He is a *good* man, in so many ways, yet ill-*natured, unkind* and *selfish.* I feel it is wrong to prevent this new life and *he,* as honestly, *sees* no wrong; for my *suffering,* he cares *nothing;* soon over, he says. A good *moral* man, who *cares nothing* for *religion.* Drinks but not to excess; keeps liquor in the house and brings his friends home to drink and I must *seem pleased,* or *be cursed. How unlike the man I thought I was marrying.*
Mon. 29	Johnny gets *so cross* at me, for getting, *so sick,* and I *can't help it.* He thinks there should be *no children,* if one must be so sick; he is not sick any more of mornings.
Tues. 30	Went to P.O. this evening, with Johnny to work up his mail for tomorrow.

July

Thurs. 2	*Oh!* I wish I did not have to be so sick. I am still coaxing Johnny to, "*lets* have the child." Let the little one come.
Fri. 3	I never would have believed it possible for Johnny to be such an ill-natured man. He *always* went to church with me.
Sun. 5	Mr. & Mrs. Ed Hanway (Carrier) and Jim Shaw's spent the afternoon with us. Other men, seem so kind to their wives, I wonder if they really are, or whether it is all *sham* as in my case. Johnny pays me *lots of attention, before others* and makes folks think he is very sweet to me; he would never let anyone, know he ill treats me, *yet there is hardly a day passes* without *his cursing me, for the most trivial thing.*
Mon. 6	I get so sick, I can hardly do my work and it makes Johnny so cross, he curses dreadfully, but he has *halfway* consented, that there will be *no preventing* the birth of a child. I *do not see,* what *makes* him such a man; he is jolly and witty and everyone likes him yet his ungovernable temper, *loses* him friends and makes me unhappy.
Fri. 10	Johnny has *at last* given *full consent* to the coming of the

child, and I *am so happy*, O so happy, but *he growls* and *grumbles about it*. O just to *think* of *being a mother*, is *unspeakable joy*.

Sat. 11   Busy, though all thro' the morning hours of every day, I am so sick, I can do little. *What strange emotions, the thought* of *motherhood brings to one; such sweet joy and loving expectancy* and *the willingness to go thro' untold suffering*, for the *blessed joy* of being a *mother*. *O, God help me* to be *just the kind* of a *mother I ought to be*.

Tues. 14   I went down town this afternoon. God *alone knows the joy of the secret* of *my heart*. Oh! *the dear love, one feels for their unborn child*.

Sun. 19   If I could only live happily with my husband, it seems to me, I would have nothing more to ask for. He is so *very* selfish, ill-natured and usympathetic. *Loves me, yes!* as he would love a fine horse; just because it was his, and a little better than anyone else owned.

Fri. 24   Some of the Mail-Carriers are spending their Vacation on a fishing trip and are camped on an Island in the river, near the Sugar Mill. I got the Weymouth horse and buggy, and with Mrs. Herman and little Max and Ed. we drove up and stayed all night. Guy met us with the boat and took us over to the Island, where we found Fred Farnsworth, Mrs. Geo Weymouth and children. Johnny and George Weymouth came, from P.O. this evening: it is a pretty spot, but I was so sick and the long hot drive up there made me worse, but I dared not let on.

Sun. 26   Mother Shaw came out today and I was so miserable could hardly hold my head up, yet I gave no sign and tried to give her a *"cheery"* call.[3]

Mon. 27   *Utterly miserable all day. O its so dreadful.*

Tues. 28   Spent afternoon with Mrs. William Baker.

Wed. 29   Another very sick day. I suffer torture.

Thurs. 30   I wish one could become a mother, without being *so sick* and cramping of muscles and a thousand other, dreadful things.

Fri. 31   *Morning* sickness is getting to be *all day* sickness, with me. And Johnny gets so angry: says there *"wont be another damned child,"* if he has to get sick over it and me sick all the time. I don't see how he can be so wicked. *I am willing to suffer* as I do, *for blessed Motherhood*.

August

Sat. 8	I went with Johnny to Forepaugh's Circus this evening and enjoyed it very much.
Sun. 16	I get *so hungry* for *kind words* and *sympathy:* I know it is just Johnny's way, to be indifferent, and that he loves me, but he gets angry at some one at the Office and is then ill-natured and abusive at home and it is so hard to bear, especially now, that maternity causes me to be so sick and *I so long for sympathy.* But I am thankful he has at last become reconciled and *looks forward with pleasure to the coming of our little one* and does not think of it as an added burden.
Fri. 21	*No* day *without* sickness; well, it means *untold joy* after awhile, so I *shall patiently endure.* I just talk to the Lord about it every day and ask Him to *help* me bear it; I have *no mother* and *no one,* I feel *free to go to for sympathy* and *comfort,* beside, everyone has troubles of their own and *would think mine amounted to nothing.*
Mon. 31	For some time it has seemed as if Johnny's health, was failing and we begin to talk *Colorado* again. I pray God to spare me this sorrow.

September

Tues. 1	Went to Lincoln Circle this afternoon. I feel I *must* get out when I can: makes me forget my troubles.
Wed. 2	Working a little on *"Baby things" for the little treasure* thats coming to me: the *very thought is so precious* and *all so strange* and *mysterious.*
Thurs. 3	Went to see Retta Shaw this afternoon. We have not told any of our family of our *sweet secret* for we want to surprise them, but I have told Allie and Eva and a few other close neighbors.
Fri. 4	. . . . This is our *Second Wedding* Anniversary and a very unhappy *two years.*
Tues. 8	Johnny is *beginning* to *cough considerably* and Dr. C. F. Menninger says he *must* go back to Colorado again and for us to *go in a wagon* and *we are considering it,* or *Johnny is,* for *I don't see how I can take such a trip.*
Wed. 9	It seems as if my *"cup of bitterness!" was almost full. Maternity keeps me sick all the time* and Johnny's *health* is

failing and he *is so cross to me, because I am* sick and *can't help it,* and now I *must think* of *leaving my home* and *dear friends* and go to *make a new one among strangers.* I am willing to *sacrifice* anything for Johnny, *only it's hard.*

Thurs. 10 I walk the floor most of the night in pain, but Johnny sleeps and *never* knows. I keep all my suffering and tears to myself. I get a little sleep during the day in a Rocker.

Fri. 11 I wish Johnny was a strong, healthy man; he is so ambitious and plans such *great* things and I have a *presentiment,* he will *never* be *well again* and that *I will not raise my child.*

Mon. 14 We *have fully made up our minds* to *move* to Colorado and *will drive thro'.* It *breaks my heart to leave my friends here,* but we will go *where my father* and *sister live* and that *will be some compensation* and we *must go where Johnny can live.*

Mon. 21 Johnny traded a *"lot and a half"* out on Redden Ave, and a young cow, today, for a team of big gray horses, wagon, harness and some tools, and so we have *made our first* start, toward a home in Colorado. If it *were not for the hope* of Johnny's *regaining his health, I would be most unhappy.*

Tues. 22 Went to Jim Shaw's this morning and again this afternoon, to get mother to sign some papers as she and Johnny owned some Lots together.

Thurs. 24 We talk and plan, every day now, for our Overland trip to Colo. While my heart is so *full* of *sorrow,* because I *must leave dear friends,* I *smile happily,* and tell Johnny how *well* he will get (and I *am sure* he will never get well) and how we *will prosper* in our *new home* and *say all* the *encouraging things* I *can think of,* while I *feel the opposite.*

Wed. 30 All afternoon at Mrs. Baker's and Mata Magerl *taught me a pretty little piece on Guitar.* I *beg* Johnny *to go on to Colorado* and *let me stay here, until my little one comes,* but he *wont do it; says other women have taken such trips* and *I can, but it will be an unusually hard trip and so long, I do not see how I can ever stand it.*

October

Thurs. 1 We hope to *start soon* for a *new home* in Colorado and *my heart is very heavy.* Doctor says we *must go on a farm,* where Johnny *will work in open air,* and to do this, we *will be fifty miles* from a Railroad and *there will be many deprivations.* I can *have no nurse, no doctor, no help,* when *my little [one] comes.* I *beg* Johnny to *let me stay,* as our rent is only five dollars per month and my aunt Sarah Ogden a *fine nurse would stay with me* and I could *have the care that is a woman's right at such a time, beside* the *long drive will almost kill me, but he won't hear to it,* and *his selfishness almost makes me dislike him.*

Sun. 4   Have been sick nearly all day; and how will I ever endure the long hard drive to Colorado. Wish I might go on the Train.

Mon. 5   It is dreadful to be sick so much; *what a price* woman *pays* for the joy of motherhood, but I guess it is worth it.

Tues. 6   *Very cold* rain, and a few, fine flakes of snow fell, being *worst kind* of a day for Johnny. I wish our trip was over and we were in Colo.

Sun. 18   All of Jims' and mother, here today all day and they *never dreamed* of my condition. I am [in] *good shape* and *carry myself well* and have been *so sick* all the time, that I have *eaten barely enough* to *keep me alive*; so *have not taken on any fat,* in *fact am poor.*

Mon. 19   Johnny coughs so hard it distresses me and there is *no doubt* it is *consumption,* tho' he wont have it so. I pray God, to make him well and strong again.

Tues. 20   I am not sick so much, in afternoons, anymore and I am *so thankful.* I don't think anything could be worse, than this dreadful Maternity sickness.

Sat. 24   *Busy, as I am able to be,* and a *most unhappy woman.* Johnny *doesn't spare me, his curses because of my condition* and *I have to endure his insulting language* and *abuse.* But *my heart is full of joy, for the little one that is coming and I thank God, with all my heart.*

Tues. 27   I have been so sick today. Oh! if I could but be free, from this *awful, awful* sickness.

Wed. 28   *Not so sick today, but feel miserable.*

Thurs. 29   *I wish something could be done for this terrible cramping.*

Fri. 30   *Can neither eat or drink, without being dreadfully sick.*

November

Sun. 1   Been *so sick* today. I am getting so poor some are afraid, my little one will not live to come to me, but what can one do.

Sat. 7   Sewing at Mrs. Baker's again today. *Everyone thinks* it *is dreadful* that Johnny *intends to make me drive thro' to Colo.* with him *in a big wagon* and *especially this late* in *the Fall. I have asked him* to *let me go on the Train,* if I *must go at this time,* but *he won't even let me do that.* I *never quarrel* with him and he *never sees ought but a smiling face, however much my heart may ache,* but *this heartless treatment is beginning to make me lose my love for him.*

Wed. 11   Our last night in this house, and God only knows what is before me, but I shall *trust* Him to take care of me and my unborn Babe.

Thurs. 12   We ate dinner with the Bakers today, finished packing and loading our wagon this afternoon, and bid all our neighbors good-bye this evening; even the surly Geo. Weymouth, came over and shook hands with me and had kissed me goodbye, before I knew his intentions, but not a word passed between us. We drove down to brother Jim Shaw's to stay all night and we told them of our expected little one and Oh! their surprise; and so at last, it is good-bye to home and friends, and away to the West, for a *new* home and *new* friends, in a *new* country, almost a Desert. But I am *willing* to make the sacrifice, if it will but restore my husband's health. Our friends think him very selfish to *compel* me to take such a trip in my condition especially, when I could as well go on the train. This late in the Fall will even be harmful to him and I will suffer greatly. Woman will sacrifice everything for the man she loves, why will *he* not do *half* as much for her.

Fri. 13   Well at last, our journey has commenced and tonight after only a few miles of travel, I am *very* tired and the jolting of the wagon, caused me to *suffer much.* We were late in getting away from Topeka, leaving about 3 o'clock; the weather fine and a lovely evening. From our camp tonight at Mulhollen Hill, or a little West, we can see the lights of my beloved Topeka, and it makes my heart ache; when shall I see them again, if ever: my husband in poor health and at the end of a *long hard* journey, my little one to be born, without the help of Doctor or Nurse. But *for an ever present* God, I would be in *utter despair.*

Sat. 14   A cold, chilly drive. Rained all day and the roads terribly, hilly—we got "*stuck*" on one hill. With our heavily loaded wagon, we only reached Dover, 20 miles from

Topeka, at dark this evening, and I am so weary and heart sick.

Mon. 16   Passed thro' *Harveyville* at noon. Bought some good, *Home-made bread*, at a little house in the Village. Very cold today and snowed some, but we keep warm as we have a stove in the wagon; how *hard* this *shaking*, as we drive along over *rough, frozen roads* and never a word of sympathy. Johnny gets so cross, if he *even* thinks I feel badly: well, I thank God, for giving me a heart, that can keep its sorrow to itself.

Sat. 21   We passed thro' *Marian*, a nice, thrifty looking, little town, late this afternoon and are in camp, three miles West tonight. Turned *very cold* and *wind blows a gale* and only that we are in a *hollow* I believe it would blow our wagon over, heavy as it is. We see some fine country and some especially pretty place, but the trip *is so hard*, I can't enjoy *anything*. I am not so sick any more, but I *suffer dreadfully*, from the *jolting* of the wagon, so I get out and walk as much as I can, but I am getting so heavy and it is *so hard* for me to climb in and out of our high wagon over the side-boards. It is cruel of Johnny to make me *suffer such torture* by this trip.

Sun. 22   Passed thro' *Hillsboro* and *Lehigh* today and tonight are stopping over night with a young couple by the name of Drew, three miles East of Canton. They are strangers, but insisted on our coming in and sleeping in a bed and I am so *grateful*.

Mon. 23   Drove thro' the "outskirts" of Canton, McPherson Co., this morning and 7 miles beyond to the Ritz farm by noon, and are "laying over" here, to rest and visit and "re-adjust" our load, which has become badly shaken apart. Mrs. Ritz is a cousin of Mother Shaw's. So tonight again, I will get to straighten my tired body in a bed, with room to turn over, and I am *so* tired and worn I could cry, if I could only get away by myself. Mrs. Ritz had such a *splendid* supper and I ate heartily without getting sick.

December

Wed. 2   Passed thro' *Dodge City*, this morning and tonight are camped 20 miles West at *Cimarron. Cold* and the *wind blows a gale. We drove in beside a large empty store building* and are *pretty well protected*. The roads are *something terrible* and *sometimes* it is *wholly unsafe* for me to be in the wagon. The journey is *so hard,* that *many times,* I *lie on the mattress* behind Johnny and *cry my heart out* and *he* thinks *I'm sleeping.* How *blind most* men *are* and *how utterly indifferent, to what women suffer. Some times, after a hard days journey,* I can feel no life and my *heart* is *agonized, lest my little one be dead.*

Sat. 5 Passed thro' Deerfield and Lakin today: *Six degrees below zero last night* and we had no shelter whatever, but was no wind. About 4 o'clock, we came to a Ranch house and stopped to enquire the *better* road, as *two raods forked here.* It was *commencing to snow* and the people *advised us* to *stay* with them *over night,* as a *Blizzard* was *imminent,* but Johnny *would not listen* to them. Oh! *I would give the World* to *have stayed.* They said *but one* house in 18 miles and that an *empty one* and Johnny understood them to say, *but one empty house* in 18 miles. Well, we drove on and the *storm grew worse,* and *soon* was *dark* and the *little travelled* road, began to *fill,* and my *heart beat anxiously; finally* when we could *no longer follow* the *dim trail,* to *either go ahead or turn back,* and the *wind, snow* and *ice* was suffocating us and we *could hardly force our Team against it,* we *made out* a *dim black shadow,* near the road, which *proved,* an *empty* and *locked "Claim Shanty,"* so we drove up beside it and are camped, with *no other protection* and *completely lost and only those who have been lost in a Blizzard know the agony.*

Sun. 6 The wind was *blowing so hard* this morning, that I *feared* to look out of our *closed wagon,* lest the storm *still be raging,* but when I *found heart* to do so, the sun was shining and a dim depression, showed we were near the road, but Oh! the *terrible anxiety* of the past night. Lost in a *terrible storm,* that might last, on *these barren Plains, for days* and our poor horses, tho blanketed, had to *stand out in it all, as also our faithful Watch dog,* Joe, a fine Newfoundland, whom we *might* have *kept* in wagon, with us only for Johnny's *impatience*: and we might all have been comfortably housed, had Johnny but listened to the *kindly* Ranch people. I am *sure* I did not sleep a moment all night: our horses and dog suffered *dreadfully,* and Johnny *froze* his hands a little "unhitching". And we had very little fuel too: Oh! it was a night of *torture,* but God *graciously* spared us, and my unborn Babe, that I *so feared* would come to me last night God has been *merciful* and I *cannot thank* Him *enough*. We drove to *Kendall* for dinner and six miles only farther West, to camp tonight—deep snow—hard traveling

Mon. 7   We reached Syracuse, our last City in Ks. nearly noon, and found my father there, with Team, to meet us and take part of our load. And he took a *mighty big load*, off my heart, for there will be no more anxiety, about roads. After dividing our load with Pa and eating our dinner and getting some supplies, we started out on the last hundred miles of our journey. Crossing the Arkansas River and driving 8 miles S.W. we are *cozily* camped among some low, sand Hills, and I can sleep happily because Pa is here and I feel safer. He protested about starting out with us after dinner as we could reach no house, to make our camp tonight, but we told him we were used to it. He was *shocked* to think we had not camped each night in a town, where I could have had some comfort, and care if needed.

Tues. 8   Have driven *all* day, today, without a *sight* of a *living* thing; *not a bird*, bush or tree; the Plain as level as a floor, with only Buffalo grass growing; not the *slightest hollow* or *raise* of ground—just a *monotony* of *"distance"*. We camped tonight at Pettit's Ranch and my father insisted on my going in to visit Mrs. Pettit who *seldom* sees a woman in her Ranch life. I was very sick all day.

Thurs. 10   *Commenced our journey this morning before Sunrise* and reached Pa's Ranch, Belle View, at 11:10 A.M. and I *could have cried with joy*, that my *long hard journey was ended, only* I *was too tired and sick*. My sister and family (May and Lyman, and little James and Zaidee) were all at Pa's to meet us. Little Zaidee is five years old today. We were *four long weeks* on the journey, who would not rejoice at the end of it.

Fri. 11   Enjoying *blessed rest* at Pa's today; I *wonder* if it *won't seem like this* in Heaven, when our Earthly journey is ended. Not a very pleasant day, almost a storm. Oh! it's been so hard, and I am sure my unborn little one, became tired to, because some nights, after a *hard* day, there would be no pulse of life and I would fear lest my little one would *never* come to me.

Sat. 19   At Pa's, just *resting, resting resting*.

Sat. 26   We went over to Mr. James Wilson's this afternoon, to complete arrangements for the renting of his farm as doctor told Johnny to go on a farm, so to be out in open air much as possible.

Thurs. 31   Pa, Ma, Vella, Johnny and I, all went to sisters today to help celebrate, her *6th Wedding Anniversary*. Lyman is so good to her and their two little ones. And so ends another year of my life: I *think* the *most unhappy*, I *have ever known*. Johnny is so *unkind* to me, but *more* through his *selfish, indifferent, nature*, than that he *willfully means* to be unkind; but *it is not possible* to live *happily* with him and *were it not* for God's *mercy, I could pray to die*. My *greatest joy* is my *expected Motherhood* and one would *think, this coming joy*, would make him kinder, but it *does not. He does not spare me in the least:* there *is not a profane, low, vulgar, filthy name he has not called me. His vileness is almost unendurable.*

[1892]

January

Fri. 1

"*New Year's Day*". The *past* year has been *so filled* with *sickness, sorrow* and *unhappiness*, and *so full* of *God's grace to bear it all; I pray Oh! God, my Father, give me strength to bear whatever comes to me that is hard this year,* and if it *may please Thee,* to *give me peace* and *happiness.*

It has been a beautiful day, but I have been so *very sick all* day in bed; and wondered if it meant the coming of my little one. May, Lyman and the Children spent the day here at Pa's.

Sun. 3

Lymans all came down to Pa's today. I am quite myself again; But wait anxiously for the coming of my little *Girlie,* because I *know* my babe will be a girl.

Tues. 5

In our new home today. Old Mr. Wilson[1] is to board with us; quite a nice farm, well improved and everything furnished—we give a third of the crop for rent and board him. Doctor said *only hope* for Johnny was farm life and I pray, he *may be restored* to health, but there comes to me such a *strong presentiment* that he will never be well again and that my beloved child, yet unborn, will not be with me a great while. I *wish* I could get rid of such a feeling, for it is terrible and I *cannot* give up either of them; and pray God will not take them from me. . . .

Thurs. 7

Sister May, came down awhile this morning. I am beginning to get our new home *cozy,* but my heart is among friends in Topeka; however I shall be very happy here, if Johnny only gets strong and well. He may become kinder to me, if he gets *well.* Consumption is dreadful.

Thurs. 14

The weather is fine and I am resting and waiting, for the day of happy Motherhood. Johnny's health has not improved any and I fear we came too late.

Fri. 15

There is running-water and a fine Spring on this farm and a good *well* at the door; the kitchen is stone, and detached from the house; a fine large barn and hen house—we are unusually comfortable, for to be living in the West, fifty miles from a Railroad.

Sat. 16	The days seem long, till the coming of my child, whom *I* shall have *no* part in naming. Johnny says "if a boy, it shall be named for him and if a girl, he shall name it for his cousin and I can have no "say so" about it. *I* could not *be* so selfish with *him*.
Mon. 18	Little "girlie" Babe, when are you coming to mother? And you *know*, you *are* to come to us a "wee girlie" because *that* is what your father *wants* you to be, while your *mother* would *have you a boy*, only for *his* sake, I pray you *may be* a *"wee girlie"*. *Stork Approaches*
Wed. 20	My dear sister Belle's *birthday* and how I *wish* she were living, to be my little *"comforter"* for I will soon need sympathy to help me bear the pains of motherhood.
Sat. 23	*No day*, could *be more grand*, than this one has been and I felt *strangely buoyant* when I arose this morning. About *10 o'clock* I began having pains and they have continued *all* day, *increasing in severity*—but I *have had so much to do*, and *found* I could *stop* them by stooping over, so I just stopped them and *went on with my work*. *Washed* a few pieces, *ironed* a little and did *much baking* because sisters and my fathers' are coming over tomorrow. I *scrubbed* my kitchen after 4 o'clock. *Oh! how I have suffered* and Johnny *never guessed I was in pain*. He and Mr. Wilson went to town, late this afternoon, and *I* was *left alone*. It *seemed* to me, if *motherhood* was near, I would have to go to bed, and since I have been able to *endure* and *go on* with my work it surely can't be that. Tonight I was *suffering* so *dreadfully*, I *could not eat supper,* but *sat* down to the table and *held a paper* in *front* of my face *as if reading*, so they would not see my face in pain and Johnny *scolded* me, for being *"so interested in a Topeka paper, that I could not eat:" how little he knew*. But I kept everything to myself, until 11 o'clock tonight, a *most severe pain*, which I *could not hold back, made me groan* so *loudly* it *awakened* him and now he has gone for *my stepmother* and I *sit here alone*, with *everything* in *readiness* for the coming of the *little stranger*. When he returns with Ma, he will go *five miles* in *another direction*, for Mrs. Gordon who is *all* I can have to help me thro'. But she is the mother of 15 children and knows all about Babies. I am *just sitting here waiting* for the folks to come so think *I'll read, between pains*. Well here are Ma and Johnny—he

made a quick trip—Johnny has gone to sister's to get Lyman *to go* for Mrs. Gordon and Ma is *so surprised* that I am *able* to be up. And *now* Lyman has come at 1 o'clock with Mrs. Gordon and tries to jolly me. *I am still on my feet. I make all go to bed.*

"*Motherhood blessed Motherhood*"

Sun. 24   Today, at 12 minutes past 1 o'clock P.M. my *precious,* "wee girlie" came to her mother. The *dearest, sweetest, little, treasure, ever* a mother had. The *blackest* hair and the *blackest eyes, big* and *round* and *full.* I *thank* God *with all my heart* and *soul* and *being* for my darling. But *what a time we had, to get her*: there are no doctors near here and *motherhood* was *all* but *impossible*; by *stopping* my pains, I *had worn* them *out* and *nothing could be done* to *bring them* on, and *part* of the time I *lay exhausted* and *unconscious,* until in *sheer desperation,* Mrs. Gordon, *tore me,* with her *fingers* and *pulled* baby *away, scratching* the little *forehead* and *almost crushing* the *head until* was a *great ridge across* the *top, big* as my *finger* and the darling was *black* with *strangulation*—the *cord twice* around her neck. She came *without* a *pain* and *as soon as she was here, all suffering ceased* and I feel *strong as an ox.* In an *hour* and a *half* after she came, I had *eaten* a *meal, hearty enough* for a *Harvest-hand.* I *didn't suppose* they would let me, but *they did* and tonight I *know* I am *strong enough* to get *supper.* And they are *all* surprised. Mrs. Gordon, Johnny, Ma and sister were only ones with me. We named Baby, Mabel Inez Belle.

Mon. 25   A fine day they tell me, tho' they wont let me see outside and I feel as strong and well, as if there was never a pain in the World. Pa came over this afternoon, to see my dear little girlie; he had not yet heard what our precious gift was. I have written several long letters, to Topeka friends today, to tell them of my happiness, also read the papers and feel so strong and well. Oh! my sweet, blessed Babe, you are worth all the suffering you cost your mother, and more. And how proud your father is of you; but thro' it all, Johnny gave me but one sympathetic word: yesterday morning, he came to my bedside and placing his hand on my brow asked in a sympathetic voice "Are you suffering much Mattie? Well you will have to try to bear it now:" The only kindly words I have had in all the months, and they brought tears of gratitude.

Wed. 27	I wanted to name my girlie, "Inez Belle" but Johnny says she shall be *always* called *Mabel* for his cousin. We weighed the precious mite of a baby today and she weighed 9 1/2 pounds.
Thurs. 28	Mrs. Milt Gordon and baby, spent the day with me. I would love to get up, but they won't let me: and there has been no time, I have felt the least bit weak. My unusual health and strength is a surprise to everyone.
Fri. 29	I have been begging them to make my bed, as I am on a featherbed and it needs stirring but they are so afraid I will take cold, they won't do it, so this afternoon, when they were not near me, I hurriedly *rolled* out of bed and walked to a chair, across the room and sat down and told them they *must* make my bed for me, or *I* would do it. Ma and Johnny were so *shocked* at my getting up and walking, that they were *not long* in making my bed, so they could get me back into it. But I felt so good, I did not want to go back to bed. My little *sweet-heart* and me, are so well and strong and I most devoutly thank God for our health.
Sat. 30	Ma still staying with me and Pa came over and brought Vella to see my blessed baby and they spent the day with us. Baby has had a little "colic" several times, but she is such a good baby. I wash and dress her each day: in fact was the first one, to *really* give her a thorough washing. Oh! its *blessed to be a Mother*.

February

Thurs. 4	My little sweetheart is 12 days old today noon and this evening, I went to the kitchen and got supper. Johnny does not like to cook.
Mon. 8	Trying to be busy, but most I do, is to just *love* and *love* my little "hearts-ease": she is such a dear, little "ray of sunshine" in my life.
Tues. 9	When Johnny is cross, what a little comforter my baby *"treasure"* is. I *know* I have some thing to live for. Johnny quarrels with Mr. Wilson and that too makes our home life very unpleasant. Mr. Wilson is very old, somewhere near 80 and the two men cannot agree about the management of *anything* but Johnny is *almost invariably* in the wrong. Mr. Wilson has been very kind to us too, tho' has some *childish ways*.
Wed. 10	*My baby dear, you and I will love and love, if all the World goes*

wrong. Mother's own dear precious girlie, how I thank God for you.

Thurs. 11   My wee Inez, grows and grows. Her father always calls her Mabel, to contrary me.

Tues. 16   *'Tis wonderful how you grow, my loved one, but Mother's heart will always be large enough for you, however fast you may grow.*

Thurs. 18   Johnny grows into better health and stronger all the time, yet I do *almost* as much for him as for Baby.

Fri. 19   My little Inez, is so well "featured"; *tiny hands* and *feet* and the *prettiest ears: big black, eyes, so round* and *full* and the *blackest hair.* Oh! she is *a most wonderful Baby.*

Mon. 22   Am not well today: guess I should not have changed dresses to go visiting.

March

Thurs. 3   *With a World of care,* and a *home life, none too happy,* my *sweet Babe is never a burden. I bless* God *every day, for the little life,* He has *given into my care* and *I pray always that I may live worthy [of] such love.*

Tues. 8   My little "joy girl," you expect mother to do nothing, but hold you and talk to you; what a spoiled child you are. And you show much temper sometimes too, when I cannot take you immediately, my precious one.

Thurs. 10   Wash and iron and bake, make beds, sweep and dust, wash dishes, do mending, milk and churn, look after chickens chop wood too—I wonder if a woman is supposed to kill herself for a man, who has a temper like a Bear. But then one marries *"for better, for worse"* and I do not believe in divorces, tho' down deep in my heart, many times, I could wish there was a way out, when I am *cursed* beyond endurance.

Fri. 11   Baby Inez is so sweet and cute; and the *strongest* baby: tries to sit up, and not two months old. Sleeps on her stomach too, like her mother; many times I find she has rolled over on her stomach, in her sleep and I don't see how she does it.

Sat. 12   Such a lovely day, that mother and baby went out to walk about and see how Spring is coming on. Baby dear is getting so heavy, and I carry her on one arm, to do all my work, because she is so spoiled and her father won't have her cry.

Thurs. 17   I do not see, how anyone could help loving children. *My heart is full all the time of the joy of my Babe* and I can better bear Johnny's abuse, because *I have her.*

Mon. 21   Johnny and Mr. Wilson, just quarrel and quarrel; simply *cannot* get along, so we moved into a part of the house, by ourselves, and he will have the other part and not board with us any more. I wish Johnny was better tempered, for Mr. Wilson has been very kind.

Tues. 22   We drove over town this morning and then to Pa's awhile. The grandest day imaginable. What a temper my little girlie, showed at noon. I was in a hurry to get dinner, so laid her on the bed, because she is so very heavy to carry, while about my work: she is spoiled and expects to be carried *all* the time, so cried and cried until she could cry no more; almost broke my heart, but I would not give up and she finally cried herself to sleep. Mr. Wilson came in, to see why she cried so, and when I told him, she only wanted to be carried, he said "she has her father's devil in her." My *sweet Babe.*

Thurs. 24   Baby Inez, is *two months old today,* and the *sweetest, dearest, cutest, blessedest* baby ever a mother had: *She can sit alone* and she has the *dearest little chuckle of a laugh* and *crows* and *coo's so sweet*—she is *white* and *pretty as a finely chiseled piece of Marble.*

Fri. 25   My sweet baby love lets me work without carrying her, since her *"cry"* the other day. I have to milk and feed and chop most of the wood, beside all my other work, and Johnny I know is better able to do it, than I am. He is over his cough and seems well and strong and I believe, in as good health as he ever was. Yet, *I* do *all* the hard work and getting out in the storm, to save him in every way I can; and it seems like the *more* I do for him, the *more* unkind he is to me.

Sun. 27   We spent the day at Pa's. My little love grows and grows and is so strong—sits alone and can raise up by herself. I can't make her lie [down]. I sometimes wish I could take her and go away off, where we would never see her father—he curses me so and is so ill-tempered, I am afraid she will learn to do the same, when old enough.

Mon. 28   Johnny started on a hundred miles drive, this morning, to Syracuse, Ks. for some of his plows and farming utensils. Frank Tipton will go with him. Pa did not think he ought to take such a long trip, this time of year, when there is so liable to be severe storms, but he is *so self-willed*, no one can do anything with him. Joe, baby and I went to sister's, after Johnny left, to stay while he is away. Joe is my finely trained Newfoundland dog. He carried my basket and *I* carried Baby dear, and together, we walked the 1 1/2 miles up to Sister's.

Tues. 29   All day and night with my sister. An awfully windy day. In my sister's home, is "the fear and admonition of the Lord": the reading of the Bible and family-prayer. In my home, curses and abuse and I read my Bible most of time in secret, to save myself and it, more abuse.

Thurs. 31   Still at Sister's. An awful dust or sand storm, raged all day; by middle of the afternoon, had hid the sun, and grows worse; is something fearful. Baby has a slight cough as if teething.

April

Sat. 2   I came home this morning, to get work done for tomorrow. Johnny came home at 9 o'clock this evening sick with a cold, because out in so much bad weather.

Wed. 13   Went up to Sister's at noon on horse-back. She and little Jimmie came down and staid all afternoon with me. How my heart has to suffer extremes: extreme joy with my baby, extreme unhappiness with my husband. How can men be so cruel, as many of them are: Johnny's temper is dreadful. One evening he went out, to shoot Jack rabbits by "moonlight" and the dog followed and frightened the rabbits away, which made him so angry he was going to shoot the dog, who seemed to have a sense of danger and ran to the house and I opened the door and called him in, so not to let him repeat his offense; but Johnny followed determined to kill him, and my pleading for the dog's life, because Baby and I need him, when left alone and he is our only protection, only made him more angry and when I stepped between him and the dog, still begging for the dog's life, he became insanely angry and drew his gun up and aimed at me, to shoot me. I was paralyzed with fear, as I saw his look and could only turn to my little one sleeping on the bed and thought, "who will take care of my precious one" and in that instant she moved and attracted his attention, and he lowered his gun and left the room without a word. Baby had saved my life, but O the horror I suffered in those moments.

Thurs. 14 After dinner, we drove up after sister, then over to Springfield, where we had our Baby Inez's pictures taken by a traveling Photographer. She would just laugh, and crow, and throw her little hands in play, until we thought we *never would* get a picture: she was the happiest baby, and the Photographer called her a "little Brick," because the more he would *try*, to get her quiet, the *more* she would play with him. She is only 2 1/2 months old, and sat up straight in a High chair alone, to have her picture, tho' I held her dress from the back, so she would not throw herself from the chair in her play. I wanted to have her picture and mine taken together, but Johnny would not let me. After we got the pictures May & I went to call on Mrs. Miser and Mrs. Whittaker and see their *new* babies, then came home, we first taking May home.

Tues. 19 Garden-making time in Colorado, and of course I make it, and when I go out to work in the garden, I take little girlie along, in a big clothes-basket on wheels and "old black Joe" lies beside her and watches her while I work. He is a faithful old dog.

Tues. 26 Sister and little Jimmie came down for dinner today in honor of my 25th *Birthday*. Only 25 years old and think of the *world of care* I've had.

May

Tues. 3 Baby is cross and fretful, and everyone thinks Johnny is letting me work too hard, and have told him, we wont raise her, if he does not do differently: of course *he* doesn't think that way.

Wed. 4 Baby coughs, but does not seem to have more than a slight cold, but it makes me anxious.

Mon. 9 God I pray, keep my Baby well. She only seems fretful and cross, but her cold does not yield to treatment: sometimes it makes me heart-sick.

Wed. 11 I do not believe my darling has a cold at all. I believe she is "teething".

Thurs. 12 Lyman's were all here today. Lyman is helping Johnny put in the Spring crop. I have been helping "plant corn" but Baby is not well and I can't take her to the field.

Tues. 17   Lyman Gilbert family, all here again today. Baby gets no better and no worse, and still coughs, but not as if it were a cold and I am convinced she is "teething", tho' many say "too young".

Thurs. 19   My darling sweet-heart, bites on everything and bites me, *so hard*, when nursing, I am sure she is teething; she's not at all well.

Fri. 20   A very windy day. How I wish there was a good Doctor in this part of the country, that I might consult him for my little "joy-girl", instead of using *all* the remedies, *all* the old "grand-mothers" can think up, for *all* the "deseases," one ever heard or dreamed about.

Mon. 23   A lovely day and Baby seems some better. My little treasure, don't get sick for it makes Mother's heart *ache* and *ache*. My blessed one.

Tues. 24   My blessed little "sun-beam girl" is four months old today, and such a joy to her mother: there would be little to live for, without you, my precious one. Oh! God keep her well.

Wed. 25   Johnny has not been well, since his trip to Syracuse, Ks.: that is he coughs and it seems to grow worse. And baby love is not well so my heart is heavy with care.

Thurs. 26   My blessed little one seems better today. If the little teeth would only come, I'm sure she'd be alright.

Sat. 28   My little treasure seemed so much worse today, that we took her away down to Vilas, to a Mrs. M. E. Martin, a sort of "Home-made" Baby doctor, and she says, there is very little hope, that my darling can live. Could a mother ever hear more cruel words—why it stunned me, crushed me; my Baby *must* live, or I'll die.

Sun. 29   Johnny took me over to Pa's this morning where I will stay while my precious one is sick. My heart is so *utterly crushed* and *broken*, I cannot stay at home.

Mon. 30   At my father's. My "wee girlie" seems brighter today, but my spirit is crushed. I am wholly undone. I only seem to live because there is yet life in my sweet Babe.

Tues. 31   Still at my father's. My heart aches with fear for my little "joy-girlie". It seems to me, every breath I draw is a prayer to God, to spare me my precious Baby, whom I have loved and thanked Him for, every moment I have had her. Oh! God hear the pleading of an agonized heart.

June

Wed. 1	Little Inez is so sick, I hardly let her out of my arms day or night, but we think she is getting better, very slowly.
Sat. 4	Johnny went to Vilas to see Mrs. Martin today and she says, since baby has gotten along as well as she has, so far she may live: dare I grasp at this "straw" of hope?
Tues. 7	Mrs. Martin thinks Baby's trouble is her lungs and I'm just as sure it's her teeth: she seems better.
Wed. 8	Baby about as usual and we went over home this morning, to get some of my clothes, then went up to Lyman's and finished packing my trunk, to go to Topeka, Ks, with my baby, to get a good Doctor, and if she gets well, I'll be in no hurry to come back to a cross man. I shall at least take a good, long rest and am packing my trunk, with that in view. We stay all night, tonight with May and Lyman.
Thurs. 9	Johnny drove 50 miles today to Lamar, with Baby and I, where was to take 9:30 evening train for Topeka, but it is very late and we are "camping" in the wagon until morning. It has been such a hot, windy day, that my little darling has suffered from the trip, and it *breaks* my heart.
Fri. 10	I took the train at 2:30 this morning for Topeka, Ks. with my little sick darling to get a good Doctor for her. Arrived in Topeka at 4:30 P.M. and took Cab to Mother Shaw's 1217 E-10-St. It has been such a long hard trip, it seemed at times, my precious one would die. Phoned[2] for Doctor Menninger, who is out of City; but baby got easier and we wait for him.
Sat. 11	At Mother's. Dr. Menninger came this morning; says baby is a *very* sick baby, but will get well. It *is* her teeth, as I suspected, and she has Brain-fever; O it is so terrible.
Sun. 12	Dr. Menninger here again to see my "wee girlie" who is so very sick, I don't see how he can be hopeful.
Mon. 13	Baby seems better. Dr. M. came again this morning. I try to be hopeful and I pray.
Tues. 14	Dr. M. here this morning again to see Baby Inez. I do not undress, day or night and trust my child to *no one*. I only sleep with her in my arms.

Wed. 15	Baby Inez so much better that Dr. M. did not come today, but my heart is so anxious, I scarcely eat or sleep.
Thurs. 16	Dr. Menninger came again today, and baby grows better, but my heart is heavy in spite of his reassurances, for something tells me I must give up my heart's treasure. Oh! if I could but get rid of these dreadful premonitions.
Fri. 17	Still at Mother's and scarcely eat or sleep because of my anxiety, and never trust my baby a moment to any one. Dr. M. did not come today. She continues to improve.
Sat. 18	Dr. Menninger came today, and thinks baby is doing so well, it is not necessary for him to come any more and I can give the medicine he left for her.
Sun. 19	Inez is better. Johnny writes nearly every day and addresses the letters to Baby.
Mon. 20	Commenced today, to make some short dresses for my little loved one, for she is so large, and it is so hot here. Baby is beginning to play with her "playthings" again and I can let her lie in the Rocking-chair.
Tues. 21	One of the Mail-carriers (Fred Farnsworth) a good friend of Johnny's, came down this evening and brought Mrs. Eva Herman and two children, to see Baby Inez, and my little girlie played with Fred until she went to sleep. She is so sweet. O if she were only well and strong like other babies.
Wed. 22	Baby is doing nicely but had to call Dr. M. to see *me*, for I am all worn out with loss of sleep and rest, and care and anxiety and I have a very sore breast: in fact I am *sick*, all over, and had to give up awhile this afternoon and go lie down and sleep and leave my darling to the care of her Aunt Retta Shaw.
Thurs. 23	Very hot here. Baby is better and so am I, and I walked out with her awhile this evening, for a little airing.
Fri. 24	My sweet, blessed girlie, is five months old today and I put her first short dress on her. She is so sweet and some have told me, she was "*too sweet and pretty for this world*" and I would not raise her.
Sat. 25	My precious one slept peacefully and seemed quite a well Baby until 12:15 P.M. when she went into a "spasm" and by 3 o'clock had had *five very* hard ones. Dr. M. got here at that time, stayed some time, working over baby; she kept getting worse and he returned at 9:30 Baby very low. Telegraphed for Johnny, but from Lamar

Colo. the Message must go by mail and no Stage on Sunday (tomorrow).

Sun. 26   My little darling was almost continuously in spasms all last night and I have prayed with every breath I drew, to God, to be merciful and spare my child to me. She has had many hard spasms all day, but fewer than last night. Eva Herman and Mrs. Wm Baker have helped me all day. Dr. M. came and his medicine helped baby a little. I plead Oh! God for the life of my child.

Mon. 27   Retta Shaw stayed up with me tonight, and helped me care for baby and once when baby seemed dying, Retta said to me, "*she is dead*, there is no need to give her medicine," but I *could not* give up and I forced the medicine down her throat and she revived, and from 1:30 A.M., was better, and "nursed" two different times but at 9:30 this morning, she grew worse and death commenced: there were no more spasms, but one knew she was suffering dreadfully, and with a broken heart, I bowed to God's will and said "Oh! Lord, I give her back to thee: I cannot see her suffer longer." At 10:05 this evening, while I held her to my aching heart, God sent the Angels for her and her terrible suffering ended and *mine* commenced. Mrs. Pettit and Mrs. Ed Johnston were with me when baby died. Every one else were in bed asleep. I don't know when I have slept.

Tues. 28   Oh! God if You would, in mercy, take me to my child. I hardly know that I live.

Wed. 29   Oh! the emptiness of my arms, the loneliness of my heart. Oh! God, ease this terrible heart-ache. Johnny arrived, from Springfield, Colo. at 4:30 P.M. and is *crushed* by the loss of our darling.

Thurs. 30   We buried our little darling, in the Topeka Cemetery at 5:30 P.M. Charlie Conwell, Sad Hodgins, Wes Brown and Fred Farnsworth (Letter Carrier friends) were the Pall-bearers. The Carriers sent a lovely pillow of flowers and F. Farnsworth sent a "Star" of flowers: many others also sent flowers. Rev. B. L. Smith of First Christian Church preached her funeral. It seemed wicked to leave my darling in the cold, dark grave. But tonight tho' my heart is breaking, stunned, crushed I can say, "Thy will, Oh! God, be done." And in some way, I know God will help me to live, without my "wee girlie." And I do thank Him, with all my broken heart, that I've known the blessed joy of motherhood. Heaven will be a brighter place, for my little one's being there.

July

Fri. 1   At mother's today and my heart aches and aches. Johnny and his mother quarrel so, and I can't bear to hear it. Johnny and I came out to Guy Herman's to stay all night, but I am lonely every where I go.

Mon. 4   Fourth of July, and we went with the Herman's to Garfield Park, this afternoon. They need not think to make me forget. I just long to be alone and cry my heart out.

Fri. 8   We came to Mr. Guy Herman's again today at 4th and Filmore and will stay all night. I wish I did not have to meet people, for my heart is so heavy, I *could pray to die.*

Sat. 16   Today and tonight, with the Hermans. Guy Herman and Fred Farnsworth left at 4:30, with a loaded Express wagon, for Maple Hill, Waubaunsee Co. to prepare a Camp for a two weeks "outing" on Mill Creek.

Sun. 17   We have spent the day with Mrs. Herman and little Max and Ed. and will stay tonight. I am so weary of heart I could die. I do not see how I can ever live without my Babe.

Mon. 18   We, with Eva Herman and children, took the 12:50 Rock Island train for Maple Hill and were met by Guy and Fred, who drove with us to camp. And tonight, we are in a very pretty camp on Mill Creek, 1 1/2 miles East of Maple Hill.

Tues. 19   In Camp and a lovely place, on Mr. Frank McClelland's farm. The men have named the camp, *"Camp Sunset"* in honor of S. S. Cox (nicnamed Sunset Cox) who got the Bill thro' Congress, to give Mail-Carriers 15 days Vacation each year, with pay.

Tues. 26   Sad Hodgins still in Camp. Fred Farnsworth is such a good boy to have about Camp for he waits on us women like a slave and when all work is done, he goes to fish and boat, with rest of the men.

Sat. 30   Packed, and broke camp, at 11 o'clock today and Fred F. took Cal West, Eva and children, Johnny & I to Maple Hill, where we took 2:03 P.M. train for Topeka, where we stay all night with Herman's. Guy and Fred drove home and arrived at 10 o'clock P.M. We have spent twelve very pleasant days in Camp and I am stronger, but so lonely.

Sun. 31 We spent the day with the Hermans. Fred F. came for us this evening and took us to his house to stay all night. We had never met his people. Johnny went to his brother Jim's a little while.

August

Wed. 3 Are still at the Farnsworth's 201 Topeka Ave. but are saying our good-byes. I went this morning to call at Rev. B. L. Smith's then to Mrs. Kempter's, to see their new baby girl, a little over a week old. Johnny gets so angry at times, that I am afraid he will break out in a fit of temper before the Farnsworths.

Fri. 5 Johnny and I went to the Cemetery this morning to say goodbye to a precious little grave, and he cursed and swore and was so abusive, because I took some wild flowers and put on the little grave. They were all I had, and I had no money to buy any better ones. My "wee girlie" even so young, loved flowers and I've seen her hold and look at flowers and play with them and reach for every flower she saw any one have. From Cemetery we went to the Hermans', and Farnsworths' and to Post Office to tell all good-bye. After dinner, Mother and Jim went to Santa Fe depot with us, and with a last good bye, we took 2:40 P.M. train for Colorado. Train was terribly crowded and very hot. But I was almost insensible to any discomfort for my heart was so torn with grief, that I must leave even the body of my precious one; that I must go so far from that little grave. I wonder how I've lived these weeks without her. Oh! just because I cannot die. Oh! if I *might* lie beside her, to stop the pain of my heart.

Mon. 8 We went to Pa's this morning and will stay until can make other plans, for I just *cannot* go back to the house where my "wee girlie," my little "joy baby" was born. Oh! it seems as if my heart would die within me, my baby, I want you so much. My baby, my baby.

Tues. 9 At my father's: there seems *nothing* to live for.

Wed. 10 At Pa's. I am all smiles to friends, that they may not be pained, to see my sorrow, but God knows, how my hours of the night are filled with tears, while others sleep.

Sat. 13 We are still with my father. I try to be brave and not let any one know, how my heart hurts, for I know it makes them all feel badly, to see me grieving. I cannot even go to Johnny, because he worshiped our little one, and her death has seemed to make an "*Infidel*" of him. So I give them my smiles, write my sorrow here, save my tears for the night hours, and pray that God will change Johnny's heart and make him a christian man.

Mon. 15   At noon today, our Party started for a pleasure-trip down on the Cimarron River, to hunt, fish and gather wild Plums and Grapes. There are 11 of us. Pa and Vella, sister May and little Jimmie, Florus Friend and wife, Mr. & Mrs. Milt Gordon and baby Elinor, and Johnny & I. We drove 8 miles South and camped for the night on the level prairie. All slept in one large tent, making beds on the ground. Saw one lone Coyote this afternoon.

Wed. 17   Carrizzo Springs is a pretty, romantic place, once a town, but now only ruins without a living soul; and not even a *whole* house left standing. But the grandest Spring coming out of the solid rock, strong enough to turn a Mill. About 40 Cow Boys camped near our tent last night, on their way to "Round up" Cattle. We left early this morning for Tukaloke Canyon, which we reached by noon and went into Camp. Also a fine Spring here, called "Dripping Springs" because it drips from a great shelving rock, high overhead, falling into a large pond beneath. All about and everywhere is great quantities of Maiden-hair Fern. This is a wholly uninhabited country, wild and romantic and most wonderful scenery; more than a hundred miles from a Railroad, and almost inaccessible.

Fri. 19   We drove by the mouth of Guyenas Canyon this morning, passed "Robbers Roost," and Road "C", reaching Mr. Labriere's Ranch at noon, where we went into Camp, in Pat Canyon. The men killed two Rabbits, 52 Mountain Quail, and caught 70 fish, in about an hour's time. Mr. Labriere and family live in a nice Sod-house and we were the first women Mrs. Labriere had seen in *six months*; it seems terrible to live clear away from everybody and everything, yet they are happy and well, and I am not. My heart never ceases its longing for my little one: and Johnny has been so abusive today, that my sister told him she would not live with him if it were her.

Mon. 22   Resting from our trip, on which saw much beautiful country—all wild, rugged nature. I am crocheting a Lace Bed-spread and Pillow Shams, for the "World's Fair" to be held in Chicago.

Wed. 24   My sweet Mabel Inez, would be 7 mo. old today, if living: and today is the 6th Anniversary of the death of my dear sister Belle. Oh! I'd be so happy if they were living.

Thurs. 25   My heart is so lonely, I could pray for another child. I am almost frantic at times, to be a mother again, but Johnny's health is so poor I dare not think of it; it would be wicked.

Fri. 26   Sometimes I almost think God did not know how lonely my heart would be, and how it would just ache and ache, and hurt me so, or He would not have taken from me, my *"wee girlie"*

Sat. 27   We have made up our minds to move into Springfield, because I cannot bear to go back to the house where my precious baby was born; and then Johnny is not strong enough to farm—the work is too heavy.

Mon. 29   We are still at Belle View Ranch, with my father. It seems to me Johnny tries to see, at times, how unkind and brutal he can be to me, but he *never* has the satisfaction of getting me to "talk back" so he can quarrel with me.

Wed. 31   We moved today into Springfield, a mile and a half from Pa's, and I was compelled to go to the Wilson farm, to pack our things. The house seemed *haunted* with Baby's prescence. I am very tired tonight and heart sick. Oh! it's very hard to live without my Baby and yet I cannot die. How can one live when the heart almost bursts with pain.

September

Sun. 4   We spent today at Sister May's. The 3rd Wedding Anniversary of Johnny and I and life is miserable—Oh! if Johnny would only be a little kind, but I never know when to expect a kind word.

Tues. 6   So little to do in a small home, and the hours drag, heavy with sorrow: if I only had a kind husband, to whom I could go and cry out my heart's grief, I think my heart would not get so weary, but on these pages is the only place I dare *let go* of myself. To every one, and in every place, my grief must be concealed, and I must be all smiles, as if there was no such thing as sorrow.

Fri. 30   Johnny says now, that we will go to Calif. soon. He is so restless and not well.

November

Tues. 1   Johnny is determined to go to Calif. and I hate to go so far away from friends especially, with one who is so unkind.

Fri. 4   Johnny is so abusive, he has driven from my heart all love for him, and he does not *dream* that his cruelty has killed my heart and it cannot love him. I would be so glad of my freedom. Oh! this is such a terrible thing, but the human heart is not capable of enduring every abuse and continuing to love. I stay with him, simply because, I believe as a Christian, it is my duty to do so. I do not believe in divorces. I do not quarrel with him—always I give him kind words and a smiling face. I've left nothing undone I could do for him. I pray for him but my love is dead.

Sat. 5   Johnny left for Lamar Colo. this morning with a load of Rye to sell: will also sell our Team, as farming is too hard for him. We will move to a "good sized town," where he can get lighter work. He left home so ill-natured this morning.

Mon. 7   A busy day at Pa's. The load on my heart is so heavy, I could willingly die, yet God in His mercy, helps me to bear it, so that I need not let anyone know, and there-by, save from heartache those who love me. I *can't* let them suffer by knowing.

Tues. 8   Election Day and I *hope* Harrison and Reid will be elected. Democrats bring hard times.

Thurs. 10   Johnny has sent me no word, as to how he got along on his trip, and I could almost pray he would never come back, but would run away and leave me. Oh! for freedom—

Fri. 11   Still at home with my father. Pa went to town this evening to hear "Election news" and find Cleveland (Dem.) is elected President of the United States, owing to a liberal use of the Shotgun in the South and "Fusion" with "Peoples Party" throughout other States. What a shame such a man should get such a high position.

Mon. 14   J. and I, home with my father. Johnny says he will divide with me what little we have and I can go my way and he will go his, and Oh! I could shout with very joy, at the thought of freedom from such a life, but I feel it is my duty to stay with him, so I turned down his offer: it is the first time he has ever hinted he was unkind, or talked about our unhappy life, and I told him I would stay with him, because if he was to get sick, he would need me, and not every one would stand by him. I know that consumption has fastened upon him, and no change of Climate will ever cure him, because he *will* drink and takes no care of his health.

Wed. 16   Busy day at Pa's. How I long for another Baby, but I can never hope again for the joy of Mother-hood. Johnny's health is gone.

Tues. 22   Very busy getting ready to go to California.

Mon. 28   Went up town with Pa and Johnny this afternoon to pack our household things. This settling in a new home, and so soon "tearing up" and going again, takes the heart out of one: it is so hard for me to give up my friends. We could have the Post Office here, and there is, at least, a good living in it, and an easy one, and Johnny's health will be as good here as anywhere. No one wants me to go away with him, but if *he* insists on going, I feel it *my* duty to go with him: no one else would look after his welfare as I would.

December

Sun. 18   Good-bye to everybody. Very early this morning, Lyman started with us on the fifty mile trip to Lamar, and dear little Jimmie crushed my heart right in the beginning. He is a baby of few words and seeing his papa hitching up the team supposed he was going to take us back to my father's and turning to me said "Home Shaw"? Dear baby heart, he could not realize how *very far* from home, his aunty was going. Ground is white with snow. We reached Jack Ford's on Clay Creek at 6:30 this evening and stay here over night—too cold to camp.

The next three days record her trip cross-country to Los Angeles. The trip is uneventful, but interesting to her because she sees her first mountains. En route the conductor tells her that Johnny "can never live to reach the highest mountain point and better go back."

Thurs. 22

We awakened this morning to look out upon green lawns, bright flowers, trees in fruit and bloom: the fragrance of Orange blossoms, and the songs of birds in the air: a blue sky and bright sunshine over all. Great dark mountains, snow-capped, loom in the near distance, and it's a beautiful sight; a *grandly* beautiful one, but a weary, home-sick heart, cannot enjoy these things. I would give it *all* to be back where a little grave is covered with snow, in the home-land. Johnny is delighted with all this Tropical beauty, but to me, Oh! my heart is too weary, but God will help me to do my duty. The air was chill and cold this morning and while Johnny started out to look for rooms, I went to a near-bye fruit store, where fruit of every description was to be had: many kinds I had never seen before but I was not slow to ask the name. I finally bought some large fine looking Pears, only to find on reaching Hotel, they were hard, woody things that I could hardly get my teeth into and utterly impossible to eat. Johnny returned and took me to see a number of rooms and we finally decided on a nice large room in the Penny Block, corner of Temple & Metcalf; has every convenience and we only pay $2.00 per month: we then bought some "house-keeping" things and after a hard day, tonight are in our new home, 1252 1/2 Temple St. Room 9. Today is Johnnie's 33rd Birthday.

Sun. 25

"Christmas Day" and what a mockery it seems to me. Strangers, in a strange land, among strangers, more than a thousand miles from home, is not conducive to a very happy Christmas, and today I am *very* lonely and heavy hearted: has been raining all day, which makes it seem more gloomy. I have spent the day writing to relatives and friends away over the mountains, in the dear Home land, but none of my heart-ache goes back in my letters. I only send them my smiles and a cheery good word.

Mon. 26

We went down town this afternoon, to the Post Office, with our letters and to walk about the streets awhile. It is all so strange, to come from the snow into the sunny summer time. The flowers are pretty, but like our own at home. The Pepper-trees along the street are the most beautiful of all: the Palms too are pretty and the Hedges of Calla-lily. The Orange and Lemon trees look much like our cherry trees at home. It is all beautiful, but no more so than our own, dear, old sunny Kansas with her prairies and her sunflowers. The glory of the sunflower is more brilliant than any thing I see here and there is never a familiar face.

It is like we had gone to another world.

Tues. 27 We went to see a Dr. this morning about Johnny's lungs: he told us one lung was entirely gone and the other badly affected, but could cure him. Johnny believes what he said about *cure*, but *I* know it's only a question of time, until consumption will end it all. How strange this place seems. Cable cars, instead of Topeka's Electric-cars—the Chinaman instead of the Negro and every-where a strange babel of tongues—so many foreigners here.

Wed. 28 I have not been out of the house today: but where would one go, when one is unacquainted. And Johnny can make life as miserable here for me as any where else.

Sat. 31 Just a quiet day at home. Today is the last day of the most *miserable* and *unhappy* year of my life, and I'm not sorry to see it go.

[1893]

January

Sun. 1   "New Years Day" and a bright, sunny day, warm and beautiful—would that it might be an "omen" of my life for the coming year, but I know whatever comes, God will give me grace to bear. Johnny and I went for a walk after dinner, but how could it be pleasant, when you know not a soul to say "Howdy-do," to. A population of about 65000. I don't like the place too many hills—seem like mountains to us.

Wed. 4   Finished my lace Bed-spread today—crocheted it and pillow-shams of Glasgo twilled lace thread and its very pretty: going to send it to the "World's Fair" in Chicago.

Fri. 13   The sun did not shine much to do. The mornings and evenings are very cold and we *have* to have a fire—we heat our room as every one does here, with a couple of small "drums" on the gasoline stove, but it is not a very satisfactory way of warming. I prefer the snow of Kansas to this kind of cold weather.

Sun. 15   We went for a walk this afternoon out Temple to Belmont Ave and down Belmont to 7th and return—too cold. My heart is with the home folks today: here every face is a strange one—never any one to speak to, but Johnny grows stronger and if he can get well, I shall not regret the separation from loved ones. The love has all died in my heart, but I am just as much bound to him as if I loved him and shall ever do all in my power for him and pray every day, God will restore his health.

Mon. 16   Johnny gets out and is getting some acquainted but I stay at home alone and am lonely.

Sat. 21   I went to town this afternoon, and then to see a Mr. Busath—whom Johnny met recently—about work, for *I have got to go to work.*

Sun. 22   Such a lovely morning, that Johnny and I went for a walk. At noon while getting our dinner, little Mrs. Busath came for me to come down to the St. Angelo and help wait on their Boarders at mealtime and I went down at 4 o'clock. Was a big crowd for Supper and while

I am so thankful for the work, pride made it embarrassing for me.

Mon. 23 I went down to the St. Angelo this morning at 6 o'clock to help Mr. Busath wait on his Boarders for Breakfast, stayed to help with Lunch at noon. Came home at 2 o'clock, went back at 4 o'clock and got home again at 7 o'clock after helping with Supper, or Dinner here. I am to do this each day and receive $20.00 per month and my three meals a day, which will be a big help. Our money is running short and Johnny is unable to work. Mr. Busath has so many Boarders, he has three others beside me to help wait on them at meal-time. I could get a place, to Clerk in a Store, but could have no time at home: and this way, I can get Johnny's meals for him and be home afternoons so it is much better, every way.

Tues. 24 I walked down to work this morning at the St. Angelo— came home this afternoon, back for dinner and home again at 7 o'clock. I find it very embarassing to meet so many strangers but they are all so lovely and Mr. & Mrs. Busath so kind. Mrs. Busath will be a mother soon and how I wish I could know this great joy again. My "wee girlie" would be one year old today, if living. O little "joy girl" how mother's heart aches for you.

Wed. 25 Went to the St. Angelo as usual today: it is 17 blocks and I walk it four times a day, so night usually finds me tired. I get home in time to get Johnny's Lunch at noon. Leave things so he can get his own Breakfast, when he doesn't want to go to town and get it and I get his Dinner when I get home in evening.

February

Thurs. 16 To and from work at my usual hours. This evening Johnny and I went down thro' Chinatown, thro' their *old* Joss House and to an entertainment at their Y.M.C.A. Missian at 214 Wilmington St. It is the Chinese "New Year" and their narrow streets were filled with "sight see-ers." Plenty of police, everywhere, but I could hardly feel safe among these strange people.

Sat. 18 To and from work as usual, except that Johnny met me after Lunch, and we went down thro' Chinatown: were very courteously treated, everywhere, to tea, candies fruits and nuts. Delicious tea was served in the tiniest cups. Went into their *new* Joss House, which is a wonderful place, the most striking thing being the God with tapers of incense or "punk", burning about it. Everything is wonderful strange and weird in Chinatown. Punk burning everywhere, in the buildings and along the sidewalks and "fire-crackers" used by tons: the streets were covered like a carpet with those that had been used. We looked into their Theatre, but was so crowded and choking with cigarette smoke, we did not enter.

Sun. 19   To and from work as usual today. It seems hard, to have to be from home all the time, yet I believe it is a blessing, in that I do not have to be so much with Johnny and run the risk of taking consumption, for he coughs dreadfully and the smell from his body is sickening: smells like his body was dead: wish I did not have to sleep in same room with him.

Mon. 20   To work at 6 A.M. Home again at 2 P.M. back to work at 4 P.M. and home at 7 o'clock for the night. 17 blocks to the St. Angelo walked four times a day, is 68 blocks, or more than five miles a day, beside my work at home and the St. Angelo, *all for a man* who gives *me many curses* and very few smiles. I give *him* my heart's sincerest prayers. In Colorado, I could have the P.O. with salary for a good living and be with my loved ones; instead I am here doing this, not for love, but because I am trying to live aright and believe it my duty as a Christian. I will not leave a thing undone.

Wed. 22   To and from my work at usual hours. Drew my first month's wages this evening when Mr. Busath gave me a $20.00 gold coin, which I brought home and gave to Johnny, and was happy to do so.

March

Fri. 3   To my usual work today. I have met some very wealthy people here and made some very pleasant friends. Mrs. Morey, whose hands are covered with diamonds—she wears *ten fine* diamond rings on one hand—has just about such a husband as I have: he is about same size and looks much like Johnny: *he* also has consumption and is cross and cranky as can be. Well, *she* and *I* are *friends* and sympathise fully, with one another. *She* is rich—*I* am poor, but her wealth makes her no happier than I am, and we both are *miserable*. Her home is in Philadelphia.

Sun. 19
To and from work as usual. Heavy fog and cloudy all day. I received invitation Cards, saying my cousin Henry Anderson would be married today to Tillie Koerber back in my old home, Floral, Cowley Co., Kansas I hope they will be very happy, but so far as *I* am concerned "*Marriage is a failure*".

Sun. 26
Working as usual. People live like a "*whirlwind*" in this country, so "*fast and hard*" yet everyone is kind to me. I have met Mr. & Mrs. John Riley, (brother of James Whitcomb Riley) very plain, unassuming folks whom every one like, tho' few here like the Poet as he proved to be a "snob" on a recent visit here.[1] I've never seen him myself.

Fri. 31
Working as usual: another awful fog. Johnny sick—in bed most of time. I am so afraid I will come home some evening and find him dead. He thinks when the rains stop, he will get well again, but I know it is the beginning of the end and there is no hope, but I dare not let him know. I must keep him in good spirit and cheery, *if cranky*.

April

Wed. 19
At my usual work. Chinese dish washer "Big Jim" (Lin-Wong-Sell) has become much attached to me because I help him with his Bible-lessons—there is something very pathetic about the friendship of these people, it seeming almost the friendship of a dumb animal. "Jim" is deeply religious and working hard to learn his Bible and "English" so as to go back among his own people as a Missionary. I have seen him take his Bible and go to some one, ask them the pronunciation of a word and its meaning, they *deliberately* tell him wrong and laugh at him, then in mis-trust he would come to me, so now he *always* comes, for he has found I am honest with him and sincerely interested in his soul's welfare and work he is trying to fit himself for.

Thurs. 20
Working as usual. I took an Art lesson in Crayon, today, from "Anna" who knows little more than I do, about it. "A Dogs Head" was my "study."

Sat. 22   Working as usual only didn't go home after Lunch.
Finished my "Dog" picture. After Dinner went to town
with Helen Glennon to do little shopping, then came
home alone. My experience with Jim the Chinese dish-
washer, has not helped "Foreign Missions" with me. If
the Heathen at our door were properly taught the Foreign Heathen would be well cared for. Thousands of
Chinamen and other Foreigners here in California, un-
taught, and many making every sacrifice, to learn of
God, and become workers for their own race, yet not
getting help they should, and the "cry" is ever, for
money to preach the Gospel in "Foreign Lands." I say
preach the Gospel to the neglected Heathen in our own
land and send them out among their own Race.

Sun. 23   Working as usual, except did not go home after Lunch,
as was not feeling well. I overheard "*Jim*" the Chinaman
at prayer the other day: he had gone off into a little
room alone, here in the St. Angelo, and thought no one
heard him, as he put all his heart into prayer but I
caught these few words, "*Oh! Lord make-ee me, sabe-ee you,
make-ee me 'bey-ee you*" and I wondered, how many of us
prayed the Lord to *make* us *obey* Him—we like so well to
have our own way.

Mon. 24   Working and home after Lunch—usual hours. Johnny
grows *worse* in health every day, and there is no chance
of recovery—the only question is "how long can he last."
I would gladly give him my health, take his dreadful
disease and die, if God would let me. Took another Art
lesson today "Stork among Cat-tails".

May

Tues. 2   I came home after Lunch today. "Anna" of the St.
Angelo left this afternoon for Chicago, and she told us
of her life, before leaving. She was born Anna Manning,
near the "*Killarney Lakes*," *Ireland* on the *River Rhine*, the
tide from which came up into their back yard. At age of
16, she *crossed* the *Ocean alone*, coming to her brother
Tom in San Francisco, who had preceded her, several
years: here she *met, loved* and *married, George Hamilton*
(the *reprobate son* of *Lord Hamilton of England*) after *twice
following* him to Australia, on the ship upon which *he was
a Sailor*: he has abandoned her, but she won't give up

and is going to Chicago to meet him, taking her "savings" to him, for she must work, as he does not support her, and only occasionally writes her, and very seldom sees her: has not seen him for more than a year still she is *"daughter-in-law to a Lord." Bosh!*

Fri. 12 St. Angelo. Came home after Lunch. Thunder shower at 5 o'clock—are having some Earthquakes too that are pretty lively.

Mon. 22 St. Angelo on usual schedule. Got a $20.00 gold piece this evening, my month's wage and took it home and gave it all to Johnny, after paying our rent. There is demand for nurses and I could make a fine salary nursing, as some advise me to do, but I must do the work that will leave me most time with Johnny.

Tues. 30 *"Decoration Day."* St. Angelo—not home after Lunch, as went with Helen Glennon to town to seé Parade, but only Salvation Army paraded, however it made a nice showing. Another disagreeable morning of drizzle. After the Breakfast hour, I went to town and bought a *nice Guitar, in a Pawn-shop, for $5.00* some of my *tip-money* and why not, when Johnny buys whiskey with my wages.

June

Thurs. 1 St. Angelo on usual schedule: another "drizzle" day. Johnny is so dissatisfied here, because of so much cloudy, damp weather, he wants to leave and go to Redlands or somewhere in Mountains, but we are simply *not* able to travel about so much, and tho' he does not suspect it, *I* know there is no cure, for him no difference where we go.

Wed. 7 A clear pretty day, for a change and it is a *treat*. St. Angelo on my usual schedule, tho' Johny is often away when I get home—he grows weaker too.

Sun. 18 St. Angelo as usual, but not home after Lunch. Drizzle fog, as usual; O for the much vaunted sunshine of California, lest I come to believe the State sunless. Mrs. Jack Terrell left for Arizona, today, with the body of her little boy, the baby having died of Pneumonia. They *did not* call *a Doctor*, depending *wholly* on *Christian Science*, of which this country is full, tho' I believe "Spiritualism" leads.

Wed. 21   St. Angelo the usual schedual, today. I pity Johnny so; I
           wish he could get well, tho' I would not *live*, with him, if
           he did, for his abuse is almost impossible to bear; but he
           is sick and it would be unchristian to leave him helpless,
           so I will take care of him: work and support him until
           the end. My Bible and prayer my solace.

Tues. 27   St. Angelo. After Breakfast, went to town to shop a
           little: not home after Lunch. Just *one year* today, *my baby*,
           my *wee girlie* died and my heart never ceases to long for
           her. Johnny talks of Topeka and our return, much of
           the time now.

July

Thurs. 20 St. Angelo and home as usual today—little sprinkle of
           rain this morning. Johnny so poorly I must soon quit
           work, and I don't know how we will live. Death is so near
           my home, I shudder. Away here among strangers,
           working and sacrificing to make a living, and seeing
           Death coming nearer every day. O God spare me this
           blow—I don't see how I can bear up under any more.

Sat. 22   St. Angelo and home after Lunch. My month is up
           today, and good Mr. Busath paid me my usual $20.00
           gold piece—it won't last long, for tonight after Dinner I
           quit work, and am home to stay, for Johnny has grown
           so much worse, it is not safe to leave him alone any
           more; and any way, we will soon go home to Topeka, if
           he lives until we can arrange things. He thinks he will
           get well when we get back home, where it is warm and
           dry.

Sun. 23   Home all day with Johnny except just long enough to go
           down to Kalliwoda's Drug Store, this morning and get
           him some wine.

August

Tues. 1   A letter from Mother Shaw, brings money to go on. Mrs.
           Barkey and Mrs. Swezey, both former Topekans to
           whom Johnny used to carry mail called this morning to
           see us, having just found we were here, and *we* did not
           know *they* were here and we start *home* tomorrow. I
           called at Mrs. Cook's (also former Topekan) this after-

noon, then to town to buy a few necessities and dispose of our few household effects to "Second-hand man" and make final arrangements for our trip home, then over to St. Angelo, to help for last time thro' the Dinner hour.

Wed. 2   I went to the St. Angelo this morning, and to Mrs. Finley's, Mrs. Barkey's and Mrs. Busath's, to bid them all *good-bye*. . . . Mrs. Swezey & Mrs. Barkey came with a large lunch basket, filled with a nice Lunch and fine fruit and to go to train to see us off; and Mrs. Cook came with her carriage, to take us to the Depot. Johnny with some one on each side of him, to half carry him, managed to get down the stairs and to the carriage, almost in state of collapse. At Depot, Conductor picked him up in his arms and carried him into the train, which at 5:15 P.M. pulled out of the new, A. T. & S. F. Depot (dedicated last Sat.) with us aboard, occupying Berth 9—lower—bound for Topeka and home. I *came* here with a heavy heart because of loved ones and many dear friends I was leaving, and now I *return* home, with a heavy heart, for again, I am leaving many dear friends and most of all because I know, just ahead a little way, death is waiting to claim the one to whom I'm bound: it may come on way home and my heart almost failed me. I scarcely could get courage to make the start, but the sick one so longed to get home, so I've made the start and pray God for strength and to take us safely all the way.

Sat. 5   This morning I awaken, with only the day between me and home, and still my husband lives, tho' awearied and much worn. . . . We arrived in Topeka about 5:30 P.M., one year to the very hour, from day we left. Dr. White and another man carried Johnny to a Hack for me, and we soon drove to his brother Jim Shaw's, 1217 East Tenth St. and our long hard Journey was ended—Were not expecting us and no one at home, but Willie and Frankie soon came, then the others. Mother Shaw came down this evening to see us. Oh! so weary.

Wed. 16   Johnny slowly grows weaker and I am with him day and night. Have not undressed to go to bed, since I left Los Angeles. He won't let anyone else care for him, so day and night I sit by his bed-side, getting what sleep I can in a rocking-chair, and I never seem rested.

Thurs. 24   Home with Johnny, who will hardly let me from his bedside, long enough to eat my meals. I wish he was a Christian; it is hard to see him dying an unbeliever, an *Infidel.* I pray God to change his heart.

Sat. 26   Went up town on an errand this morning. Johnny grows weaker and cannot raise himself up in bed and I must lift him so much and turn him.

Thurs. 31   Home with Johnny, who is so ill-natured and abusive to me, that his brother goes after him, sometimes and *"hushes him up,"* telling him he ought to be ashamed of himself for abusing one who has done so much for him and does all in her *power* for him, day after day, uncomplainingly.

September

Mon. 4   Today is Johnny's and my 4th wedding Anniversary and what a long, *miserable, unhappy,* four years it has been. "Four years full of tears," and I have tried so hard to get J. to be kind to me, but he can't be kind to any *woman.* He abuses his mother, more than me and she is such a good woman. A Christian woman in every way, and so generous and kind to every one. I went up town this morning, for a walk in the air, and to see the "Labor Day Parade," which was good, what there was of it. Retta and I went to Church at Tent this evening and 15 united with the Church.

Sun. 17   An *awfully* windy day. Johnny grows weaker each day, but has a wonderful vitality. I have prayed and prayed for his return to health, and I still pray that God will give him *my* health and let *me* take his disease and be the one to die. He wants so much to live: he thinks too he is going to get well and told me, he knew he had not treated me right, but when he gets well he will make it all up and will be good to me.

Sun. 24   Johnny so weak I dared not leave at all today; it seemed almost as if the end had come.

Tues. 26   Johnny is quite himself again and gave me permission to go to church tonight, with Retta and he would let his brother sit by him, until my return. 10 united with the church tonight.

Wed. 27   Went up town for "morphine" this morning, as Johnny has to have it all the time; the only thing that keeps him alive.

October

Thurs. 5   Over Johnny all day. Two months this afternoon, since we came home and not *once* in all that time, have I had my clothes off, only to change to others, nor have I been in bed. I sleep in a chair beside the bed, that I may minister to his every want. Several times I have lain down on the floor on a pallet, but he does not like to have me do so.

Tues. 17   Johnny's conscience seems to *give him a twinge* once in awhile and he *feels remorse*, for his *unkindness* to me and he said to me today, "*that I had done everything in the world, for him that a woman could do* and *no other woman* would ever have *lived* with him and *done for him*, as I have, and when he *gets well*, he is going to *join the church*, and will be a *better man* and be *good to me*, and *do many things for me.*" Ah poor man; my heart is *filled* with *pity for him*, but he *crushed my heart long ago; killed all the love of my heart.* I could *never love him again, never* and could such a miracle happen, as his restoration to health, I *would not live* with him. I stay *now*, because *he is sick* and *helpless*, and it is *my duty*, as *one who tries to be a Christian.* But he *died to me, long ago.* When I felt *my love dying*, I *fought* to *retain it*, but *no love can live under such cruelty.*

Fri. 20   Johnny is a *very* sick man today, and how my "heart jumped" this morning when I discovered his feet had commenced to swell: I know *death* is very near; just a question of how long his vitality can fight it off. He has been very "flighty" today.

Sat. 21   Johnny has been real "flighty" all day. Just about half conscious. I sat up *all* night, last night alone, with him, not daring to close my eyes.

Wed. 25   Johnny apparently better, but I dare not hope. . . .

Wed. 26   Who but *God* and *those* who have gone thro' the same experience, can *know* the *strange, conflicting* emotions of my heart. *Tonight I am utterly alone* and *miserable. Tonight I am a widow. I am free. My heart* would *cry out in very joy, because it is freed from a wretchedly miserable life*, and *my heart is breaking with pain, heart-ache and utter desolation*, that *thro' death must come its release.* It has been such a *fine* *day* and Johnny *wanted* me to go to town on an errand, so mother came and staid with him and at 2 o'clock P.M. *I kissed him good-bye and went to town,* he saying as I left, to *"hurry back for I like to have good-looking girls sit by me." When I came home, he was dying.* I called Dr. Lewis at 5 o'clock. J. became unconscious about 6 o'clock and *died at 10:5 P.M.* and tho' the room was full of *people,* I was the *only one* at his bed-side. Mother and I staid rest of night with Mrs. Johnston, but I could not sleep.

Fri. 27   I went up town this morning with Jim, to get some necessary things for the funeral. Rev. B. L. Smith preached Johnny's funeral and the Mail-Carriers acted as Pall-bearers. His brother Jim would not consent to keeping the body until Sunday, because he died of consumption and so we buried him this evening at 6 o'clock: and *tonight I am so wretched,* that I *feel dazed* and *as if I must awake from some terrible night-mare. Four years ago a Bride, hoping to be happy. Tonight a widow in abject misery.* I *know* my *heart aches* as *much over his death,* as if *I had loved* him, *for it is terrible* to *have one die not a christian,* and *especially one who was much to us at some time in our life.* But *God knows* the *tears* of *my heart* and *the prayers of my heart for this man.* I have striven to do what God would have me do.

Sun. 29   Went up the Cemetery this morning and took the flowers to Johnny's Grave and some to put on my *wee girlie's.* . . . I spent the evening with the Pettits. I can't be content anywhere.

Mon. 30   I am keeping house for brother Jim and two little boys, as Retta has not yet returned, and I washed a very large washing this morning; washing bedding and Johnny's clothes, and putting things away and burning many more, that I may have no reminder of my unhappy life. My Wedding Veil and gloves were buried with Johnny.

November

Wed. 1   Oh! so lonely, for tho' unkind, yet Johnny was the father of my child, the one ray of sunshine in all the four years of my married life.

Thurs. 2   I must be looking about me for something to do, because Johnny left me no means of support. I miss him more than anyone can know, for he has been a constant cause of worry and anxiety to me, having, practically, been sick the whole of our married life and now I feel as if a great load had been lifted from off me and my freedom is actually a joy, tho' I sincerely grieve, that death should be the means of this thrill of pleasure, at being free from such a miserable life.

Sun. 5   Went up to the Cemetery this morning, to Johnny and baby Mabel's graves.[2] I am so alone I hardly know which way to turn: I am as a girl again, with the heart-ache of a terrible experience added to her life; 26 years old and think of what I have passed through.

Thurs. 16   I went up to the Cemetery this morning to Johnny and Mabel's graves. How I wish I could hold my "wee girlie" in my arms again. From the Cemetery I took a car and went to spend the day with Mrs. H. W. Farnsworth, 201 Topeka Ave. Was introduced to her son Jim who is home on a visit, from El Paso Texas, and I thought he looked so much like Johnny, tho' larger.

Sat. 18   Home with Retta today, helping her clean and bake. I have given her all my silver-ware and blankets, bedding, feather bed, bedstead and practically everything, I had left in the housekeeping line. I have given away and burned up, *everything* so that I might not *have a thing* to remind me, of the old unhappy life: it is such a nightmare, that I shudder at the sight of anything that reminds me of it. Oh! that I could make myself forget it all.

Sun. 19   Fred Farnsworth came for me this morning and took me up to his Mother's, to make arrangements to stay with her as a nurse, as her daughter must go to her home in Calif. From Farnsworth's took a car to the Cemetery, to Johnny and "wee girlie's" graves, then to Jim Shaw's. Retta is 25 years old today.

Tues. 21   In my new home today, 201 Topeka Ave.: I have only had a short rest, but I need work and don't expect Mrs. F. to be so hard to nurse as Johnny was: certainly not so unkind.

Mon. 27   I find my Patient kind and considerate; very affectionate. I am with her thro' the day and at night every one goes to bed and if she needs anything Mr. Farnsworth waits upon her, so I get my rest at night. She seldom 'wakens all night long.

Tues. 28	I am getting rested here, in this quiet home: spent my evening writing letters. Fred went to see his girl.
Wed. 29	Tonight Fred F. was home and we had a very pleasant evening's visit, really our first visit since my return from California.
Thurs. 30	"Thanksgiving Day", again and although my heart has been so burdened with sorrow and trouble all the year, yet I have *so much* to be thankful for. My work, in this pleasant home, is something to be especially thankful for. I wanted to go over to the Cemetery this afternoon, but it was so cold; foggy too. Fred went to see his girl, so Mr. & Mrs. Farnsworth and I had very quiet afternoon and evening.

December

Fri. 1	Oh! how good it seems, to have everyone kind to you; how restful. I never hear a complaining, nor unkind word and I feel as if I had been let out of prison; I almost wonder sometimes, if I have not been sleeping, and will awaken, to find it all a dream. Mrs. Farnsworth seems to think so much of me.
Sun. 3	Today is Mr. and Mrs. Farnsworth's 38th Wedding Anniversary. I went to Church this morning, but it makes me sad, for it brings up memories of the days, when I thought I was going to be so happy and instead of Heaven in marriage, I found Hell. Fred went to see his *girl* this evening, so I had a very quiet evening alone. I hope Fred gets a good wife some day, for he is such a good boy; just the kind that most often pick up a crank.
Sun. 10	I went to Church this morning, Fred going as far as 5th St. and from church, I went to J. M. Bair's for dinner. Fred asked me this evening, "if the right man came along, if I would not marry again." *Oh! dear.*
Wed. 13	Covering Fred's gloves with Chamois this afternoon, as I sat with my Patient. Mrs. F. goes to her room, after Tea, and Mr. F. sits thro' the evening with her, so it leaves Fred and I alone for the evening and he is beginning to look at me, in a rather strange way and to say "funny" things. Tonight he said we would go to Calif. together next Summer, on his Vacation. Now if he means that seriously, I am sorry, for I cannot think of

marrying again. Oh! such misery. I could never trust another man, tho' I know Fred is a splendid fellow, but he is a "moderate" drinker like the other.

Fri. 15 Mrs. F. is failing every day. Fred asked me this evening what Johnny said when he "Proposed." Now Fred don't *you* try Proposing to me for I will have to say *no! no!! no!!!*

Sat. 16 I am afraid Fred is "smitten" for when I came down to Breakfast this morning, he met me and asked if I did not say last night, that I belonged to him. Oh! if he could only realize, how I *hate* the thought of marriage. He and I have always been the best of friends, and he is so good, but I simply cannot love or trust any man again. It makes me shudder to even think of it. He is not home tonight.

Wed. 20 Mrs. F. is failing so, that she takes almost my constant time, and each night I must stay in her room over night, except that Mr. F. stays with her for couple of hours after supper.

Tonight Fred said to me, "I was wondering how long it would be, before you could marry." I can *never* marry. So far as *waiting* is concerned, I could marry now. I staid with the other and took care of him. He was so brutal and unkind, he became repulsive to me. I loathed him, yet I staid with him and took care of him, as I felt it my duty to do; but now I am free to marry if I wish. I do not want to. Oh! the horror of it.

Sat. 23 Both Mr. and Mrs. Farnsworth very sick and I go constantly from one room to another. Fred staid with them about two hours, after supper, that I might get a little sleep as I barely got a doze last night.

Sun. 24 I wrote letters, to all the Farnsworth children tonight, to tell them of the dangerous illness of their parents. We don't know what a moment may bring. Fred went to see his girl and we had to send for him. Dr. Munn here until late tonight. I was up all night last night and must be tonight.

Mon. 25 "Christmas Day" and Fred has half holiday and is home; while some of the neighbors came in this afternoon, to stay with my Patients to let me get out in the Air, Fred walked with me: I took a very short walk to river and back as I do not feel like leaving my two Patients even a moment.

Wed. 27 A Rainy morning. Cousin Nellie Dick and Ned Adams married today and as we read the account in Paper this evening Fred asked if I did not wish it was he and I. Poor Ted, how can I ever love or trust anyone again, enough to marry them, when I found married life so unhappy.

Thurs. 28   My Patients much better and Mr. Farnsworth can be up so Ida looked after them long enough for me to ride to town with Fred after dinner, to go to Express Office and get my Bed Spread, just sent me from the World's Fair, where I got a Prize on it of $3.00. I walked home.

Sun. 31   Standing with me, by his mother's bedside, this evening, Fred said I could set my own time to be married. Oh! Ted when will you ever quit talking so, to me. I cannot trust any man enough to marry him. *I am afraid.* I have been so unhappy, that now my greatest joy is to be free. Fred is so good and our friendship has *always* been such a happy one, I don't want it spoiled by the thought of marriage. I could never be so happy as now in my freedom.

Tonight closes a most unhappy year in my life. So full of care, sorrow, misery. God grant the New Year may bring more of joy.

[1894]

During this year Martha moves back into the round of visiting and entertaining that had been her life before she married Johnny Shaw. She is gradually regaining her happy outlook, and there is none of the complaining and regret-ting that so marked the Shaw years. She notes that she admires a sixty-year old "maiden lady" she knows, but does not indicate that the single life would be a realistic option for her.

January

Mon. 1   Today begins a new year in my life and I pray God, for grace and strength to live it, as He would have me live it, and Oh! that it may be His will, that more of joy may come to me this year, for the past one has been so full of *bitterness.* Never-the-less, not *my* will, but *His*, be done, in all things concerning me and I know He will ever keep my future years, as the past ones, always in His own good care.

I did not go to bed at all last night, but sat alone all through the night, in a rocker, beside the bed of Mrs. Farnsworth holding her hand. I slept when she slept. She just will not let me out of her sight. Mr. Farnsworth was able to go down to dinner today.

Thurs. 4   Mrs. Farnsworth is much weaker and there is a slight rattle in her throat today, which I am sure 'tokens death.

Sat. 6   Mr. Jim F. staid with his mother, while I went to the Market this morning. I was weighed too, at the market and weighed 138. Mrs. Farnsworth grew rapidly worse from 2 o'clock P.M. until 7:45 o'clock P.M. when she died; I was the last person she recognized and talked to, being unconscious almost all the afternoon: her sister Miss Lucy Stoddard, Mr. Farnsworth, Jim and Fred, Sad Hodgins, Mrs. Geo. Bauer, Mrs. John Mileham and myself all with her when she passed quietly and calmly to rest.

Mon. 8   Mrs. Kate Akin came from St. Louis, this morning at 10:30 and Mr. Coit Farnsworth came from Chicago at

Hiram W. Farnsworth, Kaw
Indian agent, 1861–1865,
and member of the first
Kansas Senate. (Martha's
father-in-law.)

noon.[1] . . . And the Funeral was held at 2:30 P.M. being
preached by Rev. L. Blakesly: was a very, very large
funeral and such large quantities of the most beautiful
flowers. I rode with Fred, Mr. Coit F. and Mr. Hodgins.
After the funeral this evening, Fred went to his father
and told him "he was going to marry Mrs. Shaw." And
now whatever will I do. I never told Fred I would; I
cannot consent to marry anyone, and yet if I do not now,
Mr. F. will think I have encouraged the boy and proved
false to him. Oh! Ted what an embarassing, position
you have placed me in. The Farnsworths are such excellent people and I think the world of Fred as a friend, but
the very thought of marriage is repulsive. Fred is so
persistent and I suppose thinks "all is fair in love and
war," but he has put me in a mighty awkward position.

Tues. 9   Mr. Coit Farnsworth went home to Chicago this afternoon. He is such a nice fellow and indeed one could not
help liking all the family, but I don't want to be one of
them. Fred is such a dear, good friend, but I am afraid
to marry him. Oh! Teddy I *can't.*

Thurs. 11   Such lovely weather. I am to stay at Farnsworth's some
time yet, as nurse and housekeeper. Mr. F. still needs

care and there must be a housekeeper, so for awhile, I shall act as both. Fred gave me a nice comb and brush today. He, as well as all the family, consider us "engaged" and he acts very "lover like" but I *cannot, simply, cannot,* marry. He is so good, and if I only could trust him I am sure I would be very happy.

February

Fri. 2   At Mrs. Bauer's and Mrs. Mileham's this morning. Fred brought me some beautiful flowers this evening, when he came from work. White Hyacinth, white Carnations, Purple Heliatrope, dark pink Begonia, Yellow Jonquils and Similax. *6:15 P.M.*. Upstairs writing this, Fred came to me says "what are you writing, your Diary?" Gave me a kiss and said "put that in it." Such a lover; he is just all *gone*: is certainly as devoted as any heart could wish, but Oh! my heart, will you ever believe in another man. Can I ever trust another?

Tues. 6   . . . . Of course, every evening, Fred and I spend together.

Tues. 13   Home, Ted is all devotion and a person could hardly help loving the boy, but Oh! the *trusting*; will he be the same after marriage. We have had such a happy evening together.

Mon. 26   Fred and I are taking care of little Ed Herman, for Eva, because her reprobate husband, Guy Herman, ran away and left her and the two children, last Fall; ran off with another's wife, the mother of *five* children. I walked down to Jim Shaw's this morning. The Farnsworths and me, have such happy evenings together:

March

Sat. 3   Went up town this morning to Register for the Election, and again this afternoon, Mrs. Akin went with me, as I went to City Prison to vote at Rep. Primary, for nomination of Col. James Burgess for councilman from Fourth Ward, then Minnie and I went to Copeland Hotel to call on Mrs. Sam Remington and Mrs. Cope Gordon. Also called at Mrs. Durein's Minnie says my "widow's costume" is *very becoming to me*, but I hate it.

Wed. 7   At 6 o'clock this morning went with Minnie in a Hack, to

U. P. Depot N. Topeka, where she took 7 o'clock train for Kansas City, and I returned home in Hack: Raining hard. Minnie said she came down hoping to persuade me to marry Fred, immediately; but I was not to be persuaded. I don't feel that I can ever marry anyone: it is *fear*, nothing else for Fred is good as gold, but a child who has been burnt will be *very* careful, not to put its finger in the fire the second time, and that is way I feel, tho' could one marry *rightly* I think, the married life would be the Ideal life. But *Oh! how I fear it.*

Thurs. 8   Eva, little Ed and I, called on Mrs. Chas. Kerle this afternoon, then Eva came home with me for rest of afternoon. Fred told me this evening that Sam Robinson, an old Mail-Carrier, said to him today, that *"Mrs. Shaw was the loveliest woman he had ever met in his life, here or anywhere else"* and said I *was a good, true woman,* or I *would not have staid by John Shaw as I did:* said *not one woman in a thousand would have staid with him.*

Fri. 16   Went to Drug store, 6 & Top. Ave. this morning and little Ed. H. with me. Coming home, stopped to talk with Mrs. Mileham. She and Mrs. Bauer, are making big plans for Fred and I to marry. Going to give us a *"Wedding-breakfast"* etc and I just told her how I felt about marrying. Everyone knows how I dread the thought of marrying and they all say Fred will be so good to me. I believe he will but I am afraid to trust him.

Mon 19   Misty, cloudy, cool day. Fred took Ed. H. and I to Frank McClelland's out at Maple Hill today, an 18 mile drive. Left home 9 o'clock this morning got here about 4 o'clock P.M. cold and hungry. Fred took liquor along, which I did not know, on leaving home; and drank and smoked all way out here; so lost his way and I did not know the road. He was staggering, by time got in the house and went right to sleep. How my heart ached: if I am to marry him and have him *drink* like this, there is another miserable life before me. *And I will not do it, that's all.* I'll just pack my trunk and leave, I don't care how nice the rest of the family are.

Tues. 20   Fred is sober today and heartily ashamed of himself; so am I ashamed of him and I have been very indifferent toward him all day. . . .

Fri. 23   Home today. Very cold. I feel like running away, since seeing Fred drink so the other day, but he has promised faithfully, he will never drink another drop. I don't trust any man, but I'll see how Fred keeps his promise for awhile, and very first time he breaks it, I go from here.

April

Mon. 2   I am making what I suppose will be my *"wedding dress,"* yet I keep hoping Fred will change his mind: he is dear and good, but I have such a fear of marriage. Eva staid all night with me.

Tues. 3   Eva here all day helping me sew. After dinner I took Ted to the P. O. then came home for Eva and took her to Mrs. Walker's, Mrs. Van Vliet's and down to Jim Shaw's. She will stay over night with me. I got a letter from Oren Kettlewell today and one yesterday; poor, old Kettlewell; he and I use to be sweethearts and after I turned him down, he married; now he is begging *me* not to marry; says he is miserably unhappy and would get a divorce, or do anything, to get me. I pray God to help him; if I have spoiled his life, I am sorry, but I felt he had done wrong and could *not* be trusted, so I could not marry him *then* and my religion would not let me marry a divorced man, if he should get one and I am afraid of *all* men, even dear good Teddie, whom I shall likely marry, unless I can get him to change his mind, and that is not likely.

Wed. 4   Eva here all day, helping me make what will be my "wedding dress" if I finally consent. . . .

Thurs. 5   Home working on my dress. Eva called this morning. How I *dread* the coming of the *"2nd of May,"* the day Minnie Akin set for *Fred* and *I to marry*, it being *her wedding Anniversary, she having married on the 2nd of May, year before* Fred *was born*. I tell Fred, I *won't* be married that day, but he *clings to the day* and *urges it*.

Fri. 6   Home with sore throat. Mailed a letter to Oren Kettlewell. Fred makes an *ideal lover*; *all devotion*; and if I could give him a year's trial as a lover, I think I could make up my mind to marry him. And too people in Topeka did not know much of my unhappy life with Johnny and will *think* it *strange* I could marry so soon after his death—about 7 months—I *always shielded* J. and *no one knew* how I *loathed him*; how he *killed my love long ago*.

Sun. 8   To Church this morning, with Mr. F. Got a good letter from Jim Farnsworth today. I had written him how I dreaded my coming marriage and he writes so good of Fred; thinks Fred will always be good and kind, because it is in him: it is just that I fear he will drink himself to death. I *know* he will *not* be unkind, even when drinking, but he could kill me with neglect: I have a horror of drink. Fred has not drank a drop since our trip to Maple Hill and says he never will again. If I could only trust him, I would be happy. Rained hard this afternoon. My throat still sore and my face some swollen.

Mon. 9   I find myself in possession of a *good big dose* of "*mumps*", which have taken from little Ed. In bed all afternoon with high fever.

Thurs. 12   Have been up all day, but mumps are not much better; have a fine looking face, I tell you. Mrs. Zimmerman came in this morning to look upon my beautiful countenance; now I would think Fred would change his mind and look for a "handsomer girl". I think he will do to "tie to" if he sticks to me through these horrid "*mumps*". . . .

Mon. 16   Real sick today and dear Ted stayed home with me, all afternoon; he is so devoted. Brought me a "wedding-ring" this afternoon. Two pearls and a Bohemian Garnett; *very* pretty. The two pearls had been mother's, given her by Will F. of Guaymas, Mexico, having been brought from some of the South Sea Islands.[2]

Fri. 20   Got a letter from Mrs. Kate Akin today: the whole family are urging me to marry their "Teddie"; they all like me.

Tues. 24   Ted is 28 yrs. old today and time he was marrying, but not me Teddie; go get some other girl. You are the *best boy ever was*, but my heart fears *all* men. Still I went to town this afternoon and bought my wedding-hat, a very pretty "chip" with roses and lace; a cream and gray straw, very becoming.

Thurs. 26   I am 27 years old today. Went over to the Cemetery this afternoon and took flowers to Johnny and my little Mabel girl's graves. . . .

May

Tues. 1   Ted home all day not well. . . . Fred and Mr. F. walked up town with me a 1:30 P.M. I have coaxed Ted all day, to find some one else to marry and let me go free, but he won't. I have *felt blue* all day; and he is so good too.

Wed. 2   *At last* has come the *eventful 2nd of May* and I am *frightened to death*! Bright and beautiful day, and was up early. Fred *made me tell* Mr. Farnsworth, we would be *married at noon* and Oh! how *happy* Mr. F. *was*. Fred went to P. O. and left his horse for Substitute Carrier, then went for Marriage License and Minister. Little Margarette Pierson, Eva and little Ed. came this morning. Eva and I took Ed. up town and had his pictures taken, during the morning.

At noon, Fred and I *were married* by Rev. B. L. Smith; *Sad Hodgins* and *Eva Herman* standing with us.[3] Oh! how I *shook* and almost fainted: Oh! it seems so terrible. *Frank Carey*, friend and Chum of Fred's, was only other guest. *Mr. F.* and *little Ed., Katy Brady*—our servant— and little *Annie Butterly*, being only others to see us married; just a quiet wedding. After dinner, Eva went with Fred and I, to Leonard's Photo Gallery, where had *our pictures taken*, then to Santa Fe Depot, where Fred and I took 2 o'clock train for Kansas City, and as we drove by Zimmerman's, Dolly ran out *pulled off her slipper* and *threw it at us*. And tonight we are with Fred's neice Mrs. Brook Brown, 1709 Forest Ave, Kansas City, strangers to me. They have such a *sweet Baby boy*, Leland 17 months old.

Thurs. 3   Spent a very pleasant day with Mr. & Mrs. Brook Brown, in Kansas City. After dinner, Mr. & Mrs. Brown took us on a car out to West-port, where we saw Baron Nelson's fine home: we sat about on the green grass, hunting "four leaved" clovers. I found two, which I take for a "lucky omen." Perhaps I am a luckier girl than I feel: not one of the others found any "four-leafs." We had a lovely ride and came back to Brown's for supper and spend the evening, then took Car to Union Depot and took 9:20 P.M. Santa Fe train for home, arriving there about Mid-night to find house all lighted for us, but every one in bed. On the centre-table we found a set of dishes, as a present from Mr. Sad Hodgins, and a nice glass water set, from Katy Brady, our girl. Fred's happiness shines right out of his eyes and I think mine will, when I get over the fear caused by the unhappiness of my first marriage.

Fri. 4   Being very tired and getting home late, we did not get up this morning, until about 11 o'clock. Fred home with me: we are sending out our "*At Home*" cards. Has rained all day, in showers. *Not one* of my friends or relatives, nor even any of my acquaintances, know I am married, or even thinking of such a thing; it has been a happy day for both.

Sat. 5   Fred went to work today; we are "poor folks" and can't spend many days idle. Sent out more of our "At Home" cards. Fred is such a good boy, I'm sure we will be very happy; I am trying to "trust" and to drive out all fear from my heart. Mrs. Farnsworth told me a long time ago, that she was going to give me one of her boys, but I never expected to take one; that was before I was a widow and now it seems almost to have been prophetic; well I *love* the whole family. We received a letter of "Congratulations" today, from Brother Coit and wife of Chicago.

Thurs. 10   Went to Hamilton's Hall this afternoon, to State-meeting of "Woman Sufferagists". Miss Susan B. Anthony, Mrs. Childs of Iowa, Mrs. Anna L. Diggs and Mrs. Congressman Otis, spoke.[4] Mrs. D. made fine talk, full of fun. She is so cute and sweet. This evening Ted and I went; was music by Alhambra Mandolin Club, and speaking by Mayor Harrison, Mrs. Theresa Jenkins of Wy. and a splendid address by Rev. Anna H. Shaw.[5]

Tues. 15   Fred and I take charge of the home today—we will "run things" and Mr. Farnsworth will board with us. Mata Magerl spent afternoon with me. This evening, Fred and I went to the "Grand" to hear the new Star, Miss Ellen Beach Yaw—who is proving a rival to Patti—in Grand Opera, supported by Maximillian Dick Violinist and Miss Georgiella Lay, Pianist. It was just splendid and Miss Yaw is *such* a sweet singer and has most wonderful range of voice.[6]

Wed. 16   Mrs. Zimmerman called this evening. The Milehams and Bauers were offended, because *we did not ask them to our wedding*, so they have not called yet. We did not *ask any one at all*, to our wedding so they can get glad again. I met Fred at W. A. L. Thompson's, this evening, after work and we bought a new Gasoline Stove. Paid $24.00 for it and it is a fine one. Our *first purchase*, since marrying, in household furnishing. Ted and I came home together from the store.

Fri. 18   Cold today, had a *killing frost* last night. It seems so nice

| | to belong to some one who is kind, yet there is the old dread and fear that clings to me. I feel as if I may awaken to find my good husband just a dream. |
| Sat. 19 | Miss Lula Elliott called this P.M. Some few criticize me, for marrying so soon, but *Mr. F. says they are not worth minding, or paying any attention to. They do not know,* how I staid with, worked and supported a man who was so brutal and unkind, that he made me loathe him. A man who himself said no other woman would ever have staid with him and one whom many advised me to leave. I staid and took care of him, because I try to live a Christian life and now am free to marry whom I wish and *have married a good man*, in a *good* family and one I *believe* will be *good* to me. |

June

Sat. 2	. . . . Fred and I married one month today and we are not sorry we married.
Sat. 30	Went to Miss Brown's this morning to "*try on*" my new dresses, she is making for me. A very pretty white dotted swiss and Pink Chambray. I have got the "*Goodest, bestest*" Teddie. He just makes love to me all the time. He is so good and kind and gentle.

July

Tues. 3	The days all pass so happily, I have nothing to write. I can't free myself from the old horror of my other married life, but I think that the happiness of my present life will eventually drive out the memory of the other.
Fri. 17	I canned one Bu. of Tomatoes today and made 17 glasses of Grape jelly. This is work I do not trust the Girl to do.

August

| | |
| Thurs. 23 | I went up town this morning with Anna and Emma Durein. Fred, Anna and I rented a Bicycle and this evening, commenced to learn to ride. Fred went at it, with a *vengeance*, and *fell all over the wheel* and it *fell all over him* and I laughed until I had a *splitting head-ache*, so |

did not try to do much riding myself.

Fri. 24 Spent the forenoon with Anna D. and the Bicycle, over on Harrison Street and there mastered the machine, without any falls, and learned to ride alone. Fred and I took the wheel back to the store at 11:30.

October

Mon. 8 Fred and I went down to Jim Shaw's this evening; got weighed while there. Fred weighed 132½ and I, 122. Fred is 5 ft. 11 ¾ inches high and I 5 ft. 4 in. and have weighed 150.

Sat. 20 Cousins May, Jennie, Bessie, Fred and Frank Van Orsdol, came for supper this evening, after which, Fred and I went with them to Grand Opera House, to see "Uncle Tom's Cabin."[7] Brother Jim Farnsworth of San Marcial, N. Mex. came while we were away at the Theatre.

Sun. 21 Went to church this morning with Mr. Farnsworth and this evening, Fred and I went to Santa Fe depot, to meet Grace Akin—Fred's neice—from St. Louis. And I am afraid she has "queered" herself with me; anyway she hurt me very much by telling me I was "*very foolish*" to do my housework, instead of keeping a girl. Now my Fred is not able to hire help for me as long as I am able to do the work. I never saw Grace, before this evening.

November

Thurs. 1 We spent the afternoon at Ingleside, with Aunt Lou, and this evening went thro' a hard rain to the Theatre, to see Jim Corbett in "Gentleman Jack" and he was good too.[8]

Sat. 3 Big Republican Rally today. I belong to the "Woman's Republican Club," and so rode in the Parade this afternoon. Went up town with Fred this evening to see the Flambeau Parade.

Mon. 19 Busy with home duties and I have a large 9 room house to take care of.

Tues. 20 . . . . I have been made a "*District Visitor*" of the *Associated Charities,* and I spent all afternoon visiting the poor; found 3 children *out of school* for *want of clothing.*

December

Sat. 8	We again went to Mr. Stanford's this evening to a "Seance" and lots and lots of "Spirits" came, even to see me. And "*slate writing*" too. *Fraud* such *fraud*.
Fri. 14	Fred is certainly a model husband.
Sat. 15	Fred and I went up town this evening and done lots of shopping: one thing, I bought a new hat, black felt, with "black tips" Cerise-ribbon etc, quite becoming.
Thurs. 20	Went up town at noon to pick out a piano and after Fred got thro' work in late afternoon he took me among the Poor to distribute "Candy tickets" from Associated Charities, then took me up to E. B. Guild's where he bought me a "*Stark* and *Strack*" Piano, for Christmas present: solid Walnut case, $275.00. Plain, but pretty.
Sun. 23	Too busy to go to church this morning, so father went alone and just after he had gone, and Fred gone to Post Office, here came brother Coit and wife from Chicago; Angie I had never met before. Sister Minnie Akin, husband, and son Harry from Omaha: I had never met Henry nor Harry either. My breakfast dishes were not washed, nor much of my other work done, for I was cooking and looking for them this evening. But we have had such a *jolly happy* day and *I am glad* they *are here. They are all so lovely.*
Tues. 25	"*Christmas Day*", *cold* and *cloudy*, but our *happy hearts made the day seem all aglow*. While sitting down to dinner, my cousins Manley, & Henry Anderson and wife—Tillie—came from my old home, Winfield, Ks. and so I have them all and *the house is brimful.* Mr. & Mrs. Geo. Baur and Mr. & Mrs. Mileham, spent evening with us. Minnie brought Fred candy and me a Lunch-cloth, Angie gave me a Pin cushion and Coit gave Fred a neck tie. Oh what a jolly happy Christmas, has been this, the *first* Christmas of our married life. And this was my dinner. A *14 pound Turkey*, cooked to a turn, *by my own hands, as was all my dinner,* fried oysters, mashed potatoes, peas, celery, radishes, lettuce, salad dressing Cranberry sauce, Apple butter, Grape jelly, Pumpkin-pie, Mince Pie and layer jell cake. And of course bread, butter and gravy. And all pronounced my dinner *very good.* My house is so full tonight, I was almost at my "wits end" as to how to sleep them but have gotten all to bed and now, happy tired and sleepy I go to my own.

Mon. 31   I ironed all afternoon and am tired tonight. And tonight I say goodbye to the "old Year." *1894* has been so happy; one of sweet content because of a husband who is *very* kind: is thoughtful of my comfort and gentle, always; yet the *spectre* of my *wretchedly unhappy* life with another, still haunts me; it *will come up* and make me afraid, that I will awaken to find my present happiness only a dream.

[1895]

"Just a busy day at home" sums up most of this year; she is settling comfortably into her marriage. Martha kept herself occupied by constant visiting, and taking care of the house. She also did a great deal of canning. Most of the entries for June, July, and August are records of food preparation, and have been omitted. There is no reference to pregnancy during this year. Many of the entries are very short, indicating that she had little time—or perhaps inclination—to record her days. Throughout the year Martha attended various lectures and concerts. She was eclectic in her taste, and apparently eager to hear any lecturer (especially on temperance) or artist who was in town.

January

Wed. 9 — Lots of skaters on the river these days. My father never allowed me to skate when a girl at home, lest I get hurt and now my husband is going to teach me.

Thurs. 10 — My good Fred *bought me a pair of skates* today and this evening we went to the river skating. A most beautiful evening—full moon—and warm. Several hundred skaters on the river and *how much I enjoyed it*, tho' only learning.

February

Mon. 11 — Fred & I, with Anna D. went to the river to skate this evening. *Very dark* and *many holes* and was *really dangerous*; ice was not safe, in many places, for us to skate together, but a good many skating and the danger only seemed to add *zest* to the sport. Anyway *we had a fine time.*

March

Mon. 4 — The care of my home has kept me busy today.

Tues. 5 — Just a workin' today as usual.

Wed. 6 — We "Associated Charities" workers met in Mr. T. H. Bain's Office this afternoon, to *investigate* our President Mr. Russ, whom some acuse of wrong doing. We found him *free of any guilt whatever. I have perfect confidence* in him. Mrs. Durein, Anna and Emma Fred & I went to the Grand this evening to see *Louis Morrison in Faust. Good.*

Fri. 8   Busy as usual. How I wish I could forget I had ever been married before—it haunts me and the *horror* of that *unhappy* life, casts a shadow on my happy life now.

Mon. 18   Busy and happy; have the best husband ever lived; wish I could love him, as he deserves to be loved.

Tues. 19   Another busy day. Fred is so good and has the dearest father; a Saint if there was *ever* one.

Wed. 20   A quiet day, in a quiet home, that is a blessing to any woman. I feel I have passed thro' trials, that have made an old woman of me *and I am but* a girl in years.

Tues. 26   A beautiful day, but very warm. "Hootsy" our lovely Maltese kitten, became a mother today, of 3 "measley" little kittens; one is black and white, the other two on the brindle order, *and my! but she is a proud* mother.

April

Mon. 1   Rained most all day and snowed some about noon. And now comes trouble in the family. Kate Akin wants to bring her daughter Minnie Brown up here, from Ponca Okla. to be confined. She did not write me, but wrote father just as if Fred and I had no right here. We have full charge here, yet she completely ignores us. Minnie would pay board, but she says nothing of her own board, and I would have all the added work to do, which I simply cannot do: it would be too much expense for Fred and more hard work than I can do: beside father does not want them to come and there is no need. No reason why she cannot be Confined at home; and if there was, she could go to her husband's mother. I wrote Kate today we could not take them, *but would move and they have* the house.[1]

Tues. 2   Have commenced to clean house and must do the work alone.

Fri. 5   I drowned two of "Hootsie's" kittens this afternoon and it nearly broke my heart; but I don't want so many cats on the place and thought *one* was enough for her; Fred has promised to do so, nearly two weeks, but could not get up courage, so I did it myself, and no one need tell *me* cats *can't count*; our Hootsie cat *can.* I went to her "nest," while she was absent and took out the two kittens, and this evening I went to her home nest, to look at the other kitten and she was curled up happy with all three: she had missed her two babies and hunted for them, found them in the bucket of water, fished them out and carried them back to her nest but they were dead. Oh! it was so dreadfully pathetic and so almost human I *vow* I will *never* do such a thing again. I made Fred bury the kittens while she was again absent from nest.

Sat. 6   A rainy day; Our "Hootsie" cat, misses her two drowned kittens and comes in the house, looking about everywhere, crying pitifully. Father noticed it and asked the reason and when I told him, he said *"Oh! poor cat, poor cat;"* then looking at me said, *"lets have no more drownings."* We all feel dreadful about it.

Sun. 7   And still our "Hootsie" cat comes in the house, crying for her two drowned babies; it seems almost *human intelligence* and *mother love*; she still has one kitten why not be content, but no, she must come crying, to the house and look all about for the others, and *break all our hearts* with her *pitiful wailings*; catch *me drowning any more kittens.*

Sun. 21   . . . . Fred and I went to church this evening—First Christian—and Fred *"made the good confession"; united with the church by Confession and I'm so happy. We walked home with Mrs. James Burgess after church, she having no one with her.*

Mon. 22   Busy, busy, busy.

Tues. 23   Hot day and I was out all afternoon trying to sell tickets for Church entertainment.

Wed. 24   My good hubby is 29 yrs. old today. . . .

Fri. 26   Today I am 28 years old and my Teddie brought me a sweet gift, of a great quantity of Pansys and Carnations. I *feel* like a kid.

Sat. 27   Baking and cleaning and my usual Saturday's work, has made a busy day for me.

Sun. 28   Father and aunt Lucy went to Church with Fred and I, this evening and after the Sermon, *Fred was Baptized* by our minister Rev. B. L. Smith, who married us a year ago. Also married me to my first husband and preached his funeral and preached funeral of my little daughter.

Most of the entries for June, July, and August are records of food preparation.

June

Wed. 12   Went to Depot, after dinner with father who took the 3:35 P.M. train for Santa Ana, Calif. and other points, on a visit to his daughter and other relatives, and tonight Fred and I are alone, for the first time in our more than a year of married life: father goes over the Santa Fe.

Sat. 29   A drizzily day: went to town in afternoon and Fred met me at the "Fair"—store—and gave me $40.00 dollars and I went to Building and Loan paid $14.41, then to Dreyer's and paid $22.00 Grocery Bill, he paid some other bills and we had $2.05 left out of $80.00 some dollars. He had lots of debts when we married.

Sun. 30   We went to Transfer Sta. after dinner to meet Mrs. Herman and go to Garfield Park, but she did not come and we came back home. Got letter from home saying sister has 11 pound girl born 27.[2]

August

Sun. 11   Quite worn out today. Mr. & Mrs. J. Mileham spent afternoon with us. My Teddie makes me sad because he tries to keep things from me: he is a boy who has never saved his money, and when we married, had many debts; he knows I worry over "Bills" and trys to keep the amount of his debts from me and how am I to be of help to him, if he does not confide in me: he is so good too.

September

Fri. 13   . . . . Fred's half-sister—Mrs. Kate Akin—came from Okla. at 5 o'clock to visit us awhile.

Sat. 14   Emma Durein went down town with me this afternoon. I went to the Buildg. and Loan Association and paid $35.41 on the home place—the 4 Boys built the House for their parents—and Fred is paying *all* this month and may continue—I met Fred at P.O. and rode home with him. Uncle Marian Van. came to dinner today and gave me a Bu. of apples.

October

Mon. 14	A lovely, bright, warm, Fall day: Mrs. Boyle called this afternoon: she is so pleasant, but has such a Scotch brogue is hard to understand. Coit Farnsworth writes, we should pay $25.00 per month rent to father and says it is our duty to stay here and do it: we now keep up all the expenses of the place and make double payments on the house and I think that quite enough; and beside, it would be very foolish for us two young folks, just starting in life to pay such a rent, when we could take a small house for $6.00 per month, by going out a little way: and I do not intend to pay any such rent. We had far better buy a home and make payments on it. Coit don't show much business tack, to suggest such a thing, or else must think me a fool. He is too "bossy." But it is Kate and Min's doings. Kate would not come keep house for father when he wanted her and now she *wants* to come and he would rather have us and she is determined to run us out.
Wed. 23	Got a very *saucy* letter, from brother Coit today. Now if *he* is going to *run* things, we will move out, and he can *run* the house in the ground if he wants to.
Sat. 26	Fred and I drove down to John Lowe's on Chandler St. this evening, to see him about a piece of property he owns out in Lowman Hill. Are just beginning to get Fred's debts straightened out and now we will have to go in debt to buy a home, but it will beat $25.00 per month rent and we will be independent. We have not got but *five cents* in our purse tonight, but the Good Lord will help us get a home and we are willing to work hard.

November

Fri. 1	Busy very busy and troubled because Coit must be so unfair and I know it hurts father, who is very fond of me and wants us to stay with him.
Wed. 20	A most beautiful day. We drove down to Mr. J. Lowe's this evening to tell him we had decided to buy his property at 1017 Brooks Ave, for $600.00. A pretty 3 room

Cottage and two lots, East front. We will build another room. And yet we have not a cent to do a thing with, but I'll manage it with the Lord's help.

Fri. 22   Very cold—such sudden changes. And now I am busy planning for the new home. I am sorry to leave father, but Kate and daughter Grace will keep house for him.

Thurs. 28   "Thanksgiving Day" and in spite of our troubles, the unfairness of brother Coit and Kate's selfishness, and unjustness of the whole thing, we have a World of blessings to be *thankful* for and we had Aunt Lucy S. come spend the day with us. Of course I had Turkey and a fine one, and Cranberries, Celery, Peas, Potatoes, Mustard Chow Pickles, Currant Jelly, Honey, Biscuit and Ralston Bread, Peaches, Fruit Cake and Mince Pie.

Received a letter, telling me of the death on 24 inst. of a very dear cousin—Sada Anderson—almost 17 yrs. old, of Typhoid; this saddened the day much for me cloudy.

December

Tues. 10   Received two *hind quarters* of an Antelope, today from my father in Colorado. My! but it is fine. Pa is a great man to hunt, and a fine marksman, and when a girl at home we use to live on wild game.

Wed. 11   Busy day. Oh! how we are enjoying the Venison Pa sent us tho' Antelope is not nearly so good as Buffalo-meat, which we *lived on* away back in the '70's, when I was a little girl and Kansas was all Buffalo and Indians.

[1896]

By this time Fred had become active in the First Christian Church: much of their spare time was spent going to church services, and Martha often went several times during the week to Bible classes. Fred was not so avid in attendance, but he went often enough to be considered an active member, and Martha did not fault his absences.

January

Fri. 24   Our neighbor, Elwood Mileham, died at 2 o'clock this morning, and little George Roehr died at 4 o'clock this afternoon. My little Mabel Inez, my own "wee" treasure, would be four years old today, if living: my heart will never cease its longing, for the *precious one*.

February

Mon. 3   A fine day and Mrs. Matthews called this afternoon. Fred & I went to Mr. A. D. Robbins Office—Notary Public—this evening at 7:30 and Met Mr. & Mrs. J. A. Lowe and made the first payment—$50.00—on our new home, 1017 Brooks Ave. It seems too bad, to leave father and to take Fred from the *only* home he has *ever* had, but we can't pay $25.00 per month rent and keep up all expenses beside, and sister Kate will keep house for father tho' will make it expensive for him. But it is all her and Coits doings and we shall be glad to be free from so much expense and one is *so* independent in their own home.

Mon. 24   Grace Akin came at noon from Omaha and her mother will come later: are getting in a hurry to push Fred and I out. When father wanted Kate to keep house for him, she would not do it, and now she is out of a home with her son-in-law, she is determined to come here and make Fred & I get out. Well we are very willing, only do not like the manner and hate to hurt poor father, as it will. Cousin Manly Anderson came this afternoon and staid over night with us.

March

Fri. 27   Fred not working this afternoon and we went to Case's Law office, to meet Eva Herman and her Lawyer, Mrs. L. O. Case and over to Court House at 1 o'clock P.M. where Eva's divorce trial was to be tried. Eva's divorce was not contested and she was granted *everything*: her husband ran off a year ago, with another woman, who was the mother of five children. When we got to the Court House, Mrs. Tillie Sloan-Hitt, who sued her husband O. J. Hitt, for divorce, had her trial called first and it being contested, took the whole afternoon. Ol Hitt was a brute and ought to have been ashamed to have appeared in Court; he was caught stealing from his employer and his employer was in Court as witness against him; he was proven an adulterer, by the girl he wronged appearing against him. Eva's trial was called at 5:40 and divorce granted in five minutes. Eva with us to Church party this evening at John Gardener's in Lowman Hill. Had a good time.

April

Fri. 3   Warmer today. Fred had an awful heavy mail and did not get home for dinner until 1:05. We drove out to our home this evening to make some more garden. Kate Akin came on the evening train and now we won't be long in getting out. Grace has done all she could to hurry us out; giving me many hints to hurry up: she is so disagreeable.

Sat. 4   We moved a load of our "stuff," (canned fruit, empty cans etc.) out to our home tonight, on Brooks Ave. We just have built on a new kitchen and live in that until our renters can find a house to move into.[1]

Wed. 8   Fred "laid off" this afternoon, to finish our moving. He took me up town, where I made a few necessary purchases, then took car, and *he* drove out, to our new home. *Oh! how hard it rained.* And tonight we ate supper in our *own home* and are *independent* of any one. Spent evening, in with Robys.

Thurs. 9   A beautiful day and I have been cleaning and settling our few possessions in our one room, and tonight we are quite "cozy": the Robys who live in the house, have not yet found a place to move and we are living in one room until they get out, but they let me put my Piano in their parlor. We have a set of dishes and few silver-spoons and a splendid Gasoline stove, then we bought a kitchen table and two kitchen chairs and with these we will do "light housekeeping" until we get our house in the shape we want it; we will just camp for this Summer: we have a mattress and plenty of bedding and will put right down on the floor as have no bedstead, and we will sleep "soundly and well" and are Oh! so independent; here, Coit cannot say "do this or that" and Kate cannot come in and "run us off." Coit, Kate, Grace and Min, thought we would have to pay $25.00 per month rent; we had nothing and could not buy a place, but while we *have* nothing, yet we have bought a place, tho' some of them doubt it and think we are lying, but they don't know who they are dealing with. I am able to run my own affairs. I can take care of *myself* and Fred too, if I have to.

Fri. 10   *Home* yes spent the day in my own home, mine and Teddie's, and made garden, for we have two lots and can have a good, small garden. Awful windy. The home at 201 Topeka Ave was the only home Fred ever had and only place he ever lived until we bought this and to move from that large pleasant home into this "little Cottage" must make him lonely, yet he seems so happy and contented; but I know it hurt poor father very much and I dared not tell him we were going to move; had to just "run away." We all ate dinner together and when Tea-time came, Fred and I were gone and father did not know; it hurt me to do it, but I had to; father just *would not* consent to our going, and Kate & Grace were determined we had to and lied about us, to friends. Father told me if Fred & I ever left, we left *against his will.* He wanted us to stay and keep house for him and Kate to move into her own little home and he would help her there but she *absolutely would not* and thought she had a right to come in and drive us out.

Sat. 11   Another awfully windy day; So nice to be in our own home; why I have nothing at *all* to do: cook for two, wash dishes for two and play rest of time.

Sun. 12   Rained most of the day and I visited in the rooms of Mr. & Mrs. Chas. Roby with they and Bess Roby. This evening Fred & I walked down to Church; we have some distance to go now.

Mon. 13   "Love in a Cottage" and *what happiness* it brings, when that *Cottage* is *yours*.

Sat. 25   Am reading Camille by Dumas. Don't like it; terrible Book I think.[2]

May

Sat. 9   We have nothing in our home, and are very "close run," yet we are buying our home and are happy. I have my bare floors as white as soap, hot water and a scrub brush will make them. I have one pretty Wolf rug, which I placed in front of a Bench I made myself and covered, then I have a box, covered and two chairs. I got at grocery, common manila wrapping paper and made window shades, and we have our Piano, and we have music in our home and are happy: we are just "camping" this Summer; we will "furnish" this Fall, when we have "saved up" enough money.

Tues. 19   Rained awful hard at noon, almost cloud-burst, flooded everything and water broke thro' Cement of cellar and filled it about 3 feet. Became so dark, really needed a lamp. Glad Fred was home for dinner.

Mon. 25   Called on Mrs. W. C. Baker this afternoon, but not home. Mrs. Fell and little "sweet Marie", Harry Bair & family and Frank Roby called this evening, and later we women folks went across to Charlie Roby's where we met a *real live Morman*: Mila's cousin, on a missionary trip from Utah: a fine looking young man, but Oh! the Mormons. *Adulterers.* His name is Bair and seems very pleasant.

June

Sat. 27   Little Freda Gilbert, one year old today. And 4 years ago today, the Angels came and took, my "wee" precious, girlie. Oh! that she might come to me again.

Mon. 29   We went down to father's this evening. He is such a dear old man. I wish I felt free to go see him often; but Kate and Grace are very cool, and seem to resent our coming and many times go away, perhaps intending to before we came, but anyway they don't like me. Kate says, I "have too much dirty, nasty independence"

July

Tues. 28   Fred got his "over-time" money from the Government today, $139.00 so I went to town with him and took the money to pay some bills, and then went to Mr. Donnell's where I finished paying Mr. D. for the carpenter work he did for us. I then went over and bought an oak lounge and a little oak rocker, of Mrs. Chas. Roby, as they leave soon for Calif. and are selling their household goods. . . .

Wed. 29   Just a workin' in my own little home, for a man who is very good to me.

October

Sat. 3   I had such a *frightful* dream last night; in it, I stood with my sister, beside a coffin and an open grave in Floral, our old home: the coffin was in a pine box and I could not see who was in it and while I had the impression her husband was in it, all day long I have been very sad, for I have wondered if it might not mean that death was near to me, for I have not been really well all summer and many have thought I was going into Consumption. I worked so hard all day, packing our trunk and cooking to start on our happy Vacation trip, to Colo., Monday next and at 4:35 P.M. a "Messenger Boy" galloped past the house and instinctively, as if some one said to me, "*he has a Message for you*" I ran out and called him back and the message *was for me*, answering my dream. A Telegram, telling me my sister's husband was dead. Fred came and we took the 11:45 P.M. Santa Fe train for Winfield. Oh! how terrible the shock of it, *no one can know.*

Sun. 4   Oh! such a sad journey. After leaving Newton Ks. this morning the Conductor came into the car and I told Fred he was my uncle: some way I recognized him, tho' had never seen him in my life and never but once saw a picture of him and that many years ago. Fred asked him his name and found indeed he was my uncle Harry Wilcox and when we told him who and where we were going and why he said he had a funeral party in the Coach ahead and it proved to be my sister and little family and stepmother; we had ridden many miles with them, we now having passed Wichita and their car joined our train at Newton: it was a heart-breaking meeting. We arrived in Winfield 8:38 and were transferred to the Frisco to go out to Floral. Met Sam Gilbert and family here and having 3 hours to wait, Fred & I walked out to aunt Till Weber's. Aunt Till and cousin Emma Adams went with us to Floral at 11:45 P.M. arriving at 12:10 and going direct to Baptist Church where funeral was preached: large crowd. From Cemetery we all went to uncle Joe Anderson's and staid all night.[3]

Mon. 5   Oh! my heart aches so all the time; it is so pathetic to see my sister, only 27 left alone with 3 little children and she so like a child herself. Yesterday, as in my dream, I stood with my sister beside an open grave in Floral, a coffin in a pinebox beside the grave, but I was not in it. *But how gladly* I would have taken Lyman's place in the Coffin: my poor sister needed him, so very much more than Fred needed me. And the poor fellow looked forward so much to our coming on a visit to them. He had been complaining some time, but only in bed about 10 days with Typhoid fever and only two days before, my father wrote danger was passed and he was doing fine, then the shocking news of his death, which I received first in a dream. Ma, May & children and Fred & I have been at Uncle Joe Anderson's all day. And my heart aches so with sorrow. We stay over night here tonight again.

Tues. 6   Uncle Joe and aunt Mat Anderson took us, in a big wagon, all over to Uncle Zeke Rogers this morning, to spend the day and we stay all night tonight. It is so sad I can hardly live. We drove by the old farm, this morning, where I grew up: strangers are there now. We also drove by Prairie Grove school house where as a little girl I passed many happy days in school, but the old school house, full of sweet memories grew too small and is sitting away to one side and used as a dwelling, while a new School-house, larger and finer and with a Bell in its Cupalo takes its place. And too the Prairies, where I use to herd cattle and be my father's "Cow Boy" for 7 or 8 years are now all under cultivation. I saw no Antlered Deer, bounding acros the Prairies; no Indians passing, to say "How! How!" to the white man's Pappoose sitting on her Pony, watching her father's Herd. No, *everything* is changed now.

Thurs. 8 Yesterday in all our drive I did not see a single Haystack and prairies used to be dotted with them, and I had many a hard run to keep the cattle away from them, so not to tear the hay out with their horns. And many and many a time I have "shinned" up these stacks and turned a "Summersault" off of them and slide down until do almost as much damage as the cattle. And with many girl friends, who were "Cow boys" like myself, I have run many a horse race on these dear old prairies and many a "Jack Rabbit" has panted for breath before he got away, for some of my ponies were fleet footed. I could wish for those days again only one would *again* have to "grow up" and go thro' much sorrow. . . .

Mon. 12 We with May & children took 8:30 morning train up to Winfield and went to cousin Henry Anderson's where we spent the day and stay tonight. This afternoon we took the children up town and had their pictures taken and little Freda—named for Fred—14 months old could not be kept still a moment: she is a wonderfully bright child. May and I also had our pictures taken together. My sister does not look as if she could live a great while: poor girl.

Sun. 18 We arrived in Topeka, at 4:30 this morning and walked out home, 3 miles, went to bed and slept until noon. Oh! so tired. Fred went to P. O. after dinner and got our mail and received a half-rate Pass to Colo., from Mr. C. S. Gleed. . . .

Mon. 19 Very busy packing our trunk and getting things in shape to leave, for another two weeks, for now we have a Pass, we are going to Springfield Colo, to visit my father. We went down and spent the evening, with father Farnsworth and from there to Santa Fe depot where took 11:45 P.M. train for Newton, Kans.

Tues. 20 Arrived in Newton, Ks. at 5:40 this morning and at 8 o'clock went out to Uncle Harry Wilcox and gave them a surprise. . . . At noon, Ma, Sister May and children, came up from Winfield. . . . We with May & children and Ma, took 4:30 train for Colorado, all going to depot with us.

Wed. 21 Arrived in Lamar Colorado at 3 o'clock A.M. and few minutes later Pa met us there and was greatly surprised to see Fred & I as did not know we were coming. We all went over to the Hotel and after Breakfast, started "overland" 50 miles for Springfield, Colo., down in Baca Co. Being so many of us, was too much of a load to make the drive in one day, so we camped this evening on Butte Creek. Such a lovely day.

Thurs. 22 We were all up early this morning and on the rode: is very cold and looks like snow, and Pa hurried his ponies over the fine roads, until we reached Mr. Smart's ranch, where we all got out and "warmed," then continued our journey reaching Belle View Ranch,—Pa's place—at 10:30 A.M. and glad to be home so can get a little rest.

Fri. 23 We, with Pa and Vella, went over town with May and children this morning and staid at her house for dinner, but all came back to Pa's for supper and to stay over night. And now begins the hard part of life for poor little sister; to battle with the world for her bread and butter and care for three little children, the oldest 10 years and youngest 14 months. She has a little home and a little store that did well, with a man at the head of it, but she will never be able to continue it.

Tues. 27 May & children went over to Springfield and Fred and I went home with her and stayed all night: her little home seems so lonely and I do not see how she is ever to live in it alone. Lyman was such a good man; and did everything in the world for her; humored and petted always and he bore all responsibility for everything so that she practically had "not a care on earth" and now, I am afraid the burden will be too great for her to bear.

Thurs. 29 Snowing and blowing awful, but *not at all cold*. May & children and Fred and I all came to Pa's to stay all night. Storm cleared away, by middle of the afternoon. Everything is Politics and we must hasten home, that Fred may not lose his vote for we are hoping for McKinley's Election.

November

Mon. 2 We took the train, at Lamar, Colorado, at 2 o'clock this morning and arrived in Topeka, over the Santa Fe, just 14 hours later, at 4:30 and went directly to the P. O. where Fred reported for duty tomorrow-morning, got his horse from Substitute Carrier, and went with me to W. A. L. Thompson's, hardware Store, where we bought a "Majestic Range" then to get a few groceries and home. Election tomorrow, has every one strung to high tension. The Democrats are sure of their man, while we Republicans are sure of McKinley's Election and hope and pray for it, but all is unrest.

Tues. 3 Election day and excitement runs high. Fred went to work today. Our new Range came out this morning and makes my kitchen look like a Parlor.

I pray McKinley may win in today's Election.

Wed. 4 Some time after Mid-night, last night, I *dreamed* my *sister came* to *me* and told me, *McKinley had been elected* President of U.S., in yesterday's Election. The dream awakened me, I turned over, *fell asleep* and *almost immediately, dreamed* that an *Indian came to me* and *told me McKinley was elected: it was all so vivid that I awakened* Fred and *told him* of *my two dreams* and told him if *I dreamed* it *again*, I would believe the *"news" true*. I again went to sleep and *dreamed* that *a very large, colored woman* came to me and *told me* that *McKinley was Elected*. And after Breakfast and Fred had gone to work, as I stepped out the kitchen door and saw Mrs. Dilbert (*a colored woman weighing nearly 300*) passing thro' the alley and asked her if she had heard any Election news. She replied that *had heard McKinley was elected* and *hoped to the Lord it was true, so we would have better times*. I rode to town with Fred at noon.

Thurs. 5 Kansas has gone to the "Pops," but McKinley was Elected and we Republicans are "too full of joy for utterance"; Oh! it is such good news.[3] We spent the evening with H. and Lizzie Bair.

December

Thurs. 31 The Old Year of '96, is leaving us, as in sorrow, for bitter tears are falling, (a heavy rain.)

Has rained very hard most all afternoon. We thank the dear Father for the many blessings of the Old year, tho' are hearts are heavy with sorrow over Lyman's death and we cannot understand *why* such a good man was taken from his family, who need him so much.

[1897–1902]

The years 1897–1899 were generally uneventful ones for Martha, and have been cut in the interest of space. She continued to make daily entries throughout this period, and the concerns evident in previous and future years are here: she marks the anniversaries of her sister's death and her child's death, she continues to be very active in the church, the Democrats still cause most of the country's woes. Her failure to have more children is a constant source of sorrow for her, and she comments on the loneliness of a childless household. She deals with this sense of loss by working in her lodge, The Knights and Ladies of Security, getting elected in June of 1897 to the second highest office, and by taking up painting in 1899. Running throughout these years too are repeated comments on Fred's kindness and generosity; her marriage is a happy one. The extended family continues to be central; she and Fred spend a lot of time with Freda Gilbert, their niece, and both are saddened by the death of Fred's father on July 26, 1899. In September of 1899 they start to build the house at 220 W. 10th Street that was to be their home for the rest of their lives. They move on November 28th, and one must assume that some of the next year was spent arranging the new house.

Unfortunately, the diaries for 1900, 1901, and 1902 are missing. The volumes written in later years give little clue to her life during this period, except for one newspaper clipping on Carry Nation dated Feb. 18, 1919. Martha has inscribed on the side of this clipping: "I was one of her 'crusaders' and took food to her when she was in jail for smashing. She was a good woman."

Other events of these years that might have interested Martha: In January 1900 a woman killed herself and two children because of whiskey; Buffalo Bill's Wild West Show came to Topeka on September 23, 1900; McKinley was reelected in November of 1900; in January of 1901 Topeka women successfully fought a bill designed to rescind their municipal suffrage; Carry Nation extended her activities to Topeka, was charged with malicious destruction of property, got hit over the head with a broomstick by the wife of a "joint" keeper while followed by a howling mob, on February 5 smashed up the Senate saloon, and on Feb. 6, 1901 caused the closing of all Topeka bars; Queen Victoria died (January 23, 1901); McKinley was shot (September 7th); Teddy Roosevelt became president; in 1902, the Boer War ended and Kitchener received 50,000 pounds for winning; in July of the same year meat prices soared, and by December 25 smallpox had broken out in Topeka. One less public event was the arrival of sister May and her three children. Martha's earlier comment that a

Left: Poster of Carrie Nation. *Right*: Hall of Fame Saloon, Topeka, 1908.

woman could not manage the store in Colorado alone evidently proved to be correct. May, Zaidee, James and Freda are all living with Fred and Martha as the diary resumes in 1903.

[*1903*]

January

Thurs. 1   A cloudy day, but not cold: Sister not home today and I made no big dinner so we were alone with Zaidee, James and Freda. Fred and I spent the evening at Mr. C. Goddard's, playing "*Ping-Pong*". . . .

The past year has been one of many blessings, as well as one of much toil and sacrifice and I pray the good Master to prosper us throughout this year.

Fri. 2   Home and very busy as I have all the work for a family of six to do. Sister is away all day and many evenings and Zaidee also, not returning after school until her mother returns. I get no help from her.

Mon. 5   Washed rather a large washing this morning and ironed all that was needed then went to the Beardsley Studio and painted all afternoon.[1] How I love painting. Uncle Geo. Van Orsdol of Silver Lake here to supper this eve.

Tues. 6   Spent all afternoon at the Beardsley Studio painting. Mr. B. and his mother gave me a lovely Boston Fern.

Mon. 12   Down to Zero this morning first time this winter, and a wind that makes it seem colder. 18 years ago today, I was proposed to by W. A. Finch. What a funny world; then I thought him quite *the* one. I've married twice since then and he is married, and neither of us at the old home.

Tues. 20   Clear but cold wind blowing. I took Oneta G.[2] to town in afternoon and up to Ladies of G. A. R. where I was re-obligated having been suspended for dues. We drove thro' City a little and then home it being too chilly to enjoy driving. This is 33rd Anniversary of my Mother's death and sister Belle's birth.

Wed. 21   Fred & I took the children, Oneta G. and Russell W.[3] to the Mid-Winter Exposition at Auditorium.[4] A very nice show it is and we all enjoyed the evening very much.

Sat. 24   Chilly but otherwise a nice day. Eleven years ago today, the dear Lord gave me a precious baby daughter, which he soon took Home again and left me broken hearted.

Mon. 26   Took Onita Gilbert down to the Beardsley Studio where

	I painted in afternoon, then took her to "Mail & Breeze" office and left her with sister, then came home and got supper.[5] Russell with us, yet.
Tues. 27	Have been very busy, as 8 in family would make any woman who does all her own work.
Fri. 30	Onita went home, today—noon, to Arkansas City, and I took her to the train. Mr. Wilcox came home this eve, took supper with us and Russell went home with him. So tonight we're alone.
Sat. 31	A most beautiful day. I washed & ironed and scrubbed and baked seven *large* loaves of delicious bread. Freda churned and we had nice butter and fresh buttermilk. Children went to town and Fred & I alone for dinner.

February

Mon. 16	Snow, snow, everywhere; white and beautiful; with a bright sun, shining overhead; calm and quiet, but coldest morning of the winter: 6 below Zero.
Tues. 17	Very cold—12 below Zero this morning. Fred commenced his vacation this morning so not out in the cold.
Thurs. 19	Still cold but 4 above Zero this morning: didn't go to Club today because Fred was home all day with me: he is such a good husband, I would not leave him home alone to go to *any* club.

March

Sat. 7	I've been lazy today, doing nothing but my tatting,[6] since I did not feel extra good. I had a "*proposal*" 19 yrs ago today from Maurice Carmen.
Sun. 8	A *most beautiful* day Fred's day at home so he staid home and "made love" to me.[7] Sister & children went away for the afternoon and evening.
Wed. 11	Another nice day and I spent the afternoon painting at the Beardsley Studio; finished a large pretty Homestead piece.
Wed. 18	A grand day except for the wind; had garden plowed. With Mr. & Mrs. Mathews, went all thro' the *Santa Fe Shops* in the afternoon and also *Wolfe's Packing house.* How *very* wonderful are both: how very great the ingenuity God has bestowed upon man.
Thurs. 19	Mr. Mathews left us this morning. Had a very hard rain

last night and much cooler in consequence. I spent the afternoon at Mrs. Forsythe's at meeting of our little Coterie Club to meet her Sister-in-law and niece, Mrs. Forsythe and Miss Kate. We were entertained with *Graphaphone* music. I cannot *begin* to conceive, how the mind of man could *invent* such a *wonderful* machine. Mrs. Henderson and Carl and Mrs. Holt and children spent the evening with us.

Fri. 20   Bright and clear but cool. I kept little Robert Holt this afternoon, while his mother went to the Studio to paint.

Sat. 21   Home all day: not doing much. I felt nervous and bad all day because my sister whom we have been keeping for nearly four years with her three children, has made up her mind to move. We've done so much for her and she does not seem to appreciate it at all. She does not act kindly toward us and has not for a long time; going to work this A.M. said not a word to us, but children commenced packing things to move. I cannot conceive of any reason for her acting so. I'm most sorry for James—12—and Freda—7—who will be much neglected.

Sun. 22   Fred's day at home: sister busy all day packing her things. She works all day in Mail & Breeze Office and will be away from the children all day and so I can't see why she wishes to move. She is a *most strange* woman. Treats me always more like a *stranger*, than as a *sister*, who has made many sacrifices for her.

Wed. 25   Fred got Mr. Cook's delivery wagon and took big load of things to sister this eve. I gave her a heating-stove, Bed-lounge, dining chairs, small table, little coal dish-pan and ten dollars worth of groceries.

Fri. 27   Cold and sort of rainy. Children took horse and went after their uncle Fred after school and he took them down home to their mother near 5th & Jackson where they have 2 upstairs rooms, a very poor, shut in place for any one, much less children.

Sun. 29   A very pretty day tho' little cool. Fred's day to work. The house is very quiet without the children, but their mother sees it is best for them to finish the two months more of school out here, and so has decided to leave them with me, and they will come out in the morning again. The children came out this evening instead of tomorrow-morn: they seemed as glad to be back as tho' gone 2 months instead of less than 2 days.[8]

May

Sun. 24   Cloudy; rained last night. In evening Flora and I left children with Fred and we went with Mrs. Potee and Mrs. Carpenter—both colored—to the colored M.E. church, to hear the Quadroon Evangelist, Isabelle Horton, who is but 16 years old. She is very pretty and a most earnest speaker, tho' her voice is most too childish and shrill. She preached a very good sermon.

Fri. 29   Has rained most of day. River is away out of banks. Terrible flood. I pray for safety of our loved ones.

Sat. 30   River is more than 6 mile wide: most of County bridges gone. All North Topeka flooded and more than *four thousand* homes in water; some ten thousand people compelled to move out of their Homes. *Terrible terrible.* This being *Decoration Day* Fred has half Holiday and we drove down to the river; the flood can never be described. I have 5 families of relatives in the flood and know not their fate. We called at Durein's and at Mr. Luce's to see the Carey family rescued from N. side.

Sun. 31   Commenced raining at dark last night and continues now, at bedtime. All day it has not ceased and many must perish of cold and exposure, who are on roofs and in tree-tops. Fred went down but could hear no word of our relatives. Rescue work has gone on all day. Oh! if I could but shut out the terrible sight of those ugly black waters: they say the river is from 6 to 8 miles wide and many houses are being washed away. My heart aches as if it would break with sorrow for those poor people.

June

Wed. 3   Cold and cloudy. Aunt Nan spent day with us. She and uncle Frank Van Orsdol were rescued Mon. afternoon, but can hear no word of any of others.[9]

Sat. 27   A beautiful day like the one, *eleven* years ago today, when God sent his angels to take from me my precious Babe; my little daughter the only child He ever gave me and allowed me to keep her such a short time: five months, I kept and loved and cherished with all the love a mother's heart is capable of, then God took her Home again and all these years I have so longed for her. I wonder sometimes, why mothers are given such love and cannot keep these Babes.

September

Wed. 9
Rained hard most of forenoon and Mrs. Goddard and I drove thro' it to Court, at Court House where we were subpoenaed as witnesses as to character of a neighbor girl, Mary Davis who has a child by Ira O. Guy. Case was not reached and we came home: stopped at sister's.

Thurs. 10
Mrs. Goddard and I again drove to Court at 8:30 A.M. Case not reached, dismissed until 1:30 P.M. so went to sister's to have her meet an early afternoon train, as we looked for children from Colo. at 4:30 P.M. and I dreamed last night that they came and none of us met them and as I would be at Court, went to see sister and have her go to earlier train. Went to sister's at 11 A.M. and there were the children and my stepmother. They arrived at 8 o'clock A.M. on a train none of us knew about and so none of us met them; just as I dreamed. Brought James and Freda out to dinner, after which Mrs. G. and I went back to court. Cecil G. and Freda going to sister's where we called for them in eve. James went off with some boys.

Mon. 21
Took Fred to P.O. and James home; got Freda, bought crate of peaches and Plums to Can and came home. A beautiful day, but too busy to enjoy it. I have a lovely home and the *kindest, most patient* and *loving* husband in the world and so find my busy life a happy one. The only thing to make it *perfect* is lacking; *children*; God gives us none, yet we have with us much, some of my sister's.

The remainder of this year is much like the first months, except that they finally get indoor plumbing—("a bathroom and its accompanying conveniences") in October.

[1904]

Martha's year was filled with the usual visits and church going, along with regular painting afternoons at Beardsley's Studio. She celebrated her tenth anniversary in May, and was chivarried with tin-ware by her friends. Oren Kettlewell visited in July, and smelled of liquor, so Martha was relieved that she had not married him. Entries for much of October and November have Martha revelling in the good weather. She also recorded that the neighborhood children played in her yard, much to her delight. She and Fred, not her sister May, celebrated Halloween with James and Freda, once again illustrating their devotion to the children. Freda spent a great deal of her time with Martha and Fred during this year. They went to concerts together, and Freda often spent the night. In fact, on October 1, Martha noted that James and Freda went to "visit" their mother. Zaidee, however, stayed with her mother. As was her custom, on December 31st Martha swept the entire house, "that I might begin the New Year clean."

[*1905*]

January through March entries are devoted to the usual attendance at church, and a week-day routine of working in the morning and painting at Mr. Beardsley's studio in the afternoon; he played the piano while those present painted and sang. Martha noted on January 24 the birth of her child thirteen years earlier, and in June on the anniversary of her death records: "I have spent much of this day in tears. My heart cries out in bitterest anguish for my little one; it aches and hungers with mother love that can never be satisfied and yet 'God knows best.'" In August a tornado struck the city but missed her house, and in September she got a heavy shock from lightning, but was not hurt.

August

Fri. 4 Freda and I walked to town this morning,where I spent the forenoon shopping. In evening taking Freda, I went for a drive with the colt—Don Jaime—pronounced as if spelled Hy-me—Spanish for James—Drove nicely for awhile, then concluded wanted to come home, which I would not let him do, and it ended by my getting a Colt down, a broken Shaft and generally tangled up, however I conquered; four men came running (as if I needed help) helping unhitch and get him up. I then strapped the shaft together, hitched up and drove home, one of the men offering to drive *if I was afraid.* O! my. I've never seen the horse, I was afraid of. *Man* is the *only* creature I'm afraid of.

November

Wed. 1 A grandly beautiful Autumn day and the Woods near us are gorgeous in their Autumn colors. We stand, up here, on the hill alone and so have an uninterrupted view of all this autumn glory. I walked to town after dinner to pay some bills, do some shopping and leave an order, to have a Telephone put in our house. Went to the Historical rooms in State House and got a book for sister Minnie Akin, in Omaha. Got weighed in Mr.

McLatchey's Coal office—weigh 136; want to gain four pounds more, then I'll be satisfied.

Thurs. 9   Went over to Mrs. Swendson's after dinner and from there . . . to Mrs. J. V. Rowles 1121 Harrison St. to a meeting of the Good Government Club.[1] Mrs. Jones and myself were voted into the Club together with Mrs. E. Hoch—the Governor's wife—. . . and several others. Had a splendid meeting. . . .

Mon. 13   A grand day. Men here stringing wires for a Telephone which I don't want but my neighbors want me to get, so as to visit over the Phone.

Wed. 15   Spent most of forenoon at Phone talking to friends and telling them my number. Mr. Guild came out after dinner to notify us our monument was up.[2] And we are *very* glad it is. James—my nephew—came out to supper.

Thurs. 16   Such grand weather one can hardly stay in house but I've spent whole day, between the Telephone, jollying my friends and writing letters.

December

Fri. 1   Cold old morning. I walked down to sister's and went to the "*Skating Rink*" with her, and Mrs. Risen, cousin Belle and Freda.[3] Spent all forenoon at Rink and did not fall once, tho' my first time on Rollers.[4] This afternoon I washed a large washing. My good Fred suffering so with tooth-ache, could not work this morning. I was so sorry for him.

[1906]

Most of January was spent doing the usual housework and making almost daily visits to the Studio to paint. The telephone, installed the previous November, had already begun to make changes in her personal relationships.

February

Fri. 16   Went to *Roller Skating Rink* this morning for an hour's skate with cousin Belle Van Orsdol, and just as I was taking my last round, I *fell* and *broke my left arm* at *wrist, also dislocated it. I didn't faint but my! how it hurt,* tho' *tooth-ache* is *worse.* They called a hack and sent me to Dr. S. A. Johnson's Office, where I was *examined under X-Ray,* by *Dr. Johnson, Dr. J. C. McClintock* and *Dr. W. F. Bowen* and *two X-Ray* or *Coil Photos* taken of *my arm,* which shows a *very bad, oblique fracture* of the large bone. Dr. Bowen then brought me home in his buggy, followed on car by my sister and Dr. Johnson. I was then *chloroformed* and *bones set,* but *don't give* me much *encouragement.* It was *2 1/2 hours before* my arm *was set.* . . . A most beautiful snowstorm this evening.

Sat. 17   I rested pretty well last night. Mrs. Swendson came in this morning and combed my hair, also Freda's and swept sitting room, dining-room and kitchen. Mrs. Jones spent afternoon with me. Mr. Jones, Mr. Howlett, Mrs. Carpenter and Port Henderson called. Port came to do the milking, as Fred doesn't know how. Zaidee came out for supper. Many friends called by Telephone. *While I am not a moment without pain and suffer greatly at times, I thank God it is no worse.* Ground white with snow this morning, but gone by noon and so bright and sunny I walked out in yard, *carrying my broken arm on a pillow.*

Sun. 18   A grand beautiful day. Had many callers and Telephone calls. *Doctors Bowen and Johnson came at 4 P.M.* to take off *the "splints"* and *put my arm in a Cast* but found *the bones had slipped apart* which means "*Chloroform*" again and *work all to do over which is a bitter disappointment* to me. *I suffered torture all last night,* but feel *easier today.* . . . .

Mon. 19 A pleasant sunny day. Dr. Johnson called after dinner and *informed* me I *must be taken* to *Hospital, my arm cut open* and *bones wired in place, so can be no more slipping. No one can know how I dread it,* but *"What can't be cured, must be endured"* so *no use to think farther about it.*

Mrs. J. Tullock and Rev. and Mrs. Finch, called to see me, and many, many called by Telephone. Gertrude Harris called this evening and *brought* me *a pretty Cyclamen in bloom.*

Tues. 20 Raining slowly all forenoon. . . . Dr. Johnson *'Phoned me* this afternoon that I must be *at Hospital* by *8:30 tomorrow morning.* Mrs. Goddard *is going to give me "Christian Science" treatment and says they will not cut nor wire* my arm as they intend to do.

Wed. 21 Such a *beautiful* day. Mrs. Frank Washburn came at *8 o'clock this morning* and took me to *Christs Hospital,* Fred and Mrs. Jones coming later, on a car. I had Fred go home *just before I was taken to Operating-room.* Mrs. Jones went into Operating-room with me, where I was *put on the table at 10:45* and *under Chloroform one hour,* coming to, in time *to hear clock strike 12.* Dr. Bowen told me before I went into Operation-room *that they would have to saw out an inch* of *bone before wiring.* But I *opened my eyes after Chloroform* to find it had not been done nor my arm opened, *nor no wiring done; Christian Science triumphed.* Fred came in to see me after dinner and he and Freda spent evening with me and Dr. Kiene "gave away" the fact that my *arm was broken. Fred had only known* it was *dislocated. He is so sympathetic,* I knew he would suffer *so much in sympathy I did not want him to know for awhile.* Dr. McClintock set my arm with help of Johnson and Bowen. Dr. Kiene and Hill gave the Chloroform.

Thurs. 22 A grandly beautiful day. I *slept some* and *rested quite well* last *night,* tho' the nurse came in *every hour to examine* my *arm,* which disturbed me some. My *good hubby came* to the Hospital this morning to see me and *again at 3 P.M.* with Mrs. F. Washburn *in her carriage,* to bring me home. Mrs. C. Goddard was at house when I got home. Had *swept my rooms* and *filled them with pretty flowers.* It is *good to be home.* I feel like I had been gone a *month* instead of *two days.* Am still *a little the worse for the Chloroform.* Though it *did not make me sick* neither time I took it—I feel some *dizzy from the horrid stuff.* My Hospital Bill *was $17.14* and my Surgeons charged me *$100.00* which seems pretty steep. Mrs. Swendson and Mrs. Jones called after I got home and Mr. G. O. Beardsley and Mother came out and spent evening with us, and *brought* me *some beautiful roses. I am so tired and exhausted tonight* but *thank God my arm was not opened,* nor shortened.

Sat. 24   It is nice to have my hubby home with me, tho' sorry his Vacation must be used this way. *This is first time in my life, I was ever helpless. My first accident,* and *is most inconvenient, but am free from pain.* Mrs. E. Bowman called in afternoon Harry Seiler spent evening with us.

March

Thurs. 1   . . . . My arm seems to be doing well and *I'm praying I may not have to* go back to Hospital, but Doctors have *given me no hopeful word yet.* They think I'm gritty; and every one says I am mighty brave, but *why should I not be. I am well* and *strong* and do *not suffer.* There are *worse* things than broken bones.

Fri. 2   A pretty morning, but rained and snowed all afternoon. Dr. Johnson *Phoned me this morning,* I could have a *sling for my arm* and *I'll tell you I was not long getting it.* It gets mighty tiresome carrying a pillow every step one takes. Mrs. F. Washburn spent morning with me.

Fri. 9   *Swept* the stairs and *hall* and *scrubbed my kitchen* this morning *all with my one arm, also churned.* Mrs. F. Washburn came after dinner and *took me* to *Coterie Club* at *Mrs. Seiler's.* Dr. Johnson Phoned me this evening to *come Monday* to his Office, prepared *for to take Chloroform.* Must *have no food or water that day.* The last Photos do not show my arm to be satisfactory.

Sat. 10   *I haven't the heart today to do anything.* I had hoped *my arm was alright* and *it may be,* but *doctors want* to *examine it again* as Photos show something wrong: they do not tell me what they mean to do. But I *shall trust God,* and *not allow myself to worry.* Freda went to her mother's last night and I'm alone today. Election Primaries today: *sleeting and snowing.* Mrs. Goddard spent some time with me this morning. Mr. A. E. Jones called at noon.

Mon. 12   *Cold, cloudy* and ground white with snow. Mr. George

Moore called just after our dinner. Mrs. A. E. Jones *came at 2:30 P.M.* and went with me to *Dr. Johnson's Office*, where he and Dr. *McClintock gave me another X-Ray examination.* They called me down, to *break my arm over again*, but after *today's examination, decided it would not be best to do so,* tho' found bones *had slipped 1/8 of inch*, and my arm is *to be allowed* to heal *in this manner*: it *being broken in three pieces.* Dr. M. says the slip is so small it will never *bother me* and *my arm will be useful*, the *first hopeful words* they have *ever given me.* But I must wear my *Cast three weeks longer.* After leaving Doctor's office Mrs. Jones and I called at Beardsley Studio, where Mrs. Beardsley *gave me a glass of milk, my first food today.*

Sat. 17   Just after dinner, Mr. A. E. Jones took Mrs. Jones and myself to *Good Government Club*, meeting with Mrs. Estey, at *Presbyterian Manse*, 819 Harrison St. *Election of Officers* and I was *unanimously elected Treasurer*: I feel highly honored, it being largest Club in the City. Mr. Jones called and brought us home after Club.

April

Fri. 6   Dr. Johnson called me this morning *to come have cast taken off* my arm *which I did at 3:30 P.M. My arm looked awful, positively repulsive*, tho' *straight and no lumps showing*, but *so shrunken* and *some swollen and stiff.* Dr. J. C. McClintock says *best result he has ever had.* Took another Photograph of my arm, bound it up and I came home feeling *"like a bird out of a cage."* . . .

Wed. 18   Fred went to work this morning. Got word at noon that San Francisco was destroyed by an Earthquake at 5:10 this morning and City burning. How terrible.

Thurs. 19   We still get terrible news of the San Francisco Earthquake. The City is still burning and many lives lost. The suffering will be *awful.* Mrs. Strickler called this morning while I was gathering Dandelion for greens. Mr. Guild also called to see about our colt, but I don't want to sell him and Fred is not over anxious. Called at Mrs. Howlett's this afternoon. Mr. H. has been very sick, with Apendicitis. Brother Coit Farnsworth 43 today.

May

Fri. 25   Swept and cleaned from "Cellar to Garrett" this morning, then after dinner, to rest me, I went to Mrs. C. W.

Kansas Avenue at 8th Street, Topeka, 1906.

Thompson's to a meeting of the Coterie Club. Mrs. L. Seiler brought Mrs. McLatchey and me home after Club. After supper Fred, Freda and I, with the Joneses and Mr. & Mrs. Racliffe, attended the *Novelty Theatre*, to see the "Moving Pictures" of the *San Francisco Earthquake*. The pictures were good, tho' some were dim, but showed the *awfulness* of the wrecked City; *falling buildings, fire* and *discharge* of *dynamite*.

Wed. 30   *"Decoration Day"*. With Cecil Goddard, and Freda I took flowers and went early to the Cemetery, to decorate the graves of our loved ones. I took flowers for *father and mother Farnsworth, aunts Maria and Lucy Stoddard Fred's neice, Della Akin-Sperry* and my father's aunt, *Deddy Dick* and my *Great-Grandmother, Mary Ogden*. To the *one spot, most sacred of all to me,—the grave of my own sweet Babe—I did not go. I never go there in company with others*, but the *mother love ever yearns* and *longs for the wee heart buried there*.

A very large crowd in Cemetery and we left too, just as the real crowd commenced coming. Fred had half Holiday, which he spent home with me.

June

Wed. 27   *. . . . Freda is eleven years old today.* And it is also the Anniversary of the death of my own, sweet little daughter. *Oh! my heart aches* and *aches and no one knows. If I only could have my precious one,* but *God knows what is best. His will be done.*

September

Fri. 7   Canning tomatoes this morning, and after dinner doing sister's Office work in at Robinson and Marshall's,[1] while she and Freda drove out to uncle Marian VanOrsdol's— Silver Lake 15 miles—to stay all night. We wanted to give Freda a little "outing" before school commences and we could not all go, so I looked after things while they went, and tonight I am alone for first time since Fred and I married more than 12 years ago. The first time he has been from home without me. Walked home from work this evening.

Mon. 10   Spent the afternoon with Mrs. Ward Burlingame, looking up material for a club paper, which I must write. Brother Will Farnsworth 50 years old today. Called at Mrs. Munson's this evening.

Tues. 11   Making peach preserves and Plum-jam. Walked down to the City Library after dinner, and home again. I got Fiske's "Critical Period of American History," to use in writing my Paper.

Wed. 12   Canned a Bushel of tomatoes and made a basket of wild grapes into grape juice and bottled it.

Thurs. 13   "Topeka Day" at the Races and Mr. & Mrs. A. E. Jones took Mrs. S. A. Swendson and me. *Mrs. Swendson gave me tickets.* A fine day, and fine Races. *Ten or eleven thousand people present.* Ostrich Race.

Fri. 14   Spent a very happy afternoon at the Races again today, with Mrs. Swendson and the Jones's who took us in their carriage. We got a splendid position in the Quarter Stretch and saw some of the *finest Races* I ever have seen. The *Ostrich Race was very amusing.* The crowd not so large as yesterday. Threatened rain but got home at 6:30 before it rained.

Sat. 15   Spent the afternoon at the Good Government Club, which met with Mrs. S. A. Swendson 1127 Morris Ave.

Had a *most enthusiastic meeting*. I had charge of the Program and read a paper about the District of Columbia and Washington City. After coming home this evening, I killed a couple of young chickens and sent down to sister by Freda; also sent a loaf of bread, I baked today.

Wed. 26   Fred, Freda and I spent the evening with Mr. & Mrs. Harry Bair in N. Topeka to visit Oren Kettlewell, who just came this evening to bring his little son Glenn, to leave with them, that he may have a home and go to school, the mother being dead. Oren is an old sweetheart of mine.

Thurs. 27   Oren Kettlewell and Glenn came over this morning for a little visit and I asked them back for supper and to spend the evening. Oren came back after dinner for a little while, saying he must leave the City this evening, so none of them came to supper. *Nineteen years ago he and I were Sweethearts*. We quarreled and when he came for me *two years later* I *sent him away* and this is our *first* meeting, when we could visit, in *seventeen years*. We met two years ago, just for a moment, but in all the seventeen years we have been as strangers; he married *once*, and I have married *twice*, and still he suffers because of the "*old days*". *How I pity him, a wreck of his former self. Once a young man of good habits and full of hope*, now a *dissipated wreck*. He said to me today "*You have wrecked my whole life. Our separation hurt us both, but you stood up to it and lived a good life and I went to the dogs. I had not the stamina to live down my sorrow.*" I *pray God to help him.*

October

Sat. 20   Attended meeting of Good Government Club, at Mrs. E. E. Roudebush's, in Potwin walking over and home again. Had good meeting but in "Current Events" the *Negro question* was brought up by Mrs. Lee Monroe, who said some quite bitter things against Negroes who were defended by Mrs. L. O. Case and arguments waxed warm for awhile.

Sun. 21   Fred and I spent the afternoon at the Jones', being invited there to dinner with Prof. Geo. O. Beardsley and his mother, who have just returned from a summer spent in Colorado.[2]

December

Mon. 31 Spent afternoon down town shopping and went in to see sister in "Robinson & Marshall's." Earnest R. gave me a very pretty Calendar, representing a Cuckoo Clock. Freda came out tonight to stay all night—has been visiting her mother during Holidays.

Today closes another year, which has been full of God's goodness to us; a year of hard work and sacrifice, but health to do the work and grace for the sacrifices leaves nothing to be desired. Our one piece of ill-luck, the breaking of my arm in a most dreadful way and thro' God's goodness its perfect healing, leaves us with grateful hearts.

[1907]

During 1907 Martha became increasingly active in politics, especially through the Good Government Club. As her activities increased, her longing for her child received less attention: the diary mentions Freda's twelfth birthday, for example, but does not commemorate either the birth or the death of her own child, even while noting on August 24th the death of her sister Belle twenty-one years before. Bert Freeland, an old beau of twenty-two years before, came to Topeka in February to preach a revival (he had become a Nazarene minister) and Martha spent much time with him, attending most of his two-week series of meetings. Her most revealing comment on his stay is: "During his sermon he made this remark—that I cannot fully agree with—'I believe that temptations are good for you.' Now I do not believe they are good for me. It was such a good sermon, but I came home with a very heavy heart." Oren Kettlewell also visited in October, and brought his two sons to see her. While visiting he reaffirmed his love for her and charged again that she had ruined his life by turning him down twenty years ago. Martha responded with genuine pity and an admonition that he join the church. Her attitude throughout the year was one of general well-being.

[1908]

January

Wed. 1 Such a *beautiful, bright, warm, sunny, day*; I pray it may be an omen, of what my life is to be throughout the year. God give me strength, to live each day as He would have me live it, go with me every step of the way, that I may live to His honor and glory. Mrs. E. Bowman, came in on an errand this morning and staid "chatting" for some little time. Mr. Guild also stopped in passing, to use our Phone. Fred having a half Holiday, was home this afternoon. I am not at all well and ate nothing all day, but took a "nap" during the after-noon and this evening Fred and I went to an entertainment at the Railroad Y.M.C.A. gotten up by Mr. G. O. Beardsley; it was very fine, the decorations beautiful and an immense crowd present. We got home just about 11 o'clock.

Sun. 5 Freda and I walked down to Sunday School together this morning, she going to First Methodist and I to my own—First Christian—where I have "Class No. 5" in the Junior department; a Class of Boys. We met in our new Basement this morning, with Mrs. Settle Supt. . . . Ralph Davidson, Ronald McCord, Claude Swendson, Billy Badger and Alva Edson are the boys in my S.S., given me permanently this morning.

Mon. 13 Sunny, bright day, but a cold wind. I met by appointment, Mrs. S. A. Swendson at 9:10 A.M. at Alderfer's Store and together, we walked to Mrs. Lee Monroe's 9th & Harrison St. to meet Good Government Club—about 75 present—and all went in a body, to State House, to call on Governor Hoch and present him a Petition, asking him to endorse the Woman's Suffrage Bill, to be brought before the Special Session of the Legislature, which soon convenes[1] . . . .

Fri. 17 I went down to Mrs. Lee Monroe's this morning—9th and Harrison—at 8:30 to a Business meeting of Men and Women, interested in "Presidential Suffrage" for women. We are hoping the Bill will pass at this *Special* Session of the Legislature. This evening Fred and I went to a dinner Party at Mr. A. E. Jones' for Mr. Nat Franco.[2] Prof. Geo. O. Beardsley and Mother and Miss Clora Lanham, were the other invited guests. Mr. Franco and Miss Lanham each gave a "reading" before he had to go to the Theatre for the evening performance and we had to come home early, for we had told Zaidee and James—my neice & nephew, they could have their "Success Club" meeting with us, so when we returned, we found 22 young people in possession of our home and having a most happy time.

February

Sun. 2   Ten above Zero this morning, tho' it seems much colder; I had Freda who came out yesterday, take a car down home, because so cold. She said to me yesterday, "Aunty you are the kind of a Mamma I want." . . . .

Sat. 8   Freda came out this afternoon to stay all night. I churned and did lots of Baking this forenoon and had the finest luck with my Bread and Ginger Cake: also made some fine Cream Candy to give one of my Sunday School Boys, who has a Birthday tomorrow (Edward Myers who will be 10 years old) Little Mrs. Williams spent the afternoon with me. I have not known her long, but like her; she seems such a sweet little body and has taken a fancy to me. The poor little thing is to be a mother in a few months and is almost "wild" about it and was in tears most of the afternoon; came to me for council and advice and sympathy; her people do not live here. Her husband is fond of children and she does not like them at all and naturally is a *very miserable* little creature. I pity her so; because she feels so bitterly about it and because she cannot realize her blessings. I would give all I possess, endure anything, could I but be a mother again and I cannot *understand* how *any one* can feel so badly, when such a blessing comes to them. I did my ironing this evening.

Sat. 22   Washington's Birthday and Fred having a half Holiday was home this afternoon. Freda came out this morning, bringing her friend Pearle Head, and both staid over night and are two very happy "kids". We left them alone this evening, while we went to the Auditorium to hear W. J. Bryan; he is a pleasing speaker and told many amusing Stories, as a "take-off" on the Republicans, but

I could not see that he made any points worth while, tho'
we did not stay late. His arguments could never make a
Democrat of me.[3]

Wed. 26   Painting all afternoon at the Beardsley Studio. A cold
day and *awfully* windy. Fred at home all day, having
another day of his Vacation and helping Mr. Dunlap
measure his lines, and get ready to move our Barn and
other outbuildings on the ground we keep for our
home. It seems so good to have our Home paid for. I
paid off the last note of $278.38 yesterday, when Mr.
Dunlap paid me, for the 6 1/2 lots he bought of us, and
my Teddie and I are both very happy and *very thankful*
to God, that He has made it possible for us to own such a
nice home; it has been a *long hard* pull with much of toil
and sacrifice and we are so thankful, the last payment is
made.

May

Sun. 10   Had a very heavy rain this morning soon after we "got
up" but it was fair and pretty by Sunday-school time and

Martha and four boys on front steps of her home, June 1908.
First Sunday School class picture. Second boy from the left is
Roy Penwell, whom she adopted but later gave up. From her
photograph album.

Freda and I walked down together; my class of boys all present but Ralph Spurrier. Roy Penwell is a new pupil. Mrs. Swendson and I walked home together after church, and after a hurried dinner I took car to "*K. L. of S.*" Hall where I drilled with the Degree Staff, from 2:30 to 4 o'clock, then walked home and of course am tired; but the Staff is to be sent to the National Convention, at Philadelphia, June 6th with all expenses paid, so must do lots of hard Drilling and have to use Sunday because the only day can have the Hall, with 2 evenings.[4]

A *very, very* hard rain came up soon after I got home and has rained all evening.

June

Mon. 1   Freda came out this morning; now that school has closed, she will be with us most of the time. The robes for the K. L. of S. Degree Team came today and I had to go to the Hall this evening to be "fitted;" the Robes are pretty, but mine is prettiest of all: red velvet with green and gold silk front; gold cord and gold braid trimming; bright, showy and pretty; and *becoming* to my *black* skin. . . .

Wed. 3   Went to town this afternoon to do some shopping and to the Court House to see the County Commissioners about some "over-valuation" of property belonging to Will and Coit Farnsworth. . . .

Sat. 6   *The eventful day.* Bright and sunny; Fred got the afternoon off, as half day of his vacation and at 3 o'clock went with me to Santa Fe Depot, where about 35 of "Knights and Ladies of Security" met to take the 4:55 P.M. train to the National Convention, in Philadelphia. Some others are going too, and we have a *Special* train. We are to meet other delegations along the way and altogether there will be between eight and nine hundred of us. In our especial "bunch" from Capital Council No. 1, K. L. of S., are [24 names follow] My sister Mrs. M. M. E. Gilbert and myself, and we were a mighty jolly set. We left promptly on time and was a big crowd to see us off. I hated to come away and leave my good Teddie, for I know he will be *dreadfully* lonely, as we have not been away from one another 24 hours, since we were married, more than 14 years ago. But I felt it would be foolish to "*turn down*" such a trip, when it was *free*. All expenses paid, for the whole bunch, going, coming and while in the East, by the Lodge. Zaidee, James and Freda are to stay with Fred while I am away. The river is very high—reported within a foot of going out of Bank; and every one is "anxious" fearing another *flood*. . . .

Mon. 8   Awakened this morning—after a good nights sleep— just as we were entering Hamilton, Ontario at 4:30 A.M. A pretty place and large, but has very narrow streets. Such pretty country all about and quaint homes. We travelled 65 miles an hour last night and for a way 82 miles—a terrific speed and I do not like it. All the way to Niagara the scenery was beautiful; crossed the Niagara river about 7:30 A.M. and spent an hour and fifteen minutes in Niagara and at the Falls, walking to the Falls from the depot. Oh! the Falls—so grand—so beyond any words to describe them; what *must* Heaven be like, and we are told Heaven is grander than all this. The morning at the Falls was "perfect." And about noon we came to a dear little place, Geneva, New York, beside pretty Lake Geneva, along which we travelled for 50 miles, tho' I believe it is called Seneca Lake, part of way; but it is a beautiful body of water and the scenery pretty, tho' the little patches of tilled yellow soil on the hill-sides are a very striking contrast to the broad acres of black soil of our Kansas prairies. "Scare-crows" stuck up all over their fields—or their little, gravelly patches, which seem to be mostly cultivated by hand; men, women and children hoeing, with an occasional one-horse plow in the field. A great Vineyard country. Along in afternoon, we came to Wilkes-Barre, Penn. in the great Coal region and it seemed as if we were in a Foreign Country. A very large place; and so many foreigners, with the buildings so odd, so foreign looking. *Coal, coal, coal,* everywhere and of course saloons of which we have seen many; we travelled all afternoon thro' the most beautiful scenery, along the grandly beautiful Susquehana river on the Lehigh Valley Railroad—some of trainmen said it was Lehigh Valley river—Crossed the Allegheny mountains, which were covered with beautiful flowers and the most exquisite Ferns, growing as thickly as our Alfalfa grows at home. Oh! but it was Heavenly, this pretty scenery. At South Bethlehem, we had a change of Conductors and lost the very pleasant one (Mr.

Stevenson), whom we had from Niagara and ran on down into Philadelphia, over the Pennsylvania and Reading arriving about 9 o'clock, several hours late and going to the New Central Hotel, 31-33-35 N-15th St. . . .

Tues. 9 Well, it seemed strange to awaken this morning so far from home and Teddy, but here I am and I shall certainly make the best of my time and see all of this noisy city possible. After a Breakfast of Oatmeal, glass of milk, Broiled steak and potatoes, I went with our Degree Staff and Officers, to Odd Fellows Hall, over on north Broadway to practice our drill, for tonight. Our Capt. Johnny Bauer, had been drinking as usual and our President Wilson asked him not to drink any more, until after the Contest tonight; there was a big row and a "cry" all around then things smoothed down, people got in good humor and we proceeded to drill, going thro' three times, then we were turned loose; some back to Hotel to rest, but I with Emma Evans and Grace Greenlee went to John Wanamaker's Store, over to City Hall and took in all we could with our eyes; saw fine new Newspaper building 20 stories high on Market St. *Wanamaker's of course is fine.* Saw many men and boys selling roses 5 cents doz. that at home would be two or three dollars; Carnations *five cents* for *two doz.* and when I left home, we had to pay a dollar for *one doz.* I don't see how they sell such beautiful flowers so cheaply. The streets are so narrow here, some no wider than our Alleys at home and paved with cobble stones, make them so noisy one can scarcely hear. After our Lunch at noon we all rested until 4 o'clock, when all again went to I. O. O. F. Hall, for practice, after which returned to Hotel and found Adam Weber, (a friend since childhood) there to see sister and I: after supper all went to Odd Fellows Hall and entered the Contest against Pueblo, Colo. mixed Team, St. Joe Mo., women's Team and Reading Pa. men's Team. We were only given 3rd prize of $800.00 although ours was only Team that went thro' the work without a mistake and the other Teams and all the audience conceded First prize to us. Our uniforms were not bright and showy and so scored against us; and too, our Capt. was "full as a tick" which also counted against us. We came back to our Hotel very much disappointed. Almost Mid-night when we got to bed.

Wed. 10   Oh! such a busy day; crowded so full of sight-seeing. A fine day, tho' some what warm, but everyone was *"stirring"* early. I was up by 4 o'clock and wrote a letter to my good Teddy at home, and cards to many friends, then called the girls, and got our Breakfast early and started on our round of "sight-seeing." We could not get together, and *all* agree on same places, so I took the lead, with one crowd, . . . and we went first to the "Academy of fine Arts" where we saw many beautiful Paintings, some by the old Masters. "The Birth of Venus" by Cabinel was my choice, if one could make a choice of such beautiful paintings. "The rejection of Christ" by West, was another beautiful painting. Oh! it was so full of good things. Oils, water-colors, Statuary, exquisite Tapestry. One would thrill with the beauty of it all. We hurried from this delightful place, to the "Betsy Ross House" the birthplace of our beloved Flag and again the thrill of Patriotism and the awe of this sacred place, brought the tears to our eyes; one could not fail to go back in Spirit, to the "dear dead days beyond recall" as they stood in that little historic room and trod the *same board floor*, of Betsy Ross days. But we could not tarry, and so hastened on, stopping in an old, old Cemetery and standing beside the grave of Benjamin Franklin and other old families of ancient times. Oh! one lived in such an air, as they stood here by these graves; but we had not time for dreaming, and again hurried away from the history learned in our schoolbooks and passing the old "Friends Church" hurried down to Washington Pier, where we took the Steamer "Pleasant Valley" down the Deleware, to Washington Park and return. We could see the big Boats at League Island also up the river to Cramp's Ship-yards where the Battle-ship *"Kansas"* was built. Also saw the Battleship, *"Michigan"* lying in Dock in the New York ship-yards where it was *christened* last week. We saw a British "tramp" steamer, and another large British Steamer come in loaded with Bananas; also saw the U. S. Dispatch-boat used during the Cuban War or war with Spain and a fine, big American Steamer, whose name I did not learn. The water and the Boats were so grand; I believe *I* would like to be a Sailor. We saw a Sugar Schooner come into Port and tug-boats, motor-boats,

sail boats and all kinds of water craft; it seemed like
Fairyland. After our return from our Boat trip down
the Deleware (the Capt. took us all over his Boat) we
went to Christ Church, a very old and historic place
where our first President Gen. George Washington,
Betsy Ross, Benj. Franklin and many other Notables,
used to worship and we went into and sat down in each
of their pews; one felt they were treading on holy
ground. I could hardly enjoy walking down the aisles
over the graves, buried there; we are not accustomed to
such things at home and I felt continually like going out
around these graves. There was so much of interest in
this old Church and its ancient churchyard, but time
was limited and we hurried on to Independence Hall,
with its blessed Liberty Bell, and here indeed, our feet
trod upon sacred ground, as we went from one relic to
another, in this store-house of beloved memories; one
fairly breathed the "spirit of 1776," as they stood upon
this holy ground and one could not help feeling the
thrill of Patriotism "well-up" in them, but again inexo-
rable *time* compelled one to tear them-selves away from
all this deeply interesting spot, and we hurried to our
Hotel for Lunch, passing by "Carpenter's Hall" of
almost equal interest. We had but 15 minutes for Lunch
and then took car to Fairmount Park, the old Centenial
Grounds and into Memorial Hall, another storehouse
of good things; as one enters the door an exquisitely
beautiful Chandelier, costing five thousand dollars and
never lighted but once; the Centennial grounds and
buildings in miniature and grandly, beautiful things, to
numerous to mention. But most exquisite laces that I
could hardly get away from and *Tapestries*; how *can* one
tell about them; one at $40,000.00 and several at
$30,000.00. And *paintings*! Why one would almost melt
into tears before such lovely works of Art—the Rubens
of 1577, Murillo's, Ippolitoda, Scarsella 1551, Van Dyck
1599 and many, many others. Oh! it was such a *"feast of
good things"* Why, I felt as if I could live with out eating,
forever, to be in such an atmosphere, but one was compelled to go on, and we took a car to Willow Grove,
passing Girard College, Gen. U. S. Grant's Cabin and
many points of interest, and after an hour's ride,
reached Willow Grove Park, a pretty place similar to

Vinewood at home, and returned to Hotel 7:45 after a most strenuous day; but it has all been so happy and grand.

Fri. 12 .... I wanted very much to go down to New York, but could not get the "bunch" together.... After Lunch we went on a shopping tour of the big Stores; thro' John Wanamakers a fine store, opened with prayer each morning. A fine Pipe-Organ, theater, resturant etc. Simply grand. I enjoyed very much the fine Paintings. The clerks "stare" at us so, knowing we are "Westerners." Was in Snellenberg's, also a fine store, where did most of our shopping and here we were questioned by some of the Clerks and a nicely dressed young woman shopper, who said she *"would like to come West, but was afraid of the Indians and Cow-boys."* I could have "screamed" with laughter only did not want to embarass her; the people in the East seemed so "densely" ignorant of the West. I can't understand it, for we of the West are not ignorant of the East and I asked them too why it was; we found many who had never heard of *"Kansas"*; just think of it—had no idea *"Kansas"* was a state, nor where it was. And one of our crowd was approached and this said to them "You don't look like we thought people in Kansas looked." After going thro' the Strawbridge Store, we came home to the Hotel had supper and proceeded to "pack up" preparatory to our return home. And I wonder "if they miss me at home." I have had one letter from Freda and *one Postal* from Fred and I have written him a letter *every day* and sent him from three to a doz. Postals each day. *Old rascal.*

Mon. 15 It is nice to be on a nice clean train again and now we are nearing home and there is water everywhere; from Carrallton, Mo. on in to Kansas City, the flood was so terrible, it was heart sickening. Crops all under water—many homes deeply in water and the Missouri River, running swiftly over many farms and miles and miles wide—a most pathetic scene and fearful to look upon and *very dangerous* to travel through. Reached Kansas City at noon and found Electric cars being hauled about the streets, thro' the water, by mules and people going about in Boats—Water was up on step of our train which was taken by way of Ottawa and Baldwin where we were held one hour, and some of the many Law students aboard bought us a most acceptable Lunch, and tasted mighty good to our hungry stomachs. From Baldwin we ran on into Lawrence and everlastingly got into the Flood—From there on to Lake View, it was simply dreadful, the water being so deep that it almost put fire out in the Engine; I have lots of nerve, but this was almost too much for even *my* nerve. The women were brave, and the men were brave for the women's sakes, but it was such a dangerous risk, that had the Passengers known what they were being taken into, they would have rebelled and never have taken such a trip; it was wicked for trainmen to subject its passengers to such a risk and the water miles each side of our train was a terrifying sight; however we reached Topeka safely at 9:45 P.M. after being ten hours getting here from Kansas City. A terrible strain on one's nerves. Sister and I took car out home and all were in bed but Zaidee, not dreaming we could get in, for the flood. Almost midnight and we tumbled into bed.[5]

Sat. 27   Freda's 13th Birthday and I fried her a chicken, made Caramel ice-cream and Caramel cake: had sister and family to dinner. . . . Rained. The 16th Anniversary of the death of "my wee girlie" and someway the longing for her just will not wear away. I can't forget.

July

Fri. 31   Splendidly cool and pleasant, but things have just seemed to go wrong all day. Mr. & Mrs. A. E. Jones came this evening and took us all in their carriage, (Fred, James, Clara[6] and I), out to Gages Park. Mr. Guild came out this morning, for the Monument design which I made in pen and ink. He pretended to be much pleased with it, but you never can tell how much a man *means* of what he says. Fred thought it good, but then *he* thinks everything *I do* is good. I know *I* was not altogether pleased with it.

August

Mon. 3   "Monstrously" hot today. James selling and packing his mother's household goods, to move to Boulder, Colo. and never gave me a hint of it when they left a week ago, for vacation. My sister always treats me with just such "contempt" and I do "everything under the sun" for her that I possibly can; do with out needed things, to buy things for them and we virtually support Freda, but she just won't be kind to me and nearly breaks my heart; I wish she were different.

Tues. 4
A worse day still and busy baking and ironing when James came in at 11 o'clock and announced he was ready to start for Colo. Clara and I put up a hurried Lunch and hastily helped pack a few things and the boy was off on the 12:05 Santa Fe, for a new home in Boulder, Colo. and I am alone; no near relatives and these with a father are all I have. I do not see why they could not have been content, for both James and Zaidee had good positions in Santa Fe. And they have not been, since very little folks, where they could not come to "Aunty" for anything they wanted and this *breaks my heart.*[7] Ray Spencer ate supper with us.

Sat. 22
Cousin Gene[8] stayed until after dinner, then went to his father's. Fred went to 8:50 P.M. train and met cousin Minnie Weber-Farrell, who stops enroute home to Little Falls, Minn. for a couple of days visit. And Ray Spencer and Emma Evans, came out to spend the evening, and get my help to settle the "*marriage question*" and it *ended by sending for Rev. Holcomb* and our dressing Emma in Clara's white waist and my dotted-swiss skirt and *their being married at 10 o'clock*—the wedding to be *secret* for a while, for it was a sort of an *elopement.*[9]

Sun. 30
. . . . "*Mr. & Mrs. Ray Spencer*" came out this evening, to stay all night with us. Our little "Bride and Groom" are having a hard time of it; they have told the mother, who is very much "wrought up" about it.

September

Wed. 2
Ironing today and fixing Lunch for Ray and Emma Spencer, who are to leave tonight for Denver. Ray here for dinner and most of the day. Emma's parents are raising—well raising all kinds of a fuss and say she can't go with Ray and the poor boy is nearly crazy. Fred, Clara and I went to the depot (Santa Fe, at 9:30 but poor Ray had to go alone at 11 o'clock. Emma would not go because her folks didn't want her to, but will later. She

makes me tired—it was her duty to go and she ought to have gone: her folks were trying to compel her to marry a fellow who happened to have a little money, instead of Ray, whom she loves and now they are raising a terrible fuss. I fixed for their Lunch, a Basket (with handle wrapped in 2 inch white ribbon and tied in two big bows) filled with fried chicken, "Angel Food" and "sandwiches" each one cut "heart-shape" tied up with white 1/2" ribbon and a big red paper heart under which was slip of paper on which was written an appropriate "Toast" first one being "Who so findeth a wife findeth a good thing." First on top of the Lunch was "Pen and ink" Stork carrying a Baby, then a row of 12 different sized little children, strung in a row, on which was written "May these be all your troubles" and a little package of Rice done up as Sandwich, which would shower all over them when opened. Fred got a half day of Vacation, this afernoon, and went to the Masonic Temple at 4 o'clock and took examination for 3rd degree which makes him a "Master Mason" member of the Blue Lodge.

Sat. 5   Mr. Cy Evans called at noon, to see us about Emma's marriage to Ray Spencer—he is making a big "kick" and says may take it to Court—the only thing he would accomplish, would be to give some Lawyer a good roll of his "Greenbacks" for they were married "*good* and *hard*." . . . .

Fri. 11   Had a letter from Ray Spencer and his sister today in Denver. Poor Ray—Emma's folks have made her write him, she would not live with him. Well I will see what I can do with persuading her to go to the man she loves. Fred took Clara to see Queen Ester at Auditorium this evening and I am alone and as it is now nearly mid-night guess I will "turn-in"[10]

Mon. 14   Washed this morning and just after dinner Ray Spencer came from Denver; he came to help get his wife from her parents. I went to Mrs. Goddard's to Phone Emma to come out, not telling Ray was here, but she could not come, so he went down to see her and at 7 o'clock Phoned for me, saying it was fight for life or death. Poor Ray he is so good, and has no parents, so I sort of take him into my heart, as a mother. Clara had gone *out* to supper, so while Fred ate *his* I dressed and we took the

7:30 car for Evans' meeting Ray and Emma near the house: We left them, to go to the house and try to persuade the parents they should let Emma go with her husband; soon Emma, Ray, and "Jack" Stewart her former sweet-heart came and there was a "scene," a *mighty* "scene"; in fact, it was *Hell, Hell, Hell,* for the next three hours; Her parents declaring she should not live with her husband and her father in a wild frenzy, cursing and abusing everybody, and "Jack" declaring he would travel the World over but what he would take her from her husband; her father declared he would have her put in the Insane Assylum. Oh it was all so dreadful, but I fought for Ray, 'till the last minute. Emma promised to see Ray, tomorrow, so at 11 o'clock we came home bringing Ray with us; the poor boy is sick with worry and trouble. I don't see why Emma does not assert herself and go live with her husband; she is past 21 and need not listen to such cranky parents, who have not even "good common sense."

Tues. 15   Very busy day; "packing" for visit in Oklahoma. Ray Phoned Emma this morning and the mother answered Phone, saying Emma left town last night, then he went to the house and found it "closed" and got no response to his "ring", consequently the poor boy, is beside himself with grief. I have tried to comfort and encourage him all day. I had him go see Sheriff Wilkerson, who advised him to get a gun and go kill "Jack" and the whole police force of Topeka would stand behind him. Jack is to blame, for he continually urges the parents against Ray and makes them abusive to Emma. At train time tonight 11.25 Ray had not yet found Emma and was suffering untold agony, because of it, yet to please Fred and Clara, I had to leave the poor boy, who needed me so much and take the train with them, for Oklahoma. I would not have left him, only we are all hoping that the Sheriff tomorrow will help him get his wife.

Our train is a very long one and had to put on an extra Coach, just for the crowd getting on here in Topeka, but it was a horrible old rattle-trap of a Coach and very uncomfortable; lighted by *one lone Candle.*

Wed. 16   Passed through dear old home town, Winfield this morning; how the memories pull at ones heart-strings. Train stopped at Arkansas City for Breakfast. A most beautiful day and as fine a country as one could wish to see. . . . At Red Rock a large crowd of Whites and Indians got on train, going to Perry to 15th Anniversary Celebration of opening of the Territory. Passed thro' Guthrie the Capital of Okla. a good looking town too. Saw many fine fields of Cotton, Corn, Kaffir[11] and Alfalfa. Our brother in law Tom Willits got on train with us at Guthrie. All the Passengers took Fred and I to be new married couple and asked Clara if we were not. We saw the absurdity of the "Jim Crow" law this morning when a *neat, clean* colored woman was made to leave our Coach, and *greasy, dirty* Indians left in it. Arrived at Waterloo 45 minutes late at noon and were met by Tom & Louis—twins—and Coit Willits and drove one mile West to their home—a nice place.

Thurs. 17   Fred & sister Addie, and I went over to and thro' their Cotton-field, this afternoon; it is a fine one. We are enjoying some fine melons here at Tom's. We are both very much in love with Oklahoma, but the red soil looks odd to us; and all the streams we crossed in coming looked like rivers of red ink and I could not help laughing at the sight; but there had just been heavy rains, was why; they tell us the streams are clear as any water, except after a rain. But even nature tells us, it is the Redmen's country, for the rich dark *green* of the Cotton-fields and prairies the brilliant *yellow* of the wild flowers and the flaming *scarlet* of the soil, are the colors of his War-paints.

After leaving Oklahoma, they go to Winfield, Kansas.

Thurs. 24   All day at Uncle Joe's.[12] Carrie and Manley only ones home now—Oh! *what changes* the years bring; if they would but stand still and let us be children awhile longer. Growing fields of fruit and grain, where once it was broad prairie, and I a little barefoot girl herded my father's oxen and then as the "settlers" could afford it, the cows of our own and neighbors; and then I began to ride horses and there was nothing I didn't ride. And many a time, has a flock of Deer come in among my cattle; some great fine antlered ones. And to see a wolf as I often did, frightened me half to death, but worst of all, when some Indian would come jogging along on his pony and say "How" to the little white Pappoose, my heart would almost stop beating.

Martha and Fred return to Topeka on the 28th.

Mon.28   . . . . We took the 3:20 train for home and arrived in Topeka about 8 o'clock and got a car out home, where found everything alright. We have had such a happy two weeks visit. O such a happy time. The *parting* is the one unhappy thing about visiting. Oh how glorious will be Heaven, with all our loved ones, and "We will never say Good-bye, in Heaven." I thank God for this blessedly happy visit.

Wed. 30   In the thick of House-cleaning Mrs. Greenlee called this afternoon, and told me what a time they had with Ray and Emma. Emma did not consent to go away with him, so after everyone thought he had left the City, he bought some poison and came out to our house to take it—quick silver—and Grace Greenlee—not knowing we were away—called on a errand, found him with a note written to me, and the Poison ready to take; she Phoned for her mother and Emma and some others, took his Poison from him, and took him to a friends for the night, then to E. Wilson's for a few days and got his wife with him without her folks knowing it and she finally went to Denver with him after a big row with her folks.

November

Thurs. 12   I walked to and from Bible Class this evening; coming home, had Brother Finch for company as far as his home, but there was a beautiful moon and I am not afraid anyway, and if I was why, I carry *two* "hat-pins" than which there could be no better weapon.

Sun. 22   Walked to and from Sunday-school and Church this morning. Rev. Ritz of Maryville, Mo. preached us a good sermon, but we want our own Bro. Finch and the Maryville folks are trying to take him from us. The morning was foggy and threatening, but fine afternoon. We got letters from my sister, and Zaidee and Freda. My good Teddie and I miss our Freda whom we had for nearly ten years.

December

Tues. 1   Walked over to Bible Class at Cent.[ral] Cong.[regational] this afternoon, then went to town shopping. Bright and sunny but very cold: 15 degrees above 0. Mr. J. Ramsay called this morning to talk Politics, but I am going to "cut out" Politics. He is working for Swendson for 3rd Ward Councilman and Col. J. W. F. Hughes for Mayor, both men I would support, but I shall take no part in Politics this time. Men will work the women to death in Politics and yet refuse the Ballot to them, and if we are not good enough to vote, we are not good enough to help get votes. Fred and I went to Knights and Ladies entertainment this eve.

[1909]

January

Thurs. 14   The "Copeland" Hotel burned very early this morning: a *terrible* fire; one man, (a Mr. I. E. Lambert of Emporia) is known to have perished in the fire and may be a number of others. After dinner, Mrs. Swendson and I took car to town, to "have a look" at the ruins, and it was a pitiful sight; most of the guests were rescued in their night clothes and compelled to walk thro' snow, barefoot, to places of safety. We met Mrs. Tallman-Bailey, and together we three went to the "Woman's Sufferage Headquarters" in the State House, then visited the Legislature, both Houses, for a short time, then walked home, for it was delightful to be out. We met in the State House corridor, Dr. Bancoft, who travels and Lectures on "*Lincoln*". He saw Lincoln assassinated and helped carry him from the Theatre. Dr. Bancroft is tall and "spare-built", with white hair and whiskers and of kindly bearing.

Sat. 16   Spent all afternoon down town shopping. Was to have met Mr. L. M. Penwell and have talked over with him "plans" for my taking to "raise," his Nephew (Roy Penwell) but Fred thinks I had better not take the boy, so did not keep my appointment. *Awfully sloppy.*

Mon. 18   Washed this morning, in spite of the "foggy and freezy" weather and the clothes froze dry. After dinner Mrs. Swendson and I went to Mrs. Lee Monroe's 909 Harrison St., to help her in some "Sufferage work" for the Legislature, but she was compelled to be at the Auditorium so late, that we went on over town to do some shopping and then came on home and will do our portion of the work another time.

Thurs. 21   A regular California day, fog so thick you could "cut it." I walked down to my own Church, to Bible Class this evening but I came home on a car, because the fog was so densely thick, I did not feel it safe, to come so far, even if one had a dozen "hat-pins," for protection. Had a letter from Freda today, asking us to send her *three-dollars* because "she wants to go to Denver with her Class and Mama won't let her have the money." Well we will send it: we raised her from a baby and she thinks we will give her anything.

Fri. 22   Just the busiest, busy day and all outdoors so grand with sunshine, but I had no moment to step out in it, because of the much I had to do within. O well my home is *full* all the time, anyhow, of the *sunshine* that comes, with the kindness of a *good* husband. My Teddie is so good to me, that it keeps my home full of *Sunshine* all the year 'round.

Sat. 23   After dinner, I took some candy in to "Robinson and Marshall's" to some of my friends, then spent rest of the afternoon painting at the Bearsley Studio. He [Beardsley] is such a queer fellow, but I like his pictures. Very many do not like either he or his mother, but I have always gotten along with them, in spite of their peculiarities.

Sun. 24   A fine day and I walked to and from Sunday-School and Church this morning. Took Candy and a picture I had painted to Walter Bowell, one of my Class, in honor of his Birthday. And today my *"wee girlie"* would be 17 years old if living. O the years have been *so many between the day you were placed in my arms and this*; and I was allowed such a *small portion* of *Heaven's joy* in your possession—*five* short months *and then you were taken from me.*

February

Thurs. 4   Sunny, but rather "blow-ie" day, and so in the midst of hard study, and right at noon here came aunt Sarah Ogden, bringing Ida Harper, of Kansas City, a cousin of my father's whom I had never seen, yet the moment I opened the door I knew it was Ida Harper and I had never even seen a picture of her. I wonder what it is within me that causes me to know people instantly, when I meet them for first time. I often, and sometimes on the street, see people who I know *by name at once*, and never have seen them before. This *Power* (or whatever it is) causes me to wonder, often, what there is in me. I must be a sort of a Telegraph apparatus or "receiving

Machine." Well, any way, while I was wholly unpre-
pared for company, we had a pretty fair dinner, and a
most happy afternoon together, and Bro. Finch Phoned
that examination questions did not get here, so no "examination" tonight and I am at home.[1]

March

Thurs. 11   Painting at the Beardsley Studio again this afternoon,
with the usual crowd. They are "packing" to move soon
to Denver, Colo.[2]

Sun. 14   Cold wind blowing, but bright and sunny. I walked to
and from Sunday School and Church. *Brother Finch, in
his sermon, lauded* the women, saying they were the *best
thing God ever made*, etc, then *proceeded* to *roast them,*
saying they *were not doing much* for *their race* because *they
thought too much* of *fine clothes, Automobiles,* playing *Bridge*
and *"sipping Cock-tails."* And after the Sermon *I* went
after him, for not also *criticizing women* who *exhibit Bull-
dogs* at *dog Shows,* meaning Nan Herron, whom *he is too*
fond of and some *patted me on the back for saying it.*

April

Eastern Star

Sat. 3   . . . . Teddie and I went to the Masonic Temple this
evening and were initiated into the "Eastern Star". . . .

May

Sun. 9   . . . . Cora, Mrs. McConn, Miss Berry, Idola Runyen,
Fred and I went to the "Daily Capital" building, met Mr.
Runyen and Winfield and were shown through the *fine*
building by Mr. De Armond and Mr. McConn; it's
grand , *wonderful.* Cora, Fred and I took a car home and
I have walked so much today, I am tired. Had a talk with
Mr. L. M. Penwell this morning about taking to raise his
nephew, Age 10 yrs. Guess I'll take him.

Fri. 14   Mr. L. M. Penwell and brother Frank came out this
morning, bringing the Papers to be signed up, for our
taking Homer La Roy Penwell (son of Frank) age ten
years. He is to be our boy until 21 years old; the mother

is dead and the father drinks, until he is unfit to have the care of his children. . . .

Sat. 15   A bright, beautiful day—an *ideal* one. Mr. L. M. Penwell came out this morning and brought his nephew (Roy) and now we have a *boy*; he is a bright, fine looking little fellow and I am happy to be his mother, but it is always sad that a child must grow up among strangers, and forget or grow indifferent to his own people. The boy has been in my Sunday School Class for over a year and I do not anticipate any trouble, but the responsibility is very great, still I feel sure God will bless my efforts to rear him a good man.

Sun. 16   A fine day and this morning, son Roy and I walked to Sunday School and Church and Fred came to church and walked home with us. Mrs. A. E. Jones also walked home with us. Post Office opens earlier on Sunday morning now and Fred will get to Church oftener. Roy seemed very happy—we do not give him our name, because I do not think it fair to take a child's name from them, when as old as he, but he is ours by Contract, his father signing away all right to him.

Thurs. 20   I went to town shopping this afternoon as the weather was *ideal*. Had to buy a new Umbrella, as Roy broke mine yesterday.

Sat. 22   A fine day and such a busy one for me. Had a letter from Freda today noon asking me to buy her a white dress for Graduation from 8th Grade; she is only 13. I sent her a new dress and ten dollars just after Easter, but she wrote her folks "borrowed" it, which simply means her mother took it from her, for something she wanted herself, instead of buying Freda the shoes and hat we intended. It makes me *tired*. Well I went to town right after Supper and bought a fine French Lawn, a bolt of lace also insertion and some pretty "hair-ribbons" then met Fred and Roy and went to the Grand to see Mrs. Fiske in "Salvation Nell"; 'twas *excellent*.

Tues. 25   "Sunshine and rain," "clouds and chill" and yet the day was not bad. My good "hubby" said to me, "I *love* and *love* and *love* you," and I replied "why do you" and he said "because you are so nice, and I like to watch and listen to you, when you are talking to others".

I have the most adorable of husbands; just *courts me*, as if *I were his sweet-heart* and *this, after 15 years of married life with him; he makes love to me until he almost wearies me only it is so blessed to be loved by a good man.* Roy was standing at the Barnyard gate this morning watching a Guinea very intently, when he looked up at me and asked "what kind of a *chicken* is a *Guinea* anyway."

Wed. 26 . . . . Let Roy go to Schwartz to play, after supper, and with the boys he was playing with, got into a little "*scrap*" with some negro boys, and came home frightened half to death; was afraid to go from one room to another without me; afraid to go to bed, and so frightened, it made him remember to say his long forgotten prayers: it was really pathetic to hear the little fellow, say, as he crawled into bed in great fear "I use to say my prayers but I guess I've forgotten them" then try to go thro' his prayer. But I am rather glad he has had the lesson, for I only recently told him to let the negroes alone and to always treat them in a respectful manner. I guess he will now.

June

Tues. 1 A busy day and I hardly know how I find life so full, when but three of us; our boy seems a happy, contented little fellow and we are very happy to have him in our home. I have loved him from the first moment I saw him and now I adore him; how well I remember the first Sunday he came into my Sunday School Class. I did not know he had no mother, but how I did wish he was my boy: he was such a sweet, pretty, little fellow; blue-eyed, yet so dark that they are hardly blue.

Thurs. 3 Another rainy, busy day, but stopped this evening and Roy went to his "Boy's Club" at Grant Laxman's, 4th and Buchanan. He is a mischievous boy but in a *good* way; at my heels all the time. Fred and I spent evening at Mrs. Armstrong's.

Sat. 5 Roy helps me always with the dishes and this morning helped me sweep the house. This afternoon he and I walked down to the Church to practice for Children's Day, then walked home and this evening Fred and I went to "Eastern Star," while I let Roy go to stay over night with Claude Swendson.

Wed. 9 Gave Roy his "*first*" Music lesson, this morning and he did pretty well. Lucille Sheafor and Marie DeArmond came out this afternoon to play Croquet with Roy. I love my Boy very much and a thousand dollars would not tempt me to give him up.

Fr. 11   Roy said today, he *never* would live with his Aunt "Ell" again, she was too cranky—was always "cranky" and never said anything to him but crankiness. He seems to be very fond of me and I hurt his poor little heart this evening too—he was "tagging" me and got a little rough in striking, and I had to speak rather firmly, to make him stop—he broke into tears, saying to Fred that I was angry with him. I soon kissed away the tears and brought back the smiles. We think so much of the Boy. I went to Rev. Finch's to 2nd Division, C.W.B.M.[3] meeting, this afternoon, 318 Topeka Ave. Mrs. A. E. Jones and I served the *refreshments* (ice-cream and Nabisco's) Roy came at 5 o'clock and I took him to town and got him a new tie and some collars.

Mon. 14   . . . . For almost a year Fred and I have been alone and it has been so still all about the place, but now we have a boy, there is plenty of noise again and it sounds good to hear it—nothing like children in a home; it makes home *real* and life worth living. And O my the questions Roy can ask. He said to me the other day, "which of you asked the other to marry, I'll bet *you* did, because you are jollier than Mr. Farnsworth"; meaning *I* talk more than he.

Sat. 26   Such a hot day and more than busy. Mrs. W. P. Armstrong and Fronie took Fred, Roy and me to Gages Lake, tonight again, to Swim: we all went in, and had the jolliest time. I can't "swim a lick" but the water is glorious. Roy went in, for his first swiming lesson tonight.

Sun. 27   . . . . Our dear Freda is 14 years old today and writes she "*gets so lonesome*". We miss her so much; and my own "wee girlie" died 17 years ago today, and I have prayed, and begged and plead, that God would give me another, Oh! the heart-ache and *longing* in a *childless* home.

July

Thurs. 8   No rain today but hot and stickey; 101°. My boy is "crazy" about swimming and keeps begging *me* to go; I told him, *he* could go, but *I* could not; he objected, saying "*we can't have any fun unless you go too.*" I hope he will always care as much for me: he objects to my working so hard and said to me the other day, "*you just work all the time and never go any where, not even to the neighbors*".

Fri. 16   Fred home this afternoon for half-Holiday, so to do some needed work at home. Mrs. Armstrong took us, and the usual crowd, to Gages tonight for a swim, and we had a grand old time. I swim pretty well with water-wings and find I can swim a little without them, tho' swimming is not yet easy for me.

Tues. 20   Fred having another day of vacation today and this evening Mrs. Armstrong took he and I, for a swim at Gages. Roy walked out earlier. Big crowd. And I am *first* woman who has ever swam across.

Wed. 21   A good breeze blowing today. Oh! how I did enjoy my swim last night and the distinction of being the *first* and *too*, the *only woman* who *has ever swum across Gages*. Of course I used my "wings" but no one else has had the nerve even with "wings", and I swim some without "wings" anyway. I could hardly sleep for the joy of it all and perhaps excited too. Spent afternoon at J. W. Dunlap's to see Mrs. Harry Dunlap, who is here from Clay Center with her two fine babies. The usual "*bunch*" went

Martha on Fred's back, clowning. From her photograph album.

swiming this evening and had our *usual* fun and good
time.

Fri. 23   Another fine day and quite cool, but Fronie, Mrs. Armstrong, Obed Goddard, Fred and I went for a *swim* at
Gages Lake, and *never* had a *finer swim*, and I had several
long swims without "water-wings." Had to *"Punish" my boy
today*, by having him *wash* his *pants, shirt* and *underclothes*,
and it almost *broke his heart*. Yesterday, he and Dewey
Goddard had a *"dust" fight*, and his clothes were *something dreadful*.

Thurs.29   . . . . Laurent Schwartz and Dewey Goddard here to
play Croquet with Roy and I had to give him a "strap-
ping." He can't bear to be a "loser" in any kind of a game
and won't play fair and when I spoke to him about his
unfair play, he became extremely *"saucy."*

August

Thurs. 12   Fred, Roy and I, walked out to Gages Lake this evening
for a swim: one and a quarter miles walk, seems a long
way to walk on a hot night, but the swim is so fine, one is
more than paid. Roy has a dreadful temper, and children
are getting tired of playing with him. I do not know
whether I shall ever be able to teach him to control it or
not: he and Dewey have quarreled dreadfully today.

Fri. 27   Well it actually rained a little today, but not enough to
settle the dust. Roy in his anger, attempted to stab one of
his play mates (Dewey Goddard) this evening and I had
to take his knife from him and give him a whipping too.
His terrible temper is his only fault.

November

Sat. 6   Another grand day, and a busy one. Had to give Roy a
whipping, because he got *saucy* and refused to do some
work I told him to do. He has to be handled with strong
hands; has an ungovernable temper, but lots of good
in him and I am sure will make a fine man.[4] We went
to Eastern Star this evening—Initiation and Oyster
Supper.

Fri. 26   Busy with my Sunday School work. Wednesday, when I
had all my Preachers here, my Pastor, Rev. Finch, told
the Evangelists that *I, "was the most wonderful woman,"*

with boys, that *I could do anything with them.* And Mrs.
Finch, told them *I had taken a Class, that had been the
despair of every teacher, and had gotten them under perfect
control and interested in their lessons.* The work with and
for my class of Boys has been very hard, and it seems
good to be commended, tho' I feel very deeply, my
unfitness and unworthiness. I love the work and love my
Boys into being good, but I do not feel I am fitted for the
work. I wish I was more worthy. Mr. Sam Gilbert of
Arkansas City called to spend evening with us. Fred at
Lodge.

December

Thurs. 16   Met "Jonesie" and Mrs. S. A. Swendson at 4:15 P.M. and
went to a Reception at Mrs. Judge Lee Monroe. I have
nothing decent to wear, and there were some very
"swell" costumes and our Governor's wife, Mrs. Stubbs,
in the Receiving line, but Mrs. Monroe is so sweet and
gracious that she chooses her friends for themselves
and not for their clothes, and I had a *very* happy time.
There are few women like Lilla Day Monroe.[5] Got home
about 6:30.

Fri. 31   Well the old year ends today, and is going out white and
cold, tho a great deal warmer than usual. I have spent a
busy day baking: and baked some "ginger-bread" men,
for some of my neighbors' babies and for Roy. The past
year has been filled with the invaluable blessings of
health and *happiness.* My good Teddie and I have had to
work hard and economize closely, but we have had the
strength and health to do it, and enjoyed a happy year
together, beside helping others and giving a home to a
motherless boy, so I feel the year has been one of great
blessing to us, and pray the New Year may possess as
much for us. I have *tried* to live a consistent Christian life
and God in his boundless mercy will forgive wherein I
have come short.

[1910]

January

Fri. 14 Received an invitation today, to my niece's (Zaidee Gilbert) wedding. James home all day half sick.[1] Mr. James Ramsey came out this morning on Political business, in the interest of Col. J. W. F. Hughes, for Mayor; while I am a Hughes "*man*", I am not going to mix in Politics this year; these men will work you to death in their own interest and yet refuse you the Ballot.

Mon. 24 Partly cloudy and quite warm; washed and my clothes got dry. James not home yesterday nor today. Came home this evening and is working for McSpadden Grocery. Mrs. M. H. Strickler and baby Herbert came in this afternoon. Herbert is the sweetest boy and *cries* to come see "Nannie", as he calls both Fred and me. The Stork left a baby boy at Mr. Spooner Goddard's this morning—everywhere but our house and my heart has *starved all these* years, for babies. My own "wee girlie" would be 18 years old today, if living, and O, I can't forget. I want my baby, my loved little one.

> But Ah! the dainty pillow next my own
> Is never rumpled by a shining head!
> My precious birdling from its nest has flown
> The baby girl I used to kiss, is dead.
> No child can ever be so dear to me
> As thou wert, sweet
> And yet *all* childhood is more dear to me
> Since I have kissed thy feet,
> My babe—who bode with me so brief a space.
> Because of one dear infant head
> With raven hair,
> To me, all little heads
> A halo wear;
> And for one saintly face I knew,
> *All* babes are fair.

Got another look at the Comet this evening, thro' the clouds. I called to see Mrs. Armstrong this evening whom I found much improved and called to see Mrs. Gleason who was taken sick at noon.

Mon. 31   A fine day, and I washed and ironed. Today is "Passing" day, at school and Roy passed with a Fair grade, or rather *Good*, as he received all "G" 's but two, which were "F's." He also got a very *saucy spell*, on him this evening and I had to give him a *lickin'*. Our new Comet still shows up tho' getting dim, but each evening by 8 o'clock, it shows an *immense* tail, straight up in the air and bending in a graceful curve, to the South. It is the *third* Comet I have seen.

February

Wed. 9   A most beautiful day and I spent the afternoon with my friend "Jonesie." They are going to move to Florida, and I don't like it a little bit: big land *boom* on down there and they will lose all they have got; just a "get rich quick" concern, but *some* won't be *advised*.

Tues. 15   Am reading "Rienzi" and have done little else today, but read; it is most interesting.[2] That nephew of mine did not come home today and Phoned he was going to commence work in morning at Santa Fe Depot.

Thurs. 17   James came home last night after we had gone to bed—says he is "pastry" cook, at Santa Fe Depot but I *doubt* him some way; I believe he is only "loafing" around town: O these boys that can't be "reasoned" with and lay

Fri. 18   James came home this morning, for his "good clothes" saying he was going to the Theatre tonight and would not have time to come home and dress after work; from his manner and seeming ill at ease, I believe he was "lying." I had already asked Fred to come home at noon, by way of town and look for him at Tromp's "*Smokehouse*" and sure enough, there he found the Boy loafing, instead of working as he told me. I sent Fred to Santa Fe Depot this evening and found he is not working there, nor hasn't been. Now *why* should he lie to us. We have done *everything*, under the sun, for him. It worries me sick, and neither Fred nor I can scarcely sleep or work. I feel sure he left town this afternoon, to go to work perhaps some where else. O such a boy.

Sat. 19   A beautiful day and I washed a very large washing, cleaned etc; busy, *very*, almost every moment of the day. I wish I knew where James is tonight.

March

Sat. 12
A grand day; Received letters from Zaidee and Freda—neither they, nor we, have had a *line* from James yet, and he has been gone 3 weeks. Roy said to me this morning "your bread is *finer* than "Weston" bread," which is very complimentary for "Weston" is a very fine "Bakers" bread; but the child thinks I am a great cook.

Sun. 13
. . . . Eddie Phoned us this morning, James was working as second cook, in the Eating House at Elsworth, Kansas and is working his way home, to Boulder, Colo. Think he might write us.

Sat. 26
. . . . Roy has been cross and ugly as a Bear all day and I had to give him a hard whiping this morning. I guess I let him play too much and do too much for him and so have rather spoilt him. I painted a lot of Easter eggs this afternoon for Roy.

Sun. 27
"Easter Sunday" and a mighty fine day. Roy and I walked to and from Sunday School and Church. Had most excellent Music this morning, and the Church very prettily decorated. I put the eggs I painted for Roy in a circle, about his Breakfast plate this morning, as a surprise and he seemed very much pleased. A large "double yolk," I painted with a grinning face, showing teeth and called it the Giant. One unusually small one, I painted with a smiling face and black hair and painted on the name "Ethel," for his girl at school; a slender white one, I painted with "tow"-colored hair and named "Marie", for a "*tow-headed*" neighbor girl who is more "*smitten* with him, then he with her: and as luck would have it, my hens layed a brown, *very* speckled egg and this I painted with red hair for his Red-headed, freckled face "Lucile" down at the church, a very sweet girl, whom he cares a great deal for: then another was a frowning, angry face, to represent himself when angry, and two more bright smiling faces represented two boy friends, Warren and Dewey; and he was very happy with his egg family.

April

Thurs. 7
Finished a new *Shirt waist* and some collars for Fred. Roy has dreadful cold. An old cattle buyer here to buy my cow and wanted me to keep her up and *stuff* her with all

dry food she would eat and give her *no water* for 24 *hours*, as if I would *starve anything* that way. I told him, he *could not have her*—that "I would not starve *my cow* to help *any* man, sell a few pounds of water to the Packing Co." I would not be so inhuman nor dishonest. I *try* to practice what I Preach. He made me decidedly weary.

Tues. 26   *My 43 Birthday.* Old Father Time empties his Hour-glass so fast, that the years "whizz" by, until one can scarcely count them: It seems but yesterday, since I was a little girl, *splashing contentedly* in *all the mudholes* I could find to get into, which in the vernacular of Whitcomb Riley, were our "old swimin' holes."[3] And it was just as much fun to *slide down a slippery-bank*, into a *mud-hole*, as if the water had been cleaner. Youth is not discriminating: *Wonder why there were no "germs"* in those days; one would be loth to stick their fingers in such water now days, *lest they catch a Germ.* And the poor little Sunfish we caught in those ponds on Pin hooks, was as exciting fun in those days, as pulling a whale out of the Ocean would be now. And *bear (bare) skin bathing suit.* Walked to and from Bible Class this afternoon and made a short call at Mrs. H. H. Bair's as I went over and at Mrs. M. H. Strickler's as I came home. This evening, Fred, Roy and I went to the Auditorium to hear the Minneapolis Symphony Orchestra. It was very fine and we enjoyed it *very, very* much.

June

Thurs. 2   Another *perfect* day. Fred brought home my glasses from Dr. Cutsingers at noon and now I'll see how they benefit me. I *haven't* enjoyed them this afternoon—don't like anything hanging on my nose.

Fri. 3   A rainy day, yet I *washed* and got my clothes dry. *The last day of school* and now I will have *trying time* if we *keep* Roy as he will want to be gone from home to play all the time. But he is so saucy and ill-tempered and his father has annoyed us so much, we think we will give him up.[4]

Mon. 6   "The day is dark and *cold* and dreary
            It *rains* and the wind is never weary"[5]
            but I got my washing dry just the same.

Tues. 7   More *cold* and more *rain.* At 5:30 P.M. I took Roy to U.P. depot and sent him to Rossville to visit his father: *guess will let him stay.*

Wed. 8   O but it has rained today. Roy's father phoned me today and it is settled that he is to keep Roy: it is too bad: he was a great trial, yet I was much attached to him and didn't like to see him go. O, I so pity the poor child.

Thurs. 9   Had a terrific rain and some hail today. I went to bed at 8 o'clock last night with out my Supper and *cried all night*, over Roy's going away: the poor boy will get so homesick. I have felt *wretchedly* lonely today, but know its best he has gone, for he was a great trial. His uncle LaRoy wrote me a nice note today and made me a present of twenty five dollars.

Sat. 11   *O so cold* but no rain and the sunshine was fine. Our neighbor Harry Dunlap was married today—his wife has been dead about ten months but he needs another to care for his two babies and I do not blame him. I sent Roy's trunk to him at Rossville today and now we live alone again.

Tues. 14   Another fine day and another most busy one. Ironed, put up few Raspberries and washed beding. Roy has been gone a week today and I miss him greatly. He was the most stubborn and high-tempered child I have ever known, yet I had splendid control of him. I hope his father can find a good home for [him] and his having to go from the good home we gave him will be a splendid lesson to him, to be a better boy. I so pity the child.

July

Mon. 25   Another *scorching* day: 109 and seemed hotter. I did my washing tho' and made Plum jelly. Mrs. Armstrong here this morning and again this afternoon: she has little to do and gets lonely. I never have trouble to find enough to do, to keep from getting lonely. I often wish the days were double their length, so I could do all I find to do. *Fronie Armstrong* is *18 years old* today, and *Mrs. Brown* (a dear old colored woman) *is 79 today* and some of her friends gave a Party for her, at Mrs. Birds on Woodward Ave: she came over and invited us, so we went over and ate some Ice-Cream and drank some Punch with her. We think a great deal of Mrs. Brown.

August

Mon. 15   Did my usual washing and ironing, and washed fruit jars all afternoon. Our neighbor Harry Dunlap came home this morning with his run-away-wife: it seems now that her mother compelled her to leave him and the poor child is in a bad way with nervous "break-down." Mrs. Otto D. found her unconscious at 11 o'clock this morning and called me: we worked with her an hour and could not bring her to consciousness then called Dr. Sams, who thinks she has been given poison: she remained unconscious until 5 o'clock this evening.

October

Mon 17 ⸱⸱⸱⸱ Cousin Emma Adams is still with us and she and I have visited hard all day. She tells me she is a Spiritualist and Medium: I wish she would let it alone—I believe it to be wrong. I know that on my mother's side we have a gift of "*Mediumship*" and that *I* have strong Mediumistic powers and Clairvoyant too, but I will not develope it or have anything to do with it, because my Bible teaches me not to—that it is all wrong. My good hubby had to go back to work this morning.

November

Wed. 23 Another fine day and I have nearly wasted it. I should have spent the whole day on my Sunday School lessons, but spent almost half the day reading "The Price of the Prairie" Mrs. McCarter's new Book. I am glad to have the Authoress for an acquaintance and fellow Club member.[6]

Thursday 24 "*Thanksgiving Day*" and such a fine day—too warm for *wraps*. We went to the Second Christian Church (colored) and bought our dinners, and got a mighty fine dinner for a quarter. Working in yard all afternoon.

December

Sun. 25 "Christmas Day" and a most beautiful one. Warren Remington walked down to Sunday School with me. My Class of Boys gave me a most beautiful hand-painted Bread plate, this morning. I was taken completely by surprise. We have been *promoted*, and next Sunday are to be *big* folks upstairs; I ought to stay in the Junior

Department and they would like to keep me there but as soon as my Boys found it out, they found a piece of wraping paper, wrote out a Petition, all signed it, and presented it to the Superintendent: it read as follows. *"We want Mrs. Farnsworth or we will quit."* The music at Church this morning, was unusually fine. Fred came home from P.O. for dinner but had to go back and work up his Mail, so has put in most of the day at the P.O. and it has scarcely seemed like either Christmas or Sunday, only for our many presents coming in: Candy, China, Books, handkerchiefs, neckties, Baskets, Doilies, Money, Silver Thimble, Calendars, and Christmas Cards, by the score: we feel Santa Claus was good to us and we have tried to be good to others by giving some useful presents.

[*1911*]

February

Tues. 7

O, such a fine day. I put in the morning writing letters, and this afternoon called on Mrs. Darby and Aunt Delia Howard: this evening, Fred and I went to State House to Legislature. House passed Suffrage Amendment.

Wed. 8

An ideal day and at 9 o'clock, I went to Mrs. Swendson's and she and I walked down to the State House, where we attended the Senate of the Legislature and heard a most tiresome discussion as to whether they should pass the Suffrage Amendment that was passed in the House last night—they succeeded in getting it put off and called for a recess: it's too disgusting. Well Mrs. S. and myself went up town and shopped awhile and "ran on to" Mrs. Armstrong, who brought us home in her buggy; and tonight I see by the paper, that the Senate did after all pass the "Suffrage Amendment" this afternoon: and by 27 to 12. The House passed 94 to 28—and most of us are feeling good tonight. We were only opposed by a few "thick skinned" Democrats—the better Democrats were for us; of course Republicans were.

Wed. 15

Another ideal day and this evening I went to the church to Supper: the Junior Department of the Sunday School gave Supper to the other Department Teachers and to the Scoville Evangelistic Party. I had a talk with Dr. Scoville about my Class of Boys. From the church we all went to the Auditorium to preaching. Were 16 "confessions" tonight and a most splendid sermon.[1] I came home on a car; my Teddy could not get off early enough to go to the Supper. Dr. Scoville said in his sermon he didn't believe God ever meant for man to smoke or He would have turned his nose up the other way for a Flue.

Sun. 19

Light snow falling most of the day. Warren R. came over and went to Sunday School with me; we took car because of deep snow. Dr. Scoville was at S.S. at the close of which he made a short talk and gave an "invitation" asking *who would be first* and *immediately I stepped into the*

Aisle, with my Class of S.S. Boys and *when he saw me coming down the Aisle with a string of Boys,* he said *"isn't this a pretty sight, lets cheer them"* and *every hand in the house commenced clapping.* Every boy in my Class who were not already members of the Church, except Victor Carrell and he wasn't at S.S. this morning: as soon as I asked my boys to make the "good confession" this morning, the most of them immediately promised to do so: two made the promise after I had talked with them a little: and so tonight *my heart is full of unspeakable joy,* that *God has given me these precious young souls for my hire: I have prayed much for these Boys;* that *God, thro' me, would lead these Boys into the Kingdom;* but when, this morning before starting to S.S. I knelt in prayer, once more to ask of Him that He would help me to lead them to Christ, I little dreamed that the victory was so near at hand: that even then my prayer was answered.[2] *Ralph Davidson 13 years, William Jackson 14 yrs. Billie Badger 13 yrs. only needed to be asked,* while *Ronald McCord 13 yrs. Purl Bernard 13 yrs.* and *Robert Sympson 13 yrs. I needed to urge a little. Claude Swendson 13 yrs. Fred Brackett 13 yrs. Lyman King 12 yrs.* and *Warren Remington 12 yrs.* are already members of the Church. This has been *one of the happiest mornings of my life.* I struggled hard to keep back the happy tears, and *in my heart I have thanked God all day long.* So many came to me and congratulated me, and Dr. Scoville said *"I will never forget that Teacher and these Boys."* I went to Auditorium to morning Services with Ralph D. and Lyman K. then took car home.

March

Sun. 5

Walked to Sunday School this morning at the Church, then Ralph Davidson and Lyman King went with me to preaching at the Auditorium, where was a good crowd and about a doz. "confessions." Scoville's special theme of denunciation this morning was *dancing,* which he styled, "hugging set to music." I am afraid *he* never danced any, and does not know all that he thinks he does, because a respectful young man would no more hug a young woman in a dance, than at church or anywhere else. I danced, constantly, when a young woman and *never* was hugged in the dance. A *respectful* young man, will be respectful *in the dance* and a *disrespect-ful* young man, will be disrespectful, wherever he is: he could not be trusted any place. . . .

Mon. 20   The "Scoville" Meetings, closed last night with *1008 Converts*. He has done both *good* and bad: I do not like him, and many more feel as I do. He takes much credit for many things that I am sure God will not give him credit for: for instance, he will authorize the report to be sent all over the world, that he made, "*1008 Converts* in the Topeka Meeting," while the facts are, on his sermons alone, he would not have made one third, possibly one tenth that number. . . .

Thurs. 30   Edison Co., thro' H. B. Howard, sent men out this afternoon to "wire" our house for Electric-lights. Fred and I very foolishly this evening, decided to attend the *opening* of the New Mills Store and got into *almost* a dangerous jam: it was so dreadful, we got out of it soon as possible and came home, without seeing anything except a very little on first Floor: no more *Openings* for me: it almost made me sick.

April

Wed. 26   Rained most of forenoon, but afternoon was nice and I took Pearle[3] down to the State House to look about a bit, and get some Historical data of our Ancestors, in the State Historical Rooms, then up town to "Shop" a little. O how our tongues have run today—we haven't near tongues enough to say all we want too, in the short time she will be here and the tongues we have are about worn out. Today is my 44th Birthday and I am still fond of Singing, whistling, dancing, boating, riding horse-back and on Bicycle, tennis, hunting, skating and above all swiming. Pearle gave me a "cut-glass" drinking-glass and Warren Remington gave me a potted Heliotrope and my Sunday School Class of Boys, gave me a very pretty imitation Rookwood Vase. They are a great bunch of boys.

May

Sun. 28   . . . . Topeka Post, G.A.R. No. 71, had their Memorial Sermon preached at our Church this morning, and the

Martha and seventeen of her Sunday School boys on her porch roof. From her photo album, May 1911.

son of a Confederate Soldier, preached it. Rev. Cantrell of Omaha, Neb. It was fairly good, but *some way there seemed a certain restraint*—there didn't seem to be the sympathy and enthusiasm a Northern man would have called out. *As hard as I tried not to, I felt a certain antipathy* to this Son of a Confederate speaking to the men, who had to *suffer untold hardship*, because *his* people were *determined* to *destroy the Union*. And yet my mother's people were *Southern Slave-holders*: my father A Northern man, *fought for the Flag. . . .*

June

Tues. 27
Another pleasant day: Thermometer didn't reach a hundred all day; but no sign of rain. Today our neice, Freda Gilbert, whom we had almost ten years, is 16 yrs. old—in Colo. now with her mother, who takes no pride in making anything of her: she neither goes to school nor takes music. O our little girl, its too bad, for we kept her in School, gave her music and painting and did all in our power, to make a fine woman of her.

19 years ago today, my own sweet "wee girlie" went home to Heaven and thro' all the years, my heart never forgets. Who, that ever has sat in deepest anguish, beside a precious child and watched the "lamp of life" go out, can ever forget. God alone has known how my heart has hungered all these years.

July

Sat. 1   Another 112 day. Well we people who live thro' the heat of this Summer, will at least be proud to say, "we lived in Kansas that Summer, that the doors of Gehenna were opened on us." Kansas is sure a State that goes to the extreme of extremes. I wrote some 50 cards and letters for Minnie today. From time we were girls I've had to write for her, when she was near.[4]

Sun. 2   And still another day *at 112*. . . . Too hot for even a Diary, or to write in one.

Mon. 3   Minnie went to Kansas City today, so early this morning she and I took her grips to Santa Fe Depot, "checked" them bought her ticket, then walked back up town to shop awhile then to Mills store, where I wrote some 50 Postal Cards and letters for her, then went up to the Tea Room, where we got a nice dinner then wrote some

Birthday party invitation. From her photo album, 1911.

more, walked to the P.O. then to Depot, where she kept me writing until train pulled out. She would write a person to death: says I write better than she and have a talent for it. I get tired just the same. Her train left at 1:40 and I came home.

Mon. 24   So cool today one almost needed a fire, but I kept house closed instead. I washed and ironed, both, today. Got letter today from the Christian Pub. Co., St. Louis, Mo. to write them a twelve or fifteen hundred word article, about my Sunday School Class, which is becoming quite famous as the P□G or "*Play Square Gang.*"

Wed. 26   At Mrs. Armstrong's awhile this morning. Frank Shaw (my nephew), Mrs. Strickler and Herbert were in this morning, so I did no writing on my Paper until this afternoon. Mrs. Jim Shaw and Jessie have the Small-pox: the South East part of town is full of it and many deaths occurring.

Fri. 28   Writing all day and this evening finished my Article, ready to "copy" and succeeded in cutting myself down to 1395 words. Hard work but it seems to be a woman's way to want to say too much.

August

Tues. 1   Ironed and went with Jonesie at 8:30 this morning to a "Sale" at Mills and it was good as a Circus. I never attended a sale in my life before—don't believe in them and I just had to stand and laugh to see women so undignified as to run, actually race thro' the building and up the stairs, reach the Counters they wanted and all "grab" for the same thing, then pull and haul until goods would almost be torn in two; blacks and whites, all pulling same goods.

Thurs. 3   Had hard rain last night. Mr. Jones took Jonesie and I to town Shopping this morning then to the Sewing School and brought us home at 5 o'clock. About 7 o'clock Mr. & Mrs. Cornelius came for me and took me to Frank Shaw's 1104 E-8-St. His mother died at 9:30 of *Smallpox*. O its so horrible, so horrible.

Fri. 4   I did not get home last night until 1 o'clock and am tired with grief. Frank Shaw was not able to see his mother and took her death very hard—poor boy, I pity him so. He had Mrs. Wooley Phone for me to come down. Said he just had to have me—his father, brother and Uncle were quarantined at home with his mother and brother Jesse, who is also very sick with Small-pox. We are having a dreadful scourge of it here. I went with Frank to his father's and talked with them all, out in the yard, but did not go close enough to expose myself to the disease. Poor Retta was dying when we went there. They said she was a solid scab all over. Dr. Munn said it was the worse thing he ever saw in his life—just horifying. Retta was buried at 7:30 this morning. She was a dear, good woman, loved by every one who knew her and it is too pitiful to think about—makes my heart ache. The Remingtons brought sister Kate Akin out this evening to stay all night with us. She is a fine little sister.

Thurs. 17   Awfully hot and dry. I put in most of day making "Pen and Ink" invitations for my Sunday School Class. Mrs. Schwartz, Remington and Armstrong in today. Poor Jim Shaw died at 3 o'clock this morning of Small-pox: he was such a good man—always took my part and many times scolded Johnny for abusing me. He was my first husband's brother and as good a man as ever lived. Retta, his wife, died two weeks ago this evening with Smallpox. Mrs. Armstrong sent for me to come over this evening—had a *fierce* sick headache. I stayed with her until 10 o'clock when she got better.

September

Wed. 6   Writing all day. Getting out a 2000 word article, on Sunday School work, for the "Round Table", Christian Pub. Co. St. Louis by request of R. P. Shepherd, one of the Editors.

Mon. 11   A most awfully hot day, but I got my washing out early, and had no hot work for rest of day. Saw my first "*Aeroplane*" this evening as we sat on the Porch. It had flown from the Fair Grounds to the State House and was on its way back. A very pretty flight.

October

Thurs. 12   Went with Jonesie this afternoon to Good Government Club at Miss Kline's 103 Western Ave. A fine meeting. I was on Program for "Sufferage Notes" and all said my notes were good. A number congratulated me warmly. The papers had announced the defeat of Sufferage in California but just at close of our meeting, Mrs. W. A. Johnston got a Telegram, announcing "Victory for Women in California." We all shouted for joy, some hugged and kissed one another, some cried and some jumped "up and down" for joy and all joined most heartily in singing "Praise God from whom all blessings flow." O we were a happy lot. Had hard rain this evening.

Tues. 17   A fine day. Mrs. Strickler and Herbert over this afternoon and Mrs. Wm. Baker-Lovall who was my neighbor on Lincoln St. 20 years ago, spent the afternoon and evening with us. She is quite broken hearted over the death of her daughter Mrs. Rhodes, who died in August, with Smallpox. Mrs. R. fearing the disease left Topeka and went to Bazaar, Ks. where she was stricken and was quarantined in a Tent in an Alfalfa field and had a most terrible experience.

November

Sat. 25   Ironed until almost noon, and busy as always on Sat. Mrs. Sherman came in this morning for some Sufferage Literature, I being Chairman of Good Government Club Literature committee. Well, one hears many comments of satisfaction over the Electrocution of Henry Clay Beatty Jr. for murder of his wife and the conviction of the men who Tarred Miss Chamberlain—a pity *they* could not be electrocuted, for men who will do so horrible a thing, will do worse: Man a woman's protector? Well, not in these days; he is anything else.[5]

December

Sat. 23   Just an ideal day and I have worked hard all day— Ironing, sweeping, cleaning and decorated the house, for Christmas. Fred's work was heaviest he has ever had—he worked all day without getting time to eat either dinner or supper and it is a shame: almost 9 o'clock when he got home, and he was so awfully tired, could hardly eat. . . .

Tues. 26   Sleeted last night—snowing this morning and cold, but

the afternoon was sunny. Fred didn't get home to dinner today. Hired a man with horse and buggy two days
last week, and all day yesterday, and this forenoon, to
help him with his mail, just to deliver Packages, and had
to pay him *five dollars*. It is to be hoped the Government
will do more for their men, some day.

[*1912*]

January

Wed. 3   Another cold day—we are having Winter, all in a lump; I finished reading "The Calling of Dan Matthews" today and cannot conceive what a man is like who will write such a book—no Christian would write such a story: it is wholly against the Church and christian people and I shall destroy the book, or return it to the one who gave it to Fred for Christmas. There is no room for such a book in my house.[1] The day has been glorious with sunshine and "Sunny Jim" Strickler was over, for awhile this morning. I cut out two night-gowns.

Thurs. 4   Making some new gowns for Fred and myself. We went to the "Grand" tonight to see Thomas Jefferson in Rip Van Winkle and enjoyed it very much.[2] A cold and "sun-shiny" day and an exquisite night: cold and crispy with a great, full moon, hanging in the cloudless sky.

Mon. 8   Snowing hard when we got up and found the weather 8° above zero. But long before noon the sun was shining gloriously. You can't keep the sun out of Kansas: it just will shine in spite of anything. Fred did not get home to dinner—Mails very heavy.

February

Sat. 3   Cold, very cold, but I used my new "suction sweeper" this morning from the Daily Capitol and soon warmed up: it's the finest thing *under* the sun, if not "new" and most certainly revolutionizes "house-cleaning"; in thirty minutes I had gotten about a bushel of dirt—(more or less, but any way, enough to astonish one) from under the carpets, and wore out the muscles of my back and shoulders and made myself lame in great shape.

March

Thurs.14   Mrs. A. E. Jones and I went to Good Government Club at Mrs. L. F. Sherman's 109 East Tenth St. this after-noon. Election of Officers and I was elected Treasurer, a job I hate, but we are to make a hard fight for Suffer-age this year and all will have to work hard and I must do my part, and too I am associated with some mighty fine fellow officers. . . .

April

Tues. 16
Fred home again today on Vacation; he and I spent the after-noon down town Shopping and went in to Dr. Cutsinger's and had my eyes tested again and "glasses" changed.

The morning paper and this evening's, were filled with news of the *horrible* disaster to the Titanic Sunk by an Iceberg and nearly 2000 lives lost. Oh! it is *beyond* my heart and mind to comprehend the *awfulness* of it. My heart is *sick* with the horror of it and *breaking* with all *sympathy* and *sorrow* for all the sufferers.

Fri. 19
Another cold day—And at last the terrible suspense of Titanic wreck, was partially relieved by the Carpathia getting into New York last night with those it had res-cued from Titanic. Oh! its shocking. Horrible—beyond all words to describe. And I have cried my heart out, in sympathy for the poor sufferers. Cried until I have no more tears to shed—its just all dumb anguish now.

July

Thurs. 11
Fred and I went to Leavenworth today, with the Good Government Club, leaving Topeka at 7:40 A.M. We had a most delightful trip. Stopped at Lansing and were shown thro' Penitentiary by Warden Codding—(A most pitiful place) then we had dinner at the Soldiers' Home and later went to the Fort, a most beautiful place. Home at 10:30 after a most splendid day.

Sat. 27
Spent the morning down town shopping and put in a most busy day, and it was a scorcher. This evening Fred went with me to A.K. Rogers to see Aunt Sarah Ogden, who is near death from heat prostration, then to a "Woman's Suffrage Meeting" at City Park, where Judge Garwood of Denver Colo. spoke.

Sun. 28
Another warm day. Warren R. walked to S.S. with Fred

Suffrage cartoons. From the Topeka *Daily Capital*, Sunday, October 27, 1912.

Martha (far left) in suffrage car in Topeka Automobile Club parade, 1912. Topeka *Daily Capital*, October 27, 1912.

and me. Only about 18 of my boys present; fearfully sultry—so much humidity. We took a car home after church. Anna Rogers phoned me soon after we got home, that aunt Sarah Ogden passed away at 10:45 this morning. She is the last of all her people, except a few nieces and nephews and their children, and was 86 years old Apr. 10—last. It must seem good to her, to be again united with her loved ones. And it was a blessed going home—just went to sleep and did not wake up again.

Wed. 31   A fine day and a very cool evening. The Good Government Club met with me this evening and we had a pretty good crowd: many being "luke warm" Sufferagists, just the kind we want to have come so we can talk to them. We had a fine meeting tho' not as many men as we wished.

August

Sat. 24   Scorching hot day but almost *cold* this morning. . . . Spent afternoon with Mrs. Monroe making up a Book of Mother Goose Rhymes.[3]

Sun. 25   Just 100 today, so Warren R. and *us* took a car to S.S. and home again. . . . I had to make a Cartoon for "Mother Goose to date," Jingle Book, by Mrs. Lee Monroe.

September

Sun. 22   Cold this morning. Warren R., Fred and I took car to S.S. this morning and I was so "bum," did not stay for church, for I needed rest, but just after Lunch, Mrs. Lee Monroe Called me, and I went down and with Mrs. E. E. Roudebush and Mrs. E. S. Marshall, went in the big Auto. Parade. Mrs. Monroe decorated her car in Sufferage banners, and penants and her regular Schauffer would not drive but her son did.

Mon. 23   A fine day and I was quite busy with doing my washing and having my stoves repaired, by Rudolph the Socialist. Also bought two Bushels of tomatoes for 75 cents.

October

Tues. 8   Rained quite a little this morning, and a sort of disagree-

able day. This afternoon I went to my Bible Class at
Y.W.C.A. and at 3:30 to the Auditorium to meet some
of Good Gov. Club ladies and distribute our Sufferage
Campaign Literature to the crowds of men gathered to
see and hear Gov. Woodrow Wilson of New Jersey, the
Democratic nominee for President. We found the
majority of men for us, and almost every one courteous:
occasionally there was a "smart aleck." But Wilson's
train was delayed and it was almost 6 o'clock when he
reached the Auditorium, so I took a look at the man and
hiked for home.

Wed. 9   A mighty busy day, but it is nice to be home and busy—
no one loves home more than I do, yet we "Sufferagists"
have got to work if we ever get the Ballot.

Wed. 16   Making Cartoons for the Sunday Capital which we
women of the Good Government Club are going to
publish on Sunday the 27 inst.[4] Are having ideal
weather.

Thurs. 17 Still busy with my Cartoons and don't feel very good,
beside my right eye is troubling me very much. Such
beautiful days.

Fri. 18   A grand day and I so wanted to be out doors but it was
my day to stay in the Good Government Club Booth, at
the Cooking School held this week in the Auditorium,
so I was there all afternoon and until 11 o'clock at night.
Requa Rinner, Ruby Long and Lena Anderson in Costume, helped me distribute our Sufferage Literature
and sell Buttons etc. Fred came down after Supper and
stayed with me.

Thurs. 24 A grand old "Indian Summer" day and I have been so
busy. Fred home today painting the porch for his Vacation. I went to Good Government Club at Y.W.C.A. this
afternoon. . . . 7 o'clock when I got home. O we "Sufferagists" are working most strenuously these days—working to the death and praying to win on Nov. 5. at the
Ballot Box.

Sat. 26   Fred went to work this morning again and I was most
awfully busy all day. This evening met Good Gov. Club
at Mills and went in the Sufferagist Parade at 7:45,
riding in the Clevenger car. . . . Gov. Stubbs car headed
the parade and we were lead by the Knights and Ladies
Band—After our parade, on the Ave, we went to the
Auditorium, and sat on the platform during the address

of Rev. Anna Shaw, on Sufferage. And she made a fine address.[5] Big crowd.

Sun. 27   Another most beautiful day. . . . At 2:30 . . . walked out to Central Park to have a business meeting of the Board of Good Gov. Club. . . . Got home about 7 o'clock. We women certainly are working ourselves to death whether we get the Ballot or not.

November

Fri. 1   A beautiful day and sloppy of course: that is, I thought it a nice day; it may have been cold to some. Fred did not get home to dinner and I had to go to our Good Gov. headquarters and help Mrs. Roudebush get out 730 Campaign letters.

Sat. 2   A bright, sunny day; and I worked hard all day; had to neglect the house a little to address 230 Campaign letters, to send out in our Sufferage cause. Fred's mail so heavy today, he did not have time to come home to dinner and I did not take time to eat any.

Sun. 3   A day of sunshine, but the wind blew fearfully and whipped and whirled the leaves into every nook. . . . And we were barely thro' dinner, when six of my Sun. School boys came. . . . Never a Sunday passes, but some of my Class come out and we enjoy them immensely. Today they locked John in the barn and he got mad and broke a window: they all love to tease him, because the poor boy has a dreadful temper. I have not been able to impress upon them the wrong of teasing him: I had to go to Mrs. Monroe's 909 Harrison, to a business conference of Good Government Club, at 4 o'clock and leave the boys here with Fred, or it would not have happened.

Mon. 4   What I call an ideal day, but my how I had to hustle. Was all thro' washing at 9:30 and cleaning up. Had no time to eat dinner and Fred's mail too heavy for him to come home, so I took a "sup o' milk" and hurried away at 1 o'clock to the Y.W.C.A. to "stand in line" for the Good Government Club "Tea Party". A Sufferage affair of course and we had an immense crowd; about two thousand called between 2 and 6 o'clock. And tonight closes the Campaign, and I'm *more* than glad.

Tues. 5   Up early, got Breakfast, but only took time to eat a wee bite and hurried away to the Polls for it's Election day and we women are to make a last stand for our enfranchisement. I was at the Polling-place (2nd of 6th Ward) before daylight and handing out Cards: no one came to help me for several hours, then Mrs. A. E. Jones came: the morning was cloudy, damp and chilly and I got quite chilled and was most grateful for the *hot-brick* and chair, brought me by old Mr. Donnell. I did not get relief until 12 o'clock when Mrs. Lucia O. Case and Mrs. Clark came, then I came home and got dinner, and not having to go back, laid down on the couch and rested. A terrific rain and thunder-storm came up at 5 o'clock. I only had 3 men refuse to vote: one a negro.

Wed. 6   *"This is the day after."* And so bright and sunny—a glorious day, and "there is sunshine in my heart," for while I went to bed last night a *slave*, I awoke this morning a *free woman*: My vote counts as much as any negro's—as any dago's. Oh! it's glorious. I got up and came downstairs in my gown and went to the Phone and heard the good news. Of course I was sorry the Republicans lost, and I feel only *contempt* for Roosevelt, but my vote will help change things, four years hence. Suffrage won in Kansas by 50,000 Majority.[6] And the papers say it won in Michigan, Oregon, and Arizona—only Wisconsin losing.

Thurs. 7   Another fine day, and I'm trying to rest, but Mrs. Monroe called me at noon, to make a "Transparency" or Jack o'Lantern, with the word Citizen on the sides, so I spent the afternoon making a good big one from a box .Fred's pants came in, and after supper, Fred took me to Mrs. Monroe's and then went to a Picture Show, while a hundred or two of we women gathered at Mrs. Monroe's for to celebrate our *victory*! With a man with a drum to lead us, we paraded around State House with our lanterns and "votes for women" Penants, then back to Mrs. Monroe's, where had few short speeches, sang "Praise God from whom all blessings flow," were served Coffee and wafers and went home happy, my good hubby coming for me just at the "Coffee serving stage" and we slipped away home, neither of us caring for coffee. It was a happy evening.

Fri. 8   A splendid day, and I worked very hard, sweeping and cleaning my long neglected house and it was a joy to work—*Victory* makes all the hard work of the Campaign worth while. I went to town shopping this afternoon and rode down in Automobile with Charlie Tullock. Election returns do not yet tell who is Governor, but Wilson is President.

Sat. 16   A fine day and a most awfully busy one. And still we do not know who is Governor. What an Election it was. Well, "United we stand and divided we fall" and we fell; hard too. But me and mine did not help to cause the fall—we were satisfied with good old Republican Party and had lost no "Bull Moose" to run after.

Thurs. 28   Beautiful day, tho' cold wind. Our Thanksgiving dinner was the "*scraps*" left from last night's dinner, but there was abundance of everything and we had a feast. But we have everything to be happy for and most thankful—God has blessed us most graciously in every way. Thirteen years ago today we moved into this house, which we built. Today Fred has the whole day for a Holiday. The Post-Office for *first* time, closed *all* day instead of a half-day. . . .

Sat. 30   Cloudy today and balmy as Spring, so of course will be colder. Baked beans, roasted a fine young pullet, made pumpkin-pies and very busy with the usual Saturday work. Tonight's paper says Hodges is our new Governor. I am not a Democrat, but I'm mighty glad he defeated Capper, just because Capper went over to the *Bull Moose* and still kept his name on Republican ballot.

December

Tues. 10   A fine day, tho' rather cool. Crocheting all day. 40 years ago today I came to Kansas—to Cowley Co, 12 miles North of Winfield. I should not want to go thro' the hardships of a pioneer life again, tho' I was only 5 years old. I very distinctly remember the Indians, Buffalo and Grasshoppers and the hardships.

Wed. 18   At last our Freda is back with us, after 4 years absence. I met her at U.P. Depot, 8:15 this morning. (Cousin Belle Van came with her) and she has grown to be a woman— a little girl when she moved with her mother to Colorado. It's good to have her back. I had my Sunday School boys out this evening to practice a Christmas Song and parts of two classes of girls. Most of my boys were here—(a few could not come) and they sang splendidly, then later played games and had a jolly good time.

Tues. 24   "Twas the night before Christmas and all about the house, not a creature was stirring not even a mouse". And Oh! the glorious night—a great full moon and I thought it might be like the glory of the night two thousand years ago in Bethlehem; we know *that* was a glorious night, when angels sang "Peace on earth, good will to men." My poor Teddy was too tired to go to the Church this evening, but Warren and Jennie Remington and Freda and I walked down together and had a fine evening. The exercises were splendid and many presents and food brought for the poor.

Wed. 25   "*Christmas Day*" and such a fine one: almost like Summer: not a cloud and a blessed day. About 10 o'clock this morning, [seven names follow] came bringing to me as a Christmas present a lovely oak Piano-bench. I think I have the most blessed bunch of boys any Sunday School teacher ever had. Freda played for them and they stayed until after 12 o'clock, when Freda and I dressed and went to 7th and Lane, to Mr. Clarence Radcliffe's to Christmas dinner. Fred came right from work and my! what a dinner we had, and how we enjoyed it, and what a happy time. Mr. and Mrs. A. E. Jones were there too and in the midst of dinner we were called out to see Phil Billard in his Aeroplane and he was certainly making a most beautiful flight and very high—*its wonderful.*[7] We

Phil Billard barnstorming over Topeka c. 1912.

spent the early evening at Radcliffes and Miss Spencer and Mr. Allen and Mr. & Mrs. Dickhoots and Mary also there—Freda played and also Miss Spencer and several sang. O it was a jolly evening alright.

Fri. 27 A grand day, warm and sunny. This afternoon I went to Mrs. Lee Monroe's to a meeting of the Executive Board of the Good Government Club—we are going to erect a Woman's Building as a Memorial to winning our Enfranchisement at last Election.[8] I went from Mrs. Monroe's to do a little shopping—gathering up the "tagends" of Christmas, tho' it is past.

Tues. 31 The finest day of all and I spent the morning down town shopping then put in all afternoon working hard, getting the house in readiness for a "Watch meeting," I gave this evening for my Sunday School Class of boys and two classes of girls, tho' many could not come, because no cars run at midnight and too far to walk home—but we had a fine bunch and a fine time, and drank the "Old Year out and the New Year in," with cider, as we flung the door wide, and all gathered on the front porch. It was a glorious night as well as a day. . . . And so the Old Year went out with merriment and we welcomed the New, in like manner: it has been one of my most happy years—most of my time given to my Class of boys.

[*1913*]

January

"*New Years Day*". Again I stand on the threshold of a new year, and cannot hope for a happier year than the one just passed, but I *do* pray with all my heart and soul and being, that God will help me to live my life more perfectly before him: will guide and lead me, and give me strength to live without offense, before Him and in like manner bless all my loved ones and each boy in my Sunday School Class, who are so fast growing into young men and will so soon enter into the life of the World and of necessity must go out from me, but may the love of God ever abound in their hearts and lead them thro' the years, unto everlasting life. And these are the Boys for whom I pray, every night and every morning, as I would pray for an own son. . . . I feel very deeply my responsibility to these boys: that I must answer to God for what I teach, or fail to teach them, of His word. I feel so helpless and so dependent on God. They are a wonderful "bunch"—so worth while: and at times try me sorely, because of their inclination to play and be noisy. And how I love them all. I wish I could make Missionaries of every one of them. We had a "Watch-meeting" last night and it was nearly 1 o'clock this morning when the last one of the happy, noisy bunch left and we hurried to bed for a few hours sleep and up again at 5:30 A.M. And such a bright, beautiful New Year. Warm and sunny no mud, no snow—just grand fine weather. . . . Hazel Sillix who staid all night with Freda went home and Fred, Freda and I went to A. E. Jones' for "New Years" dinner and what a feast— a most delicious Turkey was the big part of dinner. . . . We are so glad to have Freda with us. And glad for all this happy day, and pray the whole year may be as happy. Fred got thro' with his mail today about 1:30 and had a little bit of a Holiday. O it's been a blessed day.

Fri. 24 My own "wee girlie", my blessed little daughter whom

God let stay with me so brief a time, would be 21 today, had she lived. How careless most mothers are, in the enjoyment of their daughters—not seeming to realize what a blessing they are. How little they appreciate their blessing and how little understand the ache in the hearts of those who have lost the blessing. My heart thro' all the years, never ceases its yearning.

This has been a magnificent day, and after dinner I walked to Mrs. L. O. Case's and with her to the State House where we attended the Legislature, spending our time in the House, to do a little Lobying, as we both registered to Loby.[1] . . . .

February

Sun. 2
Warren walked to Sunday School with Fred and me as usual, and after Church found it snowing so took car home and it just kept snowing all day. Robert Sympson, Fred Brackett and Verra Hanna came thro' the snow to spend afternoon with us. Oh! I had such a terrible dream of trouble last night that it has haunted me all day. Some sorrow is coming to us. About 8 o'clock this evening Aunt Kate VanOrsdol Phoned from Silver Lake, that Freda had just been taken with appendicitis, and I told them to call a doctor.

Tues. 4
O such a cold day. I phoned early to Silver Lake and they said Freda was doing alright, but wanted me, so I made every arrangement to go out on train this evening, and bring her home tomorrow morning where I can look after her; at 1:30 they phoned again that Dr. Dudley of Silver Lake said I must bring an Automobile and come get her at once and bring her to Hospital for operation—What a shock, after being told she was alright. I called the Johnson Garage, and Mr. Johnson himself was soon at my house and we left at 2:20 for Silver Lake and what a hard race with death—I hope I may never have to take another. But by three o'clock we were at uncle's and found the poor, dear child suffering agony: we soon had her in the Automobile and Dr. Dudley too and began our terrible race—death kept close beside and it seemed at times, as if he *must* win. My heart bursting with grief, I held her close in my arms, across my body all the way, to make it easy, but she

suffered terribly and when within four miles of Topeka, I saw the whiteness of death driving back the purple fever, I thought my heart would break. But at last we reached Stormont, where everything was in readiness and Dr. L. H. Munn assisted by Dr. Ernest, and Dr. Hogeboom to give Ether soon had operated. I watched the operation, which was performed in little less than *twenty-two minutes*, then Dr. Munn told me he could give me no hope whatever and any minute might be the last. I was simply "crushed" with grief, but had to bear up, because so much depended on me. Fred came, in time to see her a moment before operation and he waited in hall. I saw her appendix, a greatly enlarged, ulcerated and perforated rotten thing. Gangrene and also just a starting of peritonitis. We waited to see her come out of Anaesthetic, then we came home to do up our work and get bite to eat. I needed a moment of rest for I was exhausted from the long ride in the cold and with heart breaking grief. We left Hospital about 6 o'clock and were back before 8 o'clock and staid until nearly ten o'clock—I called Mrs. Goddard a Christian Science Practicianer and my every breath is a prayer for recovery. We went from Hospital at ten o'clock to send word to her mother and sister in Colorado, near Bryant— could not reach them by wire so had to send letter and don't know when they will get it.

Wed. 5   I was at Hospital at 8:30 this morning and waited on Freda all day—she is very low and under Opiates, so but partially conscious. Dr. Munn still gives no hope. Pulse 120, steady. She came off operating table with it at 160. I was with her all day and Fred came after Supper and we came home about 10 o'clock.

Fri. 7   With Freda all day at Stormont Hospital. She is a hard "patient" to take care of and the Hospital is full, with only 16 nurses, so they neglect Freda's bathing and I had to make a *kick*. The doctors "jolly" her, tho' so critically ill, to put some life into her. Fred comes up in the morning to see her, again at noon and then to spend the evening and walk home with me at 10 o'clock. Tonight we took car home as I was too dead tired to walk. I do not get to sit down five minutes during the day, but work over her constantly.

Sat. 8   Another hard day at Stormont Hospital with Freda. I've eaten nothing but cold lunch, and little of that, since Freda's operation. Tonight as Fred and I left Hospital, Dr. Munn said *"There was a chance"* for Freda, but she is still *very low*. Fred & I went to town this evening to shop a little, after we left Hospital. Snow all gone and not so hard to walk, but I'm so very tired and worn.

Thurs. 13   Another grand day and I went early, as usual, to the Hospital. Dr. Munn took out stitches this morning. Freda's mother and sister and little neice (my sister May and neice, Zaidee Gilbert-Mort and grand-neice, Hazel Mort) came from Bryant, Colo, this forenoon, having started as soon as got our word of Freda's illness. They came to Hospital this afternoon to see Freda who is still in dangerous condition. Mrs. Emmett Wilson and Mrs. Sillix came also to see Freda.

Sat. 22   A most beautiful day, not a cloud in sky all day. It being "George Washington's Birthday" Fred had Half Holiday and was home in afternoon. I went as usual to Stormont Hospital to take care of Freda but at 1:30 P.M. was called home to help Zaidee thro' confinement. Everybody too busy to come help us, tho' I have always dropped everything to go help others, any hour of day or night. Well, I ran as much of way home, as I could thro' deep snow, and had to "get busy" at once, and the baby (a ten pound boy) came at 2:33 P.M. I got hold of the little fellow and pulled him away, let him lay 30 minutes, then cut the cord, rolled him in a blanket and laid him aside: not a soul but her mother and I with her. Dr. Jeffries was called, but did not arrive for one hour and two minutes after baby was born, and Mrs. A. E. Jones came just a little ahead of him. Fred took care of little Hazel during the ordeal and now Zaidee has two babies as Hazel is only 15 months old, but walks and talks. I was so tired and worn, I did not go back to Hospital, but sent Fred over to spend the evening with Freda, so she would not be too lonely. Some friends give me this comfort: "Oh! well you are strong and can stand what you are doing." Yes, I'm strong, but I'm just as human as any one else and I get most awfully tired.

Sun. 23   Snowed hard until noon. Fred and I went early to Stormont Hospital, he to stay with Freda while I went to Sunday School and taught my Class—I had 25 boys present. I came home alone this evening, thro' deep snow. O, God has been most merciful to me to give me

Martha Farnsworth, c. 1913.

strength, to do and bear so much. While Freda was sleeping this afternoon, I composed a few little rhymes, to send the new baby's father, who is home in Bryant Colo.

"The new Baby"
Oh! little, Gilbert Mort, is a brawny lad,
 Who some day'll be bigger than dad;
A fine round head and shoulders broad
 That some future time, can lift a big load.
Close to the head two tiny ears, lies
 And wide apart are two big eyes;
A generous mouth, and a prominent nose
 While on each foot, are five little toes;
Two chubby fists, two long legs, fine
 And a body straight, as a plummit line.
This is the boy, who made us bustle
 Shake ourselves and get a hustle,
To receive him, and cheat us of vacation,
 On the Natal day, of the Father of the Nation.

Not so much of a verse, but then the Muse doesn't find much inspiration in a Hospital, so mine is excusable.

Tues. 25   Cold and raw—a chill in the air all day. I went to Stor-mont Hospital as usual this morning to take care of Freda, until soon after 11 o'clock when I started for home with her in Penwell's Ambulance; took us almost an hour, as had to drive very slowly and even then, the poor child almost fainted from exhaustion, as we laid her on the bed, in her own room. But, Oh! we were all happy, to have her home again. Doctor found consider-able Pus when he dressed the wound this morning and of course my heart went down again. . . .

Thurs. 27   Another stormy day and it seems like Paradise, to be able to stay at home. I dressed Freda's wound this morn-ing and it is doing fine—her appetite is splendid since coming home and *I am* resting; at least it seems like rest, to be home, even tho' my hands are more than full, since my house is a Hospital. Freda in one room and Zaidee in another and neither one able to go in to see the other.

March

Thurs. 27   Weather fine again. May, Zaidee and children went to Mrs. Gandy's to spend day. Freda grows stronger and I let her go to Mrs. Remington's this morning, and Mrs. C. Goddard's this afternoon. The first time from home for 8 weeks. Oh! we have had a siege, but God has been so good thro' it all; our hearts overflow with gratitude for His great mercies.

April

Wed. 16   Another fine Spring day. I ironed my last weeks washing and put in a busy day. At 6 o'clock we all—even to baby Jack—went to Y.M.C.A. to see Basket Ball game, between First Christian Church, Intermediate En-deavor boys, and Congregational Boys. Four of my Sunday School boys were in the game and it was a most intensely interesting game tho' our boys were beaten. Lost the game by two points. The Cong. boys were much larger and had to be called down for unfair playing several times too. Our boys played brilliantly. From Y.M.C.A., I went to Mrs. Lee Monroe's to Board-meeting of Good Government Club and home at 10 o'clock so my day has been more than full of pleasure and work.

Wed. 23   Cloudy and cool and a "wee bit" showery. I went to 1
o'clock Luncheon at Mrs. E. E. Roudebush's this afternoon—she and Mrs. E. S. Marshall entertained Good
Government Club Officers. We had the jolliest, best
time ever. We had a Board-meeting and helped our
Pres. select an Advisory Board, to work with Mayor and
Police Force. They wanted me for one, but I could not
possibly accept tho' I wanted to so badly, but knew we
women would have to fight some ugly men and they
might thro' spite take revenge on my husband and make
him lose his job.

Sat. 26   Baking just a little—doing no more than I had to. My
46th Birthday: if I feel no older in proportion when I'm
a hundred years old, why I'll be a mighty young old girl.
I've heard folks pity those who never grow up, but for
myself, I don't want any pity—I enjoy being young: why
I'm only beginning *to live*. I'm sure no "kid" enjoys a
good, old swim more than I do and I doubt if they can
get up more enthusiasm over a good Ball game. Ronald
McCord, Harry Davis and Edward Price, out this afternoon—cold and rainy. Folks came home this evening.

May

Fri. 2   A warm day and a windy one. Our 19th Wedding
Anniversary, and I'm sure we neither one have any
regrets. Fred has been so kind and good thro' all the
years. I made a chicken Pot-pie in my old Colonial
Kettle, that used to be my Great Grandmother's and I
don't know how far back in the family it did belong but it
is a precious heir-loom; and I remember how, forty
years ago we used it to cook our Buffalo-meat in, or
other meat, but we seldom had other than Buffalo or
Deer meat which my father would kill—rich meat
'twould be now, but all too common then, when even
that would pall on one when there was nothing else and
could be no change.

I went to meeting of Good Government Club this
afternoon at Y.W.C.A. and we had a very interesting
meeting. Commissioner Porter was there to confer with
us on Sanitary work of the City. Mrs. B. B. Smythe gave
us a good talk on Meat prices and Mrs. Rhodes, on
"Meat substitutes" and brought a nut-loaf, that was delicious. Most of afternoon was discussion of high cost of

living and how to overcome it. There is Graft and Trusts in everything it seems.

Sun. 18   A grand day, as near perfect as a day could be. Warren Remington walked to Sunday School with me and Fred staid home to do some packing for the folks. . . . I hurried home after Sunday School and we all went to Santa Fe Depot at 12:30 to see the folks off for home—my sister May and my neice Zaidee and two babies—well it nearly pulled my heart out by the roots, to say good-bye to little Hazel and baby Jack Gilbert. . . .

June

Wed. 11   Fine day—sunshine and cool—most too cool for fruit and garden to grow well, yet our garden is fine. I made a nice Currant pie today and had our first lovely Beans (white wax). Freda and I went to town this afternoon, I to shop a little and get my new glasses at Dr. Cutsinger's while she went to the Dentist's. She phoned out this evening, she was going to stay all night with a friend. She causes us much anxiety, for she is simply "boy crazy" and doesn't choose the best. I'm sorry she is here with us.

Thurs. 12   Another cool day and I was more than busy, all day. Freda staid away all day. I don't know what I will do with her. I cannot turn a girl into the street. She lies *to us* and *about us*. She is "sneaking" about meeting young men and girls we do not approve of. Just breaks our hearts and we have done so much for her.

Tues. 24   . . . . Paul Porter here to see Freda again this evening. I would give the World to see her marry.

Wed. 25   Been awfully hot all day. I went to town this morning to hunt up something for a Birthday present for Freda who will be 18 on Friday. I got a gold chain and locket, which I could not afford to do and would not have done only it is her 18th Birthday—paid $10.50 chain is solid gold. Paul here again tonight to see Freda.

Thurs. 26   Another extremely hot day and busy getting peas ready to can: gardens are drying up and I bought 1/2 Bu. then gathered 1/2 Bu. from my own vines. We need rain badly. Paul here to see Freda, again this evening; and yet she says she is engaged to another fellow.

Mon. 30   Hot, sticky, rainy—a light gentle shower most all day.

Had to leave my washing on line all night. Thea Baker and Jennie Remington spent all afternoon with Freda cleaning out the Barn and making a "Play-house" in the loft. They carried out bedding and sleep there tonight. Really they have quite a playhouse having used matting and old curtains to partition and make three rooms: going with the boys, yet playing in Play-houses.[2]

July

Fri. 22   The day has been pleasantly cool and I could do much work. This morning early I went to County-jail for a short visit to the Matron, Mrs. Abbot, as I was on my way to the Court House to see Sheriff Kiene, about a young man (one Jason Curry) in jail for stealing $20.00 that he might go home to his mother and Sweet-heart in Kentucky. The man from whom he stole would not prosecute if money was returned. We are poor and so in need of money, and are paying Freda's Doctor Bill, for Appendicitis, yet I felt I *must* save this home sick boy, from the Pennitentiary and give him another chance to make good. I had never seen him or heard of him, until I read of his trouble in the paper. I took every cent I had in the house and my Bank Book pittance and went to the jail, only to find in few minutes, there was another who loved boys and wanted to do good, for while I stood talking to Mrs. Abbot, Sheriff Kiene brought the boy from his cell and a man came forward and gave him a ticket home and money for expenses, and my good intentions will never be known, as I did not tell my errand except to Mrs. Abbott. The boy was blue eyed and rather fair, of good face—only 19 yrs. old and certainly the happiest boy I ever saw when he realized his good fortune—the stranger who gave him this happiness must have felt more than repaid. I'm sure I would.

September

Tues. 23   Another cool day—Fred having day of Vacation. Freda had long lessons assigned her this morning so I spent all afternoon helping her get them, and had Fred go to town and get her "Gymnasium shoes" and material for

"Bloomers" which *I* cut out and *she* made just before Supper, then we three got ready and went to Grand Opera House to see Edison *"Talking* Moving pictures" and they were *great*. I canned a crate of blue-plums and one of peaches this morning—worked very hard all day, but enjoyed, immensely, the pictures this evening—not too tired for pleasure.

Thurs. 25   Fred home today again—Vacation—putting up shelves in "storm kitchen"—a slow "pokey" fellow around the house—don't accomplish much, but best man under the sun—ought to have done in one day, all he has done in three. Quite cold all day tho' fine and sunny. . . .

October

Fri. 17   Busy with many things all day. Freda went to "Show" tonight with Guy Hilton, a young widower—I am afraid of widowers, for they Court "fast and furious" and a girl can scarcely ever escape them: beside, Freda has been persuing him for some time.

Mon. 27   An ideal day—washed a large washing. Bought a bushel of shelled Walnuts from two "Trustys" from the Assylum: one had a very hard face and one a kindly gentle face and I wondered what sin had clouded their intellect: poor unfortunate fellows, Human beings, yet not: in the world, yet not in it.

November

Mon. 24   A fair day and my big washing dried nicely—helped Freda with her "Problems" all afternoon; put in a good part of Sunday afternoon on them too. I wonder if it pays to give *all* one's time to a girl who is utterly selfish and does not appreciate the least thing done for her. She is an "ingrate that turns and bites the hand that feeds her." I have found out she lies shamefully about both her uncle Fred and me. I only bear with her hoping to make a better girl of her—no one else will do anything for her and her mother *cannot*, so the great trial falls to me.

Wed. 26   Another misty, bedraggle-ee day, and quite cool—this evening, we went to Music Hall, 6th & Quincy, to the Mail-carriers Ball, taking Jennie Remington and Freda.

About 300 present and we enjoyed watching the dancers—at one time I could not have stayed off the floor, but I haven't danced for 20 years—we came home on last car.

December

Wed. 17 · Rainy, misty, gloomy day and I've been busy planning my work and dinner I'm to give on Christmas for the Juvenile Court children.

Fri. 19 Stormy day and a stormy night. And very, very busy all the day: I could almost "scream" there is so much to do, yet I go about calmly because it's my way—a storm within me, a calm without, for I never let go of myself.

Wed. 24 Cold and snowy; O so busy and so happy, but the house was pretty, when about 4:30 P.M. Probation Officer E. Rooney arrived with about 30 of the Juvenile Court Boys, in an Auto Truck, and a little later, Mrs. Rooney and Mrs. Chapin came with two Juvenile girls (Andrews) and still later, Judge Hugh McFarland with Capital Reporter Mr. Padgett and two little boys. Mr. Harrison also came and took Flash-light pictures—Mrs. Chas. Brooks Thomas also came to take a look at the children. Miss Spielman came and brought a Victrola. We had a house brimful and everybody was very happy. I had set two long tables and they looked beautiful. Judge McFarland paid expense of the dinner and provided two fine turkeys, candies, nuts, raisons, Oranges, ice-cream, two kinds of potatoes, pickles, cheese, celery, Bread and Butter and cocoa. I gave mince pie, Plum-pudding, Apples and Spagetti: the Judge also sent out a big Christmas tree and *we* provided a small one, so we had two: and the Judge and Mr. Rooney brought toys. And the children seemed supremely happy and all our work seemed worth while, and we too are happy.

[1914]

In the first half of this year Martha continued her work with her Sunday School boys, and took up a new hobby, developing her own pictures taken with a camera given to her by her class. The "Socialists (anarchists)" in the Good Government Club attempted to change the Club's Constitution, and were soundly defeated, much to Martha's delight. She was asked by the Juvenile Court to house temporarily an abused sixteen year old girl, which she did for one month in June until the girl was sent to her aunt in Arkansas. The summer saw a continuation of her involvement with the Juvenile Court.

August

Tues. 4   Hot *all* day—and Election Day (Primary). Big ironing—thro' with my part, before 10 o'clock. Left Freda to do hers, while I went to *Vote*. Stopped for Mrs. H. D. Larimer, but she wouldn't go. I walked down to Hartsack voting precinct, and cast my *first State vote*—reproved a couple of young women Voters, for both going into one Booth, and "called down" the Judges for negligence, in allowing it, then came home where found Miss Butterfield and Miss Davis, two Mormon girls, whom I asked to stay for Dinner, also Genevieve Whitney came for Dinner, then she and Freda went to town and Freda went to Genevieve's for Supper. She and Genevieve got dinner for me at noon. The rush of a *full* day has rather wearied me.

Thurs. 13   Warming up—Making "mixed, Mustard Pickles," and was *very* busy until noon. Received, yesterday morning, some very nice Linen handkerchiefs from Mr. H. McFarland as a token of appreciation, for what little I did to help him receive re-nomination at Primary Election: *I* appreciate *his* appreciation but am sure it is the duty of every good Citizen, to do all possible to elect "clean" men to office and Mr. McFarland is of the highest character. I also received a Souvenir Letter-card, from Edinburgh, Scotland, from Mrs. Lilla Day-Monroe. I am glad she can be there at this time, even tho' the War must spoil some of her plans, for she is so

THE LADIES VOTED.

It is too early as this is written to make any estimate on the results of yesterday's primary election.

However, there are some things demonstrated by it that upset the theories of political wiseacres. These wiseacres predicted that the women would take no interest in the election.

We can not speak at this time for other localities, but when the writer went to vote yesterday morning every booth but one in the voting place was filled with women.

At that particular voting place at that hour in the morning, which was about 9 o'clock, there were at least two women calling for tickets for every one man.

Of course, we do not know how these ladies voted, but will venture the assertion that they showed at least as much independence and as much judgment as the men.

Those persons who have opposed woman suffrage, as they said, because it would lower the standard of womanhood and cause the men to show less respect for the weaker sex, should have been here and watched the quiet voting at the polls, the deference shown the ladies, and the perfect order that prevailed.

The man who asserts that woman suffrage will lower the standard of womanhood, or that it will cause men to hold women in less respect, or that it will drag women down into the mire, may be honestly mistaken, or he may be a liar, or he may be just a plain, ordinary blamed fool.

Topeka *Daily Capital*, August 5, 1914.

Tues. 25   bright, (a brilliant woman) she will see and understand much that no one else could grasp, of the War situation. Bright and fine; most awfully busy when Mr. E. Rooney (Juvenile Court, Probation Officer) came out this morning, to make arrangements with me to go to Winfield, Kansas (my old home) and take little Effie Dice to the Imbecile Assylum. So I hurriedly got ready and left on the 1:45 P.M. train with her, and found her anything but feeble-minded—she knows and understands *every* thing, is well mannered and to *me*, seems perfectly normal and as bright as any child on the train. We arrived at 7:30 in Winfield and I took a Cab out to Uncle Zeke Roger's to stay all night.

Wed. 26   Well I awakened this morning in Winfield, dear old home of my youth and what a flood of memories—what changes the years bring to one—happy school days, sweet-hearts, dear friends and once I attended the wedding of a dear friend (Mary Mount to Fred Gross) in this very house, now owned by uncle. And I remember Mary was *ecstatically, supremely* happy, that afternoon, but he was not the best of husbands and she was soon unhappy—Poor girl didn't live but few years. Some of the happiest and saddest hours of my life were spent in this town, but I could not lay abed "dreaming," so was up early and took little Effie up to the School, the Cab calling for us at 8 o'clock A.M. Effie (6 or 7 yrs. old) was very happy until reached the Gate of the Grounds then she began crying and when we arrived at the Buildings, she cried and screamed and begged and pleaded most pitifully, not to be left and had to be forcibly carried in and I had a most difficult time, slipping away; I came back to Uncle Zeke's and after dinner went with them to the "Old Settlers" Reunion in Island Park, where I saw a number of old friends and relatives—Aunt Til Weber, my mother's only living sister and uncle Bill Weber and Rev. J. H. Irvin who Baptized me, nearly 30 years ago. Oh! it was good to be there: from there Uncle Zeke took aunt Mary and me in the Auto, out to cousin Emma Weber-Adams, for short Call then we walked back to uncle's, and I went over to Cora Finch-Jenkins for Supper, then with Cora I went for a short call, to see Jim Finch and family—Jim's wife, Metta, I did not see, as she is too low with Cancer of liver to see anyone—can't live long—such a pity: they have two lovely daughters and a fine boy, 3 years old. And dear, lovely mother Finch makes her home there—such a blessed joy to see her—always a dear, good woman, she seems to grow sweeter as the years go by and she came so near to being *my* mother. She is an ideal mother and a friend to be proud of. When I left this sorrowing home, with death so near, mother and Cora walked up town with me, and I went on to uncle Zeke's to stay all night, and *we* visited, talking of many people and times and places of the old days, for I left here 27 years ago to make my home in Topeka and have only been back three times since—this being four times. No wonder old memories overcome me.

Thurs. 27   Went up town with Uncle Zeke this morning to get some

Cards, then back to his home alone. Taxi came for me 8:45 and I bid Aunt Mary good-bye and went to Santa Fe Depot where took 9:25 A.M. train for Topeka and my good Teddy, whom I know is lonely. Uncle Bill Weber was at Depot to tell me good-bye. Train a very long one, was crowded and more than an hour late at Newton. Raining wee bit, when got into Topeka; got out home about 6 o'clock—had a grand visit at my old home, expenses of trip paid by the county, but I never want to go on another such a Mission, for it looks like child desertion to me—the child knew and understood *everything*, looks and acts like any Normal child, but does not talk well; however, since her Tonsils and Adnoids were removed, I believe she will soon talk alright, and I'm sure the Imbecile Assylum is no place for her.[1]

Fri. 28

Most awfully busy all day, cooking and packing to go on my Camp trip with my Sunday School Boys. Just too busy to know straight up. Warren helped me make a Plum Pudding. Freda away all afternoon: no help to me.

Sun. 30

In the Camp of the "Oo-la-la's," camp Syckamore, Paxico. I awakened early this morning, or rather, did I

Left: Martha and Fred Farnsworth in bathing costume, 1914. *Right*: Martha at campout, 1915 or 1916.

go to sleep at all last night? For the boys were all so hilariously happy, scarcely anyone slept. A bunch of them got up at 11:30 P.M. and went fishing—at 1 o'clock Walter Polly and Charlie Clements came to Camp, having come up from Topeka on the mid-night train, and they made things lively for a time, then at 2 o'clock A.M. another bunch got up to go swimming, then things got quiet and there was possibly two hours sleep in Camp, and so passed our first night in Camp. My good Teddy came about 11 o'clock this morning to be here rest of time with us. We had dinner at noon and then had Sunday School in Camp as I was not at all well—ate nothing all day—and did not feel I could walk up town and I knew God was in our midst—the boys behaved well and were attentive to the lesson. Walter and Charlie had to go home this evening so we had Supper early. Oh! it is grand to live out in God's great out-of-doors, right next to nature.

Mon. 31 Another fine day and everybody happy—catching lots of fish, swimming and enjoying to the full, this pretty Camp. The girls have piled the straw in their tent into "mattress" shape and with their Comforts, have a fine bed—the boys, or about half of them, roll up in their blankets on straw in their tent, Fred and the others sleep "ditto" out under the trees. I also sleep like-wise, on my pile of straw over by the girls' tent—no tent for me, when there is such joy in lying out in the blessed open, and looking up thro' the foliage of the trees and watching the Stars come out, and then see the great, golden, Harvest Moon rise out of the dark and go up and up into the myriad twinkling stars in the velvet blue of night and one by one put out their light with its own shining glory. And we are taking a good many pictures of our Camp too.

September

Wed. 16 A most beautiful day and they say was an immense crowd at the Fair. Freda went to school this morning and didn't come home 'til after 6 o'clock this evening, and I had *so* much to do that she could have helped me, but she won't help do a thing she can possibly get out of.

I put up 1 1/2 Bu. of Peaches and a half Bu. of tomatoes, or got them ready and some put up. Tom Miller had supper with us, having come to see Freda about some trouble he is in, which means trouble for Freda.

Thurs. 17   Another fine day and busy with my fruit, while Freda went to town to do some shopping and then spent afternoon "packing" for after a sleepless, restless night, I decided it was best for us all that she leave Topeka, so I shall send her to her sister in Colo. She had been "running" with Jennie Warner, a girl that seemed "bad" to me—I tried to keep Freda away from her and while I could keep the girl from my house, Freda would lie to me and go see the girl—the girl had a baby, whose father, she told Freda, was a Traveling-man—since *he left*, without helping the girl, she is trying by the urging of her parents to lay the blame on poor Tom Miller and compel him to pay the expense at Hospital, and now it must go to Court and he wants Freda as a Witness, as Jennie told Freda it was not Tom's baby. He is a young Greek and seems a worthy young fellow whom they are trying to get the best of because he is a Foreigner: he told me all his trouble last night, and is nearly crazy and I have great sympathy for him, but Freda must not get mixed up in the Scandal, so I send her away. . . .

Fri. 18   A grand day. Fred "got-off" this forenoon, to go to Depot with Freda who left at 12:15 P.M. over U. P. Ry for Haxtun, Colo, to be with her mother and sister. I was too "upset" to go and any way, needed to finish up my fruit. I canned 3 gal. of Peach butter, and two Gal. of tomatoes, run thro' Colander, for soup. I swept and cleaned the whole house this afternoon and worked hard, until after 6 o'clock this evening—the house looks good, but "I'm dead"—but I had to work hard, to keep from "thinking", for it's like a funeral; I never expect to see Freda again: She lived twelve of her nineteen years in our home—we gave her all the schooling and music and art, she has ever had—always we have clothed her, paid her Doctor and Hospital bills, nursed her thro' all sickness, when every moment seemed death—we did for her all and more, than if she were our very own, and she proved to be an "ingrate," that turned and bit the hand that fed her, for she lied *about* us and *to* us and went in all kinds of bad company and caused us worry and heart-ache. And this last was too much, so we send her away.

Sat. 19   Another very busy day—I am so glad we got Freda away, before any trial: Tom read me letters from Jennie W. in which she said she never would accuse him of the parent-hood of her baby, because he was not the father; so that is all the proof he needs, but he wanted Freda as a witness, and it would get her in a dreadful scandal and bring out so much bad talk about her. O it is such a relief to have her away. Freda's mother is wholly at fault that she has not turned out well and it is a shame, for the girl is bright.

Thurs. 24   Another ideal, late Summer day, and today I mostly rested. I have been working so hard almost day and night until my neighbor, Mrs. Bettis, asked me if I never got tired: yes I do, but I never seem to wear out: however I enjoyed resting, today, and it is good to know Freda is on a farm so far from town she can't be "chasing" out nights with some tough.

October

Sat. 24   Cold and windy—took up sitting-room rug and Fred "beat" it, while I cleaned the room. Most awfully busy all day. . . . What a terrible World this is getting to be. "Wars and rumors of wars and Nation shall rise against Nation"—all being fulfilled, is it any wonder the earth is filled with woe? Such horror, as is the European War. . . .

Wed. 28   No frost this morning, and a fine day. I put in all morning writing to sister, Zaidee and Freda, a "warning." A mother told me Freda was writing some unclean letters, here to her daughter and it must be stopped or she would "prosecute", so I tried to convince them Freda would have to "straighten up", and behave herself as it was not Aunty now that she was fooling with. I spent all afternoon with my friend "Jonesie" who has just returned from a visit in Montana.

November

Tues. 10   O such a magnificent day and I got to rest some today, tho' I did tatting. We went to Auditorium this evening to hear ex-Senator F.J. Cannon, on *"The Threat of Mormonism"* and he certainly made plain the menace to the United States, of Mormonism. He speaks from personal knowledge, as he was once a Mormon Elder, his father one of the "26" an officer of the church next in command to Joseph Smith. He told some terrible things—and with sarcasm made many a hearty laugh. His lecture was most interesting and too bad the whole United States could not hear it and take warning.[2]

December

Thurs. 10   Cold—snowed all day—just lazily—flakes fell slowly and far between. *Forty two* years ago today, I came to Kans. from Mt. Pleasant, Iowa, a little girl, five years old. And well I remember the hardships of those days, tho' didn't really know they were *hardships* then. I went this afternoon to a meeting of the Good Government Club at the Y.M.C.A. We women are working hard for a much needed "Detention Home" and I was on the Program, to tell some of my own personal experiences in "Social Service" and Juvenile Court; Mrs. Katherine Booth-

Auto parade on Kansas Ave., Topeka, date uncertain.

Clibborn, (daughter of General Booth, founder of Salvation Army) who is in America to raise funds for work in Europe, and is holding a Revival at First Methodist Church, gave a splendid talk after my talk, and as she arose to begin her speech, she pointed to me and said, "I could have thought I was listening to a Salvation Army lassie, telling her experiences—that woman has laid up treasures in Heaven." How gracious of her to speak so kindly of me. But I feel I have done so little.

Fri. 18 To town very early, to "*Shop*", and every store crowded. At noon we had a letter from Freda, asking our forgiveness for all the sorrow she has caused us, and acknowledging her wrong doing and saying she was going to be a good girl and was sorry for the past.

Tues. 22 O its cold these days and snow deep. Ironed this morning, baked three cakes this afternoon and did lots of work, for tomorrow the Juvenile Court Children are to come. Judge McFarland sent out two fine twelve pound Turkeys which came after dark, so I had them to prepare and went to bed tired at 10:30. My work has not gone at all well today nor as I planned it, so that is *why* I'm tired. My good Teddy not home to dinner and worked over *ten hours*. I have the coal to carry in from the barn, the cow to feed and water noon and night, the chickens also, and the milking to do. Then the Telephone keeps one "Fox trotting" to answer it, often for a "wrong number" or "false" call. And all kinds of "calls" at both front and back doors, then its up stairs and down cellar, and so one some times has enough to make them weary. But we have so much to be thankful for; Splendid health, which is priceless, and the comforts of a good home; and too we live in a Christian land that is at *Peace* with the World, and so one often fails to be thankful enough.

Wed. 23 Cold—down to Zero, and nine inches of snow on the ground, "My busy day". Up before 5:30 A.M. A big Turkey in the oven at daybreak and another ready—all kinds of "hustle and bustle," for tonight was "Christmas" for the poor, needy Juvenile Court Children, that at least some of them may get in an *extra* Christmas, tomorrow night—at Provident Association or Salvation Army. Mrs. Ida Lovell came out early and we hurried to "decorate" with Alabama Smilax and Holly everywhere, then Parlor strung from all corners, with Silver tinsel and white bells. The sitting-room, with tinsel and red ropes, and red paper Bells and Balls (*very* pretty) then the dining-room, red, crepe-paper ribbons with tinsel: it was pretty and "Christmas-sy". I set two tables to seat 30 as they phoned me they would bring that many boys. I used white crepe-paper table covers with pretty Christmas napkins; the tables were pretty. I tried to have every thing as pretty and "homey" as if they were my own children. Mrs. Lovell and I worked like a Steam-engine all day, and every thing was ready to "dish up" when at 6 o'clock Probation Officer E. Rooney, in Mr. Hinkson's big sign Automobile came up to my door, with *thirty seven*, instead of *thirty* "bad boys" (?) and for a moment my heart was dismayed as I saw the regiment of boys filing in, but I soon felt sure I had prepared enough, for from *seven* years constant association with my Sunday School boys, I have learned the capacity of a boy's stomach. I asked Thea Baker and Ruth Holt to come and play the Piano, and they kept the Piano going all evening. I asked Rev. Geissel of the Episcopal Church to come, because he is interested in boys; he sang with Mr. Padgett, for the boys. Judge Hugh McFarland came out, with Miss Ann Ballard, Mrs. Cha-pin, Mrs. Padgett and Mr. Padgett, who is a Daily Capital Reporter. Mr. Paul Harrison came out and took a "Flashlight" picture, and Mrs. Parsons called to see the "sight", so there were "*fifty-two*" present and "49", (*forty nine*) at Supper where I expected not more than forty. And hungry, why everybody was half starved. Judge McFarland said he had never been so hungry in his life: the boys ate ravenously. *Every thing* was eaten up clean— the bones picked so clean, they would not make Soup. One boy said after leaving the table, rubbing his stomach "if I only could go to sleep now": warm, comfortable, his hungry stomach filled with good things, sleep was all he wished for. But Judge McFarland gave them candy and nuts and a present for each boy—*Happy* does not begin to express it, yet there was a quarrel or two, but my! it was to be expected—Every shade of black, up to the white, tan etc; red-headed negroes and red-headed white boys—every nationality, from good homes and bad, from poverty-stricken to the well to do; the bright mind and the dull; the boy struggling to make good, the boy a born criminal—Boys came with no shoes on their feet; just old stockings, several pairs, so the holes of one pair came in a different place from the holes in the other pair, and gunny sacks sewed about their feet, to keep them from freezing. Boys came in overalls and thread-bare shirts: boys came who had to wear their over-coats all evening, because their clothing would not hide their nakedness—overcoats given them at Salvation Army, or else-where—"cast off." Boys whose lives are filled with the greatest hardship, everything at home against them, yet are "making good," many of them; many wore "cast off" shoes that were not "mates". But few wore clothing bought for them, yet all were jubilantly happy and after their supper all stood about the Piano and sang, and my! *how* they sang; especially the "street" or popular Songs, and their heads bobbing, their hands beating time, in all kinds of gesticulations, bodies swaying, feet shuffeling, showed that, "music is no respector of persons" or environment—The heart pumps its music thro' the soul from the lips to the ends of the toes, of the poor boy as well as the rich—from the "down and out," to the one on a higher plane, the good and the bad, tho' the really bad has little music in his soul: the boy who sings is not often a bad boy. O, tonight so much was hard, pathetic; my heart was all atremble with tears that dared not come to the surface for all must be happy and jolly for these boys not one of whom I know. One dear, handsome lad was brought out, as a "guest" of the Court because his lot is so hard at home—a little "newsy" about twelve years old, the fifth in a family of seven boys and seven girls, the youngest a baby six months old. The boys ranged thro' every size of tall—short, fat, lean etc, but all were happy and went home about 9 o'clock shouting "Merry Christmas" till out of hearing. I did *all* of the cooking, but am not really physically tired—but mentally, am almost nervous, thro' the strain. So many things to plan and do, that every thing might make for the best and then the awful pull of sympathy on my heart. Mrs. Lovell stayed all night with us. We left all dishes for tomorrow.

[1915]

January through October of 1915 were relatively uneventful months for Martha. In February she went to hear Helen Keller, and found her "intensely interesting," but "not pleasant to listen to." Cousin Minnie came through in March with her usual scribal demands, this time asking Martha to write "cards and letters to married men—something crooked, somewhere," Martha records. In May she mentions having eye trouble, and on June 2nd notes "I have but one eye. (the other probably can never be restored)": she is never clear about the nature of the problem, though she later mentions that she has a cataract. In September she and Fred visited her father in Springfield, Colorado. She notes: "the country has changed little in my nineteen years absence."

November

Fri. 12   A most splendid day, tho' cold. Working hard all day cleaning. My good husband at home, nursing a sore heel; poor fellow it is very sore and he is so patient. Mr. Henderson came up this morning and made me a Magazine-case, after dinner I tore it to pieces and made it over and like it better—put in two more shelves too.

Tues. 16   A fine day and I let my ironing go, to get my house in order, and I got lots of work done: my "house-cleaning" almost finished, thank goodness. My good Teddy went to see Dr. Menninger this afternoon, about his heel and finds he has Erysipelas and badly—caused by bruise from hard walking with heavy load of mail.

Fri. 26   The weather continues fine. Edwin Jones and Warren Remington were in today and played "Checkers" with my good Teddy, to help him pass the time, tho' he seems content to sit and read: he is a dear, patient fellow. We received a letter today from Freda *begging* us for money, just even a little—said they were "down and out"— Darrell could not get work: all they had for "Thanksgiving" was Beans and Bread and no butter for their bread—have no clothes and no money for rent.[1] Surely hard luck and I think, she is begining to realize how

"Top o' the mornin' to good st. Pat. Two fine fellows, you can bet your hat.

St. Patrick's Day invitation card, 1915.

much we have always done for her, and how unworthy she was.

Sat. 27   A most beautiful day and my good Teddy getting along fine. Edwin and Warren here again today to play "Checkers" with Teddy. We had Edwin take $20.00 to the P.O. and send a Money Order to Freda—she is at point of starvation and tho' Teddy is sick and don't know when he can work and we have always helped them 'til we have nothing laid bye, we are not starving, for we have the cow and chickens and a cellar full of fruit and vegetables, and we have Insurance and sick allowance Policy of $10.00 per week—we are richly blessed even in this, our trial.

Mon. 29   A fine day—got my washing on line early—took usual care of my good Teddy, who gets on fine tho' today, has complained of soreness in the large varicose vein of right leg. I had a fine rest this afternoon.

Tues. 30   Beautiful sunshine outdoors, but all darkness in our home, because all last night and today *Death* has tried to come in and take my good Teddy: the struggle has been terrible and exhausting and the shadow of death hovers very near today. Fred was feeling very splendid, when we began to prepare for bed and as he hopped over to the Couch to have me dress his foot, the last time for the night; but as he lay down on the couch I heard him breathe heavily and asked what was matter—he replied that he could not breathe good; it all passed in a moment and we came upstairs, he going in bathroom and I getting into bed: he called me in a moment and I ran to him, and found him apparently dying and half unconscious—I held him against me for a moment sitting on edge of bath-tub and rubbed him and he revived so that by half carrying him, I got him into bed. He insisted he was alright and I should not call doctor—said he just could not breathe well. But I made him comfortable as possible then ran down-stairs and phoned Dr. Menninger, who being out to Christ Hospital, had not far to come and was here in about ten minutes: after a hurried examination he told me what I already knew that poor Teddy was seriously ill and told me to phone for Dr. Owen, to come at once. I had trouble in "getting" Dr. Owen, but finally succeeded, then ran to help Doctor give Teddy five "Hyperdermics" in the veins, one after the other as fast as he could prepare them; by that time Dr. Owen came and the two Doctors began a "Tug o' war" with death, which lasted until midnight, when Fred became easier and Dr. Owen went home. Fred was taken suddenly ill at 10 o'clock P.M.—I also phoned for my good friend Mrs. A.E. Jones, who came soon after the doctors, and remained thro' the night with me. Dr. Menninger staid with us until 1 o'clock A.M. We heated irons and put about Teddy and wrapped him close and warm—Doctor says he is almost certain to have a "chill." This is what happened: enough poison from Erysipelas got into the large varicose vein of Fred's right leg, to loosen a "blood-clot" which flowed up, into his heart—this is what so nearly took his life, when I found him half conscious in Bath-room. The heart pumped this clot into his lung (right one) where vein is not large enough for it to pass thro'. Doctor says it is like tying a string around his lung: and had it been pumped to brain instead of lung, he would have lived but short time, or had he lived would have been paralyzed. Dr. Menninger and Dr. Owen both returned soon after daylight this morning and Dr. M. came again this evening. We warded off the *chill* and are giving medicine every hour:

keep his leg wrapped in hot woolens and have cotton jacket on him—rub him every three hours, (his chest) and renew hot wrappings every 3 hours. Had Mr. Carney and Thompson put heating stove upstairs for Teddy must be kept very warm. Mrs. Jones will go home tonight and Mrs. Wilcox come up. Any way *some* one will stay in house with me, so I won't be alone. I pray God to spare my kind husband.

December

Wed. 1   I am thankful that God still spares to me the life of my good husband—I give medicine every hour of the day and night: and clean the barn, milk the cow, feed and water her, take care of the chickens, carry coal for upstairs and down, and pump the water for the house—answer the phone occasionally for I can't do it all the time, so many are "calling up" to know how Fred is; and door-bell too, seems always to be ringing—I had to take it off. And many are sending in beautiful flowers—every one is very kind, and I must just run from one thing to another, until I'm almost dizzy, trying to do everything between medicines. Mrs. Idola Moore-Runyen staid with me tonight.

Sat. 4   A day overflowing with the cares of the sick room: Fred seems no worse but is no better and a very sick man. I am kept on jump all the time—Some neighbors are good to help, others don't even enquire. Doctor came twice, as usual. My most loyal friend, Mrs. A.E. Jones stays with me again tonight—she is worth her weight in gold.

Mon. 6   I got thro' last night very well, tho' Fred had quite a severe spell of pain at 1:30. All day today these pains kept coming and growing in severity—and this evening when alone, a most agonizing attack came on: I could get no one over the phone and raised the window called at top of my voice for help and blew a whistle and while I could see and hear neighbors in their homes, I could not make anyone hear me, so gave up and worked over Fred for a time, then tried again and got Mrs. Wilcox, who stayed at Phone until she got the Doctor, but when he came, he could do nothing, as had given the limit of medicine, but Fred grew easier and he left and before out of hearing poor Fred was suffering agony—for five hours he walked thro' the "Valley of the Shadow" and we did not know whether he would come back: it would have been easier to have seen him die then to sit by and see him in such agony and powerless to give him relief. At midnight he got easy, but at 3:30 A.M. he had another spell, which only lasted about an hour. Of course this is the *crisis*. The blood clot on his lung, breaking and passing.

Tues. 7   Doctor came twice today—poor Fred lay in sort of stupor all day, exhausted from last night's terrible struggle. My good friend "Jonesie" stays with me again tonight: it frightens me to even think of staying alone. I never undress and do not eat, but stop to drink a glass of milk occasionally—I have so much to do outdoors and *everything* inside. Fred must be rubbed every three hours, his leg wrapped in hot Witch hazel woolens, every three hours and medicine every hour day and night, and God strengthens me.

Thurs. 9   The day is dark and dreary and looks like snow but there is sunshine in the house today because Fred has safely passed the crisis and pulse dropped to 85 which is still improvement, but Doctor says we must remember *he is still* a *very sick man*. My good friend "Jonesie" (Mrs. A.E.) stays tonight again.

Mon. 13   A most splendid day—and I took the usual care of good husband and did a large washing, in between times. I stay alone with Fred, all time now—my neighbors all got tired, quick, and some of them very soon forgot the *nights and nights*, I sat up with their sick, and I have gone at all hours.

Wed. 15   Dark and cloudy—heavy mist falling all day. Dr. Menninger held consultation with Dr. Munn, over Fred today and decided to give him a Tonic three times a day and bind camphorate oil on his leg and in about a week, to operate on him: his leg is badly swollen and this varicose vein must be tied. Dr. Wehe was out to see him too, for the Insurance Co. I had such a fine sleep and rest last night, tho' I awakened often, thinking I had medicine to give.

Mon. 20   Very pretty day—washed a large washing and did a lot of work. Fred has "*Milk-leg*,"[2] now and Dr. Menninger says, "go back to the hot witch-hazel pack" every three hours: well I could almost give up in abject despair—will complications *never* cease to set in? We thought Fred would soon be up and now *this*—one of the most tedious and slowest of *disease*: it is dreadful.

Wed. 22   Fred seems to grow stronger as his leg swells worse—We seldom see anyone any more, but the Doctor—everybody calls by phone and it's the Holiday season and everybody *rushed*. I can't make it seem like Christmas, for I have not been outside our gate for four weeks and have done no Shopping—sent no presents—saw no Holiday decorations—nothing that looks like Christmas.

Sat. 25   Bright and beautiful, sunny and warm; An ideal Christmas, except for mud—for the warm sun *made* mud, by the use of much of the beautiful snow. Everyone so happy in their own happy Christmas affairs, that we had few callers, but we were not forgotten by my splendid boys, a few of whom came out and brought me a set of silver knives and forks, as a present from the Class: and then we had cards and letters from many who could not call in person—but the day seemed like Sunday—we could not make it seem Christmas, because we have been so shut in for many weeks: however, the day was most blessed because my good Teddy was spared to me; and he came so near being called away, that it made the day doubly blessed. Dr. Menninger called as usual. Ernest Shelden, Ronald McCord, Harry Davis, Edwin Jones came out with my present, and later Keene Saxon and my "two Bobs."

Thurs. 30   *Doctor did not come* today, the *first time* in almost six weeks. Fred sat up more than three hours today and it is so good to have him out of bed—We are alone all the time now and being Holiday week, everyone so busy with their plans for the New Year, no one comes in and I can hardly get a letter posted—all our Calls are by Phone and I almost wish I had no phone.

Fri. 31   Doctor came this morning and thought Fred much improved—I had "Jonesie" do some marketing for me, and bought a lovely dressed Duck and brought over this evening. I had made plans to have my boys here with their girls for their annual "Watch Party" but Fred's sickness prevented—as we "turn in" for the night, it is raining hard. I developed some films this evening.

[1916]

January

Tues. 4   A very warm, balmy day—all the house open. Doctor came about noon and thinks Fred improves fine—but you *have to look twice to see it.*

Mon. 10   . . . . Mrs. Calvin came over and spent the evening with us and gave me a new recipe for Fleabitus (milk leg) which Dr. Weston of Chicago gave her (and which cured her after having it for four years) and she helped me put it on Fred. "Put cabbage thro' a meat grinder, making it very fine and put on a cloth and bind on Varicose vein, with five yards of bandaging, at bed-time: next morning take off and sponge limb with good rich buttermilk and bind on fresh cabbage—use about 1/4 cup of buttermilk—the milk may be used quite old."

Tues. 11   Sleeted during the night—fine mist falling all day and freezing making it extremely slippery, and so raw and cold—did my ironing and much other work today. Took off Fred's "cotton" jackets—one thing less to make every few days. Fred's leg shows decided improvement this morning from just one application of the Cabbage poultice. But his left arm hurts him much—his hand being cold and numb—worries me much.

Wed. 12   A howling Blizzard—15° below zero, 43 mile wind from North West, blowing sleet and snow. But I was out early, and cleaned the barn, fed the cow and chickens, carried water and coal and kept everything "snug and warm," took care of my good Teddy and did my usual house work. Hard? Why, it is so hard, I almost give up at times and then I just begin and "Count my many blessings". Fred's leg showed a very great improvement this morning.

Thurs. 13   Some more snow today and 18° below zero, and I did *all* the usual rush of work that I do every day and not a neighbor came in to see how we are "making it," these bad days—well, I am glad for good health that makes me independent of them all; but *I* was not brought up to be selfish and it surprises me to see so much of it among neighbors.

Sat. 15   Cold, but moderating. The day brimful of hard-work and the blessing of health and strength, to do all required of me. Dr. C.F. Menninger came out this morning and was fairly amazed, and greatly pleased with Fred's improvement due to Cabbage poultice. He looked at Fred's leg, then said "I don't know it all and neither does any other man, and the one who thinks he does, is a damn fool." He was thankful to know about the Cabbage treatment and said to continue its use: but he sees no merit in using the buttermilk—but as it is part of the treatment, we will continue *its* use also.

Mon. 24   . . . . My baby daughter, "wee girlie" would be 24 years old today if living. And right or wrong, I wish she were. Mr. Wiede stayed all night tonight with us.

Thurs. 27 Dr. Menninger came out this morning: said no more cabbage—give Fred his clothes, dress him and let him begin to learn to walk again and we are very happy. I dressed him in a hurry.

February

Thurs. 17 Warm, sunny and fine—Fred out on porch just a few minutes. I find as *he* grows stronger *I* am relaxing— letting go of myself and my nerves are trying to go to pieces; I do not sleep well of nights, and often I find myself dropping things.

Fri. 18   Another grand day and Fred walked awhile on the porch. Freda wrote us again for money—she is sick in bed—we have only about fifty dollars to do us until Fred can work, but we sent her ten dollars, for we are in better shape than they. Mr. & Mrs. Swickard spent evening with us. I don't like him—he is so conceited. These February nights are so exquisitely beautiful "The Heavens *surely* declare the Glory of God."

Sat. 19   Grandest day of all—Fred walked across the yard for the mail this morning. Mr. Bettis took him up to Barbershop, near Morris Ave, just after dinner and he walked back; was late getting home to his dinner, (almost 3 o'clock) his back and ankles hurting, legs more swollen and stiffened up and had taken some cold, sneezing every few moments—I ought not to have let him go. My nerves are all *unstrung* today, too. I wish I could just let go of myself, and *scream*, and *scream*, and *scream*, but I know I must not, even tho' I would feel better, but it would make it easier another time to "let go," and its hard to pull oneself together again—I've just *got* to *keep holding on.* . . .

Mon. 28 A cold, gray day. Dr. Menninger came out this morning and took Fred's "blood pressure" and gave him a thorough going over: the *test* was contrary—part of it, showing acute "Bright's disease" and the rest, absolutely the opposite and his "blood-pressure" considerably below normal, being from 75 to 104—should be 120. Has put him back on medicine again: Asperin, 5 grain capsules—one every three hours.

Lizzie Roby-Bair phoned me this morning, that she had just received word from California that Oren Kettlewell was dead: nearly 30 years ago he was my "sweetheart": we were "engaged," but I had little faith in him—my *ideals* were high, and he did not come up to them, and I ran away from him, lest I should falter in my determination *not to marry him*: after quarreling by letter, for some months, he came here and tried to persuade me to marry—I could not bring myself to do it and he went away, but thro' all the years, he would now and then send me a letter assuring me of the constancy of his love, even tho' he had married and had a family—and too, would remind me that I was the cause of his making a failure of life. Poor, weak man. As a young man, so jolly and full of fun—no bad habits, but a flirt. Fond of music and with a most wonderful voice, which had he cultivated it, would with out question, have brought him *fame and fortune*. The poor fellow so lived his life, that not a tear will be shed at his funeral—*the pity of it.*

March

Wed. 22 Cold wind today—we had letter from Freda today, asking for "help" again, saying Darrell had left her and she was sick—not able to be up, had no money and very little food—I don't know what the trouble is, but am sure *she is to blame*. How truly, "one sows the wind and reaps the whirlwind." *She* is reaping a *cyclone* and my sympathies are with Darrell: I sent her a dollar, which was more than I could spare and told her to go to her sister, and I wrote her sister and told *her* to take money she owed me and send for Freda, and I wrote my father, to *see* that Zaidee carried out my instructions: what a *"mess"* and how I have worked with that stubborn family.

Donald Fay, & Robt. Sympson, Warren Remington and Ruth Hare came in for the evening. Warren in *"working clothes"* was to take Ruth to a "picture show," but both lost nerve and came here, instead. Young folks are most interesting objects on earth.

April

Mon. 3   A beautiful day and I had a good big washing, which I hoped to get out early, but had a severe attack of Vertigo, and had to lie down for a couple of hours, then finished it and lay down for rest of the day, O so sick; Mrs. Lizzie Roby-Bair called this afternoon and I was too sick to visit much.

Tues. 4   Am still some "dizzy," but churned and did my ironing this morning and went to town this afternoon to pay Bills, the Insurance men having settled with Fred for time he was sick—paid him $205.00. Dr. Menninger's, Bill was $102.00 which he discounted and made $75.00 which I paid: our Bill at Drug Store was over $17.00 and then a three months grocery Bill, so nothing left, but glad could pay the Bills. Melvern Pribble and Miss Brown called just as we were going to bed, so did not come in.

Fri. 21   Another very busy day—weather warming up. Mona Wiede and Dorothy Reddick came out this evening and brought baby Stewart with them. Fred is doing fine with his work: his back hurts him all the time and he wears a *plaster* on it: his chest muscles are very sore, as are the lower abdominal muscles; right leg wears a rubber stocking and thigh piece—left leg, wrapped with 5 yds of bandaging, between ankle and knee, and his heart is very weak, yet he is growing stronger.

Sun. 23   A beautiful day, tho' cool this morning and few clouds this afternoon, late. "Easter-Day" and every one out in new "toggery". All I had *new*, was my *old* hat which I have worn for five Summers and *I* re-trim: this year I turned the back to the front, put a bow of 39¢ ribbon and a 10¢ rose in the back and 10¢ bunch of fruit in front, and I'm quite sure it looked as good as many a "*store*" hat I saw today. We took car, to and from Sunday School and church this morning. I had 28 boys in Class, and Mr. King took pictures of us this morning on Church steps: *three* were new boys, who said would join class and keep coming. . . . This afternoon [ten names follow] were out and I took pictures. This evening, Ernest Shelden, Edwin Jones, Mona Wiede and Charlie Plath came out. Edwin gave me a "dandy" picture of himself: he is a handsome boy.

May

Thurs. 25   A very warm day—I was very busy making Teddy some new Shirt waists—and tired tonight. Don Fay, and Charlie Plath with Mona Wiede, came out for the eve-ning—we gave them big bouquets of white Peonies and Syringa and almost looked like a "Bride's Bouquet" for Mona. Our general conversation brought up the subject of "Diarys" and finding I had kept one for more than 35 years begged I would "read" to them: now I do not read my Diarys to any one, nor allow them read but I read them "a few bits," concerning themselves, that I knew would interest them. "Jonesie" and her husband A.E. Jones, 1152 Washburn Ave. have separated—he moved out today and it's too bad, but I don't know how she has stood him so long—he had become "smitten" with a Mrs. Zora W. Elder.

June

Thurs. 1   A very hot day and Fred had so large a mail, he could not come home to dinner. One of the "Subs" helped him with three blocks of his heaviest mail this morning, telling him to "keep it secret" or it would anger the other "Subs" who had all agreed to stand together, against Fred—not to help in any way and so if he was not strong enough, he could not work, would lose his job, and they would get it, or one of them would and the others be a "step" nearer to a job: it does not seem possible that any one could be so inhuman and utterly forget, that they themselves can get down sick and be out of work and at great expense for months like poor Teddy. God recompense them. Charlie Plath and Mona Wiede came out for the evening. I was in to see Mrs. Bettis this afternoon. "Blew up" fine and cool at bed time: a strong wind from the North West. I went to High School this morning to Class Day exercises and they were good.

Sat. 10 Rained most all day and so I kept busy in the house tho' I had hoped to do some work in the garden. I churned and "cleaned" all up-stairs and down. Fred brought me another dozen Plymouth Rock chicks, from the "5 & 10" store, this evening. My hens are not setting, tho' had one hatch 7 *chicks*.

Well, the big Republican Convention, in Chicago today, nominated "Hughes for President," just the man I wanted to see nominated; a mighty fine choice. And the Bull Moose nominated "Roosevelt for President": and so, "*splits*," will let the Democrats in again. But I believe "Roosevelt" will resign—he *knows* he can't be elected, for there are many less Bull Moose, now, than there were four years ago when he was defeated: Roosevelt is a conceited fellow.

Sat. 24 A very warm day. I did my usual Saturday cleaning and baking. Battery A. left today for Ft. Riley in preparation for War with Mexico. Many of our young friends going and I'm glad of their patriotism; always something worth while in a boy "who goes to War," for far too many "now adays" are weak kneed, and tickled to death when parents object to their going; if they were really and truly filled with a spirit of patriotism, parental objection could not keep them home: and so, "God bless the boys who go," but what a pity they *need* to go. Why *can't we have Peace.*

Mon. 26 Got a pretty good washing out in good time this morning and cleaned up the house and churned, then did little things, to fill up rest of day. Every topic of conversation is *War*! and we pray for Peace! Politics are being forgotten for War, which might have been averted had we have had a man for President who had a little *will* power—God bless President Wilson, that he has kept us from War so long, but had he been more far sighted, he surely would not have permitted any of the Army to cross the Boundary into Mexico after Villa or any other Mexican: *great big mistake.*[1]

July

Tues. 11   Most awfully hot, and most awfully busy which made me a few degrees hotter than the day. Baked cakes this forenoon beside other duties and after dinner went to town with Mrs. A.E. Jones to see Lawyer Schenk about getting a divorce: he says she is to have the home, all the furniture and pay her own lawyer—Jones to pay his lawyer and Court costs. May be the poor woman will get justice yet. . . .

August

Fri. 4   "Red-hot, and still a heating, "O my! my!! I cleaned the house and was very busy most of the day—Mr. George Sutherin came out this evening to see about putting in "City water" for us. I will be so glad to get it done. My! what a World we live in, when it allows such out-rages as the hanging of Roger Casement.[2] As cruel as the time of Nero—punish him if they wished, but no man, or nation or law should presume to take a life God put in this World; God gives the life and He alone should re-call it.

Sat. 12   *O so hot,* and a hot wind from the South. A very busy forenoon. So glad we have the City water in. My dear friend "Jonesie" called me over the phone, this after-noon, to tell me "good-bye". She goes with her daughter and family (Radcliffes) in their Auto to Colorado Springs starting at 4 o'clock this afternoon, and it means my dearest friend and I will see very little of one another in this World any more, for she will make her home in the West, since she and A.E. Jones have separated. It breaks my heart, and I had to have a good cry. My heart aches, to have to give her up, for she has been kinder than my own sister. I don't know what I would have done with-out her, last Winter when Fred was so sick. I don't see why Jones could not have appreciated such a good wife and been true to her and their home need not have been broken up. O my good friend

"Jonesie," my heart aches, my throat aches, with its "lump" of tears and my eyes burn with tears because you are going, and we can no more have our good times together: and may never meet again.

September

Mon. 11   .... We had a letter last week from Freda, saying she got a divorce from Darrell Houston, Aug. 1st and on Aug. 11 she married Will Baker, coming over into Kansas—Richfield—to do so. I don't know what will become of such a girl.
Fair commenced this morning in the rain, but the afternoon has been fine, so it may bring big crowds.

Mon. 25   A fine day tho' very warm. Fred home, having a day of "Vacation." I had a rather large washing and Fred "pottered" around at "odds and ends." He helped me wash dishes at noon, then we both took a "nap." He slept two hours and I about a half hour, then brought my clothes in off line and did my ironing. This evening we went to the Orpheum to see the pictures of "God's country and the woman." Splendid and yet, much of it might better have been left out.[3]

October

Sat. 14   A splendid day—rained little this evening—Mel Pribble was out just after dinner and Carrie Weide came about 4:30 and this is the "Tale" she told me, of a new married couple. The "Newly-Weds," for convenience, left their door-key with Elma Stewart while "moving in," next door; after they moved in, the following young folks, Mona Wiede, Charlie Plath, Elma Stewart, Williard Carlson, Carrie Wiede and Isabel Southerin went over in the evening with all sorts of silly placards, and baby toys, to decorate, using key to open door, and with a lantern went thro' the house. Carrie going upstairs, found the "Newly Weds" in bed and told the others who did not believe her, so Charlie went up and they refused to believe him and Williard went up and tried to pull the covers off the young married couple and none of these young folks had ever seen the "Newly Weds" before except Elma, when they left their key with her. All were strangers. No words can express my utter disgust for such vulgarity. *What is* the World coming too, when parents do not teach their children common decency. No one could have blamed the young husband had he shot some of those young folks for the indignities to his home and young wife and it will take such action if things keep on; shameful, disgusting.

Sun. 15 .... We took car to S. S. and Church. I had 10 boys in Class. ... My friend "Jonesie," also came to dinner and will spend some time with us, since her home is broken up. ... Fred Brackett has quit the Class to go to Christian Science. His mother, long an invalid, was healed and went over to Christian Science and persuaded Fred's girl to take it up and she in turn has taken Fred away from me. I hate to lose him, he has been in Class so long.

Tues. 24 Certainly, one big, nasty day; raining when we got up and rained hard all day: some thunder and colder—did little beside my ironing. Mrs. Jones is still with us and we are glad to do everything we possibly can for her, but O, how she wearies one by constantly talking of her trouble with and separation from, Mr. Jones—from morning until night, same thing over and over. She is a dear, good woman and generous to a fault, but not more than one man out of a thousand could live with her and she is innocently blind to that side of herself.

November

Thurs. 2 Another grand day. Jonesie cleaned my two carpets with her vacuum cleaner, the "Thor" and it certainly cleaned them too. Electricity is wonderful. This afternoon "Jonesie" and I went to town to "shop" a wee bit and pay Bills—Phone, Light, Water and Lodge—and we went in to Rohr's to "investigate" the Victrola: Fred wants a "music box." Well I fell completely in love with the Victrola, like it much better than the Edison and think I shall give my husband one for Christmas. This evening Mrs. Jones took us to the "Iris" to see Theda Bara in Romeo and Juliet, with Hilliard: Splendid tho' I'm not fond of Tragedy—enjoyed this.

Tues. 7 A hard, whippy, whirly wind all day and some cloudy. *Presidential Election Day* and while I have voted Municipally, for many years, today I cast my first Presidential vote and voted hard for Charles Evans Hughes; of course I believe he will be elected, tho' I feel sure the Election will be close for many have said they would vote for Wilson believing "he has kept us out of War"—far from it for we are warring with Mexico right now and no other Country *could*, or *wants* to fight us. . . .

Wed. 8   Rained hard, nearly all day, (begining about Midnight) as if the very heavens were weeping, because we must endure four years more Wilson—for he has been elected again, what a *wicked shame*. Everything Republican by immense majority, except President. And it looks as if the women did it—they really believed Wilson kept us out of War, poor fools. Mrs. Jones came back this evening. I wish she could sell her home, poor woman.

Thurs. 9   A grand, beautiful day. "Jonesie" here and most we can do is to talk over our disappointment at result of Election—it is terrible that Wilson should be at head of the Nation four years more. A fine, cultured, educated, christian man, but with no executive ability—I can't see what he will do, exept worst of harm. Jonesie went to town in late afternoon over to Christian church where we later met her, to see the baptism of one of my boys, Melvern Pribble, after Prayer meeting. I was so happy to see Melvern Baptized. It was a *"perfect night"* of *exquisite* Moonlight. A great big, brilliant, full Moon, that shined away the stars; bright almost as day; and a cloudless sky.

Sun. 19   A grand, beautiful day. We took car to and from S.S. and Church. I had 14 boys in Class this morning and Mr. Yetter came to me and asked me to take his Class of Boys, or part of them—he is Secretary and will keep part of his Class to help him in that work. His Class got so noisy and inattentive, that he could do nothing with them and so he gave up—quit the Class, was made Secretary of Sunday School and asks me to take his "noisy bunch." Oh! *what a great, big bluff* man is, any way. All men, Sunday School workers, *howl*, "*Men teachers for boys*", yet in *our* church they have been failures: Mr. Yetter being the third man to give up a Class of boys in the Intermediate Dept. Mr. King did not give up his, but they *quit* him—I took my Class at begining of their Junior year and went thro' three years of Junior with them, when they were awfully *squirmy, wriggley* fellows, but so wide awake and interested and *interesting*; then I went thro' three years of Intermediate, with them and they were so noisy and hard to hold their attention I would come home sometimes and cry my heart out; but would not give up, yet have seen three *men* (men who brag of their strength, their superiority over women, as teachers of boys, and all else) give up Classes in Intermediate Dept. since I took my Class (*me, poor weak woman, who should not teach Boys*). And now I am finishing the third year in the Senior Dept. with the same Class of boys and am reaping my reward, in seeing the "Bunch" turning into fine young manhood, and "taking the burden" and helping me, by becoming teachers in their turn—Charlie Plath, Melvern Pribble, Ralph Davidson, Fred Brackett,[4] Will Jackson and Merritte Rowell, all as teachers and sub. teachers. Yes Mr. Yetter, I will take your deserted boys in with my bunch—take the burden off your great strong shoulders, O man, onto my weak ones, poor woman, who should *not* be a teacher of Boys. But I'm thankful, that no where in His Book, does God say *a woman shall not* teach Boys. And always in my work, He has blest me richly and helped me bear the burden of persecution and unjust criticism and jealousy, because I have been a successful teacher of boys, even tho' a woman. . . .

Tues. 21 A cold, raw, dismal, gloomy day. At 10 o'clock I met Mrs. Maxwell at Transfer Sta. and went with her to Topeka Cemetery—she was having the bodies of her son and father, moved to another lot and wanted me to go with her.[5] I was thankful the bodies were moved and partly covered when we got there—her grief is most pitiful, and beginning to affect her mind, and she knows it, for as we were waiting to catch a car home, she said "Mrs. Farnsworth, I am not right mentally"—her grief and shock of the tragedy of Robert's death, is killing her, and Mr. Maxwell either does not see, or does not care; he is selfish and doesn't treat her the best. As we were leaving the Cemetery, she turned, lifted her eyes toward the hill, where Robert's body lies, held out her hands and murmured "my poor boy", with tears streaming down her cheeks. It sounded like the moan of a poor wounded animal. My heart aches for her—I wish

I could ease her heart ache. She gave me a great bundle of Tulip bulbs. Much colder this evening and misting.

Thurs. 23   A beautiful, bright, sunny day. I am making cartoons now, to use at my New Year Party for my Boys. Mrs. Maxwell told me the other day (Tuesday) that Mr. Pribble had been at their house on business and in talking of "My S.S. Boys" told them he was jealous of me, because his son Melvern thought so much of me, always calling me "mother" or "Auntie". It amuses me, and yet I understand—Many parents of my Boys are jealous, and I am sorry for it is only friendship of Boy and Teacher.

Tues. 28   Another glorious day, and I worked on my Cartoons all day—some of them amuse me much. We went to the Orpheum this evening to see Douglas Fairbanks in "American Aristocracy"—enjoyed him very much. I ordered a Victrola, today from W.F. Roehr's—$100.00 My!

Thurs. 30   A most beautiful day. "Thanksgiving Day" and O, we have so much to be thankful for. Our blessings have been so many, the past year, we cannot name them—but [our] hearts are most thankful to God for all His merciful goodness. Fred has been home all day having a Holiday. We gave the Salvation Army a dollar to buy a dinner for some poor person—not much, but would buy as good a dinner as we had—a small baked chicken, slaw, and mashed potatoes with Strawberry preserves and cream in patty shell, for desert. We enjoyed Victrola music today—Fred has wanted a Victrola for a long time, so we got it—we always do without everything in way of pleasure, we work hard and "skimp", with our noses always on the grindstone and can't "lay by" so we decided to get a bit of pleasure by buying a Victrola—we believe we will have as much in end. We took Mrs. Jones and went to the Orpheum this evening to see Anita Stewart in "The Suspect"—excellent but more dramatic than I like. Fatty Arbuckle in a Comedy was good too, but parts of it should have been censored "out." I don't like "coarseness."

December

Sun. 31   A stormy day, as if weeping, because loth to see the Old Year depart. Sleet began falling very early, but not cold—in fact melting some, and very sloppy. We took a car to S.S. and church and return. I had but 8 boys in Class this morning—many Classes had less. And a small audience at church. After dinner I had to hurry to the Masonic Temple, for a drill and re-hearsal of new Officers—had to leave there to come home and get to work at 4:30, was kept on the jump, but got thro', dressed and lay on the couch and rested about an hour, before my first guests arrived. [Twenty-four names follow.] These were our guests who came in for the evening to watch with us and make merry, as the Old Year went out and the New Year came in—some wanted to dance and turned the clock ahead to midnight, as I had told them, "no dancing until midnight when it would be "Monday morning"—we had piano and Victrola music, told their "Fortunes" on the Ouija Board and had a general good time—at 11:30 I served Graham biscuit—hot—pressed chicken, sweet pickles, Plum pudding and Cocoa, Edwin Jones, Don Fay and Merritte Rowell helped me serve. Everyone seemed to have a good time. Bob & Merle with their girls left to go to another Party, where they could dance. Chas. Plath and Bob Williard (nephew of Jess Williard, Champ. Pug.) brought their revolvers and fired several rounds as a salute to the New Year. Every one had gone at 1:30 A.M. and we went to bed at 2 o'clock. A happy closing of the Old Year, that brought us much happiness; Fred restored to health, many friends and relatives—my parents—to visit us. Blessings so many, we cannot count them. One great sorrow, the tragic death of Robert Maxwell.

[1917]

In 1917 Martha began to slow down: she no longer stayed for refreshments after every lodge meeting, nor did she go out as much. But she did continue to entertain from six to thirty young people in her home every Sunday. During this year Martha also noted: Coit Farnsworth supposedly inherited a million dollars, but did not mention it to the family; Mrs. Jones got her divorce in May; a tornado devastated the countryside in June; and Fred Brackett and Nan Osborne married in December. Her hatred of Germany deepened as war neared, but while she felt that a stronger president could have kept the country out of war, she remained a patriot. The war became personal reality as her Sunday School boys began to be called up, and she closed the year with a prayer of thankfulness for the friendship of these young people.

[*1918*]

Most of this year was devoted to good-bye parties for her Sunday School boys, to visiting them at the depot when their troop trains came through, and to writing letters to them while they were at war. She had no patience with "slackers," the non-volunteers, and was outspoken in her criticism. Nonetheless, she records with sadness in June that "for the first time in nearly eleven years, I did not have a boy in Class. All have volunteered and gone to War except the 'slackers'. . . ." The occasional visits of the boys' girl friends mitigated some of her loneliness, and she filled some of her time by being president of the Good Government Club. But she prayed fervently for the war to end, for the Allies to win "glorious victories over the accursed Huns—O that the Hun race might be annihilated."

November

Wed. 6   A fine day—warm. Election Returns tell of a wonderful Republican Victory all over the country—a regular landslide, and I am wondering what our "*spineless*" President thinks about it. He *must* think it looks as if *he would not get to be Kaiser of America.*

Thurs. 7   Cold and rainy. And word came at noon or 11:30 that *Peace* had been declared, and bells rang, guns were fired, people quit work and simply went crazy with joy. I was home alone, when I heard first whistle just before 1 o'clock but knew instinctively it meant "Peace" so hung out my flag and went down on my knees, and thanked God. Teddy did not get home for dinner, so I dressed and went to town—the streets were a jam of "people and noise"; joyful, happy noise—noise made by every conceivable thing that noise could be pounded out of. The "Kaiser" was hung in effigy at 8th & Kansas Ave, and shot to pieces—and some one else had a "Kaiser" tied behind their automobile and dragged, kicked, beat, shot etc. It seemed impossible for the people to find ways enough in which to show their joy over Peace declaration, and their hatred of the Kaiser, the *fiend incarnate.* And this evening we hear that two speeding automobiles crashed together about 5 o'clock, at 7th &

Topeka Ave and hurt many people, two among them our lovely Katherine and Betty Harmon—a sad ending to a *hilariously happy* day. But tonight, the noise of a spontaneous *Peace* demonstration continues. We are staying at home however, content in the day's happiness.

Fri. 8   A beautiful day. Have been very busy all day, tho' I went down to the church this afternoon to a Committee-meeting—David Owen, May Roberts, Don Osborne, Rev. Schell and myself. And *now* they tell us, there *is no Peace*—the announcement was premature. But *I believe it is true*. Our Harmon girls are both very low and little hope for their lives, due to the dreadful accident yesterday.

Mon. 11   A *grand* day, an *ideal* day, and *World Peace* at last—Germany has signed the "Peace" terms. At three o'clock this morning, or to be exact, 3:15, I was awakened by the blowing of whistles, I knew it meant a fire in Santa Fe shops, or *Peace*, so I got out of bed to look at the clock and it was 3:15 which would be 9 o'clock in France; the Germans were given until 9 o'clock, Nov. 11, 1918 to sign the terms of Peace, or there would be no Peace so I *knew* the whistles were blowing for Peace. And almost immediately, guns were being fired, bells rung, people shouting and a tremendous din everywhere—no sleep but it was glorious to lie in bed and listen to the city's expression of joy. When we got up I hung out "Old Glory", the Tri-color and Union Jack. I did my washing as usual and cleaned up the house; Teddy was to be in the "Peace Parade" so hadn't time to come home to dinner. I received a telegram from Elmo Madden (one of my old Sun. School boys) that he would pass thro' Topeka at 2:45 P.M. enroute from Eugene, Oregon to Camp Taylor, Kentucky, so I dressed and left house at 1:40 and walked the three miles to U.P. depot in North Topeka. His train was on time and held here a long time, blocked by the Peace Parade so that I had a fine visit with Elmo. Teddy left the Parade at the depot and stayed with me to visit with Elmo—also Dewey Goddard, an old Topeka boy, now of Calif. enroute to Camp Taylor. Sure was fine to see the boys again—both looked splendid. After the Parade and the boys had gone, Teddy and I walked back to Transfer Sta. 8th & Kansas

Ave, where we waited for the Street cars, and rode home. All the cars quit running at 1 o'clock P.M. and began again at 4 o'clock. A big, big parade, made up of everything imaginable noise and Bands and people—wholly indescribable—noise pounded out of everything that noise *could* be pounded out of: every kind of whistle and bells, strings of old tin cans, whoops and howls and yells, big and little and old and young, every color and nationality—and the streets jammed, going in every direction everyone hilariously happy because *we licked the Kaiser*—we *helped* with America's best young men—flags, flags, flags, every where: O it was all wonderfully thrilling and wholly indescribable: began at 3 o'clock this morning and continued until mid-night, tonight Teddy and I went to the Orpheum—after Supper—to see the War pictures and see John Barrington and Lois Meredith in Movies.

Thank God for Peace, and may it be an everlasting Peace.

December

Mon. 2   All golden sunshine and blue sky overhead, with a bit of snow and green-lawn beneath, the "make-up" of a "Perfect Day" in Winter in Kansas. Mrs. Amos called me Sat. to tell me my *onetime* friend "Jonesie" (Mrs. A.E. Jones) divorced, is married again—lives in Denver—has now *two divorced* husbands and a living one, or the *present* husband—well I hope she has a *good* man, for *she* is a *good* woman, but there is no man living that she can get along with. Mail heavy and Fred not home to dinner at noon. I spent the whole day writing—put off writing [working?] to write my Soldier boys.

Tues. 31   Sunny and cold. Deep snow and heavy mails and my poor Teddy had to work all day with no time to stop to get anything to eat. His foot is very sore and the P.O. authorities won't let him off to take care of it. I wish it were possible to make the Postmaster and the various Superintendents work as the Carriers do—that there could be a law passed, compelling *them* to go out and wade the deep snow, the same long hours without food, with the heavy loads on their backs, sick and hurt or injured—what a lesson of mercy it would teach these

Government *task masters*, who would be arrested, did
they *dare* treat so in-humanely and over-work the mules
and horses used by the Government. So many of "Uncle
Sam's" men of authority are *brutes*—that is, those con-
nected with the P.O.—especially here in Topeka, and
under Democratic administration. But a man has to be a
selfish brute to hold Office under Burleson, who President Wilson seems to love(?) because he *is* a hell cat.
Teddy came home very tired tonight, haggard and
worn. We will go to bed early that he may have a good
night's rest. So many of my dear Sun. School boys are in
the Army, that I am not having a "Watch Party" this
year, and it is a very lonely ending to the old Year.

[*1919*]

Wed. 1   Again, God in his mercy has kept me thro' a year of
Time and let the Cycle of months bring me to the
threshold of a New Year, where I stand this morning,
with deep thankfulness for the many blessings of the
past year, the greatest of which is that the awful tragedy
of War has ceased, tho' the World is still in a chaotic
condition of revolutions; Anarchistic, Socialistic,
Boleshevistic.

And with all my soul I thank God, that He spared the
lives of my Sunday School Boys, who have been in the
thick of the fighting, with the 35th Div. in France. . . .
From all of whom, I have had letters, since the "Signing
of the Armistice." Ah who *dares* to say God does not
answer prayer? I have kneeled and petitioned the
throne of Grace every morning since they left for the
War, and see how graciously He has answered, by preserving their lives thro' awful Battles where 50% and
more of their comrades were killed or wounded. "O ye
of little faith," *I* know that God *does* answer prayer. And
so I pray for Divine guidance for the New Year that I
may live my life in accordance with His will—that I may
be strong in all righteousness.

A warm sun shone down on a snow-enshrouded
earth, all white and beautiful, but very cold. The Carriers had to work all day, being denied their lawful
Holiday because of heavy mails, and the deep snow
preventing for some time, two deliveries of mail a day—
so my poor, tired Teddy with a *very* sore foot, was
compelled to work full *eight hours* today with *not a bite to
eat*, while *everywhere, everyone* was *feasting* and happy,
supposing their Carriers were also enjoying the Day
with half Holiday as Newspapers announced. Well *I*
wrote the *truth* of it all and mailed to the Newspapers to
publish that the public might know the *straight of it*.
Seeking no notoriety, I signed a Nom de Plume, using

Expenses, March 1919, from Martha's diary.

Cordelia—my middle name—and "Vandol"—my maiden name with three middle letters (Ors) left out—VanOrsdol—also gave fictitious street No. and made myself a "Mother in Law"—It "worked" fine and was only fair to the *hardworking* Carriers. Fred came home tonight almost exhausted and his foot much worse, yet P.O. won't let him off to "doctor" it. We had no New Year festivities this Year because most of my beloved Sun. School boys are in France. It is very, very, cold tonight but our "Inglenook" is warm and cheery and our "blessings are so many we cannot name them". Our hearts over flow with thankfulness.

Mon. 6   *Awful* cold, but sunny day. I wrote letters all day. Did not wash. Teddy's foot alright again and he back to work—not home to dinner and very tired tonight. Mona

Wiede, Miss Myers and Frances Scott, Christ Hosp. nurses came in for the evening. Received a good letter from Scott Brown today—he sure is one dandy boy. "Theodore Roosevelt" died this morning—most dreadful shock and loss to the *World,* for he was a great and wonderful man and so badly needed, just at this readjusting time of the World's affairs: a man who did *great good* and *great harm* in the World—a man whom *all* the World *loved* or *hated.*

Wed. 8   Bright, sunny and sloppy. Received package of Souvenirs at noon from Harry Davis in France—a Crucifix made of French rifle shells and two vases made of French one pound Shells, from Verdun and Forrest of Argonne—so good of Harry to send them and so thoughtful—I'm so glad to have the uncanny, gruesome things.

Sun. 12   I went to Sun. School this morning and Fred stayed home to rest. . . . The boys wanted me to have a Class again, as *all* will soon be coming home. . . .

    Mrs. Benjamin called this afternoon, on business connected with Jewish-Armenian Welfare work. I am to be one of the canvassers in the *"Drive"* as I have been in all the others—Red Cross, all the "Liberty Loans", "War Work", "Seven in One" etc.[2]. . .

February

Fri. 28   A howling old North-West Blizzard swept down on us last night at bed time—*Awful* cold and blow and snow, and til noon today—deep snow and great drifts. I went to State House at 4 o'clock as part of delegation of Women, to meet Legislative Committee to protest against the Bill lowering the majority rights of girls, from 21 to 18 years of age.[3] Got home 7 o'clock—Fred not home at noon.

April

Wed. 30   A fine day, but cool. I worked hard all day—baked a lot of *cookies* of all kinds for *my* soldier Boys, for today is a big day in our old Topeka town—the 110 Engineers came in late this evening and stopped three hours in the city enroute to Funston for demobilization. The

"Creamery Co." whistle, or siren blew "Home Sweet Home" at 9 o'clock as the Troop train came into depot—of course only wives, mothers and fathers could meet the train, the rest of us had to meet them at State House, so Fred and I with a big basket of cookies went down early, met Thelma McComas at 10th & VanBuren. We rode down with neighbors, Stricklers. Topeka was all *alight*, and *decorated*, and *whooping, howling yowling mad-glad*. Such a jam and mob of people we did not go up on the Avenue but waited at State House and it seemed like they would *never come*, but what a grand, glorious sight, when our Hero Soldiers finally came marching up the street, to music of the Bands. It brought tears of joy to see the beloved, *living*, home again and tears of sorrow, for the beloved *dead,* who will *never* be home again—the broken ranks—the beloved dead who sleep beneath the stars, in France tonight—and I hope the stars *are* shining as brightly there, as they were here, tonight. And in the great heartthrob of *joy* in meeting our loved Soldier Boys, there was an equal heartthrob of *sorrow* for the Soldier Boy asleep "Over There." Even in our great joy we could not forget them.

Omar B. Ketchum, one of Martha's Sunday School boys, in his WWI uniform. He later was mayor of Topeka.

My beloved Sun. School Boys, home, are Omar Ketchum,[4] Earl Bunce, Charlie Clements and Frank Bunce and they looked *fine*, but tired. I was so happy to see them I could not talk, and everybody was happy. It all seems like a dream—two years ago they left for War—tonight they are home again. O God pity the mothers of Boys who did *not* come tonight, nor ever will—God bless the sleep of our Hero, Dead, in France—we *know* "Greater love hath no man, than he that gives his life for another". I *know* God answers prayer, the fervent, earnest prayer—and not one day passed bye, that I did not go down on my knees and plead with God to spare the lives and bring safe home again my beloved Sun. School boys, and He graciously heard and granted my prayers. Such a happy evening. The boys left for Funston at 11 o'clock—almost midnight when we got home, tired and happy.

May

Fri. 2
A cool fine morning—a shower at noon, and a fine warm, sunny afternoon, with a bit of "*cool*" in the air. Mail heavy and my good Teddy did not get home to dinner, tho' I cooked a *nice* dinner, because it is our "Silver Wedding" Anniversary. *Twenty five* happy years, with a *good* man. He sent me two doz. fine Carnations this morning after he went to work. . . .

Thurs. 8
Cloudy and cool. Battery A. 130 Field Artillary came in last night and this morning early one of my boys, Walter Norris, called me up and later came out to see me; (and was bareheaded) some one between Chicago and Kansas City during one of their stops, some one in crowd "snatched" his cap off his head (presumbly for souvenir). Poor Walter was so nervous, he made *me* nervous—he had a very hard time all way thro' and especially in Argonne Forest—many narrow escapes—he is a country boy and nobody's fool but has not had as many advantages as some. He sure could tell all *you* could think of to ask him, about the War and had many photographs "taken on the spot" to back up what he told. Mighty interesting to listen to. Before he left, Jack Miller came out with five Soldier Boys of the 137 Infantry who just got in this morning. We did not know any of

them, but good old accomadating Jack filled his car and took them for a ride over the City and brought them out here: also had Julia Dixon and Will Halm with him. This afternoon I went down town, to see the Army Parade— 2700 Troops in the Parade—a grand, most *inspiring* sight, and "Tears of joy that so many are safe home again—tears of sorrow that so many sleep in France, never to return." I went over onto the State House Grounds where the crowd mingled with the resting Soldiers and I hunted several hours for the many Soldier Boys with whom I was acquainted, but could not find *one*; tho met many I knew, not one was a returned Soldier—too dense a crowd. Every one was so happy today, for Topeka's own Battery A. had returned Victorious from the War. Scott Brown and Jay Banta came out this evening.

Tues. 20   A fine, cool, sunny day. I went to town this afternoon to *shop* a bit. Bought a Pork Loin Roast for which I paid $3.60 for my dinner Party tomorrow night. After supper Robert Sympson came in for about *two* minutes, a long call for him to make on any one but Helen Leeper. He grows more eccentric every day. This evening Jay Banta with Hazel Manehan, Scott Brown with Margaret Officer came in for a wee call and to dance awhile—I am doubtful of this combination—doesn't look good to me—not the right four.

Five Army Aviators in town this evening—saw some very pretty flights—looked like five big brown hawks flying—the whirr-r-r of their motors were so even, one was assured they had good machines, and so made me wish for a ride in one. I would far rather ride in an Aeroplane than an Automobile—think them *safer*.

Wed. 21   A grand day—saw some more very pretty Aeroplane flights this morning, made by the visiting Army Planes. Worked on the jump all day, getting up a dinner for Virgil Scholes, this evening. Six boys and five girls. . . . I could not ask a girl for Edwin, because he had to go to his Law Class at Washburn College. We had a jolly, jolly time, but the "kiddies" ate so much, they did not do much dancing after Dinner. I just gave them a dinner without any "frills"—a fine Pork Loin Roast, mashed potatoes, creamed corn, tomato-cucumber salad, graham biscuit, honey, sun-preserved cherries, green tomato preserve, radishes, beets, cheese, very fine lemon and pumpkin pie, and an excellent Lady Baltimore cake. And milk to drink—Jack Miller drank seven glasses and I think Scott Brown went him a few better, with Jay Banta not far behind. They were a jolly bunch—it's worth a fortune, to have such fine friends among the young folks. Good old Edwin Jones came out early and helped me get things on the table—he is such a splendid helper. The girl that gets *him* will get a royal husband. But they are all fine young fellows and I hope get wives worthy of them, and have happy homes. After dinner, Teddy helped me *clear* the table and the young folks, both boys and girls helped me do the dishes, so I feel like I had not worked at all.[5]

June

Fri. 13   Very hot day but I hurried about my work and barely got thro' in time to meet the 3 o'clock train on the Union Pacific, on which came Purl Barnard and his Bride. I was so happy to see Purl—he is just the same fine fellow—not at all changed, only grown to be such a giant,

Martha and fourteen of her boys just returned from the war.

and very fine looking, but *all* my boys look mighty good to me. And I think Purl took unto himself a very sweet little wife. We had a very hard rain at 6 o'clock but we hurried about with our evening work, then Teddy and I with Purl and Grace went down to the Church to a Banquet our church gave our returned War Heroes, the Soldiers and Sailors who went to War, from our church. We had a fine time, but always dragging behind, our church waited too long—most of the boys who have returned from War have left the City to find *work*: but we had a fair crowd—nearly 200—and they held the Banquet nearly an hour, waiting for me to come and head the procession of Soldiers and Sailors, in march to Banquet room. I did not know I was to be so honored or would have been on time. Then they seated me in the centre of the long table dedicated to the Soldiers and Sailors, the only woman at the table, a *great honor* but a mistake, for every Soldier should have had his sweetheart beside him and I *know* it had been so arranged, for I had stood firm for that plan—I do not know *why* that plan was changed, nor by whom or whose authority. Dr. Claude Smith was Toastmaster and a fine one and after calling on all Soldiers to "stand, give their name, Co. etc. where they served during War etc, all unexpected he called for "a word from another *great soldier*, sitting at centre of table and only woman so honored, Mrs. Farnsworth," Oh! at first, I felt embarrassed, because of the compliment but I was equal to the occasion and told them that while I was jokingly called "a Soldier," it was no joke, for I *was* a Soldier, *28 times* (having 28 Sunday School boys in the Service) I was in the camps, cantonements, in the trenches, I crossed the seas, I was in the Argonne, at St. Mihiel etc. My heart followed every boy to France and home again—and *not one day*, did I forget to pray, for every one of them; and much more I said, and received great applause and many "compliments on my speech," after it was over, and Rev. Schell told me he was proud of me. Mr. Yetter gave a jolly comic talk and referred to me as "Major Farnsworth" and it made a hit. A misplanned Banquet but a very happy evening.

Mon. 16   *Very* hot day. Purl and Grace went to Kansas City after dinner, to visit relatives. Mail heavy and Fred not home at noon. Governor Allan signed Ratification of Universal Suffrage today at noon at Called Session of Legislature for that purpose.

Sat. 21   A very hot day and I worked very hard all day. . . . Mrs. Monroe called to present me the Pen with which Governor Allan signed the Universal Suffrage Ratification at a "called" Extra Session of the Legislature and she told me *how unwittingly, I made the Govenor to wait on my pleasure—as President of the Good Government Club, I should have been present—they called me over the phone, and I promised to go, then found I would be too rushed—they had the Governor wait, but finally he could wait no longer, as had to go out of town to give a Lecture, so signed and sent me the pen—kind of him, but I don't half appreciate honors,* since it did not *seem such a great honor.* Let Mrs. Monroe take our Indian picture to have a copy made from it for the State Historical Society. Mrs. Lilla Day Monroe is a most wonderful woman, in every way.

July

Fri. 18   . . . . I dreamed of my folks in Colorado, last night and saw a *new Baby* in the family—I wonder *who* it belongs to—I am sure its *true,* for I *don't dream, I see.*

Thurs. 24   Another *hot* day. We went out to Washburn this evening to the Flying Field, with the Elliott Calvin's. Three Aeroplanes out there and some pretty Flying. I'm crazy to take a Fly, but can't afford the price $10.00. Working on Fred's shirt today—is very pretty.

Harry's Return From War.

Fri. 25   *Very hot* day. I was most happily surprised this morning when answering door bell, I found at the door one of my best loved boys, dear splendid Harry Davis, just returned last night from overseas. I could have cried for very joy—these blessed boys of mine, *why!* I forget they are *not* my very own. I think God must have led them into my life, to help heal the wound caused by my sweet little daughter's death. I am so thankful for Harry's safe return. Frances Scott spent the afternoon with me. Harry had not seen Teddy, so came again this evening bringing his sweet heart, Thelma Huston. . . .

Sat. 26   A most awfully hot day and I've been so very busy, cleaning the house, doing my mending and Sat. Sun.

Baking. I finished Fred's silk shirt too and it's very pretty. Again the *Dream Baby* came to me last night—I can't figure where in the family it belongs—I am too tired to get the message clearly and I don't know *who* has *sent* for one. . . .

Mon. 28   102° with scorching wind, burning up the corn. I both washed and ironed as I always do, Monday. Teddy brought me a letter this evening from my adopted sister Vella, telling me my neice Zaidee Gilbert-Mort has a new baby daughter born July 26th. So *that* is where my *Dream baby* belonged. I knew it was in family some where. This awful heat, just wears me out—I get skinnier every day, but am fat enough yet.

November

Thurs. 6   Rained most all day and cold. Mail so heavy on Fred's big route, that he did not get home to dinner. I wrote letters all day. The big Coal strike is on.[6] What unrest in the World—the Strikers *cannot win* and why not be sensible and try an *appeal* to the people—too much of "Red"-sentiment among the strikers—too many of the bad Foreign element in this country.

Sat. 8   I went to town again this morning to get some curtain material for the hall—archway—everything is so high, but we just have to have them to keep out the cold. We live from hand to mouth all the time—impossible to save anything, but we are no worse off than hundreds of other Carriers all over the country. Government works its Carriers to death and don't pay enough to live on. Made my curtains and put them up this evening. *Cold* and *raining* hard at bed-time.

December

Mon. 1st   Sun came up clear, but was soon cloudy, raw and cold. I did not wash today but wrote letters all day, I owe so many. My poor Teddy did not get home to dinner. Volunteers and National Guards went to the coal-fields last night, to dig coal, so people won't freeze thanks to our Gov. Allan, who *does things* while Uncle Sam as represented by President Wilson the wishy, washy, spineless fellow that he is, fools around, thinking about it—thank God for a Governor who would not wait on "Red Tape" and was *not afraid* to walk up and "take the Bull by the horns" and he will throw the Bull too, see if he doesn't.

Tues. 2ND Awful cold: zero this morning. I rode to town this morning with Harry Crane, (took me to Court House) to pay our Taxes, $40.69 another outrage—the men in tax Dept. admit it, but *how* can we poor people help ourselves—we just have to pay it—it does no good to squeal. Fred not home to dinner—another *outrage* for the Government should hire enough men to do the work, so *all* could have time to get three meals a day—its *rotten* the way this P.O. arranges Routes.

Mon. 8 I washed, dried clothes in house and did my ironing today. *Very cold* and snowed lazily all day. My good husband not home to dinner. Scott Brown came out for the evening. Everything is "conservation" like War times. Streets are dark at night—stores open late and close early. Woodhaulers passing everyday with big loads which sell at Profiteer prices; churches, one service a day—Schools and Colleges closed—why *what* is the old World coming too—sure *fierce. We* have plenty of coal, for we had it put in the barn last Summer, but many are not so lucky. But Gov. Allan is getting out coal in great shape and things will get better.

Thurs. 25 Christmas Day, and all the World rejoices, that is, *all* the *Christian* World. We *all* rejoice that a babe was born in a lowly manger, in the little town of Bethlehem in Judeah, centuries [ago], and Angels sang "Peace on earth, Good Will to men". Yet, *evil* prevents "*Peace* on earth." *Some time*, it will come. Today is dark, gloomy and cold—a raw, chilly wind. My good Teddy worked *nine hours* then came home, O so tired. I baked a chicken and cherry, peach and apple pies. I do not get up big dinner on Christmas because Fred cannot be home and is always too tired to eat. Brother Coit Farnsworth sent me $10.00 for Christmas. Mrs. C.S. Gleed gave Teddy $5.00. And we got candies, books, stationary, handkerchiefs and many, many cards, from loving friends. And *I* received from my lovely boys, a *most magnificent* present, of a fumed oak, writing-desk; just what I need and have long wanted, yet was content with my old one, and I never thought of buying another—this *new* one is *ideal*—had I been asked to choose one, *myself*, I *could* not *possibly* have suited myself better—it is *perfect* and am *so very* happy to have it, *only sorry* the boys bought me anything so expensive. I know their good hearts were happy to do it but I wish they had gotten a less expensive present, if they felt they *just must get something*.... I never dreamed of their doing such a thing. And Fred & Nan gave me the loveliest, daintiest little fumed-oak chair to go with the desk—then this afternoon Fred & Nan came out and Nan brought me a box of lovely stationary and Teddy some handkerchiefs. Boys also gave me a lovely desk set, in brass: writing pad, ink well, blotter roll, letter opener, paper weight, pen rack and perpetual Calendar. I am so grateful—I appreciate their gifts *so much* but I was so overwhelmed, I just couldn't express my "thank you's" —I simply didn't know how to thank them, but I think they understand. They certainly are the grandest, best bunch of fellows, ever anyone could know. I took pictures of the boys, before they went home.

This evening John Keating, Mabel McKee, Edwin Jones, Ruth Pittenger, Harry Davis and Lucille Maguire came out and it made a very happy Christmas night for us. The young folks are so good to Teddy and me—we *never can* repay them for all the happiness they give us—for all the *sunshine* they bring into our home. I thank God that he put more young people in the World than anything else, and that he gave a large share of them to Teddy and me, for friends—the friendship of young folks is worth more to anyone, than all the World's gold. I would rather have the friendship of my bunch of boys and their girl friends, than all the wealth of the World. Teddy was given $8.50 in cash today, by friends. Otis Young came in for short Call this evening.

Mon. 29   A splendidly fine day. I got my washing, a small one, out early, cleaned up the house and soon after noon went to town to shop a bit and attend a meeting of the "Fair-price Committee," called by W.H. Kemper at Chamber of Commerce for 3 o'clock. Was a good audience of women, with all sorts of suggestions and experiences.

But I do not *see* how anything can be accomplished until the supply equals the demand, even then Commission men let things rot, before they will sell below a given price and always keep the price high. This re-adjusting after the awful War, is a mighty hard thing and bound to be suffering.

[1920]

January

Mon. 12 A fine day. I washed and cleaned up house and churned and wrote many letters. We went to Comercial Club rooms this evening to a meeting of Church folks, to organize for a *Drive* to help Armenia; W.A. Biby in charge. Rev. Maynard, a returned Missionary of that country told of the awful hardship and starvation in Armenia. How the people ate the dead corpses, because so starved. I wish *I* was a millionaire, to help more.[1]

Sat. 17 A grand day. Hurriedly did my cooking for Sunday, then went to town to pay Bills and Shop a bit, then went to see Dr. Cutsinger, about my eye. The Cataract has developed so I can see it with naked eye. He thinks an operation in a month or two may restore my sight but are some bad symptoms and my eye may have to be taken out. Well, whatever comes, God will give me grace to bear. I do not want to lose my eye, but even so, I won't *be* the *only* person in the world, with one eye. My! what a lot I must *do*, in the next month—so arrange and plan all business, and set my house in order, that things may be easy as possible for my beloved Teddy, if I should not live thro' the operation. I was given an overdose of Chloroform, some years ago by Dr. Kiene, when setting my broken wrist and only for Dr. McClintock (J.C.) I would not be here today. So I have the Chloroform to dread—it *could* happen again. This is a beautiful World, and my life is very happy; I would love to stay here a number of years yet; On the other hand, "it cannot be conceived in the mind of man, how glorious is the Heavenly home prepared for those who love God." And my "wee girlie" is there—mother is there and O so many of my loved ones. And Bob and Carl am very sure, would meet me at Heaven's Gate.[2] It would be all of joy—I care most for the sorrow it would cause my blessed Teddy and my beloved father, almost 80 yrs. old—it would be hardest for these two: then, my lovely young

Fred Farnsworth in post-
man's uniform, probably
taken by Martha on January
1, 1920. Courtesy Ralph A.
Kingman, Topeka.

men and girls, who are so often in our home, and my
dear uncle Ezekiel and aunt Matilda and a host of other
relatives and friends. For all their sakes, I would be
spared so tragic a death but I shall plan everything to
make it as easy for them all, as I can. The operation of
itself is easy enough—simple enough, however Chloroform in *some* Doctors' hands is fatal, so I *must* look at
both sides and prepare for the *worst,* even tho' I'm *most
optomistic* and hopeful of the *best* result. After I came
home from town, I cleaned the whole house thoroughly, upstairs and down and did a lot of mending. I
did not tell Teddy until after work this evening, of what
I must go thro'—I did not want him worried, with all his
hard work, this afternoon. And *he,* like me, looks on the
bright side, tonight.

Tues. 20   *Cold, windy, blustery* day. Wrote most of day—have so
much to do, hardly know which to do first, in preparation for operation on my eye, and the possibility of my
not getting thro' it, so must leave things in good shape
for Fred. . . . We are always so happy to have our young
folks come in. Don Fay called me, on Phone this morning—home on Furlo—good to hear his voice.

February

Wed. 18   Another grand day. Scott Brown came out about 11 o'clock and here all day—slept all afternoon.[3] He is dreadfully nervous—I think it is all due to the War—relaxing from the strain of all he went thro', and will take a long time to get over—it's too bad—Scott is a fine fellow. I had lots to do, but have not got on well with my work to-day. Wrote letters mostly, while Scott slept.

Wed. 25   A bit of sunshine, *more* of cold grey clouds and drizzling, lazily falling snow flakes. Went to town after dinner to meet some of the workers in the "Near East" Drive—we met at Mr. R. Ellis's office in New England Bldg. at 2 o'clock and from there Mrs. W.R. Zimmerman and I walked out to Summer School where we began our canvass. . . . Awfully cold, and not half the folks at home so we only got *three dollars* for the Armenians. $2.00 of the three was given me by a poor little bed-ridden woman, whom I found all alone in a very delapid[at]ed little shack, about 326 Filmore. She said she had not been out of her bed for over a year—her husband works, and must leave her alone all day except a short time at noon when he comes home to get his lunch, and take care of her. When I told her my mission, she reached back of her and from some where, drew out two dollars and handed me saying "I guess we can spare this much—it is all the *Lord's* money, anyway—we always give one tenth." Very poor, and bedridden herself, yet so sunny and sweet spirited, and so full of sympathy for the persecuted and starving Armenians. I was loth to leave; it was such a joy to visit with her, but it was night, and a storm of "snow and blow" and cold was sweeping down from N.W. and I had to get home, so I hurried away to catch a car glad I had stumbled on to this very poor home, at the close of my canvass: it made me forget the *awful* disappointment in finding out some of the *rich* who would not give one penny. The street cars were all off time and I had to wait over half hour, in a blinding snow storm, awfully cold, nearly froze. By time I got home, the storm was over.

Sun. 29   A fine day. We went to S.S. and Church. . . . . There was no Lesson this morning, the time being taken up in raising money for Armenia. I think *some* stayed away, because they *knew* of the plan to raise money to feed more than 750,000 starving Armenian babies—how can *anyone* so harden their hearts—they don't know what it means to be hungry and cold, and forget that, as "they do to one of the least of these, they do to Him." They are sure to have some loss—such *tight wads* cannot fail to lose, it is simply retribution. Teddy and I were alone this afternoon. At 4 o'clock Scott Brown and Florence Frazier came out and were here all evening. . . .The young folks sure fill our home with sunshine—I don't know what we would do without them. Today is the 5th Sun. in February and won't occur again till 1948. I wonder how many of us will be living, to see it.

March

Tues. 2   . . . at 10 o'clock this evening, we saw the Undertaker leaving Mr. Carpenter's home, just across the street, South and we know it means Mr. Carpenter is dead—he has been very sick with his heart for two weeks. He was a *black* man with a *white* soul. A splendid colored man of good christian character and we sincerely regret his death. Fred went to Board meeting at Church tonight.

Wed. 10   Foggy morning and heavy clouds—a shower at noon and bright, warm sunny afternoon—*April* in *March*. As I went to the Grocery this morning, I stopped to talk with Mrs. Carpenter, who is very lonely, and grief stricken, since her husband's death a week ago. They were such a fine family of colored people, and I am so sorry for her. Mona and Carrie Wiede came in for the evening—two of our loveliest girls—always glad when they come.

Wed. 17   A fine day tho' rather windy—a very busy morning and *so busy*, I did not take time to eat dinner at noon but hurriedly dressed and went to town, when Fred went back to P.O. I went to see Dr. Cutsinger about my eye. He *now* advises against operation solely for reason I would look queer with *one very thick* eyeglass and one thin one—said as I had gotten along with one eye for 6 or 7 years, I just as well keep on, and not look *queer*, till I *had* to and would be time enough to operate when vision of my *good* eye grew dim. I went to Dr. Iserman's and had a tooth pulled. Scott B. came out and stayed all night.

Thurs. 18   Such an *awful* day—a gale all day—A dreadful *March dust storm*, such as only our dear old Kansas can blow up. I was most awfully busy all morning, and just after dinner the wind blew my glasses off and broke them and I had to go down town thro' the *awful* dust-storm and have my eyes tested for another pair or rather just *one* glass, as only one broke—I had to pay *six* dollars, too; we just *cannot* save money for *everything* is *so dreadfully high*. Sun hid all day by dust.

Thurs. 25   Cloudy and cold, but "clearing" after the rain. Very busy "pasting" War pictures of "*my* Boys" on my new Book. Fred has a bad sore throat and a "breaking out" over all of upper part of his body—a rash, that itches—guess he has "shingles". We went to Grace Cathedral this evening to hear James Moore Hickson who heals disease by "laying on of hands."[4] Not a great speaker and only an average man, as to stature and appearance, but most earnest in his talk—sincere and of great faith—*I do not doubt*, for a moment, that God uses him as a channel, to heal all who came in faith, after doing *all* in *their* power. I believe *we* should do our utmost, after which God will do the rest. James Hickson is a *wonderful* man.

April

Sun. 4   Easter Day, and what a day—Until noon a terrific snow storm—the worst storm of the Winter—a dreadful Blizzard—everything snow bound—great drifts that one could not get thro'—street cars could not run, and *I* felt *I must* get to Sunday School—in 13 years, no storm has been so severe that it kept me home—in some manner I have gotten there, but it was *utterly impossible* today and it was a most bitter disappointment. I called a Jitney at ten minutes of 8 o'clock—they promised faithfully—I waited 9:15 and called again; and again the promise—I kept calling, but Jitneys were *stuck* all over town; stuck in the great snowdrifts and so at 10:10 I gave up and took off my wraps; and some of my boys phoned me they were at the church—Scott Brown and Harry Davis. The afternoon was cold, but sun came out a few moments and it quit snowing—our young folks could not come out, because all traffic was blockaded—so Teddy and I had a very quiet time—I read aloud all afternoon and evening, one of Margaret Hill McCarter's Books, "Vanguard of the Plains". It is not nearly so good as her *other* Books.[5] We are lonely tonight—we miss our kiddies, our blessed young folks, that bring so much sunshine into our home—And we could not go to church or Sunday School today.

On the 14th of April, another of her Sunday School class, Robert Jones, died. (Two others had died in recent years, of illness and accident.) "The doctor had said he grew as much in one year as he should have done in five and his strength could not keep up. . . ."

Sat. 24   A pretty fair day even tho' threatening rain. I baked a most excellent Lady Baltimore Cake, this morning—a very large one, with lots of "filling" and deep white icing on top and 54 halves of English Walnuts on top of that, then I baked three "Punkin" pies, stewed a good fat laying hen, *paddled* Fred 54 times, gave him 54 kisses, and hugged him 54 times, all because today is his 54 Birthday, and I wished I had an Oil well to give him— because he is worthy of it all, and more. Tonight we went to the Orpheum to see Christine Burney in "A Stolen Kiss" and enjoyed it very much.

May

Thurs. 13   Cool and half cloudy. I colored some enlarged Kodak pictures this morning of Robert Jones' grave. This afternoon I went to a meeting of Good Government Club, at Mrs. Ward Burlingame's, 624 Topeka Ave. We had a most splendid meeting with about 24 present. Mrs. Burlingame had a fine Paper on "What Women Physicians are doing," or "What women in the Medical profession are doing for humanity." Mrs. Burlingame is 82 years old, and not strong this winter, tho' does not begin to look her age and is right up to date.

Fri. 14   Very cool and half cloudy. I shopped all day only coming home long enough at noon to set Lunch for my good husband. I bought very little for we have no money these H.C.L. times, but I spent lots of time "*looking* and *figuring*".[6] I sold a Fifty dollar Victory Loan Bond for $48.00 to help pay our coal Bill and Insurance. We have just put seven ton Burlingame coal[7] in the barn, for next Winter and it's $9.00 per ton and to go higher; everything sky high but salaries.

On the 25th they leave for a visit to her father, to celebrate his eightieth birthday.

Sun. 30

A very beautiful day, tho' very warm thro' middle of the day. We were all up early this morning, to get the pigs, chickens, turkeys, cattle fed, and milking done and breakfast over so to go to Sunday School. May has a pretty place, but O the lonely life—she lives all alone day and night, and not a house in sight—just all black canon walls and prairiedogs—my father's ranch is 3/4 of a mile away, but around the canon out of sight—sister has a good pony, a good rifle and Queen a good Collie, worth a whole platoon of soldiers as a guard. When we were thro' with morning work, Pa came over, with his team and wagon, and took us to Cedar Hill Sunday School about a mile away, stopping at his Ranch for his renters, Mr. & Mrs. Harry Knox and baby. Were 50 or 75 at Sun. S. and Church—all the people in travel distance, came in Automobiles, wagons, buggies, horse back and on burros. A very wide awake S.S. with a real live wire for Supt. Mr. Johnston. My sister has a Class of boys age of mine in Topeka—I "talked" to them instead of having a Lesson. Also made short talk to the Sun. School. A Rev. Fipps (Missionary Baptist) preached after S.S. I think he is sincere and earnest but O, I never in my life listened to a more ignorant man—so uneducated it grated terribly on one's nerves, to listen to him, and he mis-interprets, thro' ignorance—they would be better off without preaching. After the Sermon taken from "John 17," everyone (having brought with them their dinners) drove several miles up the canon South, from sister's, to a picturesque rock walled canon they call "Garden of Gods the Second" where the whole crowd had a picnic dinner together on a great flat rock—the rock formations here are very wonderful. We stopped at May's on way over, and brought Pa's Victrola along, so had music all afternoon—some of the pioneer children had never seen or heard one before. About 3:30 the Rev. Fipps preached us another short Sermon taken from Galations—no "head no tail," a conglomeration of words, most horribly mispronounced—one could make absolutely nothing out of his Sermon—but he is well meaning and God will take *that,* and not blame his lack of education. We all sat on the grass in the shadow of a rock wall nearly 100 ft. high and it was cool and pleasant. We rode from the church to his place with the Platt sisters, who are homesteading here—they also took us back to sister's in the evening. I met at the Picnic my cousin Emma Weber-Adams and her husband John, and sons Orrell and Murl, who are all homesteaders out here. The drive to the Picnic grounds looked exactly like a Bill Hart Wild West "Movie" picture winding down the canon. We met some very lovely people and everyone was so cordial and kindly. Has been a very happy day—I took many pictures—took one of a young Will Johnson on his horse, it being the young Man's "22 Birthday." This has been a blessedly happy day, but thro' it all remembered my own lovely young men's Class back in Topeka and feel sure they were in Class this morning and Rev. Schell teaching them in my abscense. And today is 23 Birthday of Edwin Jones. I have prayed God's blessing on all my boys, today. Uncle Marian, Freda, Fred and I stayed all night with May again, tonight and Mr. & Mrs. Davis came over and stayed till 11 o'clock and we played the Victrola. A glorious moonlight night. It is so lovely here, yet lonely so far away from everything. No railroads, no telephones, no doctors, five miles to a Post Office with mail perhaps three times a week if one has time to go after it. La Junta 40 miles away, is the nearest trading point. No *I* don't want any of it, tho' to visit it for a time is great, but to live it day after day? Why I would die of lonliness. I *must* live where I can mingle with many people. I had my day of Pioneering when a child, 48 years ago in Southern Kansas—Indians, Buffalo, Grasshoppers—no I've had my share and want no more of the *"Fun"*!

July

Thurs. 15 A bit cooler today. I hurried all morning, with lots of work to do. This afternoon, went to a Board-meeting of the Good Government Club, at Mrs. J.D. McFarland

1100 Harrison St. And we took up the fight of giving exact age for registration. *I* am *not at all* sensitive about my age, but so many are, both men and women, so we have appointed our lawyer friend, Mrs. Lilla Day Monroe, to convince the Public and Attorney General Hopkins in particular, that *he* is unconstitutional in his ruling that a voter is compelled to give *exact* age when registering to vote.[8] . . .

Fri. 16   A *hotty*! hotty!! day. Most awfully busy—made me a new apron—wrote letters, a lot. Scott Brown came in a moment this morning—Duffie and Scholes this evening. At noon Dr. Steward told me they have a new baby daughter at their house, so late this afternoon I went over to see it—just to make a short call, and stayed and stayed, because baby was fussy, nurse was trying to get some badly need rest and sleep, and Mrs. Steward much wearied could not get the little darling to sleep. I took her up in my arms, and had her asleep in less than ten minutes—sleeping sound, all sprawled out on my lap, so "comfy." She is a lovely baby—weighs 10 lbs. Makes my heart so hungry, for my own sweet, "wee girlie."

August

Fri. 6   Fiercely hot—very busy all day. Fred and I went out to Gage Park this evening and had a fine swim—an awfully big crowd—Marshall's Band gave a Concert. We came home at 9:30 and found Jay Banta and Frances Holman waiting at our Gate they insisted on taking us for a ride, so took us back out to Gage Park where it is estimated there are 6,000 (six thousand) people. I went to Mrs. Lilla Day Monroe's at 10:30 this morning, where a number of we Club Women met and went over to the State House, to Att. Gen. Hopkins Office, to meet by appointment Mr. Zimmerman of New York, to take our pictures for a Movie Film, that will deal somewhat with Politics, something of a "Kansas Propaganda" to do with giving age at time of Registering for Election. I was most happily placed in the picture, standing shoulder to shoulder with Gov. Allan and on my left, Attorney General Richard J. Hopkins. Margaret Hill McCarter behind me, Mrs. C.I. Martin wife of Gen. Martin, Mrs.

J.D. McFarland, Mrs. Lilla Day Monroe, Mrs. W.A. Bolinger, Mrs. Fred Hill, Mrs. Whittaker, Miss Kate King, Mrs. W.H. Bombgarder, Mrs. W.H. Foster, Mrs. Purl, Mr. Arthur Carruth.[9] It was a very happy occasion. Mrs. J.K. Jones also was with us. Margaret Hill McCarter is so swelled up thought she would burst.

Sat. 28   At last we have come to the *great day* of *days* that we look forward to, from one year to the next—the day to go to the "Camp o' the White Sycamore". Just before 5:30 we were awakened by shouts and whistles of a bunch of our boys, and tooting of Auto horn to awaken us as they drove by, with Jack Miller's Auto truck piled high with tents, bedding, baggage, groceries and five boys, on their way to Paxico to our beloved Camp grounds—we got up and waved to them, as they *fairly flew* by our house—hauling our baggage up this year to save express charges—Fred and I dressed and began our preparations quickly—soon as Breakfast was over, I began making biscuit and peach pies to take up for noon Lunch. And hard and fast as I worked, we only caught the 10 o'clock Rock Island train, by calling a Taxi to take us to depot. Mr. Grundy Thompson will take care of things for us while we are away. We met a happy Bunch at depot and at 10 o'clock were off for Paxico ... *13 of us*: I am not superstitious, but could not help *wondering*. Heavy fog this morning, but all fine sunshine by time we boarded the train. Arrived in Paxico on time and was met by the boys with the truck who had Camp all in shape when we got there. We had an excellent lunch at noon, my graham biscuits were still warm, as were my peach pies, ham sausage, cheese, tomatoes. Jack gave us 26 watermelons, two gunny sacks full of Canteloupes and two baskets of tomatoes. Jack is a splendid fellow—most generous too, and has left nothing undone to add to the happiness of Camp. At noon clouds began to appear—at 5:30 P.M. a hard down pour of rain, which made our camp very wet and prevented our having our Camp fire but "We are tenting tonight on the old Camp grounds", and camp fire or not we are *all* very happy, as night settles down about us, to be here where we have had so many happy times together. . . . I am so happy to be here.

September

Thurs. 2   A grand morning, but at noon a very hard thunder
storm and blow came up—rained hard all afternoon.
Ronald McCord and his sweetheart, Ruth Lemon, quar-
relled last night—the girls came to my tent and told me
about 10:30 and said Edwin and Fred, going to take a
last look at their fish lines, found Ron on the Bridge,
crying and shaking as if in a chill—they spoke to him
and he made no answer, but not knowing then of the
quarrel, left him. This morning I watched Ron & Ruth
closely and saw they were wholly oblivious to each other,
except to eat side by side at Breakfast, after which with
fish poles they started off toward the Dam pool, as if to
fish—Helen and Nan were near me and said "O look
Auntie they have made up, and are going fishing
together". I said "no, girls, they have *not*, and when they
get off to themselves, they will "hash" their trouble all
over again and I am afraid *he* will kill Ruth; I wish they
would not leave Camp." Helen said "Auntie he is too big
a coward to do anything like that" but I said "No he
isn't—he is of just the right temperment and I wish they
would *not* go out of Camp." A little later I called Teddy
intending to send him to go look after them for I felt so
strongly the premonition of trouble but Teddy did not
hear me, and I did not call him again, thinking as the
girls ridiculed my fears, perhaps *I was foolish*; yet I could
not get away from an unexplainable weight of fear and
in about half an hour, we heard the voices of Fred,
Edwin and Harry D. coming down the road to Camp
and they had just left for town—we thought they had
met and were returning with someone coming from
Topeka to Camp, then they came into sight and we were
horrified to see Harry Davis carrying Ron over his
shoulder—I saw instantly, Ronald had attempted
suicide in the Dam pool by drowning and turned to the
girls who did not yet comprehend and said "didn't I tell
you, girls, only he has tried to kill himself, instead of
Ruth." Helen will never be whiter, when dead—the
whole Camp was dazed. The boys laid him on a pile of
straw, rubbed and worked with him til out of danger,
then wrapped him in their Army blankets and went on
to town, leaving John K. with him to watch him. As soon

as Ronald became himself, I heard him say "I want Auntie" and I went to him at once and John went back to Dam pool where Ruth was and some of girls who went to her. Ronald told me he had been worrying for weeks— not to blame Ruth, and not to let his folks know. He cried all the time—was cold and his finger nails purple. Tonight we are divided in opinion—We *all know* he is a *Fake* of worst kind and a *few* believe it was all to punish Ruth, *he* knowing John and Edith were at Dam pool and thinking John would save him and too, he knew Edwin, Harry and Fred were on way to town and nearby to *help* save him: *all this may be* true, but he almost lost his life *just the same*—he was *unconscious*, when Edwin jumped in and pulled him out, because John K. was not a good enough swimmer to do it. And he had water in his lungs. He is in a complete state of collapse. Ronald told me some thing seemed to break in his head and he did not realize *what he* was doing, nor that there was anyone near him. The boys saw him from the Bridge as he made the plunge said he raised up and just sort of threw himself forward into the water, and made *no effort* to swim, tho' he is a good swimmer—sank four or five times before the boys could make the run from the bridge. As he raised up and fell forward into the water Ruth said *he* said "here goes *nothing*". First thing he said when he became conscious was: "You had better have left me in boys and let me made a good job of it." It has *spoiled* camp for *all* of us and it doesn't seem like I would ever want to Camp here again. Bob Simpson came to Camp at noon. All the young folks went to town this evening, to dance and have a good time in general— Ruth had to go back to Topeka on the evening train so the young folks took Ronald with them and gave me a bit of rest from anxiety. Jack Miller and his cousin Marion drove in with the Truck, about 9:30 this evening and brought 36 fine melons, some cantaloupes and tomatoes. The creek came up very high and is rising all the time—we may have to go home. We had a big fish dinner at noon. After kiddies got home from town, girls put their gowns on over their dresses and gave a "Fairy dance" or tried to, but the boys paddled them into their tents again and soon ended the "Squaw War dance".

Fri. 3   Cloudy, heavy fog, muddy Camp—Water very high—

almost up to camp—boat washed away. Most of the Bunch discouraged. Harry Davis and Bob Simpson went home on 6 o'clock train this evening. And we have to watch Ronald all the time, lest he make another attempt at suicide—the "*Jinx*" sure have this Camp in their grip, *alrighty*. I took pictures at Dam pool—water almost level over the top of it and much drift wood.

Sat. 4   Grace Hypes came 11 A.M. Frances Holmon at noon. Fine most of day, but cold and muddy. We took a vote, to go home or stay, and no one wants to go home until after "Labor Day"—water going down, very fast, but no boat and too muddy to fish or swim. Had a rousing big Camp-fire tonight, and kiddies seemed very happy: laughter and song jest and pranks. But there are some couples who should be married—so infatuated with one another—so indiscreet: some of the girls have no shame, no modesty—I wonder what kind of mothers they have, to raise such daughters. Some of them are a constant shock to me, and I'm sorry they are in Camp.

Sun. 5   Last night in Camp and *what* the kiddies *didn't do* isn't worth telling about. One *thing sure* they "*tried my soul*" to the *breaking point*. The boys paddled the girls to the very point of endurance: they pounded our tents and shook them, stole my lantern, reached under the tent and got hold of covers under Carrie, Mable & Frances, and with a quick jerk left the girls laying on the straw, minus a bed—left nothing undone, til nearly 2 o'clock when they ran a fish pole under the tent almost in our faces and it had a big fish-hook fastened on end of it—this snagged Grace Hypes, Miriam Van Horn and me—brought blood on me, then foolishly I got mad, and went after them, then they settled down for rest of the night. *I* ought *not* to have gotten mad, at what was only meant in fun, but there is a limit to endurance and had been under such a nervous strain: and too, there is such a thing as carrying their fun too far, even tho' they are the finest kiddies in the whole *wide, wide* World. We had our Sunday School Lesson in Camp, late afternoon.

They leave camp the next day.

October

Thurs. 28   A fine day and O so busy. I made 48 small individual

Pumpkin pies and 112 doughnuts today for my Party tomorrow night. Cleaned all the house too—just "licked" into work all day, but I do not feel tired, tho' I was up till midnight last night making me a necklace out of the rattles from thirty rattlesnakes, which I received last night from my sister at Hoopup, Colo. She and her neighbors killed all but 5, which were killed by my father—My! it was a "creepy" mess.

Fri. 29   A swell day, tho' a bit cool. My but I have worked today and been bothered to death—enough to drive one distracted, but I have smiled and made the best of things, because I am bound to keep sweet regardless of thoughtless folks. It has seemed to me every one coming to the Party tonight have called me up to ask very unnecessary questions, and surely knew they were keeping me from my work—then early this morning Mona Plath and Frances Scott came out, for nearly an hour: and at my dinner hour, Mrs. Tucker came in for more than an hour and I *had* to do some phoning for her that she could have done as well. Then in the middle of the afternoon Scott Brown, Will Butters came out bringing two young ladies supposed to be School Teachers here for the Convention and they kept me from my work nearly two hours then at 5 o'clock Phoebe Speckmann, a real Teacher here for Convention, came out and was here for Supper and in between all these interruptions I decorated the house beautifully with all kinds of Halloween things, did my dusting and arranging, made my Sandwiches and made all plans I could for a good time, for my lovely young folks. But I had to leave out much I planned for had too many interruptions—too many coming in. But finally I had things presentable and I dressed in a blue apron much trimmed in yellow ribbons of crepe paper—long bows of it around my hair and wore my rattlesnake—rattles necklace which brought "shivers" and "squeals" of horror. Teddy wore his overalls with knee length ruffles of yellow crepe paper. And the kiddies began to come—all girls were in costume and many of the boys. Edwin Jones always comical also Ronald. And Fred Brackett handsome as a picture. And Nan Brackett was the sweetest little Sailor boy and Carrie Wiede was a "picture" in her tacky costume, Velma Howell too pretty for a clown which she *was*. And Mable McKee was so com-

Martha, Fred, her boys, and their girlfriends at 1919 Halloween party at the Farnsworth house (note Martha's false eyebrows).

ically "made up" no one scarcely would recognize her, even tho she did not mask. Each one looked fine—no one could have decided *who* was best. I had Mr. Hill come and take a flashlight picture. Otis Young and Frances Scott were both made up as negroes and looked natural as life. Nearly 40 here and all said had best time they ever had here at a Party, and I think it was the happiest time *I* ever have had with them—Each one was sweet natured and jolly. In a scuffle, Nan, Duffie and Lucille broke my glasses and *almost* broke my nose, not seeing me. Those who came were: [thirty-eight names follow]. I served Cracker sandwiches with orange filling, cheese, split pickles, individual pumpkin pies, cider & doughnuts and apples. We sure had one jolly good time—I think I never have seen our young folks more jolly and happy. Almost midnight when they went home.

November

Tues. 2   A most glorious day. And it's Election Day and I hope the Democrats get buried so deep they will *never* come to life again. My good Teddy at home today, having a day of vacation and fixing up the fence. We went to Vote about 3 o'clock this afternoon, out on W-6th, Hartsack Precinct. We both voted hard, for Harding and Coolidge. I stayed with sweet little baby Steward, next door, while Mrs. Steward went to vote at noon. This evening Fred & I went to the church to Evangelistic services being held by Bro. Schell who is most earnest but preaches so long and loud he wearies one. After the sermon we went to the Orpheum to see Wallace Reid and Lois Wilson in "What's your Hurry," but in reality to hear "Election Returns" which the Orpheum advertised to give all thro' the evening—We feel sure of Republican victory for all the World is tired of Wilson, the worst President U.S. ever had. All the "Returns" that came during evening were so overwhelmingly Republican as to be uninteresting, in so far as creating excitement was concerned. After the Play, the Orchestra gave a free Concert and we stayed for that, then went over to read State Journal Bulletins till that closed after enough "returns" had been received to assure us Harding was elected then we came home, a few minutes of midnight. Seems like never was so happy before in all my life—My! my!! My!!! Wilson is no better than the old German Kaiser and to get rid of him will mean untold blessing to United States.

Sat. 13   Still very cold and cloudy, but thankful is no snow. I baked tarts, drop cakes, pumpkin pies, made applesauce, baked beans, cleaned the whole house, and am quite tired enough to be a bit nervous: *feel* like I wanted to "box someone's ears."

Thurs. 18   A fine sunny day. About 11 o'clock Roy Penwell came out and here to dinner and most of day. He lived with us ten years ago. My! what a big fellow he has grown to be—6 ft. 2 in. and weighs 206: fine looking too. We were so glad to see him. He is here from El Reno Okla, to attend the funeral of his uncle L.M. Penwell, who died last night. After dinner, I went with Roy to call on Mrs. Remington—he and Warren used to play together: only two months difference in their ages. After Roy left I *sure* flew into work, and more work. A fine day. . . .

[1921]

January

Tues. 11   A grand day. I wrote letters all day. I can't seem to "catch-up" my letters but I have close to 150 correspondents.

Thurs. 20   Clouds and sun—*mostly* sun—*Very* warm. Today is *Thelma Huston's 21 Birthday*. And today is the 51st Birthday of my dear sister Belle who died when 16 years old—Typhoid. 51 years ago today my blessed mother died in giving birth to this lovely sister. O the awful tragedies of life—*I* needed my mother, yet have had to go all through life without her, and the word *Mother* has no meaning to *me*. I wrote a few letters today and have been *so busy* . . . .

New Year's Eve party at Martha's house, 1920–21. (Martha is wearing a necklace of rattlesnake rattles; see entry for October 28, 1920.)

The remainder of this year was relatively uneventful for Martha. The Sunday School group began to break up: they did not go to camp for lack of interest, and by November Martha records a Sunday night with no visitors—"the first time in "Ages'." John Keating, one of her favorite boys, was killed in April by hold-up men who attempted to rob a gas station in St. Louis at which John was working to pay his way through Washington University. In June she and Fred took a trip to Fred's birthplace, Council Grove, Kansas. Martha speculated on the difficulties mother Farnsworth must have had, passing "thro' motherhood, almost alone, just among the Indians, however friendly they may have become." In November Fred's ankle developed an open sore, forcing him to miss work, but by the end of December he was able to take occasional walks. The Sunday School class did not want a New Year's Eve party, and Fred and Martha greeted the New Year alone.

[1922]

January

Mon. 2 A nice day, and a Holiday, so Fred was home all day. Mrs. Remington came in, in afternoon and told us the new folks in the brick house (2115 W-10) were "pulled" last night for running a "still"—we knew *something* crooked must be going on there. . . .

Fri. 6 . . . The police officers were out yesterday and "cleaned" out the brick house of its "Still" and every one is "tickled to death" hoping the family (Stone, 9 children) will soon go. Nine barrels, almost a hundred gallon of near "booze" was taken. Police say biggest, most complete yet found. *Awful.*

Tues. 24 Cold and dark and gray. Fred not home at noon. Writing all day. *Thirty* years ago today, was bright and warm and sunny in Colorado (Springfield) and O my heart was happy, for blessed motherhood gave to me my sweet baby daughter, Mabel Inez Belle. And the very heart o' me yearns, hungrily, for my darling who bode with me so brief a time—five months.

Tues. 31 Dark, cloudy, misty day, but warm. Mail very heavy and so Fred not home to lunch. And I just fooled away the day reading and writing when I wanted to do so much: but I felt tired—I carry all the coal from the barn to house, some distance—carry water, same distance to the cow about six or eight buckets—I feed cow, clean barn and barn yard and take care of chickens—I am always busy, *more* than busy. And *always* thankful for good health so I *can be* busy.

February

Fri. 17 Warm, sunny, and regular old March wind; whip, whirl, dirt and dust. I cleaned all the house, shook and swept rugs—worked hard and fast, all morning. Fred home at noon for lunch—I churned and had lovely buttermilk and made fine cherry pie. I went to town after dinner to pay Lodge dues and shop a bit, and really was shocked half to death at the sights I saw—"short dresses and a windy day" many a girl and *old woman* should have been arrested for *indecent exposure*; women who must have been *all* of sixty, dried up, wrinkled old hags, with skirts so short, their boney old knees and skinny legs were a *sight*, My! Set a hen this evening.

Tues. 21   Heavy fog when we got up, clearing to sunshine about 10:30 then clouding heavily at noon. Almost unbearably hot. O you California, you've nothing on Kansas—it's *Kansas*, has the lovely Winters. We went to Grand tonight to see *The Bat*—enjoyed it immensely.[1]

Sun. 26   Cold, sort of misty and snowed too—ugly, chill day. We went to S.S. and Church. I had in Class [eight names follow]. This afternoon, Edwin, Bob Simpson, Clay and Jack came out for afternoon. We had no callers this evening—are beginning to go other places for their Sun. evenings and we do not expect they will care to keep coming to see we two old folks, even if our hearts are young.

March

Fri. 3   Sunny and warm, in fact a *fine* sloppy day. I swept and cleaned all the house—baked bread. Mixed my bread into loaves then left it to rise and went to town, to meet Mrs. Lee Monroe, Mrs. J.D. McFarland, Mrs. Atchison, Mrs. Mitchner, Mr. & Mrs. W.H. Bomgardner, Col. and Mrs. Morehouse (Geo.) and few others, at Cozy theatre to censor the "Social disease" picture, "*Some Wild Oats*" which Mr. Samuel Cummins of the "Preferred Pictures Enterprises" of Chicago, is here making plans to show. And we women called to view it, cannot agree on the advisability of showing it.[2] Mrs. McFarland was shocked almost to death, while *I* did not feel the *first* quiver of shock. And it was all *so* true, and what our young people need to know, but not *severe* enough.

Mon. 13   Rained all day. Teddy not home at noon. I washed, dried clothes in house and ironed. This evening went to Community Church Training School, calling at Mrs. Taylor's, 919 W-8, on my way down. Came home in hard rain. Not many present because of the stormy night. Rev. McAffee of Westminister Presby. preached the Assembly sermon. I enjoy these meetings very much. Prof. Stout is fine in Psychology Class and Mrs. Sewell in Story telling Class.³ All well worth going out in storm for. And one finds *beauty* even in a storm. Tonight as I stood in rain at Tenth and Topeka Ave waiting for car, the White Way lights around State House grounds and all street lights seemed to gleam brighter thro' the rain. And the head lights of hundreds of Automobiles going in all directions gave double light, long shafts of light, reflected in the wet pavement and the red tail-lights of the cars were beautiful, being just a splash of red as they passed, but growing longer as the cars speed on, like a streamer of red ribbon floating out behind, while in fact *only* reflection in water of the rain in street. Some showed for a whole block in one continuous ray of red light—and the street car wires sagged down with weight of the rain til they looked like the scalloped edge of women's dresses—yes even a rainy night is beautiful to those who look for beauty and not "mud, wet, slop and disagreableness."

Fri. 17   Quite windy, otherwise a nice sort of day. I swept the whole house, cleaned the rugs this morning and went to town to "shop" this afternoon—I want a new hat, but O so expensive, I just can't get one.

The whole neighborhood is much agitated over the abuse of a little child (all colored) by a young couple recently moved into Mrs. Carpenter's house, across from us, South. The child belongs to their half sister and has been abandoned by both parents—a little girl seven years old. Her aunt makes her sweep, carry all the coal and water—compelled her to stay out in snow doing work until her feet were frozen and now has Gangrene and will lose one foot, maybe both—I reported their abuse to the Humane Officers, the Kings (Kate & Kilmours) they came out and found conditions even worse than we knew—the Kings say the child undoubtedly has Syphilis along with all the rest of its affliction—so pitiful the case, I could scarcely sleep last night.

Mon. 20   A fine sunny day, tho' cool. I washed and ironed and mended. My good Teddy not home at noon. We commence today to "dry up" the cow and so only Mrs. Kelley came for milk tonight. The poor little colored girl across the street was taken to the Hospital last night—I could not help crying as I saw the pathetic, abused little thing carried out to the car—it would be a mercy if she could die. Mrs. Strickler and Dorothy came over at supper time to find out what more I had heard about the child—the Humane Officers called me and said they found the child had been beaten badly, with a cane, all over—last Fall it was taken from them and put in Detention and *he lied* and got it back home again. Sheriff was out this evening with papers, and I hope they are arrested and punished. . . .

June

Thurs. 8   Awfully hot. I worked in garden most all day, after putting up my strawberry jam—pulled weeds and hoed. I also have 66 little chicks to look after and a cow giving over 5 gal. of milk, to milk and my hands give out on me—my right hand becomes numb. I mow the lawn too.

Tues. 13   Hotter yet, 95° today—o-o-o My! I worked in garden and very busy all day. *Chiggers* eating me up. Edwin Jones and Cecile Noftsinger came out and took us for a nice Auto ride. I picked my currants, stemmed and cooked them for jelly, big job tho' we haven't many this year. We sure enjoyed our ride this evening, my hand gets so numb can't write.

Wed. 14   A very hot day but cool and fine on our front porch, in evenings. A colored man brought us a load of hay this morning and not a man anywhere to mow it away, so *I* had to climb into the hay loft and do the work—"pitch hay" with a colored man, and *my grandfather* had *slaves* to do such work. Grandfather was one of biggest slave owners of the South and see what *I* have to do, now. . . .

Fri. 30   Hot and sticky—sun and clouds, half and half. I cleaned all the house today and had so many running in on errands I did not seem to accomplish much actual work. I wrote several letters to absent Sun. School boys. Neighborhood children by the score came in today for various reasons. Mrs. Lilla Day Monroe came in this evening for little talk. Wants me to get up something for her paper, the "Woman's Journal."[4] Also make some jelly on shares. Bob Sympson, Frankie Finney, Junior Gordon and Marie Johnson came in for the evening.

July

Sat. 22　O so awfully hot and sticky—I sure "rained" perspiration today—almost drowned myself in *sweat*. I cleaned all the house, baked some and made a new Bungalo apron. Robt. Simpson, Jack Miller and Junior Gordon came out this afternoon. Bob is determined I shall make up with Fred Brackett, who of his own volition has stayed from our home for more than 7 months, whose head swelled so after he started going to the Country Club, that he quit *all* of us. *No more* F.B. for me—he has *always* been "a thorn in the flesh"—*always* a big, big trouble maker and I have, time and again, against Biblical instruction cast *long* strings of pearls in front of him, only to have him as often, turn and rend me.

Thurs. 27　A fine day tho' pretty warm. We were awakened this morning at 5 o'clock by some one at the gate then coming to front door; Fred went down and we found it to be uncle Needham Rogers, of Aurora and Rock, Island Ill. My sainted Mother's only living relative (immediate relative) I had not seen him for more than 45 years and only recently learned his wherabouts. He is nearly 79 years of age, and being quite tired slept most of day. Bob & Ron were out this evening. Fred & Nan phoned wanting to go to Camp—I sand *No*.

On July 29th, eleven of "the bunch" went on the traditional camping trip.

August

Tues. 8　Very cool and fine—down to 60° this morning. I took pictures of uncle Needham Rogers this afternoon. I gathered from our garden this morning 1 1/2 Bu. of fine tomatoes, canned ten qts. and got the rest ready for Chili sauce—and O, the *interruptions* today. Fred and Nan Brackett came out this morning to fix up their "ugliness"—said had made fools of themselves, and done wrong by the whole Bunch, was sorry and want to come back. They may come of course but *I* (and some of others) will never feel same toward them. About half hour later came Scott Brown and father and cousin—after they left I went to store for groceries, got dinner, then went to work canning tomatoes and worked hard til 6 o'clock when Teddy came home. Scott came again for Supper, then Clay; Frankie & Dale Finney and Mrs. Kelley for milk. In meantime Clay went after Ellen Johns and when they came back, Scott took them to meet a strawride party at Gage Park, they all insisting I go along for a ride tho' I had not had my Supper and the others were eating. I ate alone after we came back, then Scott took Teddy, Uncle and I for a ride to Washburn, North Topeka and most everywhere. Scott left but came back at midnight to stay all night when he found his folks were not going home tonight. *Strenuous* and *then some.*

Wed. 16   Awful hot. Made more plum jelly and did my ironing. I am so busy can't visit much with uncle Needham but it is nice to have him here, my mother's only living relative of her immediate family—he is hard to visit with because hard of hearing, but sits in porch swing and sings much as tho' content and happy—he is neat and clean and always satisfied. However he had letter saying his wife had fallen and was hurt and now he wants to go home and hasn't the money.

Thurs. 17   Awful hot—92°. This afternoon I took uncle Needham down to State House and Memorial Hall, then for carride to Garfield Park—so hot most too much for him. Uncle Marion VanOrsdol came in for Supper. Ellen Johns and Stella Hastetter came in for short call after Supper. My days and *almost* my nights are brimful, so full I hardly get required rest I should have. And I want to write a Book about my Boys and I haven't time.

Fri. 18   Awful, awful hot. But a blow from N.W. at noon brought much dust—and a bit cooler air. Uncle became so homesick and nervous, that I was afraid he would get down sick on my hands, so I bought him a ticket home today and went to train with him. I hired a taxi to take us down so he would not get so tired—train was due at 2:20 and left three hours and twenty minutes late with him safe aboard—The Rock Island Golden State Limited. Poor old man, kindly and patient, and with ten *living* married children who do not treat him well—we had to sacrifice to help him get home, but I'm sure it was a blessing to have him in our home for a time—he is dear and kind and patient and *my mother's brother.* Stella and

Ellen came in for short call this evening and after they left, came Bob.

September

Mon. 18

I washed and ironed—half cloudy morning and at 3 o'clock a very heavy rain came up—Fred not home to dinner and when he came at 5 o'clock a very *heavy* down pour of rain was coming down like cloud burst—he brought me a letter from Cora Finch-Jenkins saying her mother and sister-in-law would arrive at 4:50, me to meet them and take them to U.P. 8:07 train—they to be here only three hours—train was already in, and a regular deluge falling—letter came too late to meet them and I could not find them, of course so we hurried about and took Street car to N. Topeka to U.P. depot thinking to see them few minutes when they would come for 8:07 train—we waited till 9 o'clock when late 8:07 train came—*they* did *not* so we came home, Fred went to bed, I sat up to read evening paper and at 10:20 Phone rang it was *they*, their train having just arrived—Santa Fe from Winfield—trains delayed because of *Strikers*.[5] I had them call Taxi and come right out to house, while I fixed their bed and made a cup of tea and tonight I have as my guests Mrs. Martha Finch of Winfield, mother of my old sweetheart, and Mrs. Will Finch of San Francisco, *wife* of my old sweetheart. I had never met her, but I think she is lovely.

Tues. 19

A cool, cloudy day, with just a few gleams of sunshine. Fred stayed home today just to visit with our guests—day of Vacation for him too—we hired a taxi and I took the folks to Washburn Country Club, thro' some of our best streets, then thro' Memorial Hall and State House, then home for Lunch, to rest and visit. I got a six o'clock Dinner then Fred & I took them on Street car to U.P. depot and saw them off on the 8:07 train about 10 min. late. I took pictures of them this morning and afternoon too. And now they are gone and *O the memories.* Away back thro' the years, I am a girl again, Will my sweet heart, our wedding day set, a quarrel, pride that would not, could not, be budged; Will on his knees with tears streaming down his face, pleading; my heart dead within me, with stubborn pride, like adamant, unyielding:

and so we parted and have never met and now today more than thirty, yes nearly thirty-five years later, I have his wife, a stranger to me, as my guest and in the few short hours, I love her—she is dear and loveable. Mother Finch I *call* mother because she came so *near being* my mother and *wanted* to be. Just one of life's tragedies that needed not to be—heart ache, heart break that ought not to have been. Will and I would have made more of life had we married; all families would have been better off. Fred and Harriet would never have met us, *so* not missed us. But today with the buried past, I am so happy with dear, blessed Fred, I know it's best and would not change the past if I could.

December

Mon. 25

"Christmas Day" once more and it's like having Christmas in the Summer time—it's so warm: no fires, and doors and windows all open—such a grand day. But it's a long day to me, for my good Teddy went early this morning, and works late tonight. I sit alone all the long day, writing belated Christmas messages—others are having their jolly Christmas times, their Reunions, their big dinners, their Christmas trees and every thing to make the day *seem* Christmas while I sit alone all the long day, and my good man is bending under a back breaking load, rushing, rushing, rushing all day long delivering heavy Christmas mail and coming home so weary, at night, he must hurry to bed to get rest enough to go with as heavy a load tomorrow. And I wonder some times, why life might not have been a bit easier for the dear good fellow—*why he* should have such hard work with a bare living and his brother a multi millionaire. But not for a moment do I complain for God has blessed us richly in health and many ways, even tho' we never *do* have Christmas—we can never find words to express our thankfulness for all God's mercies. About noon today some of my boys (Bob Simpson, Fred Brackett, Edwin Jones, Ronald McCord and Virgil Scholes) came out and brought me a lovely Mantle clock—8 day, as present from the Class—I wish they would not buy me such expensive presents—their hearts are so big, they make mine hurt.

Sun. 31   A fine sunny day, but cold enough for a fire in the grate. We went to S.S. and Church. I had in Class, Scott Brown, Larrie Brooks, Dwight Beeler, and his friend Mr. Anderson (for a visitor) Truman Hazen, Edwin Jones, Fred Brackett, Robt. Sympson and a Mr. Eccles (visitor) Friend of Grace Ellington. This afternoon, Ron, Edwin, Bob, Junior, Fred & Nan, Carrie Wiede and Martha Cundiff came out. Scott Brown came home with us from church, for dinner, so he was here too. We had a jolly afternoon—like old times. This evening the young folks came in to "Watch" the old year out and the New Year in. And it was a most happy time, except for the absence of many loved boys, who are scattered the wide world over. And where ever they are I'm sure they are thinking of us, tonight, because of the many good times we have all had together in days of the past. Those who came tonight were [fourteen names follow]. They played and sang all evening and once when I was out of room, they turned the clock and all their watches forward, to midnight so they could dance, but while it fooled Teddy, it *did not* fool me, for those blessed boys are always playing pranks on me and I guessed their "trick" at once and the carpets stayed down till midnight; then just on the stroke of midnight, the front door was thrown open and the whole bunch almost fell over one another in their rush to get out on front porch and shout farewell to the old Year and welcome to the New. And the *New Year* sure came in with a noisy welcome from this blessed Bunch: they shouted, howled, yelled, whistled, stamped with their feet, jumped up and down and made all possible noise til tired then came in and danced til 2 o'clock when all left, some for home and some to dance rest of night at Kellams.

At 11:30 I served the young folks "creamed chicken in patty shells, hot graham biscuit, pickles and cheese and Plum pudding and Punch for which I used 3 qts. grape juice, 3 qts. cider, 1 qt. heavy, thick Pear syrup and *very* heavy peach syrup 1 qt. saved from my preserving last Summer, and 5 lemons. It made a most excellent Punch.

Epilogue

It is somehow fitting, given her history of feeding so many people, that Martha's last extant sentence is a recipe. Unfortunately, the last year of her life remains a mystery—and leaves one with a regrettable sense of incompleteness. She had begun each year of her diary with a prayer of thanks for the past and hope for the future. There is nothing to indicate that 1923 would have been different. As early as 1919 she mentioned that she would like to ride in an airplane; perhaps in the missing year she did. Martha died on February 13, 1924, of malignant hepatitis. The newspapers carried an account of her final illness, indicating that she became ill on December 21 but did not consider it serious until February 2, when she entered the hospital, dying eleven days later. Her "boys" returned from around the country to arrange the funeral and act as pallbearers. A Topeka newspaper columnist on February 17, 1924 eulogized her: "What a fine heritage this kindly woman left. The good she did will live for ages. Would that we had more Mrs. Fred Farnsworths in this world to shape and direct the lives of our boys." Her grave is in the Topeka cemetery, next to Fred's parents and near her baby, Mabel Inez, although no headstone marks the baby's grave. Fred married again, and died in December, 1946. It was his second wife who donated Martha's diary to the Kansas State Historical Society, where it now resides. This, then, is the book about her boys, and her life, that Martha never had time to write.

Martha and Fred on Valentine card drawn by Martha, 1915.

Notes

1882

1. School did not resume until October 2.

2. She got the disease only one and a half months after her bout with malaria. Unlike malaria, chicken pox was not considered a reason for remaining at home.

3. Literary: "A kind of literary society or club; a gathering of persons, especially in rural districts at the schoolhouse, nearly always in winter, and in the evening, where a program is presented, such as reciting or declaiming poetry or prose selections, reading selections, engaging in dialogues (committed to memory); debating propositions, reading original papers, essays, etc. Sometimes contests in spelling are included and even burlesque trials." J. C. Ruppenthal, "A Word List from Kansas (II)," *Dialect Notes*, IV (1914), p. 325.

4. Group singing was a regular community activity.

5. To give someone the mitten meant to give him a "cold shoulder," or "the brush-off." "Girls at one time used to knit miniature mittens to give their boy-friends, as a means of informing them that the romance was officially over." Sackett and Koch, *Kansas Folklore*, p. 108.

1883

1. This is Martha's first reference to her stepmother. As the entry indicates, this relationship was a bad one; the discord was to continue throughout her adolescence.

2. A "neck-tie festival" was apparently a sort of "box supper" at which boys bid for the privilege of eating with particular girls the suppers the girls had prepared.

3. She has gone to live with the John R. Thompson family, neighbors. The diary does not discuss the events which led to this move, nor the facts and emotions of daily life at the Thompson house.

1884

1. The school year was approximately twenty-two weeks long in Cowley County, Kansas.

2. With this entry in the diary Martha inserted a card on which she listed "Names and authors of the various books I've read." They are: Mary J. Holmes, *Lena Rivers*; Augusta J. Evans, *St. Elmo*; Daniel Defoe, *Robinson Crusoe*; Charles S. Greene, *Thrilling Stories of the Great Rebellion, Scottish Chiefs, Lucille, Children of the Abbey, Life of Napoleon;* Albion Tourgee, *A Fool's Errand;* Lawrence L. Lynch, *Madeline Payne, The Detective's Daughter;* J. W. Buel, *The Heroes of the Plains*; Sir Walter Scott, *Ivanhoe*.

3. On February 1, 1883, a mob lynched Charles Cobb for shooting Sheriff Shenneman who was trying to arrest him for the murder of a deputy sheriff in Jefferson County, Kansas.

4. Helen Gougar (1843–1907), a suffrage and temperance leader, author and lecturer, wrote the municipal woman suffrage law of Kansas. She tried to vote in the Indiana state election of 1894, sued when she was forbidden, served as her own attorney, became the first woman to appear before the Indiana Supreme Court, but finally lost her case.

1885

1. The Grand Army of the Republic, a national Union army veterans organization.

2. This was a camp for a group of predominantly Irish workers who were building the railroad.

3. There is no explanation of the contents of this letter.

1886

1. "Ding donging" meant "arguing."

2. Medicine Lodge (pop. 10,000) was ninety miles from Winfield (pop. 32,000). At the same time Topeka had approximately 43,000 people.

1887

1. She lived with the Edwards family in Floral until September 19. She does not say how she supported herself during this period.

2. Zaidee, born Dec. 10, 1886, was May's first child.

3. Martha never indicated why she chose to move to Topeka rather than join her father in Colorado. She stayed with the Bairs and various relatives until Oct. 17. Harry Bair had been a boarder with Martha's father in Floral, Kansas.

4. She did not give the details of this "trouble."

1888

1. Cole Younger (1844–1916) fought with William Quantrell's Confederate guerrillas, and later was a member of Jesse James's famous gang. He and his brothers, James and Robert, were captured after an unsuccessful attempt to rob the bank at Northfield, Minn. in 1876, and, in 1888, were in prison under a sentence of life imprisonment.

2. The Kansas Old Soldiers' Reunion was held at the Topeka Fairgrounds and presided over by the Commander-in-Chief of the G.A.R. from Washington. At 2 P.M. on the 5th, eight troops of cavalry, four companies of infantry, and a light artillery battery attacked an imaginary enemy, and concluded by charging toward the grandstand of 5,000 spectators.

3. John Palmer Usher (1816–1889) was Secretary of the Interior under Abraham Lincoln. He later became general counsel for the Union Pacific Railroad and lived in Lawrence, Kansas. U.S. Senator Preston Bierce Plumb (1837-1891), Republican, elected three times to the Senate, was independent in politics. His major achievements were in land law, conservation, and reclamation.

4. Several all-male organizations in Topeka whose main purpose was to put on displays at public functions such as patriotic parades, inaugurations, etc. The members drilled in formation carrying colored torches ("flambeaux"), and also fired off rockets, Roman candles, and other fireworks.

5. Edward Payson Roe's books were written on a basic formula containing "a religious hero or heroine who labored to convert a doubter, usually of the opposite sex, to Christian beliefs, and succeeded through the intervention of some great disaster" (John L. Mott, *Golden Multitudes*, p. 148). *Nature's Serial Story* was published in *1884*.

1889

1. Alonzo T. Rodgers, 43, a well-known Topeka businessman, and his wife were shot in their home in a struggle with Nat Oliphant, who was attempting burglary. Oliphant, soon captured by police, confessed to the crime. An angry mob stormed the jail and hanged him from a streetlight pole.

2. Dwight Lyman Moody (1837–1899), famous evangelist, began his career in Chicago as a businessman and Sunday-school teacher. By 1861 he was giving all his time to city missionary work, and by 1870 was touring Great Britain and the United States on evangelistic campaigns. His preaching was simple, colorful, direct, and stressed God's mercy rather than hell-fire. In 1889 he founded the Moody Bible Institute in Chicago.

3. Dr. Charles Frederick Menninger began practicing medicine in Topeka under the tutelage of Dr. Roby in 1888. With his psychiatrist son Karl in 1920 he opened the Menninger Clinic, which under Karl and brother William, also a psychiatrist, became, with the later Menninger Foundation, a renowned center for psychiatric treatment, training, research, and public education.

1890

1. See also May 4, 1890. Martha never explains why the Pages used another name.

2. Quinsy is an inflammation of the tonsils.

3. Since 1881, alcoholic beverages had not been sold legally in Kansas. Forces opposed to state prohibition tried to "resubmit" the issue to the voters on several occasions. On the 1890 ballot it was defeated, and did not again come to a vote of the people until 1948, when a repeal won by over 60,000 votes.

4. Charles Robinson (Republican) was the first state governor of Kansas (1861-63). A free-stater, he was embroiled in the pro- and anti-slavery controversy which preceded Kansas' becoming a state. Though only fifty-five men died violently during these years (1854–1860), the strife in Kansas captured national attention, and "Bleeding Kansas" became a symbol for the greater struggle developing in the country.

5. A "dugout" house was usually dug into the side of a hill, or into the level ground so that half the walls were soil. The remaining construction was of sod, roofed with sod-covered limbs or boards.

1891

1. This was her third miscarriage. See also November 1, 1889, and October 3, 1890.

2. Elsewhere she specifically blamed whiskey and beer for his ill health.

3. She never noted why she found it necessary to hide her illness and her feelings, especially from her mother-in-law, who had always been sympathetic to her, often supporting her against Johnny. Just as strangely she never mentions consulting a doctor about her constant suffering.

1892

1. The owner of the farm.
2. Telephone service came to Topeka in June of 1879 when thirty-eight phones were installed. By 1890 there were 490 phones, in 1900 there were 910, and by 1910 over 3,000.

1893

1. James Whitcomb Riley (1849–1916), the well-known Indiana dialect poet.
2. Until Johnny died, Martha had always referred to the baby by her name for the child, Inez. Here she began to use the name Johnny had preferred.

1894

1. Mrs. Akin was Fred's oldest half-sister and Coit was his brother.
2. Will F. was Fred's brother.
3. Nowhere in the diary is there any indication of what ultimately made her take this terrifying step.
4. Susan B. Anthony (1820–1906) began as a radical abolitionist, spent much of her life campaigning and lecturing in favor of woman suffrage, and was instrumental in forming the National Woman Suffrage Association. Her interest in Kansas was both personal and political: she lived with her brother in Leavenworth in 1865, campaigned across the state in 1867 in a futile attempt to get a suffrage bill passed (it was defeated 21,000 to 9,000), and returned to the state many times thereafter. In 1894 she made three trips to Kansas, shuttling back and forth between this campaign and New York's.

Annie LePorte Diggs (1848–1916) was a populist orator, politician, and social reformer. In 1894 she was vice-president of the Kansas Equal Suffrage Association, became its president five years later, and was influential in the national organization.

Mrs. Congressman Otis is evidently the wife of U.S. People's Party Congressman John Grant Otis who served from 1891 to 1893. Nothing of note about her has come to light.

5. Thomas W. Harrison was mayor of Topeka from 1893 to 1895.

Therese A. Jenkins (1853–?) was a Wyoming writer, lecturer, journalist, politician, and campaigner for temperance and legal equality of the sexes.

Anna Howard Shaw (1847–1919) was a physician, Methodist minister, woman suffrage leader, and temperance reformer. She was president of the National American Woman Suffrage Association from 1904 to 1915.

6. Ellen Beach Yaw (1868–1947), a native of New York, made her debut in London and then toured the United States. The Topeka *Daily Capital* (May 16, 1894) described her as "a thoroughly accomplished singer, endowed with a voice indescribably sweet, melodious and pleasing. . . ."

Adelina Patti (1843–1919) was a renowned operatic soprano. ". . . history does not record a singer who was so idolized by so large a public for so long a time" (*Notable American Women, 1607–1950*).

7. Martha probably saw the favorite stage version of the book, written by George L. Aiken and first produced in 1852.

8. James J. Corbett (1886–1933) had defeated John L. Sullivan in 1892 to become heavyweight boxing champion of the world. The play, according to the

Topeka *Daily Capital*'s review, had no merit at all, but the audience had come to see the champion, and was satisfied.

1895

1. There is no explanation of Minnie Brown's desire to come to Topeka for her confinement.
2. This child was Freda Gilbert. June 27 was also the third anniversary of the death of Martha's child, Mabel Inez.

1896

1. These renters were Martha's old beau Charles, and his wife Mila. See May 9 and 10, 1886 for Martha's account of Charlie's pleas to her to marry him, just before he left to marry Mila. The Robys moved out of the house on May 5th. Martha makes no reference to the old relationship.
2. *Camille*, by Alexandre Dumas, fils, was published in 1848, but became best known in a dramatic version first produced in 1852. This sentimental story of a consumptive prostitute "may have encouraged the conception that a taint of T.B. moved men to erotic thoughts" (James Hart, *The Popular Book*, p. 87).
3. Note that this hasty funeral took place at 1:00 A.M., only two days after his death. See also Belle VanOrsdol's death, August 24, 1886, where the funeral was equally precipitous, presumably because the body was not embalmed.
4. "Pops" were the Populists.

1901

1. Carry Nation was in and out of Kansas jails throughout 1901. She edited the first issue of her newspaper, "The Smasher's Mail," which appeared in March, 1901, while she was in the Shawnee County jail in Topeka following one of her smashing crusades.

1903

1. Martha went often to paint at the Beardsley Studio, paying a small monthly fee. She met other regulars there, and the conviviality was often as important to her as her artistic endeavors.
2. Oneta Gilbert, the children's cousin, visiting from Arkansas City, Kansas.
3. Russell Wilcox, a neighbor boy staying with Martha while his parents were away.
4. The Topeka *Daily Capital* described the Exposition as "a country fair, a circus, a sideshow, and a free lunch, all in one."
5. May was working in the office of *The Farmer's Mail and Breeze*, a weekly paper published by Arthur Capper, later governor of Kansas (1915–1918) and U.S. senator (1919–1949).
6. Tatting is a delicate handmade lace formed usually by looping and knotting a single cotton thread to make varied designs of rings and semicircles.
7. Martha means that Fred still acts with the attentiveness of a suitor.
8. Freda continued to spend much of her time with Martha and Fred long after school was out.

9. All of her relatives survived the flood, in which thirty-eight Topekans died.

1905

1. The Good Government Club's constitution stated: "Its object shall be to create an interest in and stimulate the individual efforts and development of women along industrial, legal and educational lines, and to secure more equitable laws, especially for women and children." It had about 112 members in 1905–06.

2. This is a monument for Fred's mother and father. It was completed on November 8, 1905, and in 1984 was still standing in the Topeka Cemetery.

3. Freda was living with Fred and Martha, having moved in on September 11 to attend school in their district. She visited her mother on weekends. Martha never wrote in detail about her relationship with Freda.

4. After this introduction to roller skating, Martha took it up enthusiastically.

1906

1. Robinson, Marshall and Co., "clothiers and men's furnishings," opened in 1900, and by 1904 was one of Topeka's largest clothing stores.

2. Martha returned to painting in November after the Beardsleys reopened the studio.

1908

1. Gov. Hoch did support equal suffrage but the bill failed.

2. Nat Franco, an impersonator, was appearing at the Majestic Theatre.

3. William Jennings Bryan (1860–1925) was an unsuccessful Democratic candidate for president in 1896, 1900, and 1908. He later became Woodrow Wilson's Secretary of State, serving from 1912 to 1915. His famous "Cross of Gold" speech in 1896 defending the farmer and wage earner by opposing continued use of gold as the U.S. monetary standard, and his acting for the prosecution in the Scopes trial (1925) keep him in the modern consciousness.

4. The Knights and Ladies of Security, the lodge to which Martha, Fred, and May all belonged, was chartered in 1892 in Topeka as a mutual insurance company. It is now the Security Benefit Life Insurance Company, still of Topeka.

5. This flood was the worst since the devastating one of 1903. Kansas City was more severely affected than was Topeka, where relatively little property was damaged.

6. Clara Willets was their niece, from Waterloo, Oklahoma. She had arrived at their home for a visit on June 29.

7. Martha does not go into further detail about her feelings concerning the move. In fact, she does not mention the family again until August 18, when she notes James' birthday.

8. Gen VanOrsdol, from Nome, Alaska.

9. Kansas law required that a marriage license be issued before the ceremony, so the couple must have seriously planned to marry before coming to Martha.

10. *Queen Esther*, an oratorio, was presented by the Topeka Oratorio Society.

11. Kaffir: a grain sorghum grown in dry climates.

1909

1. Martha was taking a Bible school teacher-training course.

2. After the Beardsleys closed the studio Martha did some painting at home, but ultimately turned this energy to photography.

3. Christian Women's Board of Managers, organized by the national headquarters of the Christian Church, and concerned with youth work.

4. Though Roy is often mentioned as accompanying her on various errands, Martha did not discuss in any more detail their developing relationship.

5. Lilla Day Monroe (1858–1929), lawyer, writer, lecturer, mother of four, wife of district Judge Lee Monroe, was active in many women's organizations including the W.C.T.U. She served as president of the Kansas Equal Suffrage Association, and managed its 1912 campaign for the Woman Suffrage Amendment. Martha Farnsworth greatly admired her, and knew her best as fellow member and president of the Topeka Good Government Club (see note 4, 1912, page 316).

1910

1. Her nephew, James Gilbert, had hitchhiked from Colorado the previous September, and has been living at the Farnsworth home.

2. *Rienzi*, a story of medieval Italy by Edward Bulwer-Lytton, had been a best seller when first published, in England and America, in 1835.

3. James Whitcomb Riley's "The Old Swimmin' Hole" focuses, as do Martha's comments, on the changes brought by passing time.

4. Roy's father's interference is not discussed in the diary.

5. A. E. Housman, *Last Poems*, XXVIII.

6. Margaret Hill McCarter (1850–1938) was a well-known Kansas author. *The Price of the Prairie* (1910), her first novel, deals with conflict between settlers and Indians in Kansas after the Civil War. Mrs. McCarter was head of the English Department at Topeka High School, lectured for woman suffrage, and in 1920 became the first woman to address a Republican national convention.

1911

1. The Scoville revival meetings began on February 5 and lasted until March 19, under the impetus of heavy advertising of all sorts. Scoville, a well-known evangelist, had recently appeared in New York, Chicago, and Kansas City. In Topeka he held noon meetings at large business establishments as well as the nightly ones at the Auditorium, and daily advertised the number of his converts.

2. Her Sunday School class had by this time grown considerably, and was gradually becoming an important part of her life. The boys are mentioned, usually by name, in each Sunday entry. They often dropped in at her home, and she gave each a birthday party—announced with elaborate, hand-drawn invitations.

3. J. Pearle Rogers was Martha's third cousin.

4. Minnie Weber-Farrell was Martha's cousin, visiting Topeka.

5. Fifteen men were reportedly involved in the plot on Miss Chamberlain, a schoolteacher in Lincoln Center, Kansas. They stopped a buggy in which she was riding, stripped her, and applied warm tar. According to the Topeka *Daily Capital* the incident was caused by the jealousy of some women who felt that the pretty Miss Chamberlain and certain married men were "jollying each other entirely too much." The Beattie murder and execution occurred in Virginia. All evidence against Henry Clay Beattie had been circumstantial, and the possibility of executing an innocent man caused great furor until, after the execution, Beattie's priest made public the murderer's written confession.

1912

1. *The Calling of Dan Matthews* (1909), a novel, was Harold Bell Wright's bitterest attack on the Christian churches. Wright, a minister and best-selling author, wrote seventeen novels, sermons in fiction, on religious questions. He often attacked contemporary Christianity.

2. Thomas Jefferson, a movie actor, played the role made famous on stage by his father, Joseph Jefferson.

3. This sixteen-page booklet of cartoons and facetious rhymes was one of the weapons in the fight for suffrage.

4. The women, under the editorship of Lilla Day Monroe, produced a special suffrage section for the October 27 *Sunday Capital*.

5. For Rev. Anna Shaw see note 5, p. 312.

6. By this amendment to its constitution, Kansas enfranchised its women in all elections, state and national.

7. On June 13, 1940, the Topeka airport was named for this early aviator.

8. The Women's Club, a federation of several social clubs in Topeka, built an impressive club house in 1924. The building still stands at 420 W. 9th.

1913

1. Martha registered on January 21, according to state records, as a lobbyist on laws concerning women and children.

2. They lived in the "playhouse" until August 2.

1914

1. Effie Dice, age 31, died of pulmonary tuberculosis on May 14, 1938, at Winfield State Training School, after more than twenty-three years as an inmate.

2. Frank J. Cannon (1859–1933) was U.S. Senator from Utah, 1896–1899.

1915

1. Freda had been married sometime earlier this year, but this is Martha's first allusion to it.

2. Milk-leg is phlebitis.

1916

1. The action Martha alludes to came as the result of the murder of American citizens in both Mexico and New Mexico. Pancho Villa, Mexican bandit and revolutionary hero, was blamed for the attacks, and Woodrow Wilson sent General John Pershing on an ultimately unsuccessful, eleven-month punitive expedition against Villa, which badly damaged Mexican-American relations.

2. Sir Roger Casement, an Irishman, had been hanged for treason on August 3 in London, as a result of his involvement in Sinn Fein revolutionary activities.

3. *God's Country and the Woman*, an eight-reel "super feature" supported by the music of a live ten-piece orchestra, was the story of a family in the Canadian wilderness. Martha may have been objecting to part of the plot: the mother's old love affair has left her with an illegitimate child who is claimed by the daughter, so as to keep the father of the family in ignorance of the child's true parentage.

4. Martha never says what happened after Fred Brackett's earlier switch to Christian Science.

5. Her son, Bob Maxwell, a long-time member of the "Play Square Gang," had been killed in August by a freight train near Chillicothe, Illinois, while working with an engineering crew on the Santa Fe Railroad.

1919

1. The Eighteenth (Prohibition) Admendment was approved in January of this year. In October it was supplemented by the Volstead Act, which defined intoxicating liquor as any beverage containing over one-half of one per cent alcohol. In January, 1920, Prohibition went into effect. Martha did not record any of these events.

2. Seven in One was a United War Work Campaign drive to raise money for welfare work among Ameican service men. This national drive served the YMCA, YWCA, National Catholic War Council, Jewish Welfare Board, War Camp Community Service, American Library Association, and the Salvation Army.

3. See the Introduction, p. xviii.

4. Ketchum later became prominent in Democratic state politics, but was defeated by Alf Landon in his bid for governor in 1934.

5. Martha gave several such dinner parties for her returning "boys".

6. Union soft-coal miners had gone out on a national strike on November 1. In Kansas they returned to work on December 13. During the last two weeks of the strike, federal troops, the Kansas National Guard, and college students worked in the mines to help relieve critical fuel shortages.

1920

1. Enmity between Turks and Armenians had led to deliberate Turkish massacres of Armenians under Turkish domination. Perhaps as many as one million Armenians, deported by the Turks to the Syrian desert, died there while the great powers did nothing.

2. Bob Maxwell and Carl Swanson.

3. Scott, one of her Sunday School "boys," was staying with her temporarily.

4. Hickson was a well-known faith healer, and his coming to Topeka was front-page news. The Topeka *Daily Capital* reported that practically every hotel room in town was reserved by out-of-town sufferers hoping to be cured at the healing services at Grace Cathedral: "Long Line of Persons Braves Rain to Register at Guild Hall for Hickson Healing Mission Today"; "Faith Attracts Two Thousand to Healing Mission." Only two cases of "slight improvement" were reported.

5. *Vanguard of the Plains* (1917) is a romance of the old Santa Fe trail from the 1840s to about 1867. For M. H. McCarter see November 23, 1910.

6. H.C.L. is her abbreviation for "high cost of living."

7. Coal mined near Burlingame, Kansas, about 20 miles south of Topeka.

8. Mrs. Monroe was successful in her campaign: the Attorney General reversed his ruling. Mrs. Monroe argued that the Kansas suffrage bill required only that women be over twenty-one years of age to vote. Moreover, she contended, the practice of requiring that a specific age be given would discriminate against Christian Scientists, who could not register because it is part of their creed to forget time and age.

9. Notable in this list, in addition to the Governor and the Attorney General, are Arthur Carruth, managing editor of the Topeka *State Journal*, and Kate King, the Topeka Humane Officer, as well as Lilla Day Monroe, lawyer and suffrage worker, and Margaret Hill McCarter, the author.

1922

1. *The Bat* (1920), was a very successful mystery play by Mary Roberts Rinehart and Avery Hopwood.

2. Judging from an absence of advertising in the Topeka *Daily Capital*, this film was not approved for showing in the city.

3. Martha was taking these courses in order to be a better Sunday School teacher—in spite of recurrent doubts about continuing to teach.

4. *The Kansas Woman's Journal*, edited by Martha's colleague, Lilla Day Monroe, was the state's official Republican women's publication. It appeared monthly from December 1921 to October 1927, under the motto, "a square deal for every baby."

5. Railway shopmen were on strike at the time.

Index

This index is admittedly a selective one. Only those names mentioned repeatedly are listed; casual acquaintances or the myriad of people Martha encountered during the course of a day are not included unless they are central to the entry for that day. Neither is there a central entry for Martha herself, for the subject entries reflect her interests.